ENGLISH COMPOSITION AS A HAPPENING

ENGLISH COMPOSITION AS A HAPPENING

GEOFFREY SIRC

UTAH STATE
UNIVERSITY PRESS
Logan, Utah

I would like to acknowledge the generous support of David Taylor, Dean of the General College, and Terry Collins, Director of Academic Affairs, University of Minnesota, towards the completion of this book. They have made the General College a very exciting place to work.

Utah State University Press
Logan, Utah 84322-7800

"Never Mind the Tagmemics, Where's the Sex Pistols?" was originally published in *College Composition and Communication,* 48: 1. Copyright © 1997 by the National Council of Teachers of English. Reprinted by permission.

An early version of "Writing Classroom as A&P Parking Lot" and parts of "English Composition as a Happening II" were published in *Pre/Text,* 14: 1–2 (1993) and 15: 3–4 (1994), respectively. Grateful acknowledgment to Victor Vitanza.

Manufactured in the United States of America.
Cover design by Nancy Banks.
Cover photo: "Learning to Fly" by Joseph Emery. Used by permission of the artist.

Library of Congress Cataloging-in-Publication Data

Sirc, Geoffrey Michael.
  English composition as a happening / Geoffrey Sirc.
     p. cm.
Includes bibliographical references and index.
  ISBN 0-87421-435-1
  1. English language–Rhetoric–Study and teaching–Psychological
aspects. 2. English language–Rhetoric–Study and teaching–Social
aspects. 3. Academic writing–Study and teaching–Psychological
aspects. 4. Academic writing–Study and teaching–Social aspects. 5.
Language and culture. 6. Happening (Art) I. Title.
  PE1404 .S564 2002
  808'.042'071–dc21
                              2002000424

CONTENTS

To
Vera Smythe-Rawley,
Nigel, and my darling little Reggie

0

THE STILL-UNBUILT HACIENDA

I suppose the reason none of us burn incense in our writing classes any more is because of the disk drives. Smoke's not supposed to be good for them, right? But what about the sounds, the candlelight, the students on the floor, the dark? What about that *other scene* of writing instruction? Where has that gone, the idea of the writing classroom as blank canvas, ready to be inscribed as a singular compositional space?

> The next class was held in the same room; only this time I made a few alterations in the physical arrangements. There were no neat lines of folding chairs. The students sat, stood, or lay wherever they wished. When everyone was comfortable, I closed the drapes, turned off the lights, lit one candle in the middle of the room and a few sticks of incense, and played the same music as before [Ravel's "Bolero," Strauss's "Zarathustra," some Gregorian chant, selections from the Association, the Doors, Steppenwolf, Jefferson Airplane, Clear Light, Iron Butterfly, Simon and Garfunkel, and others]. The class just listened to music in the dark with the flickering candle and the scent of incense permeating the room. Again, when the period was over, the students were asked to pick up their books and leave. Some of them did not want to. (Lutz, "Making Freshman English" 38)

I begin with this souvenir—from William Lutz's 1969 writing class— because I want to reflect on the novel textures that might be brought to Composition's current course designs, the possibilities that exist for altering the conventional spaces of a writing classroom, allowing the inhabitants a sense of the sublime, making it a space no one wants to leave, a *happening* space.

Because designing spaces, I think, is what it's all about. It's a matter of basic architecture: Robert Venturi has shown that simplified compositional programs, programs that ignore the complexity and contradiction of everyday life, result in bland architecture; and I think the reverse is true as well, and perhaps more relevant for Composition: bland architecture (unless substantially *detourned*, as Lutz's) evokes simplistic programs. The spaces of our classrooms should offer compelling environments in which to inhabit situations of writing instruction, helping intensify consciousness in the people who use them. Can such intensification happen in a conventional writing classroom? The architectural design for the conventional classroom has become soberly monumental, charged with the heavy burden of preserving the discursive tradition of "our language . . . the peculiar ways of knowing, selecting, evaluating, reporting, concluding, and arguing that define the discourse of our community" (Bartholomae, "Inventing" 134). We erect temples to language, in which we are the priests among initiates (of varying degrees of enthusiasm), where we relive the rites of text-production for the nth time, despite the sad truth that the gods have fled so long ago that no one is even sure that they were ever there in the first place (in Composition, the gods are called, variously, *power, authentic voice, discourse, critical consciousness, versatility, style, disciplinarity, purpose*, etc.).

Or better, what we build are Museums, peculiar sorts of cultural temples in which students are "invited" in to sample the best that has been thought and expressed in *our language* and maybe even, like the art students we see poised in galleries with their sketchbooks and charcoals, to learn to reproduce the master's craft. Bartholomae and Petrosky, for example, seem to be only half-joking when they describe what motivated them (and, by extension, what they see as motivating many teachers) to use a canon of readings in their writing classrooms: "We thought (as many teachers have thought) that if we just, finally, gave them something good to read—something rich and meaty—they would change forever their ways of thinking about English" (*Ways of Reading* iii). Once they realized their true purpose—to teach students what to do with the reading material—they resumed the previous task of choosing rich and meaty content ("the sorts of readings we talk about when we talk with our colleagues," "selections . . . that present powerful readings of common experience, that open up the familiar world and make it puzzling, rich, and problematic" [iv]). (Mention must be made of a popular subset of composition reader, the multicultural reader, which presents the same sort of canon, only now more politically correct—like those museums that have re-hung their permanent collections to better reflect America's diversity. So, for example, John Repp selects the pieces for his collection *How We Live Now: Contemporary Multicultural Literature* according to the same tenets as Bartholomae and Petrosky: providing "imaginative literature to excite readers, inspire writers, and enliven classrooms"; readings "deeply satisfying and deeply disturbing at the same time," but overall, "so eloquently multivoiced" [*v-vi*]. A fine goal, perhaps, but the curated shows always seem to feature the same artists. We await the multicultural reader featuring a Tupac retrospective.) Underlying this trend in the Modern-Composition-Reader-as-Museum is Modernism itself. The Modern student's chief need is an awareness of tradition, which, in itself, comprises a sobering (not to mention Eurocentric) task—as Eliot wrote,

> Tradition is a matter of much wider significance. It cannot be inherited, and if you want it you must obtain it by great labour. In involves, in the first place, the historical sense, . . . and the historical sense involves a perception, not only of the pastness of the past, but of its presence; the historical sense compels a man to write not merely with his own generation in his bones, but with a feeling that the whole of the literature of Europe from Homer and within it the whole of the literature of his own country has a simultaneous existence and composes a simultaneous order. (14)

This consciousness of the past is something that must be nurtured throughout the writer's career; as Eliot phrases it (sounding much like Bartholomae when he speaks of the student's need to learn "the peculiar ways of knowing . . . that define the discourse of our community"), "what happens is a continual surrender of himself as he is at the moment to something which is far more valuable. The progress of an artist is a continual self-sacrifice, a continual extinction of personality" (17). Eliot, we know, tells not quite the whole story, or perhaps he is so clear on what he means himself that he feels no need to qualify the phrase "the whole of literature," because certainly, to the modernists, the whole of literature they're concerned with is not the entire whole. Leavis, for example, makes it clear that only some work is museum-quality; other work can't be bothered with. Indeed, since "the field is so large and offers such insidious temptations to complacent confusions of judgment and to critical indolence," "some challenging discriminations are very much called for" (9). Thus, Leavis offers what can be taken as the selection criteria for the contemporary Composition reader:

> It is necessary to insist, then, that there are important distinctions to be made, and that far from all of the names in the literary histories really belong to the realm of significant creative achievement. And as a recall to a due sense of differences it is well to start by distinguishing the few really great—the major novelists who count in the same way as the major poets [in Composition, we might add "and major essayists"], in the sense that they not only change the possibilities of the art for practitioners and readers, but that

they are significant in terms of the human awareness they promote, awareness of the possibilities of life. (10)

If we are unhappy with the dry modernist enterprise of college writing (formal, autonomous, univocal, meaning-driven), we need to
remember the way the modernist tradition is reproduced: "those institutions that are the preconditions for and shape the discourse of modernism . . . can be named at the outset: first, the museum; then, art
history" (Crimp 108). And we must remember how those institutions
consciously fight against exciting possibilities: "it is not in the interests
of the institutions of art and the forces they serve to produce knowledge
of radical practices" (Crimp 153). Our pedagogical, then, is the curatorial; we teach connoisseurship. Take, for example, the way Richard
Rodriguez's reading of Richard Hoggart's *The Uses of Literacy* becomes,
for Bartholomae and Petrosky, the masterly style, a manner to be repli-
cated, "a way of reading we like to encourage in our students" (*Ways of
Reading* 3). The composition readers themselves, as we have seen, are
miniature museums, *bôites-en-valise* without the irony, portable permanent collections or corporate-sponsored temporary exhibits of our
Greatest Hits. As instructors, our classroom activities combine the
docent's tour (explaining how the great masterpieces are put together)
with the hands-on workshop of family day (now that the gallery-goers
understand how the masterpieces work, they get to try to make one).
The scene of classroom writing is peculiarly overdetermined, then, as
Gallery—as physical space in a larger institution (Museum/University),
lying on the cusp between the curatorial and the commercial.

But the very *architecture* of the Museum, as some artists and theorists
discovered, fights against the possibility of radical meaning in the way it
predetermines the art which fits, the art that can be exhibited in (and,
hence, created for) its space. Writing instructors, then, feeling constrained by the structural determinants of the spaces (even virtual
ones) in which they practice, might do well to recall that moment in
the broader cultural field of composition when artists finally abandoned the narrow, predictable constraints of the Gallery's architecture.
Like Lutz in our own field, these practitioners felt the need for different, more evocative, spaces. Allan Kaprow, for example, realized the
cause-effect relationship between architectural space and the artwork
produced to "mean" in that space: "at root paintings, etc. could not
possibly exist in their form up to the present without the psychological

and physical definition of space given to them by Architecture" (*Assemblages* 153); the design of the gallery room, he reminds us, "*has always been a frame or format too*" (154). Those compositional formats—either the framed picture or the proscenium-delineated stage—are too accreted with associations; performance historian Richard Schechner captured the sentiment: "The single-focus stage and the framed picture are identified with the billboard and the press, and rejected" ("Happenings" 218). Kaprow was one of a group of neo-avant-garde visual and musical artists (including John Cage, Claes Oldenburg, Jim Dine, Robert Whitman, La Monte Young, Ann Halprin, Red Grooms, *et al.*) of the late fifties and early sixties who realized how the received design of the space in which their work appeared resulted in conventional product. And so these artists (compositionists-in-general, we might now name them) realized they would have to reject the architecture of that space, "ignoring the house in which they have for so long been nurtured" (Kaprow, *Assemblages* 153), if they wanted to produce a truly different composition. They practiced an art which interrupted the passivity of the spectator so that, as McLuhan & Fiore put it, "the audience becomes a participant in the total electric drama" (101). It was an art that frustrated conventions in order to allow other meanings to surface. It involved a re-appreciation of everyday material in order to complicate the distinction between art and life. This attempt resulted in new compositional forms: Assemblages, Combines, Neo-Dada works, and, most genre-blurringly, the Happenings.

As we saw with Lutz's attempt to re-style his pedagogical space, compositionists in the field of writing theory and practice in the 1960s were caught in the same frustrating dilemma the Happenings artists were—their desire to do interesting work thwarted by the constraints of conventional forms, spaces and materials. The radical gestures of the Happenings artists were not lost on writing teachers, and so articles began to appear (by Lutz, Macrorie, and Coles, among a host of others less widely remembered today) which applied these gestures (either directly or, more ambiently, in spirit) to the writing class—initially, and not so remarkably, at the level of architecture:

> The classroom as presently structured does not provide the environment in which anything creative can be taught. Physically the room insists on order and authoritarianism, the enemies of creativity: the teacher as ultimate authority in front of the room and the students as passive receptacles at his

feet. The unbridgeable gap (generation and otherwise) is physically emphasized. (Lutz "Making Freshman English" 35)

Such articles rhymed with similar sorts of texts appearing in the larger
culture—everything from the situationists' tract "On the Poverty of
Student Life" to Jerry Farber's *The Student as Nigger*—which critiqued
education for its received nature, its dull curriculum, and its passionless
tone. Farber, for example, also begins his critique of school—as the
place where "the dying society puts its trip on you" (17)—by questioning
the institution's architecture:

> Consider how most classrooms are set up. Everyone is turned toward the
> teacher and away from his classmates. You can't see the faces of those in front
> of you; you have to twist your neck to see the persons behind you. Frequently,
> seats are bolted to the floor or fastened together in rigid rows. This classroom,
> like the grading system, isolates students from each other and makes them
> passive receptacles. All the action, it implies, is at the front of the room. . . .
>
> But why those chairs at all? Why forty identical desk-chairs in a bleak, ugly
> room? Why should school have to remind us of jail or the army? . . . You know,
> wherever I've seen classrooms, from UCLA to elementary schools in Texas, it's
> always the same stark chamber. The classrooms we have are a nationwide
> chain of mortuaries. What on earth are we trying to teach? (24–25)

One of the Composition-specific articles in this genre of radical sixties
pedagogy, one which I have never been able to forget since the day I first
read it in the dimly-lit stacks of my university's library, was written in 1967
by a young graduate teaching assistant at the University of Oregon,
Charles Deemer. His article, "English Composition as a Happening," did
what many of these articles did, but did it in a formally compelling way
(the article is a collage of brief sound-bite snippets, alternating between
Deemer's own poetic reflections-as-manifesto and quotations from
Sontag, McLuhan, Dewey, Goodman, and others), and Deemer's ideas
seemed to catalyze my own discontent with what passed for Composition
during the 1980s. As I read further back into the field, saw the basic questions of language, respect, and student interest these earlier practitioners
tried to answer, current books and articles (which were written as if such
questions didn't need to be answered every time one planned a course)
began to sound increasingly hollow. I began to realize that something
questionable happened in our field in the late seventies and early eighties: our insecurity over our status as a valid academic field led us to
entrench ourselves firmly in professionalism. To establish Composition

as a respectable discipline, we took on all the trappings of traditional academia—canonicity, scientism, empiricism, formalism, high theory, axioms, arrogance, and acceptance of the standard university department-divisions. We purged ourselves of any trace of kookiness, growing first suspicious, then disdainful, of the kind of homemade comp-class-as-Happening that people like Lutz tried to put together:

> At the beginning of the second class of the semester, I gave each student an index card and instructed him not to read it until told to. Then, at a given signal, each student read his card and performed the activity described on it [e.g., Go to the front of the room and face the class. Count to yourself and each time you reach five say, "If I had the wings of an angel." . . . (Or) Be an ice cream cone—change flavor]. At the end of three minutes, a student who had been designated time-keeper called time. I asked the students to sit down and write as much as they could describing what had just occurred in the classroom and their reaction to it. (36–37)

We became Moderns. But I couldn't stop thinking about, for example, Ken Macrorie, and this book of his, *Uptaught*, which read like Kurt Vonnegut's long-lost foray into Composition Theory. How did we go from a book like Macrorie's, urging "that teachers must find ways of getting students to produce (in words, pictures, sounds, diagrams, objects, or landscapes) what students and teachers honestly admire" (186), to meditating on "Texts as Knowledge Claims: The Social Construction of Two Biologists' Articles"? Suddenly, spirit, love, adventure, poetry, incense, kicky language, and rock 'n' roll were gone. The forms and constraints seemed overwhelming, the huge gray University walls had grown tall and imposing, keeping the revelers out. As I read further through this new epistemic, Modernist Composition, I noticed something else—call it Composition's material restraint, the phenomenon by which a *de facto* "Composition Canon" forms, with the same names cropping up not just in anthology tables of contents, but in "Works Cited" lists. As article after article appeared, one could trace the waxing and waning of theoretical trends: Langer, Polanyi, Vygotsky, Odell, Emig, Berthoff, Bruffee, Bartholomae, Berlin, Anzaldúa, Foucault, and Freire. This narrow-banding is curious for a discipline that trumpets the value of linguistic richness. The texts surrounding the Happenings proved richer, more seductive to me, in the way they dealt with the same material and institutional concerns I had as a writing teacher. As I read further into them, I began to read the texts surrounding the artists who prefigured the Happenings—Duchamp and Pollock—as well as the texts of those they prefigured—the Conceptualists, the Minimalists, the Neo-Dadaists. And through it all I continued to listen to popular music (a key thread in the material of Comp '68). The truth of materialism hit home. There was all this wonderful stuff—raising and reflecting on key compositional issues—that wasn't making its way into our journals, and yet an article on how a biologist writes was. Frankly, I don't care how a biologist writes. I assume it's pretty conventional stuff, thoroughly implicated in the traditional departmental divisions that stultify the academy. If the folks in biology want to get together with me and talk about how to re-evaluate the form and subject of biology, I'm there. The way such writing represents the entrenched disciplinarity of academia makes it of dubious value as part of a material sublime. I think of what the idea of composition is: an opportunity to reflect on textuality, its craft, wonder, problems—obviously that should be at the center of any idea of academics; but thanks to the epistemic turn we are simply the eager lapdogs of the big-ticket disciplines. Our self-imposed formal and material subservience marks a sad betrayal of the spirit of verbal risk and writing-as-life that marked the best of our history.

Post-Happenings Composition never ever asks (as Comp '68 did so often) "What's Going On?" To remove any doubt about precisely what was going on, Composition undertook the classical modernist project of self-definition. Bizzell and Bartholomae helped usher in these attempts to articulate exactly what we could claim with certitude about Composition. Lindemann, influenced by these epistemic compositionists, offers perhaps the clearest summative view of the field, one which shows its newly narrowed status of allowing students practice in pre-professional discourse: "Freshman English offers guided practice in reading and writing the discourses of the academy and the professions. That is what our colleagues across the campus want it to do; that is what it should do if we are going to drag every first-year student through the requirement" (312). Composition, then, implicates itself in the contemporary re-figuring of education as training for work rather than intensification of experience. As Frank McCourt realizes, reflecting back with deep sadness on his many years teaching high school in New York City:

> There's no vision. Education's just a branch of industry and commerce. It's about scores, scores, scores—and all of this is designed to supply a workforce. We really don't give a s—about the minds and feelings of the kids. . . . In my

eighteen years at Stuyvesant High, only one parent ever asked me, 'Is my child enjoying himself?' One. ("What I Learned in School" 60)

Strict boundaries have become maintained in Composition, a separation of (profession-oriented) academy and life, one discipline from another, the specific discourse from a broader lived reality. This is not Freshman English as a Happening, this is Freshman English as a Corporate Seminar. Happenings were all about blurring the boundaries between art and life. They underscored what Cage maintained, which was that "what we are doing is living, and that we are not moving toward a goal, but are, so to speak, at the goal constantly and changing with it, and that art, if it is going to be anything useful, should open our eyes to this fact" (Kirby and Schechner 60). A view such as Cage's marks a de-determination of art, wholly at odds with post-Happenings Composition, which maintains very clear, Leavisesque distinctions between writers, texts, and contexts, so that students can join the Great Tradition. Composition, in this view, styles students to "enter the conversation of the academy and begin to contribute to the making of knowledge . . . guiding students in those uses of language that enable them to become historians, biologists, and mathematicians" (Lindemann 313). A Happenings spirit is more like that laid out by Fluxus founder George Maciunas, in one of his manifestos (the Fluxus artists being as interested as Cage and the Happenings artists in radically rethinking conventional form and content), which implies a Composition centered on amusement, Freshman English as Fluxjoke:

AMUSEMENT FORGOES DISTINCTION BETWEEN ART AND NONART, FORGOES ARTIST'S INDISPENSBILITY, EXCLUSIVENESS, INDIVIDUALITY, AMBITION, FORGOES ALL PRETENSION TOWARDS SIGNIFICANCE, RARITY, INSPIRATION, SKILL, COMPLEXITY, PROFUNDITY, GREATNESS, INSTITUTIONAL AND COMMODITY VALUE. IT STRIVES FOR MONOSTRUCTURAL, NONTHEATRICAL, NONBAROQUE, IMPERSONAL QUALITIES OF A SIMPLE NATURAL EVENT, AN OBJECT, A GAME, A PUZZLE OR GAG. ("FLUXUS" 94)

The reason the teaching of writing is permeated by dissatisfaction (every CCCC presentation seems, at some level, a complaint) is that we—bad enough—don't really know what teaching is, but also—far worse, fatal, in fact—we haven't really evolved an idea of writing that fully reflects the splendor of the medium. (Somewhere out there, for example, is a prof for whom "memo" as a verb is still a big deal.) We have evolved a very limited notion of academic writing (or any genre, really). Our texts are conventional in every sense of the word; they write themselves. They are almost wholly determined by the texts that have gone before; a radical break with the conventions of a form or genre (and I'm not speaking here about the academic convention of the smug, sanctioned transgression, e.g., Jane Tompkins) would perplex—how is *that* history writing? what community group would need *that* for its newsletter? how is *that* going to help you get a job? A Happenings spirit would begin at the point of Elbow's "life is long and college is short" queasiness with academic writing ("Reflections on Academic Discourse" 136).

To de-determine form and content means that the writing can just be; or, as the title of one of the key *CCC* '69 pieces puts it, "this writing is"(Litz). The Happening artists' basic rule was indeterminacy: nothing is previously determined, neither form nor material content; everything is under erasure. The only given, a kind of non-axiom, is the one stated by Rauschenberg, who cared not at all about control or intention, only change: "What's exciting is that we don't know. There is no anticipated result; but we will be changed" (Kostelanetz, *Theatre* 99). Once all the conventions are re-thought, the compositional scene becomes simpler, more an issue of basic being, wonder, the human heart, change. Take Happenings artist Ken Dewey's de-determination of the idea of *theatre*: "The further out one moves, the simpler one's understanding becomes of what theatre is. I now would accept only that theatre is a situation in which people gather to articulate something of mutual concern" (210). Dewey shows a basic, unoccluded desire for communion. That, along with passion, beauty, lyricism . . . why is that *not* our core? Why do we *not* insist on it? Despite all the lip service we give to empowerment in our ideological curricula, we don't really believe in the power of a composition to change the world. We have a concept of audience as construct, not as lived. Which allows us to develop all these step-by-step heuristic-templates to turn the rhetorical situation into a parlor game.

> When you consider the expectations and interests of your readers, you natu-
> rally think *strategically*, asking yourself questions such as these:
> - To what extent are my readers interested in and knowledgeable about my
>   subject?
> - What formal and stylistic expectations will my readers bring to my essay?

- What other aspects of my readers' situations might influence how they respond to my essay?
- How can I use my understanding of my readers' expectations and interests when I make decisions about the content, form, and style of my essay? (Ede 56–57)

When there's really only one heuristic that matters: the person who reads this—and it is one specific person, saturated in lived desire—will that person be changed? We think only in the abstract about how some peculiarly over-crafted college essay or some genre of "real world" writing can change a generic reader. We need to keep in mind how, not in the "real world" but in life, any small fragment has the power to truly change a person, not just (and probably not at all) some heuristic-generated, audience-strategized, oddly-voiced form that results in that weird sort of "prose-lite" essay they publish in those magazines available in the seat backs of airplanes. We need only remember what Salter tells us: "the power to change one's life comes from a paragraph, a lone remark. The lines that penetrate us are slender, like the flukes that live in river water and enter the bodies of swimmers" (161).

Rarefying materials, as Composition does (the middle-brow preciosity or academic aloofness that drives the reading selections we anthologize), only makes the possibilities for Happening Composition more remote, particularly for students. Material access is an issue, and many of the Happenings artists relied on what was available in the trash for their stage properties. It became a theoretical principle for someone like Cage: "I was already interested at that time in avoiding the exclusion of banal elements. . . . I've always been on the side of the things one shouldn't do and searching for ways of bringing the refused elements back into play" (Kirby and Schechner 60). Or take that flower garden Cage writes about: "George Mantor had an iris garden, which he improved each year by throwing out the commoner varieties. One day his attention was called to another very fine iris garden. Jealously he made some inquiries. The garden, it turned out, belonged to the man who collected his garbage"(*Silence* 263). Not only material differences, but formal ones as well, as part of the production necessary for new ideas. La Monte Young offers a simple example of the new text grammar (actually not really new, just basic undetermined juxtaposition) guiding his "Lecture 1960": "The lecture is written in sections. . . . Each section originally was one page or a group of pages stapled together.

Any number of them may be read in any order. The order and selec-tions are determined by chance, thereby bringing about new relation-ships between parts and consequently new meanings"(72). Many of these new genres arise, following the de-conventionalization of the form, from an allegorical reading, seeing one form through the lens of another. According to Dewey, "It should have been made clear that Happenings came about when painters and sculptors crossed into the-atre taking with them their way of looking and doing things" (206). So La Monte Young looks at the traditional lecture through the lens of a random generator. Or take Fluxus artist Dick Higgins, who worked out the form for his Happening *The Tart, or Miss America* (1965) by trying to apply the idea of collage to theatre. I like such practices as Young's and Higgins's, as they involve reading texts in (at least) two ways. Is Young's creation a lecture or performance art? Is *The Tart* (with a list of characters including butchers, doctors, steelworkers, electricians, and a chemist) choreography or sociology? Is this book of mine composition, art history, basic writing theory or cultural studies? Sometimes I'm not sure if the first-year writing course I teach is a course on rap, writing, or technology. Anyway, I like how that blurring messes up a stable reading; it energizes a text or scene, preventing it from becoming fixed.

I would like, then, to return to that point of disenchantment with established spaces and the desire for new forms, a disenchantment and desire that was felt historically in all fields with the idea of *composition* at their center. Much of what I hear in conferences and conversations sug-gests that we have already returned to a desire for something else (if we've ever really left—Composition Studies as a perpetual scene of disen-chantment). Contemporary Composition, as Lindemann shows, is still inflected by that epistemic turn taken in the 1980s, convincing me we need to remember what we've forgotten, namely how impassioned resolves and thrilling discoveries were abandoned and why. I'd like, then, to retrace the road not taken in Composition Studies, to re-read the eli-sion, in order to remember what was missed and to salvage what can still be recovered. This, then, is a negative-space history, one that reverses the conventional figure-ground relations to find the most fruitful avenues of inquiry to be those untouched or abandoned by the disciplinary main-stream. The disruptive/restorative dynamic of my project means both rediscovering the usefulness of some of the materials of Composition that have faded from our conscious screen, and forcing a comparison of our field with the avant-garde tradition in post-WWII American art, running that story through our own traditional, disciplined history—or better, showing our history as already-ruptured, permanently destabilized by our attitude toward (really, ignorance of) the compositional avant-garde. My key compositional theorists—Pollock, Duchamp, the situationists, the Happenings artists, punks—are non-compositionists as our field would define such; and my favorite field-specific theorist-practitioners are those now out of fashion, like Macrorie and Coles, or ones never more than minor figures, like Deemer. My re-reading of the field is really an allegory: reading composition through a particular thread (the Happenings movement, broadly defined) in twentieth century art history. Call it "writing instruction as electric drama," maybe. Of course, what I'm really doing is re-writing Charles Deemer's original 1967 *College English* allegory. Allegorical criticism—in the way allegory tells one story, but tells it as read through (or in) another—is a useful method by which to read our past, particularly for an historical review like mine, which desires to re-affirm the value in an all but forgotten era of Composition Studies, in the hope of finding an alternative to the current tradition. According to Owens, "what is most proper to [allegory is] its capacity to rescue from historical oblivion that which threatens to disappear. Allegory first emerged in response to a . . . sense of estrangement from tradition" (203). Allegory, then, serves as the perfect strategy by which to return to that stirring moment in our history, in the hopes of recapturing its intensity, because, as Owens continues, the "two most fundamental impulses" of allegory are "[a] conviction of the remoteness of the past, and a desire to redeem it for the present." Seeing the field of writing instruction through the broader compositional allegory of art-in-general connects back to Irmscher, who also suggested an art analogy as an approach to rhetorical theory, urging a focus on those artists who could de-familiarize rhetoric and change perception: "In matters of experimentation with established principles and processes, the other arts are particularly instructive, for artists continually seek to overcome the limitations and traditional agencies of their medium. . . . We can learn about rhetoric particularly from those artists who have modified our modes of perception, for what each has done is to change, sometimes radically, one or more of the components in the rhetorical paradigm so that interaction no longer occurs in familiar ways" ("Analogy" 354). A field like ours—where articles and monographs and textbooks all say basically the same thing, draw materially on the same sources—exists in much the same state as the art world in 1964, described by Harold Rosenberg as "sealed up in itself" ("After Next" 70); an allegorical reading is perfect for such a field, offering immediate fracture. Barthes, as well, affirms the heuristic power gained from the prose/painting allegory: "Why not wipe out the difference between them," he asks, "in order to affirm more powerfully the plurality of 'texts'" (*S/Z* 56).

Some have seen an effort such as this, recouping the possibilities of an avant-garde in permanent tension with the academic, as the ongoing drama of contemporary art. Foster introduces his own version of such a recuperative history in his study of American art: "[T]his book is not a history: it focuses on several models of art and theory over the last three decades alone. . . . [I]t insists that specific genealogies of innovative art and theory exist over this time, and it traces these genealogies through signal transformations. Crucial here is the relation between *turns* in critical models and *returns* of historical practices: how does a *re*connection with a past practice support a *dis*connection from a present practice and/or a development of a new one?" (x). Irmscher, then, was uncannily prescient: the history of our Composition, its failure to exploit its most radical practices, can be read saliently through the lens of the visual arts. But it is no wonder that Irmscher was ineffective (and is presently in need of reconsideration), for as Foster continues: "the avant-garde work is never historically effective or fully significant in its initial moments. It cannot be because it is traumatic—a hole in the symbolic order of its time that is not prepared for it, that cannot receive it, at least not immediately, at least not without structural change. (This is the other scene of art that critics and historians need to register: not only symbolic disconnections but *failures to signify*)" (29).

My book, then, is a kind of destiny, an inevitable rendezvous, a turning inside-out of the shadow-space of Composition, an accounting of our *other scene*, our *failures of signification*. I plan to re-open our traumatic wound in order to review the symbolic order that it ruptured, to reconsider the structural change it suggested. The interesting questions about composition asked in the visual arts only began to be asked in our specific compositional field: for example, as the visual arts struggled over the notion of what can count as *beauty*, Composition Studies shrunk from the task, falling back on the attempt to establish "what makes writing good" along very conventional lines. Other crucial issues exhaustively theorized in the more general notion of composition seen in the visual and performing arts include: acceptable materials and content;

the question of process (even process-as-product, text-as-performance) as opposed to the product/work as commodifiable; the place of the viewer as meaning-maker (the viewers make the pictures, Duchamp said), which Composition finesses with a disembodied notion of audience; indeed, the whole notion of the body; genres, and how far they can be blurred; academic conventions and institutional frames as disciplinary constructs to be worked against; site-specificity (as opposed to our sense of composition as a deracinated meaning-event, embedded with enough context so the work can be endlessly reactivated); and the general blurring of art and life. The narrowness of our Composition can be measured by how much we have shrunk from considering such issues.

It's worth tracing briefly how the history of writing instruction parallels (and where it departs from) that of the visual arts. Assume a composition-in-general, defined as the production of a work that responds to some problem, some exigency. The work itself might be thought of as having a form and content, being made of certain materials to which certain techniques are applied. That work, then, is judged according to certain criteria. In Pre-Modern art, the problem was representation: whether Altimira cave-painters or Renaissance *maîtres*, artists had as their goal the rendering of a realist image (as aesthetics evolved, we might add *beauty* as another part of the problem being worked out in such composition). The content for the image was entirely conventional: the animals the cave-painters wanted to hunt or the religious icons the Renaissance artists wanted to praise. Rendering techniques also became standardized, from two-dimensional art to chiaroscuro and perspective. Materials, too conformed to convention—again, whether we're talking about how cave painters used burnt wood and blood or how later artists mixed their own pigments (making the studio scene standard, because painters had a difficult time, until pre-mixed tubes of paint became available in the nineteenth century, mixing colors *en plein air*). The paintings were judged mainly on how well they corresponded to the accepted standard. De Kooning captured the thoroughly conventional nature of the art of this era in a comment on Titian: "But he kept on painting Virgins in that luminous light, like he'd just heard about them. Those guys had everything in place, the Virgin and God and the technique, but they kept it up like they were still looking for something" (Kimmelman "Life is Short" 22). Rendering or representation coalesced Pre-Modern writing instruction: the problem being the clear rendering or reproduction of the target language (in our case, Edited American English). Things got especially worrisome when the student couldn't achieve that clarity; so Adams Sherman Hill complains of flawed representation in 1879, of "manuscripts written in an examination room . . . disfigured by bad spelling, confusing punctuation, ungrammatical, obscure, ambiguous, or inelegant expressions . . . blunders which would disgrace a boy twelve years old" (Connors "Basic Writing Textbooks" 260). The materials, besides pen and paper and language, were textbooks, "filled with grammatical and mechanical rules and exercises" (Connors 261), and the technique those materials reinforced was "to atomize writing into small bits and to practice these bits. . . . [The textbooks] break writing down into a set of subskills and assume that conscious mastery of the subskills means mastery of the writing" (262, 265); so copying and drills became standard. The form/content was determined by the expressive, topic-sentence paragraph. And the excellence of the work was judged in large part on the correctness of its correspondence to the standard, on the presence or absence of formal errors.

The Modernist era in art is best described by Clement Greenberg. Briefly, Greenberg associates Modernism with the impulse in Western culture "to turn around and question its own foundations" ("Modernist Painting" 67). Self-reflexivity marked the turn in art, for Greenberg, from the Old Masters to the Moderns: "Realistic, illusionist art had dissembled the medium, using art to conceal art. Modernism used art to call attention to art. The limitations that constitute the medium of painting—the flat surface, the shape of the support, the properties of pigment—were treated by the Old Masters as negative factors that could be acknowledged only implicitly or indirectly. Modernist painting has come to regard these same limitations as positive factors that are to be acknowledged openly"(69). So the Modern painters under the spell of Greenberg worked to identify those properties of painting exclusive to itself. Representation became dispensable, since other arts were also representational; hence, art that was truly Modern had to be abstract. The materials, for the most part, were still oil on canvas (even if radically thinned, as Morris Louis favored). What also made a painting truly a painting (and one had to speak of the Modernist picture *qua* picture: "one sees a Modernist painting as a picture first" [70]) was its flatness on a canvas (anything else became three-dimensional, hence sculptural). Perhaps the only thing that didn't change from the Pre-Modern to the Modern was *excellence* as a criterion—particularly in historical or traditional terms (as beautiful, pleasing, inspirational, well-wrought)—to judge the work; as Greenberg noted, sounding like his fellow-Moderns Eliot and Leavis, "Without the past of art, and without the need and compulsion to maintain past standards of excellence, such a thing as Modernist art would be impossible" (77). Bartholomae, our field's most articulate Modernist, shows how the Modernist program translated into Composition theory and pedagogy. Self-reflexivity ruled: the problem became not so much expressivist representation as analytic criticism; particularly, as in the Greenbergian investigation of the essential elements of painting, this meant a formal inquiry into the medium (academic discourse) and its conventions, finding, for example, "the rules governing the presentation of examples or the development of an argument" ("Inventing" 135). The materials, newly delimited—our flat, abstract, oil canvases—are now what is strictly specific to college writing, the university continually re-invented (as the same traditional thing). So the student must work, technique-wise, on "assembling and mimicking [the university's] language," and the form/content of one's work becomes "the peculiar ways of knowing, selecting, evaluating, reporting, concluding, and arguing that define the discourse of our community" ("Inventing" 135, 134). We can speak now of what is exclusive to Composition, of the field's "historic concern for the space on the page and what it might mean to do work there and not somewhere else . . . composition as a professional commitment to do a certain kind of work with a certain set of materials" ("What is Composition?" 18, 22). Criteria no longer invoke sentence-level correctness; Bartholomae tellingly moves beyond error, as he seemingly abandons representation for criticism—but formalists, of course, never fully abandon representation. The new criterion is a kind of meta-representation: how well the work mimics the original critical text that has interrogated the tradition; how well, that is, the students "take on the role—the voice, the persona—of an authority whose authority is rooted in scholarship, analysis, or research" ("Inventing" 136). What is represented, then, is the newly refigured discourse. So, in *Ways of Reading*, for example, Bartholomae and Petrosky urge the student who has just read a selection from *Mythologies*, "As a way of testing Barthes's method, and of testing the usefulness of his examples, write an essay (or perhaps a series of 'mythologies') that provides a similar reading of an example (or related examples) of American culture—MTV, skateboarding, the Superbowl, Pee Wee Herman, etc. You might ask, 'What would Barthes notice in my examples? What would he say about these significant features?'" (36). This is writing as iterative gesture, typical of Modernist Composition (Lindemann's students, for example, "examine the texts they encounter in the academy [in order to] creat[e] texts like those they read" (314).

Happenings artists reacted to the Modernist program. The problem became not the conventional, but rather how one does something unconventional, sublime, exciting. Any material and technique was allowed, if it could produce something exciting. Form and content were equally open; as Minimalist Donald Judd put it: "Any material can be used, as is or painted" (184). The only relevant criteria was one we can also take from Judd: "A work needs only to be interesting" (184). Whether you call this postmodern or (as I prefer) avant-garde, there is very little correspondence for it in Composition Studies. Deemer, an obvious parallel, sees the problem as one of boredom resulting from conventional composition; the aim is for the teacher to "shock the student" (124). It's pedagogy as dare (Composition prefers the truth of resemblance), gambling on the sublime, "the reengagement of the heart, a new tuning of *all* the senses. Taking the first step toward poetry" (125). Materials had to be different, other: "Let [the class] discuss theology to Ray Charles records" (124). Deemer is very purposeful in his article not to describe technique too carefully, because he wants to disrupt the notion of correspondence and reproduction found in the Modernist and Pre-Modernist writing space; he wants to preserve risk: "It is with reason that I have neglected to present a more explicit blueprint for the happening after which to model a reconstruction of English Composition. In the first place, happenings happen; they are not passed down from one to another. Spontaneity is essential. Each 'teacher' must inspire his own happening" (124). Lutz's class, then, described earlier—which also used popular recordings, and had students practice almost meditative techniques while they listened, in order to bring about a sublime state—becomes a record of his own journey (as "teacher") to spontaneity and inspiration. We can consider avant-pop theorist Mark Amerika to see how these ideas might play out in a writing class. Amerika's project starts with tradition itself—particularly the conventional, media-saturated consumerist culture, and how it seems to preclude the sublime—as the problem; for Amerika, the struggle becomes "to rapidly transform our sick, commodity-infested workaday culture into a more sensual, trippy, exotic and networked . . . experience." An avant-garde technique has nothing to do with the formal, replicable, critical methods that serve to represent a discourse or produce a strong reading; rather it is a radically de-determined ambient interaction with cultural information. Text-selection replaces text-pro-duction: "Creating a work of art will depend more and more on the abil-ity of the artist to select, organize and present the bits of raw data we have at our disposal" (Amerika). Techniques now include, besides the standard freewriting, listing, drafting, etc, appropriating, sampling, copying, cataloging, scanning, indexing, chatting, and audio/video-streaming (think of these as a new list of gerunds to supercede Bartholomae's *knowing, selecting, evaluating, reporting, concluding, and arguing*). If a Happening or Duchamp's *Large Glass* or a Rauschenberg combine-painting or a Beuys multiple or a Koons sculpture are typical examples of avant-garde art, we might think of synchronous/asynchro-nous conversation transcripts, Story-Space hypertexts, Web pages, emails, or even informal drafts as species of avant-garde composition. Since the compositional arena is now more broadly cultural, which implies post-typographic, the "space on the page" has been ruptured, as well as concomitant standards of evaluation; according to Amerika:

> By actively engaging themselves in the continuous exchange and prolifera-tion of collectively-generated electronic publications, individually-designed creative works, manifestos, live on-line readings, multi-media interactive hypertexts, conferences, etc., Avant-Pop artists and the alternative networks they are a part of will eat away at the conventional relics of a bygone era where the individual artist-author creates their beautifully-crafted, original works of art to be consumed primarily by the elitist art-world and their busi-ness-cronies who pass judgment on what is appropriate and what is not.

Notions of correspondence (whether to a representational standard or a discursive tradition) are irrelevant; Arthur C. Danto caught this spirit of the inapplicability of traditional aesthetics to the avant-garde compo-sition when he titled an essay on post-modern art "Whatever Happened to Beauty?"

So the parallels between writing instruction and the visual arts, both seen as composition, are compelling. The allegory I present in this book—looking at the spaces of writing instruction through/as spaces associated directly and tangentially with the Happenings movement (including its pre- and post-history)—might best be thought of as Materialist History of Composition Studies as Gallery Tour. Benjamin has defined historical materialism as rupturing the seamless, epic narra-tive of history at many points—or rather, seeing historical works as always-already ruptured, permanently destabilized, as "incorporat[ing] both their pre-history and their after-history in virtue of which their pre-history, too, can be seen to undergo constant change" (*One-Way Street* 351). It is the dynamic Hal Foster uses to describe the movement of the historical and neo-avant-garde: "a continual process of protension and retension, a complex relay of anticipated futures and reconstructed pasts" (29). I want to tour the spaces of several galleries, spaces made from the ruptures in Composition's history—inspect the wreckage, in order to show the promise of the Happenings for Composition as well as the huge gray *longueur* of its pale post-Happenings replacement, Eighties Composition. In so doing, I hope to begin a reconfiguration of our field's pre- and after-history; my project is best defined as an alternate history. But where to begin our gallery crawl? Several theorists have already begun a materialist reading of the works of Composition Studies. Harris, for example, revisited the primal scene of the 1966 Dartmouth Seminar, finding a gap through which to view the present: "Rather than read Dartmouth as the scene of a heroic shift in the theory and practice of teaching, then, I want to look at it as a moment in which the conflicts that define English studies were dramatized with unusual clarity . . . [so] we can begin to map out some of the contested terms and ideas that structure our work in English today" ("After Dartmouth" 633). And Faigley has pried into the key date of 1963 (when important papers were presented at the conference on College Composition and Communication and both *Themes, Theories, and Therapies* and *Research on Written Composition* were published) to understand why, although "the disciplinary era of composition studies comes with the era of post-modernity . . . there is seemingly little in the short history of composition studies that suggests a postmodern view of heterogeneity and difference as liberating forces" (14). 1963 and 1966 are interesting dates, coinciding with the high times of the Happenings, but since, for the purposes of this discussion, I'm more interested in looking at Galleries and Museums than Conferences or Seminars, I'd like to push my time-travel's starting point back a bit further, to 1962, to a fateful moment in art theory, in composition theory; a moment as fully conflicted as Harris's or Faigley's; a Gallery-setting in which two competing compositional philosophies clash: a conceptual struggle between the idea of composing serious, substantive work that authentically replicates the form and content of the historical, disciplinary tradition, on the one hand, and the anti-school of thought that's satisfied to create little bits of seemingly worthless nothing that simply give pleasure and intensify one's life. The first stop on our gallery tour, then, returns us to 1962, to that very clash-site, and allows us to take as our arch-compositionist Robert Childan, the owner of that ur-gallery, American Artistic Handcrafts Inc.

Childan and his gallery are figures in Philip K. Dick's *The Man in the High Castle*, an "alternate world" science-fiction novel, the premise of which is to chronicle what history would have been like in the years immediately following America's defeat in WWII. How that alternate history relates to Childan is that the Japanese, who occupy the western half of the U.S., have become insatiable collectors of authentic American artifacts. Childan's gallery is one of the most elite on the West Coast; it sells "no contemporary American art; only the past could be represented here" (9). His customers' passion for the historicity contained in 'original' artifacts has become obsessive, as seen in an exchange between Childan and a Japanese couple visiting his gallery. Childan breathlessly informs them of some choice items he expects to receive.

> "I am getting in a New England table, maple, all wood-pegged, no nails. Immense beauty and worth. And a mirror from the time of the 1812 War. And also the aboriginal art: a group of vegetable-dyed goat-hair rugs."
>
> "I myself," the man said, "prefer the art of the cities."
>
> "Yes," Childan said eagerly. "Listen, sir. I have a mural from WPA post-office period, original, done on board, four sections, depicting Horace Greeley. Priceless collector's item."
>
> "Ah," the man said, his dark eyes flashing.
>
> "And a Victrola cabinet of 1920 made into a liquor cabinet."
>
> "Ah."
>
> "And, sir, listen: *framed signed picture of Jean Harlow.*"
>
> The man goggled at him.
>
> "Shall we make arrangements?" Childan said, seizing this correct psychological instant. (10)

Many in that alternate reality remain skeptical in the face of "the ever-growing Japanese craze for Americana" (31). To impress on a young woman that "this whole damn historicity business is nonsense[, t]hose Japanese are bats" (34), a cynic produces two identical Zippo lighters and challenges her to "feel" the historicity in one:

> "Listen. One of those two Zippo lighters was in Franklin D. Roosevelt's pocket when he was assassinated. And one wasn't. One has historicity, a hell

of a lot of it. As much as any object ever had. And one has nothing. Can you feel it?" He nudged her. "You can't. You can't tell which is which. There's no 'mystical plasmic presence,' no 'aura' around it." (64)

That man sees the absurdity in "historicity" because the object itself, if it has any worth, should be valuable for the idea it represents, the statement that it makes, not for its status as fetish. But with modernity, use-value gives way to symbolic exchange. The object is intentionally invested with a verifiable aura, signifying authenticity; its *originality*, then, only exists in its certifiability:

> "That's my point! I'd have to prove it to you with some sort of document. A paper of authenticity. And so it's all a fake, a mass delusion. The paper proves its worth, not the object itself." (65)

The above exchange between Childan and his customers shows the seductive control exercised by the fetish-object and the documentation-apparatus surrounding it.

The pressure to own 'original' artifacts (and the rewards to be made selling them) gives rise in Dick's novel to an underground of forgers, specializing in the reproduction of 'authenticity.' Childan realizes the limited life-span of the historicity business when a patron, a connoisseur, notes that an 1860 Army Model Colt .44 he is selling is imitation and asks, "Is it possible, sir, that you, the owner, dealer, in such items, *cannot distinguish the forgeries from the real?*" (58). The object itself is an artifact of a production system, made according to operative criteria (what Baudrillard calls "the metaphysics of the code" [*Simulations* 103]); and because the code can be re-activated, the object can be re-produced. But the aura can't. The aura can only be put there by a master's own hand. As such, as *something*, it can be discerned, measured. According to Crimp, the aura is "that aspect of the work that can be put to the test of chemical analysis or connoisseurship" (111). Indeed, the technician who finally determines the status of Childan's counterfeit Colt .44 through such analysis underscores Crimp:

> It's a reproduction cast from plastic molds except for the walnut. Serial numbers all wrong. The frame not casehardened by the cyanide process. Both brown and blue surfaces achieved by a modern quick-acting technique, the whole gun artificially aged, given a treatment to make it appear old and worn. . . . It's a good job. Done by a real pro. (59)

Without an aura, the work has no institutional value: "the museum has no truck with fakes or copies or reproductions. The presence of the artist in the work must be detectable; that is how the museum knows it has something authentic" (Crimp 112). But in the age of mechanical reproduction, the aura has a tough time of it, according to Baudrillard: "In its indefinite reproduction, the system puts an end to the myth of its origin and to all the referential values it has secreted along the way" (*Simulations* 112). The knowledge of how tenuous the notions of originality and authenticity are, how easily production becomes reproduction, persuades Childan to begin dealing in a different art: handmade jewelry. Even though the handmade pieces seem like "miserable, small, worthless-looking blob[s]" (172) to a Japanese connoisseur, Childan cynically realizes "*with these, there's no problem of authenticity*" (145). Gradually, Childan's cynicism about the jewelry is replaced with real enthusiasm. Toward the close of the book, when a Japanese aficionado of historicity, Mr. Tagomi, enters his gallery, looking for "something of unusual interest" (219), Childan proudly shows him the worthless blobs of jewelry, affirming to his customer (who feels "they are just scraps"): "Sir, these are the new. . . . This is the new life of my country, sir. The beginning in the form of tiny imperishable seeds. Of beauty" (219). Childan warns Tagomi "the new view in your heart" (220) afforded by the cheap-looking pin does not come at once. Tagomi, unconvinced, nevertheless takes Childan's recommendation. Later he realizes Childan's truth, the truth of form's other scene—its *informe*:

> Metal is from the earth, he thought as he scrutinized. From below: from that realm which is the lowest, the most dense. Land of trolls and caves, dank, always dark. Yin world, in its most melancholy aspect. World of corpses, decay and collapse. Of feces. All that has died, slipping and disintegrating back down layer by layer. The daemonic world of the immutable; the time-that-was.
>
> And yet, in the sunlight, the silver triangle glittered. It reflected light. Fire, Mr. Tagomi thought. Not dank or dark object at all. Not heavy, weary, but pulsing with life. The high realm, aspect of yang: empyrean, ethereal. . . . Yes, this thing has disgorged its spirit: light. And my attention is fixed; I can't look away. Spellbound by mesmerizing shimmering surface which I can no longer control. No longer free to dismiss. (223–224)

Childan's gallery is a good starting point from which to allegorically view Composition Studies of the past thirty-odd years because of the implications involved in our field's gradual rejection of that yin world of collapse and decay in its instructional theories, emphasizing instead an ethereal, code-driven, textual re-representation of authenticity and authority. The story told by American Artistic Handcrafts Inc. recurs too frequently in Composition Studies. It's the same story told in every museum's gallery: work is either a classic, desired piece (assuming it's not fake, plagiarized) or it's crude, worthless, fecal—in our galleries, for example, we teach either writers or students (and students' work can be either strong or weak). A re-appreciation of a Happenings aesthetic can reveal what our strictly empyrean formalism misses, the other scene of its vision. What we learn from Childan and Tagomi is the potential effect of a delay in standards: deferring the quick dismissal of aura-less trash, staring a bit longer, watching the light catch, opening ourselves to the new view in our hearts. Work of true beauty and artistic power, it seems, can be crafted in very basic ways from seemingly degraded materials, paying little or no attention to formal or historical tradition. Childan and Tagomi learned a Happenings lesson: to follow a work where it goes; to turn off expectations and be open to meaning, intensity, beauty. I think of Braque, who knew he was finished with a painting when nothing remained of the original idea. Composition's definition of finished writing, on the other hand, is when the original intention is perfectly realized.

And so this book, which I write out of the lull I feel in contemporary Composition Studies, a disenchantment, which I would locate both in theory and pedagogy. What should be the central space for intellectual inquiry in the academy has become identified as either a service course designed to further the goals of other academic units or a cultural-studies space in which to investigate identity politics. An enthusiasm has been lost, particularly among those entering the profession. Even the newest technologies for composition are rapidly succumbing to this lull—witness collections on what makes writing good in the digital age, taxonomies of email, or standards for evaluating web pages. The cause of our current stasis? Doubtless the major influence has been Composition's professionalization, its self-tormented quest for disciplinary stature. The price we have paid for our increased credibility as an academic field has been a narrowing of the bandwidth of what used to pass for composition. In figuring out our place among the disciplines, we have made the notion of disciplines paramount—what we talk about when we talk about writing is writing-in-the-academy or "real-world" writing that reflects (legitimates) academic departments. This streamlining of the previously disparate narratives of Composition means that less and less do our genres represent a kind of expressivist or art-writing, a writing for non-academic (or non-ideological) goals, that "first step toward poetry." To counter, then, here is my brief journey into the tenets and figures of a group of avant-garde artists who, for want of a better term, I loosely group around the concept "Happenings." It is meant as both disruptive and restorative: to interrupt the uncritical acceptance of Composition as currently institutionalized by recollecting the more open-ended, poetic theories of form and content, congruent with developments in other compositional fields, which remain our forgotten heritage.

If you desire a brief explanation or outline for what's to follow: Marcel Duchamp is first discussed as an acknowledged influence on Happenings composition: not merely for the negationist impulse of dadaism (Happenings as neo-dadaist art), but for the totality of his composition theory: the handmade artwork, connoting aura, intentionality and originality vs. the chosen, pre-manufactured readymade (evoking Benjamin's ideas of mechanical reproduction); the idea of the conceptualist, or artist-in-general; the concept of the text as catalogue (the *Green Box*, a catalogue of Duchamp's ideas and directions, as text, giving rise to notions of hypertextuality). Duchamp's enormous impact on twentieth-century art in general, the way he caused artists to re-articulate conceptions of beauty, form and criteria (e.g., Judd's sole criteria that the "work need only to be interesting"), has had shockingly little effect on Composition Studies, doubtless contributing to our relatively marginal position as theorists and practitioners of form and language. Then, a discussion of Jackson Pollock, whose Abstract Expressionist gesture played a major role on the thinking of the Happenings pioneers (Allan Kaprow, for example, acknowledged the impact of Pollock's "diaristic gesture" [26] and the way the canvases "ceased to become paintings and became *environments*" [56], on his own Happenings). Emphasis will be given to Pollock's ideas on process (as "action painter"); his insistence on the statement in a work over its form; and the way his paintings (especially the drip paintings) produce a new sort of all-over, infinite text, as opposed to an image-text carefully composed to acknowledge frame-borders. Chapter three will offer a two-tiered retrospective (in terms of mainstream art and the specialized field of writing instruction) of historical Happenings Composition; an anti-gallery tour of compositional spaces, reviewing both the formal, material, theoretical, and institutional constraints against which artists/compositionists worked to forge a new practice. Chapter four focuses on the spatial, architectural, institutional context—the Museum and the Gallery; the University and the Classroom—which Happenings compositionists strained so consciously against. To theorize institutional restrictions at the basic level of architecture, I will draw on the ideas of the situationists, contemporaries of the Happenings artists. The situationists represented the avant-garde of architectural theory, offering a poetics of architecture, one which railed against the clean lines of Modernist forms and demanded exotic spaces and buildings capable of housing passionate dream-scenes. The situationist impulse—the imperative for a new architecture, a new urbanism; the need to engage zones of passion and poetry—was that of the Happenings: a need for a new intensity. The situationist Ivan Chtcheglov's *cri de coeur* could have come from a Happenings manifesto:

> And you, forgotten, your memories ravaged by all the consternations of two hemispheres, stranded in the Red Cellars of Pali-Kao, without music and without geography, no longer setting out for the hacienda *where the roots think of the child and where the wine is finished off with fables from an old almanac.* Now that's finished. You'll never see the hacienda. It doesn't exist. *The hacienda must be built.* (Knabb 1)

It reminds one of Kaprow's similar call for a new architectonics of passion, the way no material was off-limits if it could lead to construction of poeticized spaces:

> Objects of every sort are materials for the new art: paint, chairs, food, electric and neon lights, smoke, water, old socks, a dog, movies, a thousand other things which will be discovered by the present generation of artists. Not only will these bold creators show us, as if for the first time, the world we have always heard about but ignored, but they will disclose entirely unheard of happenings. ("Legacy of Jackson Pollock" 56–57)

The next chapter explores the turn our field took from the 1960s to the 1980s, particularly in the way we abandoned this neo-avant-garde direction, while it remained a recurring preoccupation of other compositional fields. The dangers of academicization and institutionalization were not felt as acutely in Composition of the late 1970s. We turned away from the expressivist concerns of process to a taxonomizing of academic forms and contexts. While the visual arts kept unresolved the question of the frame and the museum (formal, institutional tensions), Composition

Studies cheerfully accepted both as givens—the specific, contextual constraints of a given work would unproblematically frame it, and the larger institutional setting (the academy and/or the professions) was never in doubt. Specifically, this chapter offers a reverse-image of our abandonment of the neo-avant-garde, in examining how the popular (that peculiar, post-Happenings, dadaist-inspired, negation-soundtrack of the popular known as punk) was excised from our theory (quite the opposite of the Happenings Compositionists, for whom the popular was crucial material). The Conclusion will begin to theorize the Happenings Redux: how the tenets of the neo-avant-garde can be returned to a position of useful material in our field; how we can retain a kind of neo-expressivist goal of spiritual, conceptual intensity; and how the goal of composition as art-in-general and the creation of a classroom environment where anything can happen would play themselves out curricularly.

The Happenings compositionists-in-general whom I like (and whom I learn from) have been absent too long from the history and practice of college composition. We have so much to learn from all of them: Pollock, with his idiosyncratic statement exuberantly crafted out of the everyday; Kaprow and Rauschenberg, Happenings artists proper (and their Fluxus colleagues, as well as their Performance Art descendants), with the dazzling, playful symbologies of their homemade rituals; situationists like Debord and Constant, with the labyrinthine traces of their psychogeographic ramblings through an urbanity refigured by passion; Duchamp, with his compelling redefinition of beauty; Johnny Rotten et al.'s brilliant compositions of hatred, made from the encaustic bile they dripped onto "official" culture; or John Cage, finding a profound text while staring at the side of a building in Manhattan or out of the window of a train traveling through Kansas. All of them locate composition, not in theory or an institution, but in a very specific, lived place of passion and desire. I find such grounding very much absent from Composition Studies. I mean, where is the sense of *this* in the epistemic era of Composition: of, say, gazing out the window of the St. James Hotel, and *knowing* no one can sing the blues like Blind Willie McTell? That would be a fascinating, complex project, limning the dimensions of the everyday-sublime. How can I, or my students, really be expected to be excited about having to do something like the following instead?

The mathematician Jacob Bronowski defined civilization as all activities directed at the future. Write a paper in which you explain the preparation your education has given you for citizenship and for assuming your heritage as a member of civilization in the future. Do you feel prepared to become a guardian of our future culture and values? Why or why not? What role do the humanities play in your ability to deal with the future? (Weiner, *Reading* 244)

That's the kind of assignment Johnny Rotten needed only two words to write ("no future"). So what if it's the kind of writing they'll do at college? Elbow reminds us of the relative duration of academic-life to real-life. Just because the rest of the curriculum has banned enchantment in favor of a narrow conception of life-as-careerism that doesn't mean we have to go along, does it? Can't we be a last outpost? a way station for poetry, ecophilia, spiritual intensity, basic human (not disciplined) style?

I realize any recuperative history like this will smack of nostalgia and idealization. I suppose that's inescapable—if the art and theory of the era didn't have ideals I felt were valuable, I wouldn't look longingly back to compositional ideas I feel were abandoned too quickly. But please don't think my nostalgia for those kickier times blinds me to the problematic aspects of the Happenings theorists; there are aspects about them I find troubling. The reliance on naked women in many of their pieces has already been roundly criticized (Sandford *xxii*), and there's little I can add, except to note a few cautionary points before a narrow feminist reading sees the Happenings as colored on that score: an undressing of social conventions can often be literally articulated, a return to an intimacy with nature (as Happenings/Fluxus artists like Beuys wanted) can mean a warm sensuality about the body, and, finally, Lebel and others just as often featured nude males in their work as females. In general, there is often a wide-eyed fervency and righteousness about the theorists which can be at times touching, at times embarrassing. And at times, it can degenerate into an arrogant stridency that seems to mimic the very systems of artistic purity and discrimination the artists and theorists sought to overturn; for example, in his *Tulane Drama Review* interview with Allan Kaprow, Richard Schechner complains that "places like the Electric Circus and Cheetah have sprung up: pseudo-psychedelic turn-on, packaged Happenings . . . the Broadway of intermedia" (Schnechner, "Extensions" 227–228). Do we really want to say something happening can't occur in a commercial space *per se*? Even if a space like the Cheetah was a culturally mainstream distillation of the rawer art movement, it could still be a potentially cool place, as I recall, given the music and the crowd mix. Much better is Cage's attitude of bliss criticism when coming upon things he doesn't much care for: when Richard Kostelanetz interviews Cage, he asks him if some theatre pieces are better than others; Cage dismisses the question:"Why do you waste your time and mine by trying to get value judgments? Don't you see that when you get a value judgment, that's all you have? They are destructive to our proper business, which is curiosity and awareness"(*John Cage* 27).

And take Kaprow himself, for example: besides crucial historical interest, many of his pieces contain genuine poetry, but at times he sounds like he's trying to become the Aristotle of the Happenings movement. It's one thing to affirm an open-ended tenet like "*The line between art and life should be kept as fluid, and perhaps indistinct, as possible*" (*Assemblages* 188–189), but occasionally his critical theory results in a rigidity worthy of formalism: "*The performance of a Happening should take place over several widely spaced, sometimes moving and changing locales*" (*Assemblages* 190). That he adhered so strongly to this in many of his works ultimately limits them. Or take a comment he made on the sublime Happenings of George Brecht. Brecht wrote "sparse scores," as Kaprow calls them; zen suggestions printed out and given to people who want an opportunity to re-appreciate basic life: for example, "DIRECTION Arrange to observe a sign indicating direction of travel. • travel in the indicated direction • travel in another direction" (*Assemblages* 195). Kaprow shows an odd faithlessness in mass pedagogy by his comment on this work. He, of course, can appreciate the rarefied quality of Brecht's Happenings, but

> Beyond a small group of initiates, there are few who could appreciate the moral dignity of such scores, and fewer still who could derive pleasure from going ahead and doing them without self-consciousness. In the case of those Happenings with more detailed instructions or more expanded action, the artist must be present at every moment, directing and participating, for the tradition is too young for the complete stranger to know what to do with such plans if he got them. (*Assemblages* 195)

It seems odd for an anti-tradition like the Happening to be spoken of in the privileged language of the VIP lounge. There is a will-to-genre there that disturbs; the *complete stranger*'s work should be embraced for its potential, its possibilities: in fact, a stranger would have something important to add to a genre like the Happenings, whose project is, as Robert Whitman defined it, "the story of all those perceptions and awarenesses you get just from being a person" (Kostelanetz *Theatre* 224). Kaprow further reduces the full-blown nature of the Happening's unpredictability by prescribing that those participating in a Happening "have a clear idea what they are to do. This is simply accomplished by writing out the scenario or score for all and discussing it thoroughly with them beforehand." Tellingly, he adds, "In this respect it is not different from the preparations for a parade, a football match, a wedding, or a religious service. It is not even different from a play" (*Assemblages* 197). For one who bemoaned the Cheetah, his compositional grammar is strangely bound by extant realities; instead of trying to build the New Babylon (or even settling for a detournement of the city-space), he simply inserts his compositions into existent theatres (now broadly defined). So, "A Happening could be composed for a jetliner going from New York to Luxembourg with stopovers at Gander, Newfoundland, and Reykjavik, Iceland. Another Happening would take place up and down the elevators of five tall buildings in midtown Chicago" (*Assemblages* 191). The pieces often become derivative of each other, and sometimes seem to include Surrealism for its own sake. On another note, there's a slight queasiness when one thinks of how often the final effect of Kaprow's (and others') Happenings was ecologically distasteful. This, for example, from Kaprow's comments regarding *Self-Service* (1967).

> Other of my Happenings have had far more dramatic and deliberate imagery.
>
> The majority of events involved doing something and leaving it. For example, we set up a banquet in the Jersey marshes on the side of a busy highway—a complete banquet with food, wine, fruit, flowers, and place-settings, crystal glasses and silver coins in the glasses. And we simply left it, never went back. It was an offering to the world: whoever wants this, take it. So many of the things had just that quality of dropping things in the world and then going on about your business. (Schechner "Extensions" 221)

The world, I feel, is full up already; there's enough intense, natural text to inspire already. This surreal overlay of wasteful excrescence is unnecessary. At least Rauschenberg got his props from the garbage and reused much of them in his Combine paintings and performances.

So, no, this is not wide-eyed, naive nostalgia. My project does not mark a reactionary reverence for old forms, but rather a crucial need to understand the irreverence, the disgust, for old forms, as well as the passion for rethinking forms. I certainly don't want to "make love to the past" as Cage calls it (Kostelanetz *John Cage* 25). What I want is simply to reconsider a group of artists and compositionists who wondered why texts couldn't be new, interesting, and transformative. Why they could-n't experiment with new materials and forms, blur disciplines and boundaries, and subsume the whole with a life-affirming humor. Mostly these artists wondered why their compositions couldn't strive for a sub-limity in the participants that might, in some small way, change the world. I locate my interest, then, in the definition of the Happenings put forward by Jean-Jacques Lebel. They weren't meant to recover a lost world, he claimed, but to create a new one, "imperceptibly gaining on reality" (276). Cage speaks of how art can only offer so much, can only be so consumable, and then you need something new. He fails to under-stand "people attacking the avant-garde on the very notion that the new was something we should not want. But it is a necessity now" (Kostelanetz *John Cage* 25). The forms and techniques of the past are used up, "gone . . . finished. We must have something else to consume. We have now [in 1968], we've agreed, the new techniques. We have a grand power that we're just becoming aware of in our minds" (25). But in Composition, we barely began using that grand power before we abandoned it. I want to see how and why we failed meaningfully to employ those new techniques and what that might say about our current need. It's almost too heartbreaking to read the texts of the Happenings—the scripts, interviews, manifestos—so militant yet joyful, so righteous yet open, so convinced yet innocent. That the world hasn't changed overall in their wake takes nothing from them or their the-ory. They changed me. And others, too, I bet.

English Composition as a Happening is about the need to address deep, basic humanity in this modern, over-sophisticated age. The Happenings exist as one of the 20th century's periodic attempts to revive a spirit of primitive tribalism in modernity, the aesthetic collective as spiritual cult. Performances of Happenings seemed to occur out of a felt need for new collective spiritual rituals; in staging them, old technologies were renewed just as frequently as newer, more sophisticated ones were used. "Performance art, sometimes hardly distinguishable from a casual ges-ture, emerges like an artistic regression" (Molderings 176). Macrorie's theory, Coles's classroom work, Deemer's and Lutz's materials . . . read-ing them is like sitting in a circle and listening to a patient elder gently guide us on the vision-quest, using parables and jokes and truths. It's so retro, it's become avant-garde. Their pedagogy sometimes seems such a part of the fabric of life that it's hardly distinguishable from a casual ges-ture, much like the student writing they offer as exempla. Mariellen

Sandford reflects on the renewed interest in Fluxusart and Happenings in the Preface to her republication of the famous 1963 *Tulane Drama Review* issue devoted to the Happenings. She feels the recuperation of the Happenings in the decade following the 1980s makes spiritual sense; for her, this renewal of attention responds to "a healthy need for inspiration—the inspiration to break free of a decade that in many ways rivaled the conservatism of the years preceding the Fluxus and Happening movements" (xix). Such a project, then, is desublimatory, restoring certain repressed voices to a position of innovative commentary. It was the compositionists of the Happenings era who first felt this tension in our field between deeply humanist goals and the limits of academic conventions. Macrorie's *Uptaught* chronicled "the dead language of the schools . . . [in which] nobody wrote live. Same old academic stuff" (11, 14). And Deemer felt composition to be "the rigid child of a rigid parent" (121); in order to transform that rigidity into a McLuhanesque "electric drama" (123), he urged the "shock and surprise" of the Happening, writing class now conceived of as the theatre of mixed means. The gist of my book is nicely expressed by a phrase from Thierry de Duve: "the paradoxical sense of the future that a deliberately retrospective gaze opens up" (*Kant* 86). I offer, then, these backward glances, in fervent hope: to capture the Happenings spirit for our own Composition, shaking off more than a decade of conservative professionalism; to fracture our field's genres open for possibilities, risks, and material exploration, leading to a Composition in which faith and naiveté replace knowingness and expertise; to put pressure on Composition's canon, recalibrating the field according to a general economy of the compositional arts—a destabilized site of various competing schools, undercut by an on-going, productive tension between the academic and the avant-garde; to liberate thinking in our field from the strictly semantic, re-opening Composition as a site where radical explorations are appreciated, where aesthetic criteria still come into play, but criteria not merely cribbed off an endless, formalist tape-loop. Put simply, to resume building Composition's Hacienda.

1

"WHAT IS COMPOSITION . . . ?"
AFTER DUCHAMP
(Notes Toward a General Teleintertext)

1. English Composition as a Happening (as all composition that followed him does, consciously or not) begins with Duchamp. When
Richard Kostelanetz interviews Allan Kaprow, who coined the term
Happening, "the conversation opens with Kaprow speaking of Marcel
Duchamp" (*The Theatre of Mixed Means* 102). Calvin Tomkins calls the
influence of Duchamp on Robert Rauschenberg, creator of some of the
most poetically charged Happenings-like theater events of the era, "crucial . . . , confirming and reinforcing what must often have seemed a
highly questionable use of [his] talent" (*Off the Wall* 131). There is that
amazing moment of desire, in 1954, when Rauschenberg and his friend
Jasper Johns wander amazed through the recently installed Arensberg
Collection of Duchamp's art in the Philadelphia Museum; stopping in
front of one of the works, a birdcage filled with sugar cubes called *Why
Not Sneeze?* (1921), Rauschenberg can't restrain the urge to poke his fingers through the thin bars of the birdcage to try and steal one of the
marble lumps of sugar inside. A museum guard suddenly appeared:
"Don't you know," the guard said in a bored tone of voice, "that you're
not supposed to touch that crap?" (Tomkins 130).

The scene of Duchamp, then, is typical of "Composition as a
Happening": what's conventionally thought of as a questionable use of
talent turns out to be crucially influential, poetic; what's prized enough
to steal is tediously dismissed by the guardians of culture as so much
crap. An account of Duchamp's influence on Happenings Composition,
then, is in large part a story of seemingly failed production, work which
is judged too crappy to win prizes. Failure is a fitting lens by which to view
Duchamp. There was the time, coming home in a taxi, March 1912, with
a painting that was supposed to . . . well, not win prizes, of course. It
couldn't have. It was his *Nude Descending a Staircase,* and the show where it
was to be exhibited was in Paris at the Société des Artistes Indépendants.

The slogan of this salon, open to anyone, was *ni récompense ni jury*, so there were no prizes to win, no panels to award them. But even if there were, Duchamp was out of the running before the show began. A 1953 catalogue from the Musée d'Art Moderne refers to the story: "1912. March-April. Paris. 28th Salon des Indépendants. Gleizes, Le Fauconnier, Léger, Metzinger and Archipenko, members of the hanging committee, turn it into a great demonstration of Cubism" (Lebel *Marcel Duchamp* 10). Duchamp's *Nude* was a sort of culmination; he'd taken Cubism as far as it interested him. He was at the time moving out of, away from, that particular school of painting; it implied a technology, an aesthetic, a certain problem set and certain materials, with which he'd grown bored. The show's hanging committee must have thought . . . a Cubist nude? This is a joke, right? And one they certainly didn't want played on their *great demonstration.* So Gleizes convinces Duchamp's brothers to get him to withdraw it. He does, and riding home in the cab, with this amazing work next to him, he feels some bitterness, surely, but vindication, as well, knowing he succeeded in turning his canvas into a machine. "Just the same," he smiles, "it moves" (Lebel *Marcel Duchamp* 9). Then there was the Big Show of 1917, the American counterpart to the Indépendants. Another show which was supposedly open to anyone, but another show which refused one of Duchamp's works—this one, the urinal called *Fountain.* That piece, taken to Stieglitz's studio, photographed (inscribed on glass), and then mysteriously disappearing—why, its photographic representation alone is enough to ensure its central place in art history. And finally, the later Duchamp, the one who has since left the stylistic nostalgia of painting's cult of technique (its mystic craftsmanship) behind to pursue the mechanical processes of "precision oculism," at a French trade fair in the 1930s, trying to sell even one of his *Rotoreliefs,* those fascinating revolving spirals, made for a kind of optical massage, to transport perception to another place. But his project fails. Roché recalls the scene with a certain smug glee:

> None of the visitors, hot on the trail of the useful, could be diverted long enough to stop [at Duchamp's booth]. A glance was sufficient to see that between the garbage compressing machine and the incinerators on the left, and the instant vegetable chopper on the right, this gadget of his simply wasn't useful.
>
> When I went up to him, Duchamp smiled and said, 'Error, one hundred per cent. At least, it's clear.'
>
> These *Rotoreliefs* have since become collectors' items. (84–85)

Ah, that Marcel. Even in chronicling his failures, we simply chart his success. But yet each failing must have been felt acutely at the time. "Given
that . . . ; if I suppose I'm suffering a lot" (Duchamp 23). Failure intense
enough, for instance, to warrant inscribing a theme of lament in his
most famous work, the *Large Glass* (1915–1923). Lebel reminds us of a
note to that effect scrawled in *The Green Box* (1934), concerning

> the disillusioned litanies of the glider: "Slow life. Vicious circle. Onanism.
> Horizontal. Return trips on the buffer. The trash of life. Cheap construction.
> Tin, ropes, wire. Eccentric wooden pulleys. Monotonous fly-wheel. Beer pro-
> fessor." All these terms express a single one: *ÉCHECS*, which Duchamp, with
> his instinct for inner meanings, seems in some way to have made his motto.
> (*Marcel Duchamp* 67)

Échecs, we are reminded, is the French term for "checks" and "failures,"
as well as "chess." For Duchamp, chess was "like constructing a mechanism . . . by which you win or lose" (136). So *chess*, as *failure/ success*, both
in accordance, delayed, in *check*. Motto, indeed.

Like many, I'm interested in Duchamp. I'm interested, for example,
in failures that really aren't, in works barred from gaining the prize
which end up changing the world. Brief, personal jottings that become
a litany for posterity; apparently impoverished writing that proves a rich
text. I'm interested in Duchamp, then, the way I'm interested in writing,
writing done by anyone-whoever: useless, failed, nothing-writing by
some nobody that turns out to be really something. I'm interested in
what Duchamp reveals about our era, the Modernist era, specifically in
the way Modernism is institutionalized in both the larger culture and
our particular field. I'm interested in the way Duchamp, almost from
the start, offered an alternative Modernism, one that constantly chal-
lenged forms, materials, and contexts. This was the effect Duchamp had
on the Happenings, showing how alternative technologies and strategies can change fundamental compositional questions. To represent
Modernism in our field, I'll draw heavily on David Bartholomae's piece
"What is Composition and Why Do We Teach It?", an article that exists
as his attempt at the field's self-definition. I choose Bartholomae, as
always, because I feel he manifests some of the most committed thinking about students and writing in our literature, but thinking which nevertheless results in the persistence of a very specific compositional
program. The limitations of that program I find not so surprising, given
that Modernism is all about limits, but—and this is my central point—

they may be limits we no longer want to define our composition. We have increasingly different compositional means: new tools for the mechanical reproduction of texts and an on-going electronic salon in which to circulate them. Materially, Modernism delimits choice, fixed as it is on a certain work with certain materials; Duchamp didn't:

> [I]f you can find other methods for self-expression, you have to profit from them. It's what happens in all the arts. In music, the new electronic instruments are a sign of the public's changing attitude toward art. . . . Artists are offered new media, new colors, new forms of lighting; the modern world moves in and takes over, even in painting. It forces things to change naturally, normally. (Cabanne 93)

Painting was simply "a means of expression, not an end in itself" (Duchamp 127). Modernist Composition, I would argue, the nemesis of Happenings artists, seeks to define its ends in terms of narrowly-defined means, despite the modern world's take-over.

2. In "What is Composition?", Bartholomae defines the enterprise as "a set of problems" located, mostly institutionally, around notions of "language change," specifically as those notions affect the "writing produced by writers who were said to be unprepared" (11). Bartholomae, here as elsewhere in his writings, structures his analysis of this set of problems around a few student papers—in this case, two essays from Pittsburgh student writing competitions and a travel-narrative, written in Bartholomae's introductory composition course, concerning a trip to St. Croix the writer took as member of a religious youth-group. The problem set Bartholomae theorizes through these papers concerns his general project, using textual artifacts to articulate "the sources and uses of writing, particularly writing in schooling, where schooling demands/enables the intersection of tradition and the individual talent" (12). Bartholomae focuses first on a prize-winning essay, an academic account of Pittsburgh's steel industry, which he considers "too good, too finished, too seamless, too professional" (13); he wants to open up the "official disciplinary history" to "other possible narratives" (13), suggesting this essay reads as if it were "assemble[d] . . . according to a master plan" (14). Seeming, then, to dismiss "official" composition—which would only ask of a student's revision that it "make [the writing] even more perfectly what it already is" (14), and presenting himself as a teacher who would allow a student to fracture open the text, making it "less finished and less professional" (14)—Bartholomae nonetheless manages ultimately to champion a preferred version of official composition, one whose patina is more transgressive, more outlaw, but still charged with academic cachet. The St. Croix paper is brought in as student-writing-degree-zero, which needs a hipper make-over along newly delimited Modernist lines, a remodeling (in this case) around the style of Mary Louise Pratt's travel narratives. The prose he prefers is politically more acute, so a variety of cultural-studies heuristics (like the all-purpose "Whose interests are served?" [27]) are brought to bear on the naive narrative in order to enhance it.

Analogically, Bartholomae sees most writing instruction as preparing student-artists for their juried show by having them dutifully perfect quaint, realistic sketches of traditional subject matter (in this case, simplistic renderings of St. Croix's local color); he offers instead revision as a series of treatments—a different master plan—that will complicate the sketch into a more daring work, a Cubist canvas, say. This new program nonetheless maintains a focus on the traditional compositional scene—the space on the page where the work is done and the space on the wall where it is hung and judged—a space, in general, where the writer graduates from dilettante to artist, "the space where the writer needs to come forward to write rather than recite the text that wants to be written" (14). Despite his distinction between those two verbs, in both scenarios the composition stands prior to the writer, as already-written. The juried competition is not questioned, merely the taste operative among current judges, i.e., the way "we give awards to papers we do not believe in and . . . turn away from papers we do, papers most often clumsy and awkward but, as we say to each other, ambitious, interesting" (16). The language is still the connoisseur's, now claiming vanguard status. Bartholomae claims a distinction between himself and most composition (with its "same old routine" [16]), but outside of his specific compositional space, in the space of composition-in-general—where Bartholomae is compared to, say, William Burroughs—such distinctions become moot.

So, we first must speak of prized composition. For Duchamp, art was to be rid of privilege. "No jury, no prizes," became the slogan of the American Independents, as well, of which Duchamp was a founding member. The rules for their Society stated, "Any artist, whether a citizen of the United States or any foreign country, may become a member of the Society upon filing an application therefor, paying the initiation fee and the annual dues of a member, and exhibiting at the exhibition in the year that he joins" (de Duve "Given" 190). Any artists today who want their work displayed now have an electronic exhibition-site. Though the initiation fee and the annual dues may be different, in many respects the Internet is the contemporary version of the Society of Independent Artists, a virtual museum-without-walls, a public salon open to anyone. But the academy, now as then, stands all too unaffected by the techno-democratization of the cultural space for composition. No jury, no prizes? Composition is all about prized writing, about what makes writing good; its scene, as shown in "What is Composition," always originates in a juried competition. Any artist eligible? Clearly not, for Bartholomae's theory works a very specialized field, *our field*, "writing in schooling," particularly that flashpoint, "the point of negotiation between a cultural field and an unauthorized writer" (12). There is no utopic dissembling about Beuys's dream, his basic thesis, "Everyone an artist" (Tisdall 7). Some artists will simply *not* be hung, and art, for institutionalized composition, is defined by exhibition-value. But Bartholomae's description of the juried scene delineates the confused folly that is academic judgment: Another prize-winning essay in a university contest, an essay on "Fern Hill," was

> the unanimous first choice by every judge except the one from the English department, for whom the piece was the worst example of a student reproducing a "masterful" reading (that is, reproducing a reading whose skill and finish mocked the discipline and its values). . . . The rest of us loved the lab report the chemistry professor said was just mechanical, uninspired. The rest of us loved the case study of the underground economy of a Mexican village that the sociologist said was mostly cliché and suffering from the worst excesses of ethnography. (15–16)

Such moments of disciplinary slapstick don't ironize the notion of juried writing for Bartholomae; rather, they cause him, in true Modernist fashion, to dig in his heels, insisting on the need for more discussion "on the fundamental problems of professional writing, writing that negotiates the disciplines, their limits and possibilities" (16), in the presumed belief that with enough dialogue we can give awards to papers we *do* believe in. This is composition under the sign *limited possibilities*.

3. "Composition . . . is concerned with how and why one might work with the space on the page. . . . [T]he form of composition I am willing to teach would direct the revision of the essay as an exercise in criticism. . . . I would want students not only to question the force of the text but also the way the text positions them in relationship to a history of writing" (Bartholomae 21). Such an attempt at defining the genre—finding, in this case, what is unique to composition (as opposed, say, to literature or theory, not to mention writing-in-general); doing so in terms of self-criticism or self-definition—is the Modernist enterprise. Greenberg outlines Modernism in the arts after Kant:

> What had to be exhibited and made explicit was that which was unique and irreducible not only in art in general but also in each particular art. Each art had to determine, through the operations peculiar to itself, the effects peculiar and exclusive to itself. By doing this, each art would, to be sure, narrow its area of competence, but at the same time it would make its possession of this area all the more secure. ("Modernist Painting" 68)

(We can see at once, then, how opposed to such a program the Happenings were; witness Cage's metaphor for composition: "like an empty glass into which at any moment anything may be poured" [*Silence* 110]). The specificity of Bartholomae's composition, its "historic concern for the space on the page and what it might mean to do work there and not somewhere else" (18), is the specificity of Modernism as seen by Greenberg in his notes on Modernist painting:

> Flatness alone was unique and exclusive to that art. The enclosing shape of the support was a limiting condition, or norm, that was shared with the art of the theater; color was a norm or means shared with sculpture as well as with the theater. Flatness, two-dimensionality, was the only condition painting shared with no other art, and so Modernist painting oriented itself to flatness as it did to nothing else. (69)

Both projects involve a certain kind of work (*flatness* in one scene, *fundamental problems in professional writing, writing that negotiates the disciplines* in the other) with a certain kind of materials (stretched canvases and tubes of paint, or the texts upon which "writing in schooling" is written). And both projects are subsumed by a reflexive criticism. For Greenberg, "The essence of Modern lies, as I see it, in the use of the characteristic methods of a discipline to criticize the discipline itself—not in order to subvert it, but to entrench it more firmly in its area of competence" (67). For Bartholomae, the "goal is to call the discourse into question, to undo it in some fundamental way" (14); "an act of criticism that would enable a writer to interrogate his or her own text in relationship to the problems of writing and the problems of disciplinary knowledge" (17), not in order to subvert the discipline but to entrench it more firmly, determining "the way the text positions [students] in relationship to a history of writing" (21).

4. What Duchamp offers is Modernism-in-general: self-definitions when the definitions are endless, disciplinary erosion as the ultimate in disciplinary critique, with composition as a catalogue of the ideas that grow from such work. Duchamp wanted to evolve a new language, a new aesthetics, a new physics, dissolving the conventions that would inhibit such a realization. He wanted new words, "'*prime words*" ('divisible' only by themselves and by unity)" (31). His new discourse would *utilize colors*; it would be a *pictorial Nominalism*, conflating the verbal with the visual. For how else could *new relations* be expressed? Surely not by the *concrete alphabetic forms of languages*. His entire ouevre reads like a hypertext; almost as soon as you go into any depth on one screen, you are linked to another, each with its own unique content. *The Green Box*, for example, a collection of notes written about the *Large Glass*, exists as the information stacks for the *Glass*; click on various parts of the panels to access the awaiting text. Its function: "To reduce the *Glass* to as succinct an illustration as possible of all the ideas in the *Green Box*, which then would be a sort of catalogue of those ideas. The *Glass* is not to be looked at for itself, but only as a function of the catalogue I never made" (Lebel *Marcel Duchamp* 67). Indeed, the *Glass* can never be seen by itself: "it is no more visible in broad daylight than a restaurant window encrusted with advertisements, through which we see figures moving within . . . it is inscribed, as it were, like the other image of a double exposure" (Lebel 68). "The outside world impinges on and enters into it continually," notes Tomkins (129). Composition, then, as already-inscribed: catalog the tracings and call it a text. Duchamp tells Cabanne: "For the *Box* of 1913–1914, it's different. I didn't have the idea of a box as much as just notes. I thought I could collect, in an album like the Saint-Etienne catalogue [a sort of French Sears, Roebuck], some calculations, some reflexions, without relating them. Sometimes they're on torn pieces of paper" (42).

If this is academic writing, it's writing outside the bounds of classroom composition, writing as found palimpsest: candy wrappers, say, with hastily-scrawled phrases on the back, gathered from the grounds of the Campus of Interzone University; writing already ruptured, torn, pre-inscribed. It's much like Burroughs, who describes his text as if it were an html catalog made for cutting, clicking: "You can cut into *Naked Lunch* at any intersection point. . . . *Naked Lunch* is a blueprint, a How-To book" (224). E-conferencing, web-writing, e-mail; all the false starts and lost strands, they all amount to an inscription, *a kind of rendezvous*, a meeting-site of various texts and people, an encounter, set up and waiting. The only notion of form is hypertextual, "the fact that any form is the perspective of another form according to a certain *vanishing point* and a certain *distance*" (Duchamp 45). All writing is seen as punctuated periodically with "click here." It's writer as viewer, remote in hand, clicking, cruising, blending all televisual texts into one default program; all discrete works become subsumed in the composite text, *bits and pieces put together to present a semblance of a whole.* Lebel offers an ideological overview, explaining Duchamp's grammatology of the permanently destabilized text:

> he takes the offense against logical reality. Duchamp's attitude is always characterized by his refusal to submit to the principles of trite realism. . . . By imposing laws imbued with humor to laws supposedly serious he indirectly casts doubt upon the absolute value of the latter. He makes them seem approximations, so that the arbitrary aspects of the system risk becoming obvious. . . . Evidently he finds it intolerable to put up with a world established once and for all. (29)

It's writing as surf/fiction: you never enter the same text twice. Bartholomae and Greenberg operate from a nostalgic perspective when boundaries and genres existed. But boundaries dissolve in the Panorama of the City of the Interzone: "The Composite City where all human potentials are spread out in a vast silent market. . . . A place where the unknown past and the emergent future meet in a vibrating soundless hum" (Burroughs 106, 109).

5. It might be nice to bring in some simple math at this point. De Duve shows the usefulness of Duchamp's *algebraic comparison*, as presented in *The Green Box*. It's the ratio a/b, where a is the exposition and b the possibilities. The example Duchamp had given previously, in *The 1914 Box*, was the equation

$$\frac{\text{arrhe}}{\text{art}} = \frac{\text{shitte}}{\text{shit}}$$

Duchamp is clear on the point that the ratio doesn't yield a "solution": "the ratio a/b is in no way given by a number c [such that] $a/b = c$ but by the sign (—)" (28). Duchamp calls this sign the *sign of the accordance* (28), by which all terms vibrate together in an endless troping, infinitely possible, all terms subsumed in the mechanical hum of *arrhe*. The ratio a/b, then, acts as a form of heuristicizing, allegorizing, delaying. We can see the value of Duchamp's algebra for our own field. The way Richard Rodriguez reads Richard Hoggart's *The Uses of Literacy* becomes, for Bartholomae and Petrosky, a standard, "a way of reading we like to encourage in our students" (*Ways of Reading* 3). It is, then, Rodriguez's particular exposition, of all the possibilities inherent in Hoggart's material, which becomes a measure, the criteria the jury can use in awarding prizes. So that reading becomes a way of reading we encourage of all possible student ways. We can do the mathematics of accordance on that:

$$\frac{\text{Rodriguez}}{\text{Hoggart}} = \frac{\text{a way of reading/writing we like}}{\text{students' ways of reading/writing}}$$

The specificity and limitations at work in our field become apparent in such a ratio. It is this certain reading of certain material that comes to define the field; that becomes, specifically, the way of reading we like—a specificity Bartholomae acknowledges in "What is Composition?": "I see composition as a professional commitment to do a certain kind of work with a certain set of materials" (22).

$$\frac{\text{Rodriguez}}{\text{Hoggart}} = \frac{\text{a certain kind of work}}{\text{a certain set of materials}}$$

In many fields, the generic has subsumed the specific. In music, for example, various genres or periods have evolved (after Cage) into "sound" as a generic practice. Theater, music, dance, film, and visual art are often blurred into "performance." But Composition resists being subsumed by notions like "text" or "document." We insist on the academic as a distinction; we don't make the passage to art-ness, to beyond-academic-writing-ness; only certain-styled work can count as our writing. But Duchamp, in his readymades, interrupted the easy Modernist definition: choosing a porcelain urinal, a snow shovel, a comb, a typewriter cover, anything whatever, and then announcing it as art, disrupted the entire dynamic that named only the specific, tradition-encoded as art. Happenings artists took to such a liberating gesture immediately: suddenly the world was full of potential art; as Kaprow put it, the artist suddenly "realized . . . at that moment he had enough material for endless one-man shows" (Kostelanetz *Theatre* 102). What Duchamp did with the readymade was to legitimate a wholly unique, *un*traditional situation: "you can now be an artist without being either a painter, or a sculptor, or a composer, or a writer, or an architect—an artist at large. . . . Duchamp liberated subsequent artists from the constraints of a particular art—or skill" (de Duve *Kant* 154). And yet the best theorists in our field—like Bartholomae— continue to try and determine those now-dissolved constraints on "art in a raw state—*à l'état brut*—bad, good or indifferent" (Duchamp 139).

I've tried, in the shower of discourse available through electronic media (e-conferencing, email, WWW), to dissolve the specific parameters of my own course's composition-logic and nudge it more in the direction of Composition as a Happening. I've used more easily available materials and ways of reading those materials. My first attempt to seriously interrupt that logic was simple substitution: making Malcolm X's autobiography stand for the "history of writing," and choosing what I felt were varied readings of it (Reverend Cleage's, Penn Warren's, Joe Wood's, reviews of the book from 1965 media—even sound-bites from *Emerge* magazine of anyone-whoever's reading of Malcolm, recorded for the 1990 anniversary issue), as well as letting students choose their share of materials. My rationale was to allow students a more immediate entré into the cultural flow of words and ideas. The classroom allegory is Student-as-Jackson-Pollock, "not concerned with representing a preconceived idea, but rather with being involved in an experience of paint and canvas, directly" (Goodnough 60); just putting stuff together, that's the way the Happenings Compositionist works. I didn't want to prize any one manner of academic reading/writing, and I certainly wanted to restore materials like Malcolm's book to a place of dignity in the institution (where it had been degraded for years). I used a fluxus of readings on Malcolm to show students they could position their own reading of him somewhere, anywhere. My new equation became

$$\frac{Emerge \text{ sound-bites}}{\text{Malcolm X}} = \frac{\text{a way of reading}}{\text{students' ways of reading}}$$

Am I happy with this? Yes and no. It does what I thought it would, but I want to go further, away from the specificity of Malcolm. I don't want to replace one canonical text with a new one (no matter how canonical I think Malcolm should be in our culture). So lately my students have been reading texts on an almost-anything-whatever like gangsta rap, seeing in them a range of cultural responses (from the media, the academy, Websites, and fellow-students) and writing their own. I'm happier with the new equation:

$$\frac{\text{a reading of gangsta rap}}{\text{gangsta rap}} = \frac{\text{a way of reading}}{\text{students' ways of reading}}$$

This has proven a more democratic equivalency, allowing a richer range of the possible. Gangsta is anti-traditional, anti-canonical; its force is sheer negation. Of course, the truly dissolved, wide-open flow would be

$$\frac{\text{any reading}}{\text{any subject whatever}}$$

Plugging that back into the original equation seems worthwhile, in order to set up a sign of accordance between the Bartholomae and Petrosky standard and the anything-whatever; to spin-blur Rodriguez/Hoggart on the *Rotative Demisphère*, until they blend into noise, text.

$$\frac{\text{Rodriguez}}{\text{Hoggart}} = \frac{\text{any reading}}{\text{any subject whatever}}$$

The technology, of course, allows for no other logic—anything that comes across the screen is neutralized in the electronic hum of information. We are in a post-exchange-value-apocalypse in which the only value is use-value. Duchamp chose a bicycle wheel for his first readymade, not because it was beautiful (or rare or difficult) but because it was commonplace, easily available: if it were lost, it could be replaced "like a hundred thousand others" (Lebel *Marcel Duchamp* 35). Duchamp understood the necessity for de-valuing materiality in the new art, affording *anartism* to everyone. With writing now defined as choosing rather than fabricating, all material is equal; it's whatever catches the eye. "We will sample from anything we need. We will rip-off your mother if she has something we find appropriate for our compost-heap creations" (Amerika). Material is chosen not because it's a privileged text, a "difficult" masterpiece from the "history of writing," but because it's around, on hand. It's whatever is noticed out of the corner of one's eye from the endlessly-shifting screen before one. Gangsta rap is so commonplace as to almost be a readymade, especially given the way so many rap songs are based on sampling of previously-recorded material (Duchamp called readymades he messed with a little "assisted readymades"). Gangsta is consumed by so many of my students; it's a fairly cheap, easily available addiction: "I am a consumer," pop critic Danyel Smith says of her gangsta jones, "chomping away at the brothers as they perform some rare times with a Nat Turner gleam in their eyes" (20). Could we, then, substitute an assisted readymade like "gangsta rap" for the rarer, more traditional material of Hoggart in our initial ratio? We'd then have the ratio

$$\frac{\text{Rodriguez}}{\text{gangsta rap}}$$

which exists, of course, on the Internet, in a piece by Rodriguez called "Ganstas." Is his way of reading gangsta equal to his way of reading Hoggart? Is it (still) a way of reading we'd like to encourage? But, just what interesting reading would we *not* want to encourage? What about substituting, then, the top term in our equation, the exposition? What about anyone-whoever's reading of gangsta rap? Could that be a way of reading we'd like to encourage? Could anyone-whoever's reading of gangsta be equal to Rodriguez's? Take, for instance, this print-out of some stuff, which is no more than a series of hip-hop definitions, that a student of mine found on the net. It's from an anonymous writer's web-site, which contains, among other things, a host of gangsta-terms some other unknown writers forwarded to the site. I'm not sure where it's from, exactly, or whose it is, because the print-out is incomplete, rup-tured—my student just enclosed several printed pages from the larger site as a source he used in one of his writings—but I link it into my own site here, as greedily as Danyel Smith, 'cause some of the definitions are pretty slick:

Sexual Chocolate = a dark boldheaded nigga with a proper ass car
　　and some tight ass gear
Medusa = a fly bitch who'll make yo dick turn to stone　　<kistenma>

rims = wheels for yo sweet ass ride
regulate = to creep on some sorry ass fool (see creep . . .)　　<fhurst>

Here is some stuff from the bay.
money = scrilla, scratch, mail
bad = bootsie, janky
good = saucy　　　　　　　　　　　　<crystalt>

baller = a player wit ends in a benz　　<lfunderburg>

ballin = I have game　　　　　　　<79D9407A6>

P = Pimpish, the same as tight, slick, dope   <Berry>

bammer = busted and disgusted like half the definitions
up on here   <mold7316>

All the writers on this list are doing, when they post their definitions, is *inscribing*—cataloguing words, ideas, material that might become useful for the next writer. This is Cage's discursive project: "to find a way of writing which comes from ideas, is not about them, but which produces them" (*X*, x). Or Amerika's, in which writing becomes a therapeutic cure for Information Sickness, "a highly-potent, creatively filtered tonic of (yes) textual residue spilled from the depths of our spiritual unconscious." It's the writer as possessed individual. Writing is now conceived of as drive-by criticism, rap slang; it's the *infra-thin* possibility of gangsta definitions appearing as a Rodriguez. With all writing leveled in the Interzone, every genre blurred into one, the textu(r)ality of all prose is in an accordance, best described by Wallace, when he traces the recent turn in contemporary fiction, in which the text has become "less a novel than a piece of witty erudite extremely high-quality prose television. Velocity and vividness—the wow—replace the literary *hmm* of actual development. People flicker in and out; events are garishly there and then gone and never referred to. . . . [It's a prose that's] both amazing and forgettable, wonderful and oddly hollow . . . hilarious, upsetting, sophisticated, and extremely shallow" (192).

Is a writer who posted to that gangsta list able to "interrogate his or her own text in relationship to the problems of writing and the problems of disciplinary knowledge" (Bartholomae 17)? I think so, but I wouldn't actually pose the question; the writer'd probably think I was a *busta brown* ("a fool that hangs around and isn't even wanted" <4jcf4>). Is the writing strong, forceful, able to bring about new knowledge? Of course, and Rodriguez thinks so, too: in his "Gansta" piece he describes doing rep after rep in his "sissy gym . . . the blond pagan house of abs and pecs," where he and his ilk "read the *Wall Street Journal*, [and] lose a few pounds on the StairMaster," listening to the gangsta rap that blasts on the gym's sound system, realizing the "high moral distancing" that goes on around gangsta rap among the middle- and upper-classes, how they "consign the gangsta to subhumanity." But he also knows the sheer force of raw gangsta, its ability to foster growth and change, to survive in the Interzone; he knows, if his fellow middle- and upper-class gym rats don't, "why we use the music of violence to build up our skinny arms."

Those gangsta lexicographers above used their sound-bite spaces to write about the only thing the contemporary writer can—what is already inscribed in their screens at any given moment; they're dubbers, remixers, electronically re/inscribing and re/circulating inter-texts of the rap reality that fills their inner screens, seeing no use in imposing conventional criteria on *l'état brut*. As Amerika reads it, it's Avant-Pop, "one step further" from postmodernism:

> The main tenet of Postmodernism was: I, whoever that is, will put together these bits of data and form a Text while you, whoever that is, will produce your own meaning based off what you bring to the Text. . . . The main tenet that will evolve for the Avant-Pop movement is: I, whoever that is, am always intersecting with data created by the Collective You, whoever that is, and by interacting with and supplementing the Collective You, will find meaning.

Of course, even gangsta sound-bite writing is an easy call as Composition *text* when judged against other possible texts-as-data-intersections. 'Cause what if the composition were non-verbal, or only slightly verbal—a graphics-and sound-heavy website, perhaps? Or just barely written by the student—a catalog of links, say? Not only, perhaps, are we no longer teaching words used in a special way—"writing [that] reflects on the fundamental problems of professional writing, writing that negotiates the disciplines, their limits and possibilities" (Bartholmae 16)—we're not even sure about words themselves any more. Nesbit refers to the *Glass* as "linguistic but wordless . . . cinema with the lights up . . . a language move that makes language stop" ("Her Words"). *Langage transparent*, the other image on double-exposed glass.

6. Buying a urinal from an iron-works, affixing a name to it, and submitting it as one's work is the art of the readymade. Not so much a found art as a chosen one. But there remains an aesthetic, a judgment-quality, that makes such art the legitimate subject of pedagogy and scholarship. Material is chosen from a vaster field than the disciplined one—a generic one, where all parameters dissolve, opening onto a flat, breathtaking landscape: "Regard it as something seen momentarily, as though from a window while traveling. If across Kansas, then, of course, Kansas" (Cage *Silence* 110). Cage's glass-inscribed road-trip through Kansas becomes the primal scene of Avant-Pop composition. Only those who don't listen to the silence think it's silent; only those who don't see the canvas think it's blank. (Duchamp: "The 'blank' force of Dada was very salutary. It told you

'don't forget you are not quite so blank as you think you are'" 125). Only those who don't *choose* to read the anything-whatever, the document, feel there's no beauty, taste, or critical project there. What would it mean to have a document *pose* as composition, to have the everyday *pose* as a "difficult text"? This validates not only the readymade composition (to which only a new use or perception has been brought), but its textual concomitants, too, however ruptured—composition as the *Green Box*, the *1914 Box*, writing as notes from a work/life in progress, under the sign of the anything-whatever. De Duve traces the movement from Courbet through Duchamp: "from the represented anything-whatever to the anything-whatever plain and simple . . . the devaluation of the precious, the finished, the noble . . . the correlative rise of new egalitarian values—or anti-values" (*Kant* 328). The cult of fabrication is gone. The artist (or *arrhetist*), then, becomes "a technician of the absence of technique" (330). (In an interview in 1963, Duchamp called the readymade "a work of art without an artist to make it" [Roberts 47]). All other technical-aesthetic conventions are stripped bare; readymade writing, in the fact of its appearance as art, concedes everything except its status as writing. This locates aesthetics away from the traditional-criteria-based 'this is beautiful,' to the traditional-criteria-free 'this is art.' According to the new exhibition-value, a work, the writing, is exhibited in order to be judged as basic art (is it useful, say? interesting?), nothing more; all other conventions are seen through, transparent as a restaurant window. Duchamp has termed the readymade *inscribed*; de Duve reads that as "able to be written into the register of those things onto which the statement 'this is [writing]' is affixed" (*Kant* 394). Composition busies itself with tracing not the *having become* writing, but the failings of not having become (as it would have had it be). It wants to universalize its maxims of taste and beauty. But the only beauty left in the post-beautiful Interzone is *the beauty of indifference* (Duchamp 30). The choice of the readymade is *based on a reaction of visual indifference, a total absence of good or bad taste* (Duchamp 141). The readymade, for Duchamp, is "something one doesn't even look at, or something one looks at while turning one's head" (de Duve "Echoes" 82); it's regarded as something momentarily seen (or, for the gangsta lexicographer, heard). When the mere fact of appearance is all, then making is replaced by choosing. It's not a matter of taste, as de Duve sees it, but just "some intellectual curiosity . . . some strategic desire" (*Kant* 238). Can it simply be enough to say, as Johns did of Duchamp, that *what composition is* is "a field where language, thought and vision act upon one another" (Cabanne

109)? Can it be enough for our art that it have *arrhe*? Enough for our writing that it have *writte*? Can we allow a composition that is definitively
unfinished, an "indecisive reunion" (Duchamp 26), "with all kinds of
delays" (Duchamp 32), deferring this need for writing as a revision toward
a *certain* style, toward a *certain* end? Ends (unless they're *ends in a benz*) can
bore: "No end is in view in this fragment of a new perspective. 'In the end
you lose interest, so I didn't feel the necessity to finish it'" (Cabanne 109).

The tendency in the field is still on making rather than choosing. So
Bartholomae urges a course "that investigates the problems of writing at
the point of production," in which students practice "the ability to produce a critical reading" (28), but what he offers is nostalgia, a course in
art appreciation: "the point of the course was to teach students how and
why they might work with difficult texts" (26). *Difficult texts*, of course,
means our canon, our hit-parade. The course's program becomes learning to paint like the masters, tracing their brushstrokes, learning to paint
in the grand style, "asking students to translate their sentences into and
out of a style that might loosely be called 'Pratt-like'" (26). The reason
Duchamp broke with painting was the cloying nature of such nostalgia.
La patte was the name given to the cultish presence of the painter's hand
in the work, and to avoid that cramped space of virtuosity, Duchamp
moved from a technique of overdetermined practices to one of mechanical processes: "the *Glass* wasn't a painting; there was lots of lead, a lot of
other things. It was far from the traditional idea of the painter, with his
brush, his palette, his turpentine, an idea which had already disappeared
from my life. . . . the old masters, the old things. . . . All that disgusted me"
(Cabanne 67). Bartholomae cites a passage from Bové, which sounds very
much like Duchamp, very negation-as-first-light. Bové urges a "negative"
criticism, one that would "destroy the local discursive and institutional
formations of the 'regime of truth,' . . . aimed at necessary conditions,"
but a negation that has a "'positive' content; it must carry out its destruction with newly produced knowledge. This could be Duchamp's ironism
of affirmation. But too often Bartholomae's negation is aimed only at students or at institutional composition not in his style. He has no hatred for
anything in his own composition; it's a restricted destruction, an anti-*certain*-production-strategy. His production-site is canonical; his classroom
walls full of reproductions of certified masterpieces. His production,
termed revision, implies taking the student ready-made—in this case an
essay on St. Croix, brought in under the institutional sign "irredeemably
corrupt or trivial" (26), multiplied by the sign of the clone ("The St. Croix

narrative can stand for all of the narratives the students wrote" [27])—
and working with it, running it through a series of self-reflexive heuristics
we might call the New (really, Old) Tagmemics:

> to ask questions of the discourse as a discourse: What is its history? Whose
> interests are served? What does the scene of the plantation mean? What does
> it mean in terms of the history of St. Croix? What does it mean that it is
> offered as background and color? Why don't the people of St. Croix get to
> speak? How might one not write a missionary narrative and yet still tell the
> story of a missionary trip to St. Croix? (27)

It means, he realizes, getting clumsier writing from students, a crude
rendering that will seem "less skillful or less finished or less masterful
than the original" (28), but one that is *en route* to more closely approxi-
mating the certain set of materials, one that is closer to replicating a
travel narrative à la Pratt ("Pratt's argument and her way of reading"
[28]). Duchamp might have called *genius* the "impossibility of the iron"
(*impossibilité du fer/faire*), but the iron is quite possible here—it just
needs refining, purifying, forging into the prized fetish. This takes composition back to the Greek, pre-mechanical age of reproduction as
Benjamin describes it—"founding and stamping" ("The Work of Art"
218). ("You say you hate it? *You want to recreate it!*" [R.E.M.]). The exigency is a crudely-copied masterpiece: blurred, like a fuzzy, ill-lit photo
of the *Mona Lisa* (the ur-text) taken with a pin-hole camera. Why try to
take a perfect picture of a masterpiece (unless you're a conceptual
artist, like Louise Lawler, and you want to use it materially)? Better to
just paint a mustache and goatee on it.

Composition, it appears, exists to turn *l'art brut* of the student's readymade into a form that will produce not the cool-site *wow* but the *literary
hmmm*. The focus here is training the student to develop a high-quality
hand-made reproduction of Pratt, one with disciplinary exchange-value
cachet. The nostalgia is, perhaps, understandable: there were primal, formative moments when certain texts spoke to us with authority, and we
want our students to try and reproduce that power. Composition, then,
wants to combine cult-value and exchange-/exhibition-value. But trying
to maintain the aura in repro-writing is a doomed project. The
Composite City cares nothing for aura, authenticity, or authority; in the
Interzone, art's "social significance, particularly in its most positive form,
is inconceivable without its destructive, cathartic aspect, that is, the liqui-
dation of the traditional value of the cultural heritage" (Benjamin "The

Work of Art" 221). Of course the St. Croix paper can stand for any (*faux* Pratt-like) narrative: they're all aura-less, the space of the writing deserted, to use Benjamin's metaphor (226), like a crime scene. Crime scenes are reproduced, photographed, for evidentiary purposes, in order to make historical, cultural claims and inferences (which is precisely Bartholomae's use of student text). Interzone writing in the virtual community of Composite City has only use-value, consumption-value: "Value will depend more on the ability of the different groups of artist-associates to develop a reputation for delivering easily accessible hits of the Special Information Tonic to the informationally-sick correspondent wherever he or she may be" (Amerika). In this ratio, readers = "addicts of drugs not yet synthesized," writer = "Fats" Terminal, trafficker in the ultimate controlled substance, "flesh of the giant aquatic black centipede . . . overpoweringly delicious and nauseating so that the eaters eat and vomit and eat again until they fall exhausted" (Burroughs 53, 55). It's the drug-use-value of writing; *a pimpish composition . . . dope.* "Anyone could scratch your surface now, it's so amphetamine" (R. E. M.). It's futile to hype the values of contemplation on the information-sick. The Interzone's discursive field is the *wow* of distraction, not the *literary hmm* of contemplation. Whatever contemplation there is amounts to the *pensées* of the possessed. This is very much the Happening aesthetic: there is very little buzz to be gained from conventional spaces. If we want that high, we must consciously seek it elsewhere, like rap websites. Jean-Jacques Lebel describes the Happenings' artists' search for intensity through strange spaces:

> We hope to do other things in a station, a stadium, an airplane. To be elsewhere. To be radar. To be there. The conventional theatre, the art shop or gallery, are no longer (and perhaps in themselves have never been) sacred places—so why shut ourselves up in them? Artistic activity is founded on high telepathy—a contact high—and everything which comes into its field becomes a *sign*, and is part of art. It is therefore evident that the primary problem of today's art has become *the renovation and intensification of perception.* (282)

Just as the concept of juried writing is never questioned by Bartholomae, neither is the textual genre that will decide the prize—it's a specific, authentic, highly-defined, disciplinary genre (in this case, the travel narrative). His compositional logic, then, becomes the simple displacement of one already-written text, the St. Croix narrative, in favor of another, Pratt's. A more interesting substitution might prove replacing the already-written with, say, a *wrotten written* ("*morceaux moisis*"), like, for example, the following travel narrative, William Burroughs's non-entry in Bartholomae's contest; not a Contact Zone piece, but some Special Information Tonic from the Interzone, entitled "Atrophied Preface":

> Why all this waste paper getting The People from one place to another? Perhaps to spare The Reader stress of sudden space shifts and keep him Gentle? And so a ticket is bought, a taxi called, a plane boarded. We are allowed a glimpse into the warm peach-lined cave as She (the airline hostess, of course) leans over us to murmur of chewing gum, dramamine, even nembutal.
>
> "Talk paregoric, Sweet Thing, and I will hear." (218)

Contemporary composition insists on the literary aesthetic of the Contact Zone, but electronic writing operates in the anti-aesthetic of the Interzone, where "'content' is what the mediaconglomerates deliver into one's home via the TV screen, and form is the ability to level out or flatten the meaning of all things" (Olsen and Amerika). Burroughs wouldn't dream of translating Pratt, he's actually closer to the St. Croix writer-as-recorder: "There is only one thing a writer can write about: what is in front of his senses at the moment of writing. . . . I am a recording instrument. . . . I do not presume to impose 'story' 'plot' 'continuity'" (221). Limning what is in front of one's senses, tracing what is there on the screen—the writer of the intertext underscores every line with *This is now, this is here, this is me, this is what I wanted you to see* (R.E.M.). The Web captures, in glass, this historical moment—the death of the craft of writing and its rebirth as idea (de Duve *Kant* 186). The progressive self-definition of the academy accelerated at an historical juncture much like today. As art-at-large was granted a kind of public credibility by the growth of salons, the academy, fearful that it could no longer control access to the profession, retreated into over-specification, hyper-pedantry. The Web, then, is the New Independents' Salon, Malraux's Museum-Without-Walls—built on the shards of the now-fractal Palace of Modernism. Beuys's dream has come true; everyone can now be curated. Benjamin saw this neutralization or democratization of expertise as one of the implications of mechanical reproduction. Film technology, for example (particularly newsreels and documentaries for Benjamin, though witness Robert Bresson in second half of the twentieth century), allowed anyone-whoever to be a movie star. The same held true for print technologies:

> For centuries, a small number of writers were confronted by many thousands of readers. This changed toward the end of the last century. With the increasing extension of the press, which kept placing new political, religious, scientific,

professional, and local organs before the readers, an increasing number of readers became writers—at first, occasional ones. It began with the daily press opening to its readers space for "letters to the editor." And today there is hardly a gainfully employed European who could not, in principle, find an opportunity to publish somewhere. . . . Thus, the distinction between author and public is about to lose its basic character. ("The Work of Art" 231–232)

Cinema in the Interzone is a crime-scene haunted by the death of traditional auratic "presence." All films are now read as documentaries; all cinema is *anémic cinéma* (Duchamp 115; the anagram being one of the few traditional textual strategies still meaningful). A new given, then:

$$\frac{any\ person}{movie\ star} = \frac{any\ reader}{published\ writer/expert}$$

People read their world through the glass in front of them and inscribe their interaction. Not exactly meaning their work for the marketplace, as eighteenth century painters did, writers of the electronic intertext still gear their art toward public consumption, data-interaction, supplementation: "e-mail your comments!" website after website implores. The means of production are in the hands of the consumers; the specialized knowledge of the academy becomes again increasingly beside-the-point for the now on-going intertextual salon. Increasingly new composing technologies means the media has no time to be practiced, perfected, conventionalized, ritualized. What aesthetic remains lies in capturing, choosing, from *what is in front of his senses at the moment of writing,* the hurried snapshot of life on the run, not a stylized drawing. *"The important thing then is just* this matter of timing, this snapshot effect" (Duchamp 32).

The readymade narrative, done by anyone-whoever, cannot stay delayed in glass for Modernist Composition. Any stretch of found footage is not eligible for Best Documentary. Even though Bartholomae tries to distance himself from the kind of writing as revision taught by "the process movement"—where "the primary goal was the efficient production of text . . . [in which] revision was primarily addition and subtraction—adding vivid details, for example, and taking out redundancies. The result (or the goal) was to perfect, and by extension, preserve the discourse" (27)—his goal remains an efficient discourse-production, a perfection and preservation; only now it's Mary Louise Pratt's discourse. There remains this *progression* (even as he tries to distance himself from "the legacy of the liberal tradition in composition" [15]), a process-ion away from the St. Croix narrative—a text which is heartfelt but doesn't articulate the preferred politics of a certain reading—to a better one, in which "a writer would have to ask about and think about, say, the history of North American relations with St. Croix" (27). What Bartholomae doesn't do is *delay* that progression towards the certain style—to see if the canvas is not quite so blank as we think it is, to see if Modernism could take the blank canvas as its ultimate work, the flattest canvas ever. Call it the contact zone of the art, the point where conception, *anart, arrhe*, meets aura, Modernism, art. Without a delay, a self-negation, a *SUR/cen/SURE*, a meta-irony, the on-going narrative of the discourse's tradition/production is never interrupted; the knowledge-engine never stops. There is no actual *possible*, just possible versions of the preferred. The desire of the Bride is "ignorant . . . blank . . . (with a touch of malice)" (*Salt Seller* 39). We will define that blank canvas and know it, colonize it (ignoring the touch of malice, not even realizing the *canvas* is really a *glass*). "Knowledge, like the image, was built up in consecutive layers that would reenact the progress made by modernity" (Nesbit "The Language" 355). "The question for the writing teacher, then," says Bartholomae, as he races through page after page, never stopping to dwell, "is 'What next?'" (26). The grand irony at the end of his article is his caveat that the compositionist must "be willing to pay attention to common things" (28). Sure, in order to determine what needs to be rarefied. How is the Bovéan "newly produced knowledge" going to happen if the same certain materials—difficult academic texts—are thought and written about in a traditional discourse? Duchamp located "the great trouble with art in this country" in just such an uninterrupted unfolding of tradition, in just such a perfection of a certain way of reading (say, the Pratt program):

> there is no spirit of revolt—no new ideas appearing among the younger artists. They are following along the paths beaten out by their predecessors, trying to do better what their predecessors have already done. In art there is no such thing as perfection. And a creative lull occurs always when artists of a period are satisfied to pick up a predecessor's work where he dropped it and attempt to continue what he was doing. When on the other hand you pick up something from an earlier period and adapt it to your own work an approach can be creative. The result is not new; but it is new insomuch as it is a different approach. (123)

An example of Duchamp's adaptive strategy leading to a creative new approach can be seen in his interior re-design of the Galerie Beaux Arts in Paris for the 1938 Surrealist exhibition. He designed a great central hall with a pool surrounded by real grass. Four large comfortable beds stood among the greenery. Twelve hundred sacks of coal hung from the ceiling. In order to illuminate the paintings which hung on the walls, Duchamp planned to use electric eyes that would switch on lights for the individual works when a beam was broken. Because of technical difficulties this project was abandoned, and flashlights were loaned to visitors (they were all stolen, and more traditional lighting was finally employed). At the opening of the exhibition, the odor of roasting coffee filled the hall. A recording of a German army marching song was broadcast, and a girl performed a dance around the pool. (Kirby *Happenings* 39)

It's no wonder Duchamp helped usher in the Happenings, this *detourned* gallery-space might as well have been named the first Happenings on record.

Going back to our algebraic comparisons, the logic for the ready-made writings from the Campus of Interzone University is inescapable. Bartholomae's math posits a given:

$$\frac{\text{St. Croix narrative}}{\text{all student narratives}}$$

But under the vibrating hum of Composite City, where *form is the ability to level out or flatten the meaning of all things*, we can set it equal to any reading, on any subject whatever,

$$\frac{\text{St. Croix narrative}}{\text{all student narratives}} = \frac{\text{any reading}}{\text{any subject}}$$

which, as we remember, was another possible accordance for Rodriguez's reading of Hoggart, allowing our final ratio:

$$\frac{\text{Rodriguez}}{\text{Hoggart}} = \frac{\text{St. Croix narrative}}{\text{all student narratives}}$$

The vast silent market of the Interzone effects its neutralization. That final algebraic comparison doesn't imply a movement having been made from a student writer to a master writer, a looking-backward toward the mentor-text; rather both expositions are delayed in a stasis field, in accordance. They both *appear* as writing. As exposition, Rodriguez is any writing whatsoever, like all narratives, sometimes prize-winning, though occasionally appearing *as irredeemably corrupt or trivial*; and Hoggart—as possibility—is any readymade data with which a writer interacts. All that would count Rodriguez as prize-worthy now (or

Hoggart or Pratt or the "Fern Hill" essay) is simply taste. We've seen with Benjamin how the technology of mechanical reproduction allows "any gainfully employed European" to become a published expert. It is Bartholomae's attempt to otherwise determine this that rings so hollow.

7. Composition after Duchamp is idea-generative, not product-oriented; it's data-interaction: "Take these records (these 'having become') and from them make a tracing" is its only directive. If three-dimensional objects give off a two-dimensional shadow, writing is now conceived of as a three-dimensional shadow of a fourth-dimensional process of becoming. As Roché said of Duchamp, "His finest work is his use of time" (87). The intertext, moving over time, means writing reconceived of as the teleintertext. Gervais uses the phrase *restricted teleintertext* to capture Duchamp's hypertextual strategies: "His almost systematic way of exposing at least two locations, two languages, or two sexes through pictorial and literary texts could be called the restricted teleintertext of his oeuvre: 'inter' because it makes use of at least two texts; 'restricted' because these texts were written by the same person; and 'tele' because they are often several decades apart"(Gervais 399). But instead of a restricted economy of the intertext, we'll have a general one, a world-wide economy-without-walls. Can we allow a writing that might be cracked, unfinished, but that circulates some interesting ideas? It doesn't have to be powerfully or rigorously conceptual (as some find Pratt): "please note that there doesn't have to be a lot of the conceptual for me to like something" (Cabanne 77). Just a touch will do: a drop or two of *Belle Haleine, Eau de Voilette* (1921), a small whiff of *Air de Paris* (*Sérum physiologique*) (1919), some marble sugar cubes (one lump or two?)—just an easily accessible hit. Bartholomae fetishizes a conceptual ("a certain kind of intellectual project—one that requires me to think out critical problems of language, knowledge, and culture" [24]) that's materially limited—imagine a student in his class, say, handing in a urinal as travel documentary (did Mary Louise Pratt do translatable urinals?). Under Duchamp, anyone can be a conceptual artist. The materials are readymade, common-place, easily available. What's involved is finding a new conceptual use: taking a hat rack, for example, putting it on the floor, and calling it *Trébuchet* (*Trap*) (1917) is not *materially* difficult. It simply involves picking something up from an earlier period and giving it a new function, a new thought for that object, adapting it to your own work. It's the use-value (rather than the

exhibition-value) of fetishism, an unforeseen-use-value: "it is not for walking that the fetishist 'uses' the shoe. For him it has a use-value that begins, paradoxically, . . . at the very moment it stops working, when it no longer serves locomotion. It is the use-value of a shoe out of service" (Hollier "Use-Value" 140). The hat rack, then, is not a "difficult text" as Bartholomae means it (the *Glass* is, but not in the way he means). It's rooted in the everyday in a way Modernism's program can never be. Rauschenberg, reflecting on his very Duchampian happening *Map Room II* (1965), interrogates the notion of a text(ual material) that's difficult to get; he begins at the Modernist point of limits and possibilities but inflects that setting differently:

> I began that piece by getting some materials to work with—again we have that business of limitations and possibilities. I just got a bunch of tires, not because I'm crazy about tires but because they are so available around here in New York, even on the street. I could be back here in fifteen minutes with five tires. If I were working in Europe, that wouldn't be the material. Very often people ask me about certain repeated images in both my painting and theatre. Now I may be fooling myself, but I think it can be traced to their availability. Take the umbrella. . . . After any rainy day, it is hard to walk by a garbage can that doesn't have a broken umbrella in it, and they are quite interesting. I found some springs around the corner. I was just putting stuff together—that's the way I work—to see what I could get out of it. I don't start off with any preconceived notion about content of the piece. If there is any thinking, it is more along the line of something happening which suggests something else. If I'm lucky, then the piece builds its own integrity. . . . You just mess around. The springs, for example, made an interesting noise, so I decided to amplify that. . . . [The tires] can be walked in, they can be rolled in, you can roll over them, you can crawl through them. All these things are perfectly obvious. Perhaps tires even have uses that you haven't seen before. What I'm trying to avoid is the academic way of making a dance of theme and variation. I'm interested in exploring all the possibilities inherent in any particular object. (Kostelanetz *Theatre* 83–84)

The most easily available material now is electronic information, not umbrellas or tires. The institution suspects the commonplace, the ready-made, the anything-whatever, the any-narrative-at-all: transparent trash, like those gangsta definitions, that one can just lift right off the Net—aren't there those who consider them "irredeemably corrupt or trivial"? But there are ideas there—*just the same, they move.* This is material picked up by the cyber-*flâneur*, after an electronic *dérive*. It's the *de facto* narrative brought back from situationist tele-traveling, clicking through the odd one-way streets of the Net. The situationists hated "official" travel narratives. They would have been attracted to the unofficial story of St. Croix; St. Croix *after dark*. The standard tourism-drama, no matter how p.c., was not for them: "Tourism, . . . with its crass appetites for ultravisible urban spectacle and nervousness in dark spaces of the ambient city, was as 'repugnant as sports or buying on credit'" (Sadler 91). To capture this other story, the story dealing with a space's effects on people's passions, the Lettrist International's "alternative travel agency," for example, sent people on "mystery tours".

Bartholomae's project uses "student writing as a starting point"; it exists "in relation to academic or high culture" (24). Ultimately, the Modernist focus—in composition as in art—is institutional rather than conceptual. The institution is the aegis under which the project is carried out. Knowledge of the historical apparatus is a prerequisite in order to work within the discipline, learning the style and thinking which result in a Morris Louis or a Louise Pratt. Duchamp's conceptual has nothing to do with the institutional; asked in 1966 by Cabanne, "Do you go to museums?" Duchamp replied,

> Almost never. I haven't been to the Louvre for twenty years. It doesn't interest me, because I have these doubts about the value of the judgments which decided that all these pictures should be presented to the Louvre, instead of others which weren't even considered, and which might have been there. So fundamentally we content ourselves with the opinion which says that there exists a fleeting infatuation, a style based on momentary taste; this momentary taste disappears, and, despite everything, certain things still remain. (Cabanne 71)

Our fleeting infatuations are fixed in our field's galleries—more corporate collections than actual museums, as the works are those from the artistic field deemed worthy of the well-endowed walls of our semi-corporate academies. *Ways of Reading*, then, as Composition's Paine-Webber collection. But there are other panes, other web-bers. Electronic writing, like the gangsta-sample, is the kind of raw, difficult beauty that the profession never institutionalizes (because the larger academic audience has such specific tastes). Duchamp explained the difference between reified institutional history and lived aesthetic pleasure, a use-value aesthetics rather than the museum's exchange-value. His explanation points to what's missing in the institutionally canonized texts that form our field's defining narrative:

After forty or fifty years a picture dies, because its freshness disappears. . . .
There's a huge difference between a Monet today, which is black as anything,
and a Monet sixty or eighty years ago, when it was brilliant, when it was made.
Now it has entered into history. . . .

The history of art is something very different from aesthetics. For me, the
history of art is what remains of an epoch in a museum, but it's not necessarily the best of that epoch, and fundamentally it's probably even the expression of the mediocrity of the epoch, because the beautiful things have
disappeared—the public didn't want to keep them. (67)

"That was then, but now that is gone; it's past" (R.E.M.). Composition's
Modernism revels in the trappings of history—but their exhibition-
value, not their use-value (punks, for example, were interested in history's use-value; they collaged their looks out of a pastiche of various
eras' styles). Why Duchamp's influence persists has much to do with the
actual works, but it's probably equally the result of the heuristic-value of
his aesthetics, the conceptual grammar or logic evolved through all the
texts—made, chosen, written and spoken (as well as interacted with)—
that "Duchamp" names.

The negation/affirmation Bartholomae desires from Bové is displayed
wonderfully in Duchamp, whose *prémiere lumiere* shines in his palindromic
print as "NON." The force of his negation was the *physical "caustic" [vitriol
type]* called "Possible" which he pursued through practically every compositional project, a caustic whose strength could dissolve notions of image
and text, *burning up all aesthetics and callistics.* Jasper Johns testifies that
Duchamp's "persistent attempts to destroy frames of reference altered
our thinking, established new units of thought, 'a new thought for that
object'" (Cabanne 110). Comparably, the Bartholomae/Greenberg nega-
tion/affirmation seeks simply to stabilize: it negates other art and artistic
strategies in order to refine a unique definition of composition in a specific field. Like Duchamp, Bartholomae/Greenberg want a conceptual
heuristic; there is an erotic force at the heart of them all, a repetitive
dynamic designed to lead to pleasure. With Greenberg, it's the smell of
linseed oil, the almost palpable feel of the stretched canvas's flatness, a
flatness his gaze could get lost in ("The flatness toward which modernist
painting orients itself can never be an utter flatness. The heightened sensitivity of the picture plane may not permit sculptural illusion, or *trompe-
l'oeil,* but it does and must permit optical illusion" ["Modernist" 73]); with
Bartholomae, it is the tracing, the iteration of the style and content of
those difficult texts ("I confess I admire those dense sentences"

["Inventing" 159]); for Duchamp, it's the steady hum of the precision optics—disks, palindromic/anagrammatic word-play, glass stared into for about an hour. Each strategy locates an incarnated desire, a kind of conceptualist *frottage* of the fleshy gray matter to produce the expected pleasure. For Duchamp, eroticism's universality made it a new "ism" to replace other "Literary schools [like] Symbolism, Romanticism" (Cabanne 88). Modernism could never allow eroticism to replace its critical, material practice, a practice specified by the frame: "how and why one might work with the space on the page" (Bartholomae 21); "the limiting conditions with which a marked-up surface must comply in order to be experienced as a picture" (Greenberg 73). Anything else is dismissed as inappropriate or irrelevant to its focus: "We move the furniture in the classroom, collaborate on electronic networks, take turns being the boss, but we do not change writing" (Bartholomae 16); "for the sake of its own autonomy, painting has had above all to divest itself of everything it might share with sculpture" (Greenberg 70). We know what the institution's last word on e-writing is; witness Bartholomae's article on electronic conferencing, in which any benefits it has (benefits seen institutionally, students "beginning with more familiar forms of language and seeing how they might be put to use in an academic setting . . . a transfer of this mode to written work that was officially 'writing'" ["I'm Talking About Allen Bloom" 242, 252]) are underscored by the final caveat, "a threat to academic values" (262). There is moving furniture, e-chatter, sculpture, even—then there is composition, whose institutional value is now seen as potentially threatened by new practices.

Bartholomae's St. Croix writer has written something—a potentially useful memoir of a time when a writer learned something about him/herself and others, perhaps; a narrative, a document of sorts—but it's not composition. It's like a drawing on the walls of Lascaux when compared by Greenberg with an Abstract Expressionist canvas; one is simply image, the other can be called a picture. Pre-Modernist texts suffer from being composed in ignorance of the governing conventions of the genre:

> The Paleolithic painter or engraver could disregard the norm of the frame and treat the surface in both a literally and a virtually sculptural way because he made images rather than pictures, and worked on a support whose limits could be disregarded because . . . nature gave them to the artist in an unmanageable way. But the making of pictures, as against images in the flat, means the deliberate choice and creation of limits. This deliberateness is what Modernism harps on. ("Modernist Painting" 76)

Bataille, of course, is a different sort of art critic from Greenberg. His response to the Lascaux "images" helps distinguish Modernism as an historical "ism" or literary school, one which compares *a* to *b* and gets solution *c* (*deliberate choice of limits*); as opposed to eroticism, which subsumes distinctions between *a* and *b* (*picture* and *image*) under the more general *sign*: "But Upper Paleolith man, *Homo sapiens*, is now known to us through signs that move us not only in their exceptional beauty (his paintings are often marvelous). These signs affect us more through the fact that they bring us abundant evidence of his erotic life" (*Tears* 31). Bartholomae and Greenberg prefer expensive fetishes; they limit their erotic *plaisir du texte* to exclusive, privileged materials. In their Modernism, the certain aesthetic judgment which distinguishes between an image and a picture had to be preserved. Their space for composition was that infra-thin line between writing and good writing, words and knowledge; it was a very special, *definitive* space in which the artist could work. Bartholomae: "the space on the page . . . do[ing] work there and not somewhere else" (18). Greenberg: it "would, to be sure, narrow its area of competence, but at the same time it would make its possession of this area all the more secure . . . to fit drawing and design more explicitly to the rectangular shape of the canvas" (68, 69). Duchamp abandoned that definitive space, the traditional forms, limits, concerns, and materials. He went totally off the page, out of that space, allowing thought to dictate its own laws, the resultant 'becoming' being anything-whatever: "Take these 'having become' and from them make a tracing" (33). He's interested in the appearance mainly to trace the apparition (the fact of appearing, the status as art): "In general, the picture is the apparition of an appearance" (30). The answer is not a solution (not "what makes writing *good*"), but a sign (what makes *writing*). Bartholomae's *given* is a solution, "write like Pratt," not a sign. Instead of tracing a becoming, he urges students to retrace a became. So, although he insists on "the comparison of Stephen Toulmin and a freshman" (17)—a promising equivalence, that:

$$\frac{\text{Stephen Toulmin}}{\text{freshman}}$$

—its purpose is not so ideas can become a delayed sign, but rather to find a solution, *c*, to an item in Composition's problem set. His given yields a solution enabling us to use Bové's critique of Toulmin on our students, in order to get Pratt-like text from them: we can now tell them, in so many words, "Next time, don't be so careless about interrogating your intellectual function within the regime of truth" (17). Composition, then, as a set of problems for which we articulate solutions? Duchamp: "There is no solution because there is no problem" (Roché 85). Bartholomae's distinction—between himself and the "same old routine" of Composition—is Greenberg's distinction between picture and image. The St. Croix narrative might stand for all student narratives, but it's clearly not a travel narrative in the Pratt style. Until it's subjected to the text-production strategies (whether efficient or not) of cultural criticism, it remains unfortunately a "missionary narrative" (27). Bartholomae claims the same vanguard status for his aesthetic as Greenberg does; but when the truly avant-garde art showed up—say, Frank Stella or Andy Warhol or, yes, Duchamp—Modernist Painting squirmed. It was for Greenberg what it is for Bartholomae, a question of a limited artistic context—the way the space is framed. The "cultural . . . social" context-in-general was not the specific, aesthetic determinant of Modernism:

> All art depends in one way or another on context, but there's a great difference between an aesthetic and a non-aesthetic context. . . . From the start avant-gardist art resorted extensively to effects depending on an extra-aesthetic context. Duchamp's first Readymades, his bicycle wheel, his bottlerack, and later on his urinal, were not new at all in configuration; they startled when first seen only because they were presented in a fine art context, which is a purely cultural and social, not an aesthetic or artistic context. (Greenberg qtd. in de Duve *Kant* 270)

8. Duchamp saw the problem with Modernist, criteria-based taste: "one stores up in oneself such a language of tastes, good or bad, that when one looks at something, if that something isn't an echo of yourself, then you do not even look at it" (Cabanne 94). Krauss, too, reads the desire-occluded retrojection which overlays the supposedly discerning clarity of Modernism's projective vision; for her, the blank canvas/page/screen is already filled by one's own viewing apparati, "already organized, already saturated by the lattice through which perspective will map the coordinates of external space" (*The Optical Unconscious* 54). The eye, the brain, are fleshy as well as neural, body as well as mind; hence, "the gaze is experienced as being saturated from the very start . . . the perspective projection is not felt as a transparency opening onto a world but as a skin, fleshlike, dense, and strangely separable from the object it fixates" (54). "The body exerts its demands," Krauss continues,

furthering Duchamp's notion of how taste becomes constructed, intrusive. "The eye accommodates those demands by routinizing vision, by achieving a glance that can determine in an instant the purpose to which each object can be put. It's not a look that 'sees,' it's a look that sorts" (141). Greenberg, then, doesn't see Frank Stella, he sees non-flat art; Bartholomae doesn't see the St. Croix paper, he sees non-Pratt art. Duchamp pursued any avenue, as long as it contained a hint of the conceptual. Asked what sort of art he might make if he were still making art, Duchamp answered generically: "something which would have significance. . . . It would have to have a direction, a sense. That's the only thing that would guide me" (Cabanne 106). Art that, just the same, moved. "Make a painting of *frequency*," is the note he jots to himself in 1914. That's the trouble with Composition, it doesn't move, its timing is lousy. There is past and present in Composition, but no future. The readymade was "a kind of rendezvous" (Duchamp 32). Composition's gaze on student writing directs backward, toward the already-written, toward Pratt. The time frame, then, is nostalgia—for aura, for presence; the perspective is retrojective. Without future, without frequency, Composition is not three, it is simply two—the number of the double, the copy, the clone. This bars its move to the post-beautiful: "beauty is always the result of a resemblance" (Hollier "Use-Value" 145). Writing becomes re-issue, founding and stamping; recasting, like Arturo Schwartz, creating new (highly prized) sets of Duchamp's by-then lost or discarded readymades. Imagine—recreating the readymade . . . composition as revising material into the alreadymade! "What is taste for you?" Cabanne asks. The answer: "A habit. The repetition of something already accepted. If you start something over several times, it becomes taste. Good or bad, it's the same thing, it's still taste" (Cabanne 48). Duchamp wanted art that moved—which is what drew him to chess: "it is like designing something," he said, "or constructing a mechanism of some kind by which you win or lose . . . the thing itself is very, very plastic" (136).

This chapter, then, is a plea for composition to be seen as writing-at-large, a delay in the glass we now inscribe as our writing medium. Let our default setting be Rich Text Format, the Document—such word processing terms, like *text file*, illustrate technology's ability to neutralize the ideological accrual of discursive genres. (*One may become a member* of the Teleintertextual Indeps *upon filing* . . .) The *document* differs from the compositional project envisioned by Bartholomae in the way use-value differs from exchange-value. *Fresh Widow* (1920) and *Why Not Sneeze?*

(1921) marked the point at which, according to Lebel, Duchamp "reached the limit of the unesthetic, the useless, and the unjustifiable" (47). As Roché has already pointed out, Duchamp's "gadget . . . wasn't useful." Of course not: the non-productive value of writing *is* its use-value, its inexchangeability. "Use-value cannot outlast use" (Hollier "Use-Value" 136), it's only realized in consumption, in being used (up): *talk paregoric, Sweet Thing, and I will listen.* Duchamp, like Bataille's sun, is a permanent expenditure; his gadget is a word-engine that never stops running. The *Glass* was *not to be looked at for itself* (exhibition-value), *but only as a function* (use-value). Composition is mainly about preserving form at the expense of function, or limiting writing to an endlessly simulated exchange-function—dipping back into the same River Pratt each time, coming back with the same prized treasure. It's museumification, exchange-value as exhibition-value: "The same diversion that defines the market holds for the museum as well: objects enter it only once abstracted from the context of their use-value" (Hollier 136). Composition stalls on that distinction, "the opposition which dictates that one *uses* a tool and *looks* at a painting" (Hollier 137, emphasis mine). It's the difference between the way a Lascaux ritual-image was used vs. a *picture*. Kosuth on Duchamp: "With the unassisted Ready-made, art changed its focus from the form of the language to what was being said. Which means that it changed the nature of art from a question of morphology to a question of function" (80). Bartholomae errs in taking his favorite painting to St. Croix in order to teach art, "the thing out of place is never the real thing" (Hollier 138). Cult-value, Benjamin warns, is lost in exhibition-value. Pratt becomes the transposed fetish, losing all use-value; it "no longer works as a fetish: it has been discarded and framed to be put on the market; it has been degraded to become a commodity. It is no longer used but collected" (Hollier 147). The modern museum's curatorial strategy involves not time but location; it's "the Museum of Ethnography . . . exotic, remote in space" (Hollier 151n). The Museum of the Contact Zone, not the Interzone's Museum-Without-Walls, endlessly exhibiting its impermanent collection of readymades (*what is in front of his senses at the moment of writing*), done by the Society of Teleintertextual Independents. Writing there is consumed on the spot, clicked through—a non-gallery tour, with no time for the literary *hmm*, just a quick series of *wows*; the tour itself becoming a kind of chance-inflected auto-performance art, a Happening fashioned from easily-available, already-inscribed materials.

9. Bartholomae and I have different projects. He wants to entrench, I want to dissolve. He wants the specific, I want the generic. He teaches making, I prefer choosing. He wants a writer to write like Mary Louise Pratt or Richard Rodriguez; I want writers who write like anyone-whoever, who need only be interesting. He's concerned with how one works with the space on the page, but I work on glass, already-inscribed glass behind which I can see the world pass by. He starts with the ready-made and moves to the retrograde. I would start and stop with the readymade—delaying it, there on the screen, in glass, "capable of all the innumerable eccentricities" (Duchamp 27). If he would just delay them rather than solve them, I could agree with Bartholomae on all of his givens: the travel narrative, for example, *can* stand for all writing. Whether prize-winning essay or rap slang, it's all the record of a journey. Benjamin let the film documentary stand for all art in the era of the mechanical composition. But I learn more from those travelogues that return from cool sites with new ideas (*some stuff from the bay,* say), rather than watching slides from a trip I've taken a hundred times, scenes accompanied by an already-written political exegesis. I want an aesthetic judgment, of course; but I want to judge a student's art as art, not as "critical practice" (17). Actually, I would prefer to judge it as erotic practice. Duchamp's eroticism has infinite use-value in a post-disciplinary composition. The disciplines, the professions, lie buried in the *Glass,* in the Cemetery of Uniforms and Liveries; but the *oculist charts* give those disciplinary bachelors another chance, so the Nine *malic moulds*—called by Duchamp "Priest, Department store delivery boy, Gendarme, Cuirassier, Policeman, Undertaker, Flunkey, Busboy, Station master" (21); or named by "Me Craig Harrison Cincinnati Ohio Baby" as "G-DOGG HOE PIMP PLAYA WIGGER SKATER HUSTLER MAC TAGGER"—finally have a chance to become ballers, to get some game, to replace their academic craft with mechanical precision, enabling their cemetery to become *eros's matrix.* Composition as I see it has now become a delay in glass, all writing is screen-writing. There is the artifact, which has been written about in notes, which refer to other artifacts, which contain ideas worked over previously or written about to friends, etc. *Nude Descending a Staircase,* that explosion in a shingle factory, represents composition as photochronography, each segment an exploded detail, "a ready-made continuously in motion . . . a sort of perpetual motion like that of a solar clock" (Lebel *Marcel Duchamp* 68). It's writing become real-timed, e-conferenced and -mailed, a continuously

updated home page with running discussion list; links keep recurring, moved through back and forth, refolding back on themselves, *a kind of rendezvous* awaits the reader, a *mirrorical return*. A bunch of "having becomes" that together form a tracing, a locale.

All I demand of writing is that it have *writte*; that it expose itself, announce itself, appear as writing. Writing stripped bare. Writing that wows me, dazzles me, that announces, "you're coming onto something so fast, so numb, that you can't even feel" (R.E.M.). Writing from a vast, universal field, as wide-open as a Kansas prairie, where language, thought, and vision act upon one another; panoramic writing, filled with all sorts of wonderful, useless treasures. "God damn beautiful son-of-a-bitch country," Jackson Pollock yells into the wind on one of his late-1930s road trips. He was always taking to the road, crossing the country, searching for . . . whatever. It's only fitting he dies in a crash, for the crash is the accident-al end to the high-speed search, the fatal moment when the search engine stops, the random finish to the seemingly endless hyper-cruise. The text I write from the road becomes an interaction with those other texts, a collection of souvenirs, picking and choosing what's useful, building my own restricted teleintertext. The "What is Composition . . . ?" of teleintertextual writing can be pulled anywhere off the glass. At the end of that gangsta list is a call for more definitions that reads like a new textual strategy (but an old one, actually; it reads like a note from *The Green Box*):

> Send me mail to include a new definition. . . . Make something up.
>
> Please write Definitions in HTML Format. You can include links, pictures, or whatever else you want. All I am going to do is cut and paste.

And so, a *mirrorical return* to the concept of the *assisted readymade*. The Interzone is here, now, but I know I won't live there forever; just like I know electronic writing as now practiced will lose its charm (the crash is inevitable: Duchamp writes to Stieglitz, "You know exactly how I feel about photography. I would like to see it make people despise painting until something else will make photography unbearable" [165]). Until then, sampling, linking, glass, wires, photo-transfer, sound-bites—these are the materials of composition-in-general, the teleintertext; composition as I know it and love it: as blueprint, How-To Book, a sort of catalogue or "a sort of letter-box" (Duchamp 38), *just putting stuff together—that's the way I work—to see what I could get out of it; very very plastic*. Writing full of new definitions, double-exposures; writing across all curriculums, *kicks in all genres* (Cabanne 82); amazing and forgettable, wonderful and oddly hollow; new adventures in hi-fi, just messing around. Writing I strive to inscribe in my own thoroughly-mediated academic glass. Writing I love, yes, as much as a fetishist loves a shoe, as much as some people love (is this Duchamp's term? the bachelors' grinder, right? or Rrose's maybe?) *sexual chocolate.*

2

THE AMERICAN ACTION WRITERS

To forget the crisis—individual, social, aesthetic—that brought Action
Painting into being, or to bury it out of sight (it cannot really be
forgotten), is to distort fantastically the reality of postwar American art.
This distortion is being practiced daily by all who have an interest in
"normalising" vanguard art, so that they may enjoy its fruits in
comfort: these include dealers, collectors, educators, directors of
government cultural programs, art historians, museum officials, critics,
artists—in sum, the "art world."

Harold Rosenberg

Two brief comments, made in fairly proximate places, in New York, at almost precisely the same moment in time, August 1956, revealing two radically different world views. First:

Life is beautiful, the trees are beautiful, the sky is beautiful. Why is it that all I can think about is death? (Naifeh and Smith 789)

This morose remark was made by a compositionist who'd neared the end; whose theories, forms, processes, relationships, even his own body—all had entirely worn down. His very life, in fact, as this speaker was to die about a day after he articulated this stark vision. This comment, focusing on the rupture in the symbolic order, evokes the avant-garde. The second comment:

Let your fantasy take over, make your wildest dreams come true. (Naifeh and Smith 789)

This was made by a young compositionist excited that her own program seemed finally about to take shape. According to this view, any material can be reworked into a beautiful fiction. Such a view, one which restores the symbolic order, we might term the academic.

That first quote was muttered by Jackson Pollock, wandering drunk through the town of Springs, Long Island, the day before his death, realizing his span of days had been played out. Jackson was a person always at odds with the world. "For some time after arriving in [his boy-hood home] Phoenix, he refused to venture past the kitchen door with-out his mother" (Naifeh and Smith 52). Even at the peak of his popularity, in 1950, when he had been crowned by *Life* magazine as "the greatest living painter in the United States," Jackson moaned, "I feel like a clam without a shell. They only want me on top of the heap so they can push me off" (Naifeh and Smith 628). This was a person, for example, who tried three times to sit through *Waiting for Godot* but couldn't: see-ing what seemed his own story onstage caused in him such open weep-ing and loud moaning that he had to be taken from the theatre on one occasion.

The second quote was Ruth Kligman's advice to her friend Edith Metzger on the train out to Springs: Kligman in a kind of fantastic denial, hoping that her own wildest dream of being Jackson's lover was soon to come true and so chirping the joys of optimism to a friend who was depressed over an affair with a married man gone sour. According to painter and friend of Jackson's, Audrey Flack, "[Ruth] wanted to meet important artists, but she'd never heard of Jackson Pollock, Franz Kline, or Bill de Kooning. She wrote their names down on a little piece of paper and I drew her a map of how to get to the Cedar. . . . She asked which one was the most important and I said Pollock; that's why she started with him. She went right to the bar and made a beeline for Pollock. Ruth had a desperation and a need" (Potter 228). (How often, it seems, our wildest dreams are driven by desperation and a need.)

I want to think about those two schools of thought—the academic and the avant-garde—as they played themselves out in the compositional practices of Jackson Pollock, whose story, untold in Composition (but almost endlessly reactivated in more general postwar critical theory) provides an opportunity to refocus our practices around the now-dis-carded notion of process, that once-perennial of CCCC topics, the bright promise of Comp '68 (the metonym, in fact, for that entire era of Composition Studies). Process was the key Happenings trope, as well. Kaprow, for example, recalled, "I have seen [Cage's] preparations for a very short piece that were just exquisitely done—descriptions of how he worked, the time he spent, the operation necessary to draw all the graphs. It was to me more of a Happening than the music itself" (Kostelanetz *Theatre* 113). I want to spend time re-enchanting Jackson's process, then, because it was crucial to the development of the Happenings compositionists at large—but unfortunately Jackson's was a notion of process, both as an individual gesture of material inquiry as well as a larger dynamic of cultural myth, that compositionists in our own field seemed unwilling or unable to engage. Moreover, and this is intimately connected with Composition's failure of process-nerve, recovering Jackson's production-aesthetic—seeing process as a nexus of both unique self-expression and a considered feeling for materials—allows one to affirm (rather than bemoan or fix) the processes even of those compositionists considered, as Jackson was, most humiliatingly *basic.* Composition must consider Jackson or risk self-marginalization as having no comment on the central compositional questions of the age because, let's face it, the true spectacle of American Composition began in the Summer of 1947, when Jackson put his canvas on the floor of his studio in Springs, Long Island, changing forever the way composition is made, received, and defined. Jackson, then, is Modernism's fulcrum, its 'Balancing Rock' landmark-site. According to Kirk Vardenoe, who curated MOMA's 1998 retrospective of his work, "Pollock now looms as a central hinge between the century's two halves, a key to how we got from one to the other in modern art. As the pivot on which prologue and coda balance, he has become in history, still more than he was in life, a legitimator. . . . [A]ccounts of Pollock also become litmus tests for broader philosophical and political positions about the meaning of his epoch"(17).

We can begin by naming Hans Namuth, who photographed Jackson in his Springs studio in the summer of 1950, as Composition's first process-researcher. Those photos—showing Jackson in intense concentration, wearing jeans and a black T, whirling and splattering over a canvas in his studio, cigarette always dangling from his lip—have been described in the corniest of prose: as being "the picture of the romantic Genius, possessed by demonic *terrabilità*" (Rose "Namuth's Photographs"), evoking "the image of Marlon Brando's brooding pouting profile looking down while Stella ripped his tee-shirt . . . the agonized look of a man wrestling with himself in a game of unnamable but high stakes . . . [saying], You can't talk about me. You can't explain art" (Segal in Rose "Namuth's Photographs"). But perhaps you just can't be too corny when describing photos that changed the course of art history. Those photos showed Jackson as the King of Process—in Harold Rosenberg's famous phrase, "the action painter"—and helped establish American painters, so long denigrated by academics, as compelling cultural figures, figures beginning a new chapter in the mythology of American Composition, showing "a new image of the artist in the grip of impulse, driven by inner forces . . . an inspired shaman, entirely 'other' than the pedestrian businessman who dominated American social life" (Rose "Introduction"). Jackson's art became that much more enriched by seeing the process-trace underlying the product. Artists Jim Fasanelli and Tony Smith testify to the insights into Jackson's composition that could be gained from Namuth's process-account. Fasanelli, a friend of Namuth's, speaks for the art world when he attests to what was revealed by those photos, their ability to archive (and reactivate) the passage of one person through a rather brief, but artistically charged, moment in time:

> It taught me to respect Pollock in a way I never had before. For one thing you could see, literally see, he was not dripping. That word simply does not suffice. What you saw was Pollock take his stick or brush out of the paint can and then, in a cursive sweep, pass it over the canvas, high above it, so that the viscous paint would form trailing patterns which hover over the canvas before they settle upon it, and then fall into it and then leave a trace of their own passage. He is not drawing on the canvas so much as in the air above it. He must have loved the forms and lines he could make this way. This is what is really on the canvas . . . the sign of the passage of something fleeting. (Namuth)

For Smith, watching the brief movie Namuth made of Jackson painting meant seeing his friend and fellow-artist as an organic, natural force: "he was shown [in the film] painting on glass seen from below, and it seemed that the glass was earth, that he was distributing flowers over it, that it was spring" (Namuth). Critic Barbara Rose also caught the force-of-nature quality in Namuth's composing-process data: "The style of his photographs of Pollock working does not conform to the style of the artist's portrait or the studio interior, but is related to the style of motion photography used in photographing wild animals unobtrusively" ("Introduction: The Artist as Culture Hero").

Such high romantic notions about process were transformed into a full-blown cultural myth thanks to the critical overlay of Rosenberg's highly influential 1952 essay, "The American Action Painters," which was very much based on Namuth's photos. In that article, all academic-aesthetic notions of composition were discarded in favor of existentialisms.

The painter was now seen as "living on the canvas" (23), the surface of the work having become "an arena in which to act—rather than as a space in which to reproduce. . . . What was to go on the canvas was not a picture but an event" (22). The very term "painting" itself was stripped of any terministic accretions and replaced by Rosenberg with the more indeterminate phrase "gesturing with materials" (23). Connoisseurship was dead—"an action is not a matter of taste" (50)—all that mattered was "the revelation contained in the act . . . that in the final effect, the image, whatever be or be not in it, will be a *tension*" (23). The central dynamic of the work—as local situationist archive, recording the passages, the moments, of one's life-drama—became the locus of interest, not the work's form, style, or function as critical/historical project, and critics who could not shift perspective were doomed to irrelevance:

> A painting that is an act is inseparable from the biography of the artist. The painting itself is a "moment" in the adulterated mixture of his life—whether "moment" means, in one case, the actual minutes taken up with spotting the canvas or, in another, the entire duration of a lucid drama conducted in sign language. The act-painting is of the same metaphysical substance as the artist's existence. The new painting has broken down every distinction between art and life. . . . The critic who goes on judging in terms of schools, styles, form, as if the painter were still concerned with producing a certain kind of object (the work of art), instead of living on the canvas, is bound to seem a stranger. (23)

The photos and the essay utterly changed the cultural reception of Jackson Pollock. Previously, his work, in particular the drip paintings, had been infantalized precisely by dint of its process-status: Robert Coates, for example, called the paintings "mere unorganized explosions of random energy, and therefore meaningless" (Naifeh and Smith 555). Henry McBride thought his canvases looked "as though the paint had been flung at the canvas from a distance" (Krauss *Optical* 245) and likened them to "a kaleidoscope that has been insufficiently shaken. Another shake or two might bring order into the flying particles of color—but the spectator is not too sure of this" (Naifeh and Smith 465). *Time* quipped that a "Pollock painting is apt to resemble a child's contour map of the Battle of Gettysburg" ("Words" 51). And, in 1949, *Life* cattily reminded its readers that many critics called Jackson's canvases "degenerate . . . as unpalatable as yesterday's macaroni" ("Jackson Pollock: Is He?" 42). Jackson's process, especially his signature style of "dumping" (allowing bits of the everyday to encrust his canvas), was described by *Life* as quaint eccentricity: "Sometimes he dribbles the paint on with a brush. Sometimes he scrawls it on with a stick, scoops it with a trowel or even pours it straight out of the can. In with it all he deliberately mixes sand, broken glass, nails, screws or other foreign matter lying around. Cigaret ashes and an occasional dead bee sometimes get in the picture inadvertently"(44). They summed up their characterization of Jackson's process with the petulant image of the painter "brooding and doodling" (45)— all of this in an article that ultimately raised the stakes around Jackson as cultural figure by seriously asking "Is he the greatest living painter in the United States?" For Krauss, this initial reception fixed Jackson's work in its process-status; not surprising, given the way the drip paintings can be read as an index of their process, pointing to the material condition of their production: "in places, the poured line would leach out into the weave of the canvas like a viscous, oily stain, while in others the filaments would sit high and ropey on top of one another, and in still others the paint would puddle up and dry unevenly, its crusty surface pulling into scummy-looking scabs" ("Horizontality" 97).

Ironically, though, it was finally process—only now an iconic, existential process, not Piagetian grade-school doodling—that refigured the response to the artist and his work, because from 1952 when Namuth's process-photos and Rosenberg's exegesis/essay hit, Jackson's myth became untouchable, catalyzing a generation of artists. Watching him work or just marveling at the visual traces of him in his studio, seeing the final product of such liberating practice, reading the metacommentary on Jackson's compositional scene—what Jackson provided was a kind of amalgam-text made up of process, product, and discourse. The potential of such a refigured composition—text now as scene rather than thing—was enormous. Vardenoe is only one critic who notes how the new strategies Jackson provided led to so many artistic breakthroughs. He comments on the way the paintings

> fuse the how and why, means and end, instrumental method and expressive message. It's that self-evident combination of what's left out (no familiar hierarchy of marks, no ordering constraints) with what's left in (a seemingly spontaneous, even reckless laying-on of raw skeins of liquid paint) that has been so compelling to so many artists . . . the permissions it gave have percolated irrepressibly through painting, sculpture, installation and performance art, and hybrids of all of the above (not to mention the effect on musicians and writers). (17)

The Happenings artists in particular were galvanized by the idea of what Jackson had done—these artists for whom, in Kaprow's words, Jackson became "the embodiment of our ambition for absolute liberation and a secretly cherished wish to overturn old tables of crockery and flat champagne" ("Legacy" 24). Kaprow's 1958 article on Jackson's legacy is routinely cited as a formative text for the Art of the Happening. For Kaprow, Jackson provided artists with "the possibility of an astounding freshness, a sort of ecstatic blindness" (24). Rosenberg's hype, the fusion of composition and life into situationist event-scene, proved operational. The paintings became a "diaristic gesture" of process for Kaprow (26); in fact, "they ceased to become paintings and became *environments*" (56). Because they radically re-envisioned notions of form, they provided the Happenings compositionists with a new compositional space, one read not according to conventional interpretive strategies, but according to the heuristic of the *dérive*. "You do not enter a painting of Pollock's in any one place (or hundred places). Anywhere is everywhere and you can dip in and out where you can" (26). Inside that new space Kaprow saw an "activity which our imaginations continue outward indefinitely, as though refusing to accept the artificiality of an 'ending'" (55). This new environmental effect, a blurring of the canvas and the endless space surrounding it, was an irresistible challenge now become strategy: "Pollock . . . left us at the point where we must become preoccupied with and even dazzled by the space and objects of our everyday life, either our bodies, clothes, rooms, or, if need be, the vastness of Forty-second Street" (56). It was as if Kaprow could re-enter the horizontal floor-space with Jackson, re-activate the process, be *in* the work, too. Situated thus, Kaprow could see the keys and cigarettes and matches being dumped down onto the work. His article's final litany, concluding his meditation on the meaning of Jackson's practices, became a Happenings manifesto: Jackson's, he claimed, was an art able to "disclose entirely unheard of happenings and events, found in garbage cans, police files, hotel lobbies, seen in store windows and on the streets, and sensed in dreams and horrible accidents. An odor of crushed strawberries, a letter from a friend or a billboard selling Draino; three taps on the front door, a scratch, a sigh or a voice lecturing endlessly, a blinding staccato flash, a bowler hat—all will become materials for this concrete art" (57).

The process of Pollock is received differently here. Rather than a spirit of ridicule or traditionalism, Kaprow's response grew out of an existential intensity—mesmerized, as the shimmering surface disclosed undreamed-of possibilities. Kaprow saw the work as tension-filled moment-trace, an endlessly recurring dream, able to connect us back up with our everyday, with our bodies and lived situations, with basic processes of life. Such a view diffuses the work into life, pulling against the gallery's stubborn conception of form as "what can maintain itself as vertically intact, and thus a seemingly autonomous gestalt" (Krauss *Optical* 294). Jackson's art remains intimately connected with the horizontal floor—its process-context, its production-scene. As exscription, as life-dumped text, Jackson's composition is filled with mementos of momentariness: Edward Hults, a plumber in Springs, recalls visiting Jackson's studio: "It was one of those times a canvas covered nearly the whole studio floor—hardly any room to walk around it—and it was covered with paint, but he told me to walk across it. 'Go ahead,' he said, 'you won't hurt it.'" (Potter 140).

Throughout his career, it seems, there was Jackson's ceaseless interrogation of process, always looking beneath the seemingly random tracing for the underlying tension and a way to capture it. When he first moved to New York, he'd stare in fascination at three-card monte games and even go so far as to follow the urination trails of police horses in an attempt to decode nature's patterns. His early sketchbooks show how Thomas Hart Benton, the American regionalist and Jackson's first and only post-secondary formal teacher, taught him to break down the compositions of the Old Masters into their underlying geometric shapes and lines. Yve-Alain Bois, in analyzing those portions of the sketchbooks, speculates on why Jackson kept at that exercise long after he left Benton's tutelage. He felt it showed Jackson "in search of a unitary mode of notation that would be able to transcode anything" (Review 84). That transliteration of the swirling pulse underlying life evolved into the rudiment of Jackson's composition, his line. (Ah, the search for a serviceable, non-discipline-specific compositional technique in order to record hopes, fears, fantasies; a kind of transmodal, multi-representational, plainspeak lyrical line for autoarchiving human experience—this is *my* wildest dream as a writing teacher. "Who amongst us has not dreamt . . . of the miracle of a poetic prose . . . supple and staccato enough to adapt to the lyrical stirrings of the soul, the undulations of dreams, and the sudden leaps of consciousness?" [Benjamin *Charles Baudelaire* 69]) Jackson had to develop his own line because he had a unique, personal vision to express. Dr. Wayne Barker, a psychiatrist who summered on

Long Island, got to know Jackson and realized his imperative for communication: "I think Jackson was trying to utter something almost incomprehensible to himself. I know people speak of his dancing in his paintings, but to me it's more like talking . . . the need to utter. . . . I think he had trouble saying it—a lot of people might understand him better had he been a writer—and I think as a philosopher the best he could do was an approximation" (Potter 177). Jackson's strategy, then, was most important in the way he restored content to the center of composition. If Jackson's work is about anything, it is the ultimate significance of the emotional/ideational center of the work, the rich spiritual quality of the statement. He turned to painting because it could be made into a direct gesturing with materials, and as he said, "the more direct—the greater the possibilities of making a direct—of making a statement" (Wright).

As compositionist, Jackson's was a line that evolved painfully. Throughout his life he was told he couldn't draw. His formal teacher Benton, the arch-academic, was appalled at Jackson's rendering, saying about his young student, "His mind was absolutely incapable of drafting logical sequences. He couldn't be taught anything" (Naifeh and Smith 164). Frustrated with his inability to perfect the traditional representational line, the correct line, yet needing a serviceable, functional line to express his vision, Jackson turned to other teachers, determinedly pursuing a homemade education in the technology of composition through Indian sand painters, automatic writing, Mexican muralists, Jungian analysts, obvious influences like Picasso and Miró, as well as lesser-known artists like Albert Ryder and Janet Sobel; at the same time immersing himself in an exhaustive study of traditional and non-traditional materials, "searching for a way to make the world see the world his way" (Naifeh and Smith 538). Jackson's immersion in a purposively technologized process can best be seen in his apprenticeship with the Mexican muralist David Alfaro Siqueiros, at whose Fourteenth Street studio Jackson learned how to exploit available technology in the surface of making a revelatory statement. Jackson joined the crowd of young artists in Siqueiros's loft working on political floats and murals.

> In his studio, Siqueiros generated a "torrential flow of ideas and new projects" with a child's eye for investigation and surprise. Paint itself was a source of endless discovery, especially the new industrial paints like Duco—a synthetic nitrocellulose-based paint developed for automobiles. (Siqueiros's passion for the new paint earned him the sobriquet "il Duco.") Synthetic resins like Duco

were not only stronger, more durable, and more malleable than organically based oils, they were *new*: products of the technological era. What medium could be more fitting for an art that "belonged" to the workers of that era? "Lacquer had so many possibilities," recalled [painter and friend of Jackson's during his student days] Axel Horn, "that we tried everything. We threw it around, we dripped it, we sprayed it, we chopped it with axes, we burnt it just to see what would happen." They applied it in gossamer-light veils of spray and in thick, viscous globs. For a hard edge, they sprayed it through stencils or friskets. For texture they added sand and paper, pieces of wood and bits of metal. "It was like high school chemistry class," said Horn. "When the teacher leaves the room and there's a mad dash for the chemical cabinet. You grab things and throw them in the sink and throw a match in to see what will happen." Mistakes ("failed experiments") could be scraped off easily—the new paints dried to hardness "almost instantly." Instead of canvas duck or Belgian linen, they used concrete walls, Masonite panels, and plywood boards nailed together like siding on a house—industrial surfaces for industrial paints. "As early as 1936," claims Harold Lehman [another artist and student-friend of Jackson's], "we had already announced the death of easel painting."

New materials demanded new methods, new ways of creating images. A painter should work the way a *worker* works, Siqueiros believed. In applying paint, he should use a spray gun; for plaster, a plaster gun. In one corner of the Union Square workshop stood a silk-screen frame, long considered merely an industrial tool for sign-making. "A lot of people were using these materials, these techniques," Horn recalls, "but he came along and said, 'This is all usable in art'" (Naifeh and Smith 286–287).

But such an exhaustive material quest can be frustrating. In Dec. 1936, Jackson complains to his brother, "I am at more unrest with the problems of form in art than ever. I have not yet crossed the bridge of experimentation that will put me on the road to production" (Naifeh and Smith 290). Jackson, perhaps, never really crossed that bridge; the drip paintings, for example, exploit a technology—premixed liquid paint—that had only been available for about ten years. By making experimentation stand for production, he changed the work. The critical response to such a new work becomes telling, as either the critic will develop new criteria (as Rosenberg did) or risks misjudging the work. Such misjudging might take the form of a derogatory trivializing (of the kind that first greeted Jackson); at best, it implies a recuperative misreading of the work, one that makes a strange sense of it under an established evaluative system.

It's fascinating to watch a critic like Clement Greenberg strain his own established aesthetics to accommodate radically different art like Jackson's. Such art couldn't be unique, *sui generis*, because, as such, it would destroy the force of Greenberg's critical machine; it would mean there was powerful work unmeasurable by his established theoretical mechanics. Therefore, Greenberg confidently explains all abstract art (Jackson's included) as just a logical phase in the unfolding of western art, his area of expertise: "Abstract art is not a special kind of art; no hard-and-fast line separates it from representational art; it is only the latest phase in the development of Western art as a whole, and almost every 'technical' device of abstract painting is already to be found in the realistic painting that preceded it" ("The Case" 82).

To make Jackson seem like a natural evolution in the history of Western art meant terming him "very much of a Late Cubist . . . [who] compiled hints from Picasso, Miró, Siqueiros, Orozco and Hofmann to create an allusive and altogether original vocabulary of Baroque shapes with which he twisted Cubist space" ("American-Type" Painting 217). Greenberg even glosses over the key shift in Jackson away from the easel: "Pollock was very much . . . a hard and fast easel-painter when he entered into his maturity" (217). Krauss characterizes this change as "sublimating Pollock".

> Of raising him up from that dissolute squat, in his James Dean dungarees and black tee-shirt, slouched over his paintings in the disarray of his studio or hunkered down on the running board of his old Ford. This is the posture, in all its lowness, projected by so many famous photographs, images recording the athletic abandon of the painting gesture but also the dark brooding silence of the stilled body, with its determined isolation from everything urban, everything "cultured." The photographs had placed him on the road, like Kerouac, clenching his face into the tight fist of beat refusal, making an art of violence, of "howl." Clem[ent Greenberg]'s mission was to lift him above those pictures, just as it was to lift the paintings Pollock made from off the ground where he'd made them, and onto the wall. Because it was only on the wall that they joined themselves to tradition, to culture, to convention. It was in that location and at that angle to gravity that they became "painting." (*Optical* 244)

The critical repositioning of Jackson's canvas from the horizontal (the floor, the act of creation) to the vertical (the museum wall, the act of exhibition) changes the perspective from process to product, rewriting the now-changed object according to a conventional perspective. But such a familiarization was impossible for Jackson's work, a work in which "the axis of the image has changed" (Krauss "Horizontality" 95). He denied the vertical distancing of the gallery wall, a destination whose point of origin is the upright easel: "My painting does not come from the easel," he explained; working on the floor, "I can . . . literally be *in* the painting" ("Jackson Pollock: Is He?" 45). No wonder Kaprow could so easily inhabit that scene, or that so many viewers thought of the works in terms of landscapes, nature ("Pollock loves the outdoors and has carried with him and into his painting a sense of the freedom experienced before endless mountains and plains" [Goodnough 38]); he provided a re-enterable scene. Krauss cites Jackson's *Full Fathom Five*, both for its title, as well as the residue of "dumping" contained on the surface—splashed gobs of white lead, as well as a variety of trash like keys, nails, cigarettes and matches—to support Jackson's claim that the work had to be connected to the ground, "the fact of standing over the work and looking down" (*Optical* 293). Robert Morris spent the late sixties searching for the grammar of the "Anti Form," an idea that typified the spirit of American art, which, at its best, has developed through negation: "by uncovering successive alternative premises for making itself. . . . Disengagement with preconceived enduring forms and orders for things is a positive assertion. It is part of the work's refusal to continue estheticizing the form by dealing with it as a prescribed end" (43, 46). And so he was drawn to Jackson's work because it revealed the primacy of process, of the work's "making itself": "only Pollock was able to recover process and hold on to it as part of the end form of the work. Pollock's recovery of process involved a profound rethinking of the role of both material and tools in making" (43). Pollock, then, successfully interrupted the formalist dynamic, in which process is of relatively minor concern, important only as prelude—the central focus of attention: the final work, with all its hierarchical relations and patterns; its hints, allusions, and Baroque shapes.

Concern for process has waned in CCCC, possibly because the concern for the statement has as well. In 1985, the rumblings started sounding, with Ray Rodrigues's article "Moving Away from Process-Worship," in which he seemed to realize that process-orientation in our field might become as speciously cultified as it had with the Action Painter. Its proponents were "missionaries," Rodrigues cracked, who were sloppy in their enthusiasm, trivializing process in "the use of unsystematic, open-ended writing instruction" (24). He might have been discussing process, but really he was worried about the ultimate product. Anticipating retroactively, perhaps, how indulgence in process might naturally result in the kind of drip-composition *Time* magazine in 1949 called "Jackson Pollock's non-objective snarl of tar and confetti" (Eliot 26), Rodrigues complains about process being "rather . . . like a tangled string after a kitten had played with it" (25). Rodrigues might have even been responding to an image put forth one year earlier, in 1984, by Donald Murray, in a chapter from *Write to Learn*, entitled "Writing as Process," where Murray affirms, "If we could open up a writer's head during the act of writing we might see an electro-chemical process that looks like this:"

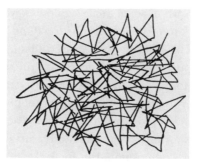

Copyright © 1984 Holt, Rhinehart and Winston

Murray, however, immediately backs off from the unwitting comparison of creativity to the Pollock dripped web, and settles back into Composition's agenda of simplification, standardization, reassuring the student that "If we could untangle that spaghetti we might find the following five primary activities taking place . . ." (7). Composition's ultimately tepid support for process proved entropic, so much so that by 1994, John Trimbur will refer to his Compositional era as "post-process," claiming the process paradigm failed because it closed on a prescribed form—a conventional, expressive statement, made in a conventional, "authentic" prose—which simply "reinstituted the rhetoric of the belletristic tradition at the center of the writing classroom" ("Taking the Social Turn" 110). A Happenings practice, though, inflects situations, revelations, tensions, over forms. It insists on the primacy of Jackson darting about the floor, what such a gesture means, over the work's institutionalization on the wall (and into academic history). The Happenings lesson to take from Jackson's art is (life-)process-oriented: his process fascinates not in order to discover how to paint like Jackson (reproducing forms, reinstituting rhetorics) but to empathize with him, to re-enter the compositional scene as Kaprow could, to consider how he solved problems (what he even saw as problems), how he met limits, considered materials, tried to make a direct statement in an interesting way—to think about what Jackson felt in the moments of composition. His process's liberatory power as radical heuristic is consistently acknowledged. His friend and fellow-painter George McNeil remarked, "Pollock is . . . one of those artists who are mid-wives: they change the course of art. The great power in his work helped all of us who were so intellectually dominated by consideration of form—it was really a tonic" (Potter 278). And the art historian Leo Lerman agrees: "Even people who don't know of Jackson Pollock see differently because of him—all sorts of visual things couldn't have happened without his influence. Pollock freed the eye and he freed the imagination. . . . He really saw the cobwebs in things and cleared them away" (Potter 279). Trimbur's sober reappraisal, in its eagerness to write the end of one chapter and review notes for the beginning of the next, stems from a curatorial gesture like Greenberg's, not a Happenings sort of process-reading which would, in this case, see Pollock as an action, an extension of being in a moment in time, as an endlessly re-activatible action. Process was too messy, too gnarly for Composition. But for Jackson, that tangled, loopy web came closest to capturing the inner life one lives. Nicholas Carone, a fellow Long Island artist, recalls Jackson arguing that it was impossible to teach art. When Carone suggested that there were certain things you could teach—the language of art and basic forms, Jackson shot back, "Well, [that's] got nothing to do with what I'm involved in, the cosmos." Carone persisted that there were certain basics that could be the subject of instruction. "Maybe you're right," Jackson said, "but if I had to teach, I would tell my students to study Jung" (Potter 197).

Trimbur critiques the process movement for closing on a certain type of representation, "self-revelatory personal essays written in a decidedly non-academic style," a style clued into by savvier students, who quickly caught on "that sincerity and authenticity of voice were the privileged means of symbolic exchange" ("Taking the Social Turn" 110). Despite Greenberg's ultimate misreading of Jackson's work, he clearly saw how easily a representational aesthetic could lead away from inner expressionism to slavish rendering; such was the western tradition of composition, which "laid more of a stress than any other tradition on creating a sculpture-like, or photographic, illusion of the third dimension, on thrusting images at the eye with a lifelikeness that brought them as close as possible to their originals . . . involv[ing] the spectator to a much greater extent in the practical and actual aspects of the things they depict and represent" ("The Case" 78–79). So the danger Greenberg sees in non-abstract art, then, lies in the way it shifts attention to a predictable, practical, "real-life" content: "We begin to wonder what we think of the people shown in Rembrandt's portraits, as people; whether or not we would like to walk through the terrain shown in a Corot landscape; about the life stories of the burghers we see in a Steen painting" ("The Case" 79).

Not so amazingly, such concerns formed Composition's actual prescriptive pedagogy for expressivism. Expressivism withered in post-Happenings Composition because it fatally conflated intensity, not with content, but reproducibility; the statement itself wasn't important, just the rendering of the setting. With expressivism in Composition defined as the faithful depiction of the "real world," Donald Stewart, for example, in his *Versatile Writer*, advocates a series of techniques for his students "to increase the intensity and quantity of your perceptions of things around you" (36). Bearing out Greenberg's reading of expressive aesthetics, Stewart wants a composition that adds depth to representation, creating a kind of hyperreal of the everyday: "Write short biographies of the persons sitting on either side of you right now. Do you know where they live? Where are they from? What are their majors? Are they married, engaged, pinned?" (41).

Elbow's 1981 *Writing With Power* invoked the same dynamic; his "Metaphors for Priming the Pump" are a series of questions (e.g., "_____ is an animal. What animal?" or "_____ is really a spy. For whom? What assignment?" [82]) designed to "help you see more aspects of what you want to write about . . . and thus see more clearly" (78). And Murray's *Write to Learn* contained a series of focusing exercises ("Look Backwards," "Look Forward" [54]) advertised as "techniques that will help you move in close and concentrate your vision" (53). Such prescriptive gimmicks made sense when the writing desired was thoroughly conventional. The one thing every one of Jackson's critics could agree on was that, for better or worse, there was never a work like his: Judd sums up the radical break he represents, noting that Jackson "used paint and canvas in a new way. Everyone else . . . used them in ways that were developments upon traditional European or Western ways of handling paint and canvas" (195). There was no rupture in Composition's traditional program by process teachers, according to Harris, "they simply argued for what seems . . . a new sort of formalism" (*Teaching* 56). Their research studies, with the type of received texts they process-traced, determined this; it would have been akin to Hans Namuth deciding to photograph Jackson early on, as he struggled to copy Michelangelo's Sistine Chapel frescoes. Their *process*, then, became a retrojection "a kind of back formation from an ideal product . . . the sort of self-expressive writing that [process teachers] value above all others" (Harris *Teaching* 63). Jackson's "action" process was projective, a working-out of his life-statement, his self-as-message. What Naifeh and Smith call Jackson's "old dilemma" was not reproduction, but rather "how to reconcile the real world with the world of his imagination" (455). "Painting is self-discovery," Jackson once said. "Every good artist paints what he is" (Naifeh and Smith 536). CCCC's version of process had more banal goals. Their notion of "helping students to write 'better,'" according to Harris, had "less to do with self-discovery than with success in the academic or corporate world" (*Teaching* 64). So forget the inspired shaman, right? Bring back that pedestrian businessman.

Reifying what can now be called a "representational expressionism," meant that process became a certain series of steps—a replicable, prescribed process—leading to a certain predictable outcome (Trimbur speaks of the "growing disillusion with its limits" ["Taking the Social Turn" 109] felt by post-Happenings Compositionists, leading them to take the "social turn" to a cultural studies curriculum). The action painter's, however, was a raw, cowboy process. A distinctly zen cowboy's, though. As cornball-Romantic as Rosenberg's description might seem, it was very close to the way Jackson worked: "When I am *in* my painting, I'm not aware of what I'm doing. It is only after a sort of 'get acquainted' period that I see what I have been about. I have no fears about making changes, destroying the image, etc., because the painting has a life of its own. I try to let it come through. It is only when I lose contact with the painting that the result is a mess" ("Statements"). This is a distinctly Happenings approach: Robert Whitman, creator of some of the most influential and poetically expressionistic Happenings, said, "You have to trust your intuition. . . . I don't think it's a good idea to be too knowledgeable about what you're doing. I prefer a situation where I make something that I'm interested in, and I'll see what it tells me" (Kostelanetz *Theatre* 225, 226). By prescribing a process, framing it as prewriting, drafting, and revising, we made almost certain that students could never come up with what Jackson did. Unlike most painters, he spurned the invention stage of preliminary drawings. Asked if he had a "pre-conceived image" in mind as he began a painting, Jackson answered, "No—because it hasn't been created [yet]" (Wright). Paint, in all phases of his work, even the pre-drip canvases, was applied quickly; watching him paint, a friend said, was like watching someone shoot craps (Naifeh and Smith 452). He down-played technique because he was concentrating on the new expression: "New needs need new techniques," he said. Technique was "just a means of arriving at a statement" (Wright), "certain basic rules you have to know, and then forget it" (Rose "Pollock's Studio"). Where painters like de Kooning revised their work endlessly, Jackson bragged of a process that would capture it all in one take, a "one-shot deal" (Naifeh and Smith 406). When he got those early bad reviews, he knew it was because critics were bringing all their determinate, obstinately academic baggage to his work. "If they'd leave most of their stuff at home and just look at the painting, they'd have no trouble enjoying it. It's just like looking at a bed of flowers. You don't tear your hair out over what it means" (Naifeh and Smith 592).

Jackson, with Namuth as his researcher, would have made a wonderful case study for the formative years of CCCC. What Namuth's photos provided was exactly what Braddock, Lloyd-Jones, and Schoer were after in 1963. Maybe they felt the Childanesque whiff of simulation in the air as they prepared their report on the status of Compositional knowledge. They realized something would be missing in trying to generalize knowledge about composition from "such indirect measures as multiple-choice or true-false tests, questionnaires, self-inventories, and the like" (24), so they instead advocated a study of the way actual writers worked, by "direct observation" (24). Namuth's was the kind of process-researcher methodology they liked: a case study (31–32), in which materials are provided and behavior recorded. A concern for simulation or replication is an important caveat as one studies process. For the composer, a thorough knowledge of process can allow one to understand materials and technologies, broadening one's own composition, allowing it to capture one's visions. Or it can simply allow one to repeat, replicate, perfect. For four years, Jackson explores the drip technology. He gradually perfects the technique: how to control effects, for example, such as streams, drops, ripples, or that smooth pooling; when to use a stick, as opposed to a dried brush; how to thin the paint to the right consistency; how much to load on. But then, paintings like "Autumn Rhythm" and "One" became almost too perfect, such obvious masterpieces; when he could control the drip technique so that the lines did exactly what he wanted, the accident was gone. He had achieved scale and control at the expense of his unruly vision and inner torment. Realizing his bind, he turned to new materials—rice paper and ink, black paint alone, glass basting syringes instead of sticks and brushes—to fight through ritual and back to real emotion.

Process knowledge is necessary for a critic or teacher as well, but here, too, lies a choice: is process studied and taught simply to replicate a certain kind of work, or rather for deeper, conceptual reasons, to understand the nature of composition, to expand our sense of what can count as work? The art critic Leo Steinberg offers an illustration of this dilemma. He goes to see Jasper Johns's first one-man show in 1958 and is utterly shaken. He looks at the canvases—numbers, letters, flags, targets (some with plaster casts of body parts attached, even a painting with a smaller frame glued in the center of a canvas, called "Canvas," or one with the knobbed face of an actual dresser drawer inserted into the canvas, called "Drawer"), most done in the then almost-forgotten encaustic technique, which fittingly seemed to gray out everything one's critical apparatus traditionally took as evaluative criteria: color, technique, brushstroke. Steinberg's reaction is complicated: he initially hates the show; but he can't stop thinking about the pictures, can't stop returning to the Castelli Gallery to look at them:

> I disliked the show, and would gladly have thought it a bore. Yet it depressed me and I wasn't sure why. Then I began to recognize in myself all the classical symptoms of a philistine's reaction to modern art. . . . I was really mad at myself for being so dull, and at the whole situation for showing me up. . . . [W]hat really depressed me was what I felt those works were able to do to all other art. The pictures of de Kooning and Kline, it seemed to me, were suddenly tossed into one pot with Rembrandt and Giotto. All alike suddenly became painters of illusion. . . . It looked to me like the death of painting, a rude stop, the end of the track. (12, 13)

What Johns's work did to Steinberg was disturb the criteria-keystones on which he and other critics had constructed their neat art-historical narrative, those "solid standards . . . set by the critic's long-practised taste and by his conviction that only those innovations will be significant which promote the established direction of advanced art" (63). Steinberg is that rare critic who went further into the disturbing composer's work to understand it; he decided a critic needed to be "more yielding . . . hold[ing] his criteria and taste in reserve. Since they were formed upon yesterday's art, he does not assume they are readymade for today" (63). So Steinberg went deeper into Johns as compositionist, exploring his technological development and strategies (finding, in fact, that some of his most interesting effects were accidents) and taxonomizing Johns's subject matter. The result caused Steinberg to radically re-determine his thoughts about art, to start fresh: "It is part of the fascination of Johns's work that many of his inventions are interpretable as meditations on the nature of painting, pursued as if in dialogue with a questioner of ideal innocence and congenital blindness" (48).

New criteria, though, are not part of the academic program. In Greenberg's steadily unfolding historical narrative there is never really novelty, never a sharp, essential break with Tradition; legitimizing a new notion like Jackson's indeterminate, infinitely expandable, non-hierarchical line would be unthinkable. All is subsumed in disciplinary historicity, working itself out genetically, according to a pre-determined code: "I fail to discern anything in the new abstract painting that is that new. I can see nothing essential in it that cannot be shown to have evolved out of either Cubism or Impressionism (if we include Fauvism in the latter), just as I cannot see anything essential in Cubism or Impressionism whose development cannot be traced back to the Renaissance" ("How Art Writing" 142). Equally for Bartholomae, novelty does not exist, even if we wish it could. "There is a student in my class writing an essay on her family, on her parents' divorce. We've all read this essay. We've read it because the student cannot invent a way of talking about family, sex roles, separation. Her essay is determined by a variety of forces: the genre of the personal essay as it has shaped this student and this moment; attitudes about the family and divorce; the figures of 'Father' and 'Mother' and 'Child' and so on" ("Writing with Teachers" 66–67).

The inevitability of Tradition's tropes and genres—"Our writing is not our own" ("Writing with Teachers" 64)—becomes the simple truth of Modernist Composition. Since there can be no rupture in the academic symbolic, what is privileged is not the exercising of an individual's creative powers, but the inescapable monolith of historical impeccability (or, as Bartholomae puts it, "the particular representations of power, tradition and authority reproduced whenever one writes" [64], i.e., *only those innovations which promote the established direction of advanced art*). Greenberg hated how art writing slighted history in praising the contemporary artist as if he/she had "come out of nowhere and owes practically nothing to anything before him[/her]. It's as though art began all over again every other day" (Greenberg "How Art Writing" 143). And so, for Greenberg, one of Jackson's "deepest insights" is that "the past remained implicated in everything he did" ("Jackson Pollock: 'Inspiration'" 249). This, despite reminiscences like the following, from fellow-painter Harry Jackson: "I wanted to paint realistically and study painting technique, and I brought him a book on the techniques of the old masters. Jack said, 'Oh *no*. You can't read that stuff. You can't do that anymore, Harry'" (Potter 204). An Action Critic like Rosenberg will call Greenberg's past-implicated work "art that accommodates itself to a prepared taste" ("After Next, What?" 72). Rosenberg even joked about how easy it was to generate a simulation-machine for Modernist composition based on a studied, detailed familiarity with the art of the past:

> the mode of production of modern masterpieces has now been all too clearly rationalized. There are styles in the present displays which the painter could have acquired by putting a square inch of a Soutine or a Bonnard under a microscope. . . . All this is training based on a new conception of what art is, rather than original work demonstrating what art is about to become.
>
> At the center of this wide practicing of the immediate past, however, the work of some painters has separated itself from the rest by a consciousness of a function for painting different from that of the earlier [artists]. ("American Action Painters" 22)

Action Painting had nothing to do with art history, and it had everything to do with offering the individual an opportunity for expressiveness, training not in an update of standard conceptions, but in how to afford even the most basic student a rhetorical-existential line capable of turning anyone's record of daily annihilations into a diary of the American Infinite, a "means of confronting in daily practice the problematic nature of modern individuality . . . restor[ing] metaphysical point to art" (Rosenberg, "Action Painting: Crisis and Distortion" 40).

But Modernist Composition never admits it doesn't know what's going on. So Greenberg insists on seeing Jackson in terms of the next stage in Late Cubism, and Bartholomae insists on seeing basic writers as carrying out (or trying to) the ongoing project of the university's unfolding narrative: to see these composers otherwise (as offering new meditations on the nature of composition, say—statements having little or nothing to do with the arbitrarily assembled "history" of composition preceding them) would automatically render the Modernist critical project odd and obsessive. No wonder, for example, language poet Charles Bernstein unnerves Bartholomae when, in a conversation, Bernstein calls traditional essay-writing, with its artificial coherence, "a kind of lying" ("On Poetry" 51). Bernstein would teach writing as drift, the *dérive*:

> If you don't account for digression at every level of teaching—from elementary school on—if you don't account for the enormous force of digression, then you end up, on the one hand, teaching some people to have an enormous facility to cut out what doesn't fit and to fit in, which is a very corporate, commodified, homogenized, bland way of imagining writing. And on the other hand, you're letting people who can't develop that facility, or have just an enormous psychological resistance to it, feel disenfranchised from their own language. (51)

Bartholomae almost stammers back a response, not wanting to consider the implication that dawns on him, about how, "if we taught the parenthesis with the same vigor as we taught the topic sentence, we'd have a different tradition of writing in this country" (52).

Just the idea of an art history tradition is amusing, when thrown into relief against Jackson's work. How could you speak of Jackson's art in terms of the past, when it looked like it came from the future? According to the painter David Budd:

> Meeting Jackson was a turning point in my work and in my life. He was a hero—the thing about him was that he was *right*, and the paintings were right. . . . That hero for me is still: I was talking not long ago to a friend and I turned on the sidewalk and there in a window was a Pollock. It jolted me like an electric shock—after thirty years it looked like it would be done *tomorrow*, it was so good. So you have to stop talking and just look. That's super power, super magic, super whatever! (Potter 193)

Clem's idea of fitting Jackson into the lineage of Analytical Cubism: such formalist fashionings of thematic continua always seem silly and obsessive-compulsive, missing the individual poetry of the work, the inner drama. "The whole evolution of Abstract Expressionism could, in fact, be described as a devolution from a Synthetic kind of abstract Cubism to an Analytical kind. . . . In the all-over Pollock and in the de Kooning of the last seven or eight years, analogous planar segments are analogously deployed (smaller in Pollock, larger in de Kooning), with the principal difference being in their articulation or jointing" (Greenberg "After Abstract" 127–128). Rosenberg had no patience for this impulse in Greenberg, seeing it as the free-world version of the kind of state-styled control of art history practiced under Communism: "The critic in a free country, who maps out the direction that art must take, does the next most effective thing: he demonstrates his accuracy by consigning to the critical rubbish heap any art that fails to take that direction" ("After Next, What?" 65). The problem with such neat notions of periodicity, for Rosenberg, is their remove from the actual creative process:

> the nature of creation is that it contains the unexpected . . . . It moves through time in a ragged, irregular order, neither purifying itself nor succumbing to an ultimate logic. (By the "logic of history," art should have ended with Malevich, and a current panel of French critics and philosophers sees it as extinguishing itself with "art informel.") Art wishes not to be historically impeccable but to exercise the powers of creation available to it. ("After Next" 66)

In our own subfield of Composition, history indeed imposes; and a writer's art must be historically impeccable. Language is the ultimate presiding logic of history to which the writer must succumb: "It is language that mediates, that stands before a writer and determines what he will say" (Bartholomae "Writing on the Margins" 72). And so Bartholomae can trace the historical implications of language's mediation in his students' papers (the tropes used, the phraseology) much like Greenberg can detail the analogous planar segments in Jackson's work. Here's Bartholomae on the White Shoes paper in "Inventing the University":

> The "I" of this text—the "I" who "figured," "thought," and "felt"—is located in a conventional rhetoric of the self that turns imagination into origination (I made it), that argues an ethic of production (I made it and it is mine), and that argues a tight scheme of intention (I made it because I decided to make it). The rhetoric seems invisible because it is so common. This "I" (the maker) is also located in a version of history that dominates classrooms, the "great man" theory: History is rolling along (the English novel is dominated by a central, intrusive narrative presence; America is in the throes of a Great

Depression; during football season the team was supposed to wear the same kind of cleats and socks) until a figure appears, one who can shape history (Henry James, FDR, the writer of the "White Shoes" paper), and everything is changed. In the argument of the "White Shoes" paper, the history goes "I figured . . . I thought . . . I told . . . They agreed . . ." and, as a consequence, "I feel that creativity *comes from when* a person lets his imagination come up with ideas and he is not afraid to express them." The act of appropriation becomes a narrative of courage and conquest. (150–151)

Poor White Shoes, having to learn the lesson the media so painfully taught Jackson: you should always be afraid to express the imagination's ideas. (The obvious irony that must, of course, be noted: Jackson *was* that 'great man' who appeared and changed the course of art history, whose life was a narrative of courage and conquest.) Jasper Johns, too, not so surprisingly fails according to the academy's criteria (Greenberg went out of his way to denigrate him in reviews); the audacity of a genre being radically made over in encaustic, with a dresser drawer sticking out of it.

The proper genre exists in Composition (it's "already there in the institution" ["Writing on the Margins" 72]); it's the essay, because historically that is the key genre of "the exemplary culture within which our students live . . . academic culture, with its powerful ways of representing the world" (79). The form and content of that essay are also historically determined; it has its "available introductions, transitions, and conclusions" (72), "its peculiar gestures of authority, its key terms and figures, its interpretive schemes" (69), which must be reproduced. Teaching, then, becomes a kind of relocation project in which a "student moves into" (72) this language. Allowing students to exercise the powers of creation available to them is laughably naive; the notion that we can "give students genuine options or transform the university system so that all styles are equally genuine" runs counter to ultimate institutional logic; it is "a utopian construction" (72). And Jackson, of course, searching for that unitary mode of notation that would be able to transcode anything, also flunks out, for teaching—even permitting—a student "to use a pure, reasonable common tongue [so that] the distinction between a professional and lay person, an expert and a novice, or school and home would disappear at the level of language" (72) is equally utopian. Rosenberg saw the simulation game of art history, where "anything can be 'traced back' to anything, especially by one who has elected himself First Cause" (Rubenfeld 239). Action Painting represented a "new motive" for painting, one irrelevant to art history. It was composition as a record

of transformation, change: "painting . . . as a means for the artist's recre-
ation of himself and as an evidence to the spectator of the kind of activities involved in this adventure into freedom" (Rosenberg "After Next,
What?" 68). Clem insouciantly dismissed Rosenberg's mythic view of
Jackson, holding firm to the art-historical line:

> Pollock's art turns out at the same time to rely far less on the accidental than
> had been thought. It turns out, in fact, to have an almost completely Cubist
> basis, and to be the fruit of much learning and discipline. . . . It was the first
> look of the new American painting, and only the first look, that led Harold
> Rosenberg to take it for a mystification beyond art on to which he could
> safely graft another mystification. ("How Art Writing" 141)

This makes perfect sense. If Jackson is allowed to be a Brandoesque
cult figure, instead of a *maître*, then Greenberg's whole theory falls apart.
Jackson is *that* dangerous in the implications of his act. (Equally, if White
Shoes was judged as high school sports hero who got a little taste of the
spectacular from the crowd at the game, it would undo the whole system
that needs to see him as a *maître maudit*, as a writer whose "skill does not
include the 'consciousness of mediation'" [78].) So Clem is especially
careful to bring hyper-connoisseurship to Jackson: to turn him into what
Rosenberg called "a fabricated 'master'" ("The Search" 58); to note, for
example, how the drip paintings "create an analogously [i.e. to Cubism]
ambiguous illusion of shallow depth . . . played off, however, against a far
more emphatic surface" ("The Jackson Pollock Market" 132). It's amusing to see whirls and lariats of paint spoken of in such a rarefied dialogue,
like hearing a punk song described as having subtle shadings or something. The mistakes of Rosenberg's first-and-only-first impression are
repeated anew any time someone fails to see Jackson's formalist genius:

> Pollock's "all-over" "drip" paintings seem swiftness and spontaneity incar-
> nate, but their arabescal interlacings strike the uninitiated eye as excluding
> anything that resembles control and order, not to mention skill. . . . His
> strongest "all-over" paintings tend sometimes to be concentric in their pat-
> terning; often the concentricity is that of several interlocking or overlapping
> concentric patterns (as in the marvelous *Cathedral* of 1947). In other cases
> the patterning consists in a rhythm of loopings that may or may not be coun-
> terpointed by a "system" of fainter straight lines. At the same time there is an
> oscillating movement between different planes in shallow depth and the lit-
> eral surface plan—a movement reminiscent of Cézanne and Analytical
> Cubism. ("Jackson Pollock: 'Inspiration'" 246–247)

Yet we can't fail to feel the tension in these lines. When one reads Greenberg on Jackson, his struggle to fit the obviously non-academic swirls into the discourse of museumification, there's always this inescapable question hovering over the critical scene: just why did Greenberg like Jackson's work, since it so obviously owed allegiance to a different, non-formalist agenda?

What Greenberg has always really wanted to talk about, one suspects, is a rapturous pleasure in Jackson's work, unspeakable by a formalist lexicon. This suspicion is confirmed in a 1969 interview. Asked, "What caused you to believe in [Jackson] when others did not?" Greenberg doesn't miss a beat: "His quality. His pictures 'sent' me" ("Interview Conducted by Lily Leino" 310). At its core, his appreciation of Jackson's gesture is a gut thing, transcending a carefully-worked-out aesthetic. Entirely understandable, given the incredibly powerful universe Jackson hoped to capture in his compositional quest. Some people, especially fellow painters, showed how effectively Jackson's meaning could be captured in terms more elemental than critical: Buffie Johnson remembers, "I saw [his paintings] as violent then because I knew the man; now I see them as still marvelous but floating and *him* more of a dreaming poet than I realized" (Potter 100); and Larry Rivers loved the effect the work had on him and his era: "His works . . . [are] like the gorgeous remains of some weird culture. He was a perfect product of that time, exemplified it, and he was full of power and contradictions. He opened up the whole idea of images with generous proportions—before that no one would have them so big" (Potter 278). Greenberg feels that kind of visceral response, obviously, and loves to use the appropriate vocabulary to capture it, speaking of the work's "mazy trickling, dribbling, whipping, blotching, and staining of paint" (247). It must feel excitingly transgressive to use those terms. Suddenly we remember Clem's infatuation with 60s pop, his favorite Peter and Gordon songs, and his serious drug use. His biographer Florence Rubenfeld notes, "In some respects Greenberg was a sensualist tarted out in positivist clothes. He once indicated a preference for Matisse over Picasso by commenting, 'I can taste Matisse's paintings. I never taste Picasso'" (303). But that sensualist impulse is held in check by his quality-centered formalism; telling his readers how the pictures *'sent' him* would be a Happenings discourse. A critic in the non-formalist camp, Thomas Hess, has none of Greenberg's compunctions; he not only admits, in poetic terms, to being sent by a poured painting in 1950, he describes in detail the place he's sent to:

The spectator is pulled into the paroxysm of creation itself, but after this shared act of violence is consummated, the image surprisingly insists on a magnificent serenity—restless, quiet, like the floor of some deep, frozen lake where life is pulsing only in the smallest organisms. (63)

Or take Bill Coles, who is quite clear about what it was that 'sent him' in his student George Humphrey's writing: it was its "incantatory power," not its traditional, formal criteria ("as an arrangement of words, the paper is not completely within the writer's control, may even be read as seriously flawed" [Coles and Vopat 326]), and so his analysis is as poetic as Hess's. Humphrey is an action writer for Coles, and as action composition exists as event or encounter, a lived tension, so Coles knows (as Namuth knew) appreciation of such must return to "the rhetorical scene of the paper" (325). An evocative power suffuses action composition ("of the same metaphysical substance as the artist's existence" [Rosenberg "American Action Painters" 23]), and indeed Coles' criticism evokes the scene of the writing along with the mythology of the writer. His encounter with the act-writing sends him to Hess's deep, silent, still place; a place that looks to Coles like the death of college writing, a rude stop, the end of the track:

We were almost at the end of a freshman writing course, one I was concluding by having students examine various ways of defining a university—almost at the end of a course, and that same spring, 1970, twenty-five miles from Kent State (as the bullet flies), almost at what felt like the end of everything else as well. It's partly a matter of what I remember of the writer of the paper too—what he had come from and through in his work for the course for one thing; the boy himself for another: filament-thin, fierce, graceless, as improbably gladdening as a crocus in the snow. And above all I remember the silence that followed my reading the paper aloud in class, deep enough in that time of that place to still the waters it seemed, to winnow heaven from earth. (325–326).

Humphrey's paper represents what action writing should be, "an extension of the artist's total effort to make over his experience" (Rosenberg "American Action Painters" 48), and so Coles rightly speaks of it in transformative terms: as "creat[ing] possibilities for living" (326), "an enactment of what I have to see the teaching of writing as being about, as having the possibility of involving" (328). The paper becomes, then, wholly *sui generis* yet also a perfect type, and Coles can only speak of it in a new lexicon, a language that constantly undoes itself: the *very complicated*

way he goes about doing what at first he seems to have avoided altogether; a place
that isn't one . . . a no-place . . . between worlds; to lose can be to gain . . . but to
gain is also to have to lose; a new whole unsuccessfully formed (326–327). (Hess
resorts to the same self-canceling prose to speak of Jackson: "Pollock
deliberately pushed violence to the point where it contradicts itself and
includes calm. The painting is made radically stable" [64]). The scene of
the late 60s still haunted Composition in 1985, when Coles wrote his commentary on the Humphrey paper. In this brief text, Coles manages to
write Composition Studies' "American Action Painters," and offers the
new anti-criteria agenda for the action writer: "to put and hold together
not just too much with too little, but all he knows with all he has" (327).

What is missed by Modernist Composition is what Rosenberg refers
to as the "trans-formal" nature of composition ("Action Painting:
Crisis and Distortion" 45). For instance: One of my favorite LP's from
1971 is David Crosby's *If I Could Only Remember My Name*. It's a real
mood-and-memory piece, capturing not only the drug-hazed idealistic
feel of the era, but existing as a sort of quiet, timeless space between
excess and the ethereal (a sort of perpetual 2:30 AM of the mind). The
lyrics might have seemed corny even then: "I wonder who they are, the
men who really run this land. . . . What are their names, and on what
street do they live? I'd like to ride, ride over this afternoon and give
them a piece of my mind, about peace for mankind. Peace is not an
awful lot to ask." But I sort of don't really hear the lyrics as great poetry,
in any tradition. Transformally, it's the sound and the endlessly activat-
able, late-night hush of a scene that signifies. It's the spirit of what the
lyrics say, voiced with the passion of Crosby's quintessentially sixties
voice, and their occasional moments of low-key beauty ("it's hard
enough to gain any traction in the rain"), along with the ringingly idiosyncratic lead guitar of Neil Young interwoven with the psychedelic-
blues filigree of Jerry Garcia's, both played against the insistent bass of
Phil Lesh. Those corny lyrics are exactly what Composition would investigate, doing a dazzlingly authoritative read of the unoriginality of their
theme and imagery and, hence, missing the entire point (anything can
be traced back to anything). The point is the way Crosby transcends
determinism to create an evocative amalgam-text. One that can change
people. Bartholomae tries to resolve the irresolvable, definitively re-fig-
ure the ambiguity. Should we read White Shoes the writer or the person? Is Action Painting the life or the work? It does no good to force

one or the other reading. Rosenberg knew that Action Painting only made sense in this transformal, contradictory context:

> An action that eventuates on a canvas, rather than in the physical world or in society, is inherently ambiguous. . . . It retains its vigor only as long as it continues to sustain its dilemmas: if it slips over into action ("life") there is no painting; if it is satisfied with itself as painting it turns into "apocalyptic wallpaper." ("Action Painting: Crisis and Distortion" 45–46).

So the transformative—the attempt to make a statement, something honest that might make a difference, might change someone or something—becomes crucial evaluative criteria: "the test of any of the new paintings is its seriousness—and the test of its seriousness is the degree to which the act on the canvas is an extension of the artist's total effort to make over his experience" ("American Action Painters" 48). Do we doubt that the writing had a transformative effect on White Shoes? It may have helped solidify his character in sports, may even have influenced other athletes who heard the paper. Are we really saying our course work is more important than that? And though I don't know if he did it each time he sat down to write, when George Humphrey sat down to write his final paper for Bill Coles, he did indeed invent the university. But not as Bartholomae would want it invented, as already-invented (as "part of the general critique of traditional humanism" ["Writing with Teachers" 71]); he invents it instead as previously uninvented, as a new place, a non-place "between worlds, the old ones undead, the new ones not quite born," as a very local critique of traditional academicism, perhaps. (Tellingly, Bartholomae shows himself a compositionist of the institution, not the statement: he wants students to invent the *university*, not *writing*. Jackson could care less about inventing the gallery, he wanted to invent painting; as his friend and fellow-artist Cile Downs recalls, Jackson "hated the whole apparatus—critics, dealers, all those schemes" [Potter 26].)

What's needed is a different grammar and lexicon. Just because we observe a composer (especially, given the contrived tasks writers perform in most research studies, when what we observe is a simulation of composition), how do we know we understand composition? Perhaps we simply lack the discourse to conceptualize the composition fully. Steiner wonders whether one's understanding of Pollock (or any composer) is limited by the discursive frames operative in the observer:

If the problem were the meaning of a painting, an explanation of the painting would enable us to experience it rather than merely see it. Experience is therefore learning a grammar; understanding is making use of one. A grammar, then, is an explanation. To *express* one's understanding requires moreover a different grammar, one that connects an object to an analysis. The difficulty in the case of Pollock may be that explanation and understanding conflate; it may be that we only understand the explanation and can only connect grammars. The sign may only be explained by a sign, so it can never be understood. Is this why, for example, when people view Pollock they see a landscape, a myth, a psychological statement by Jung, or a plate of pasta? They translate the experience of the painting into a language they already know, moving it from one verbal scene to another, or from a visual to a verbal, as though from a museum to a living room. (19)

This concern exists most crucially in our field when those taught are so-called basic writers, composers who don't seem to understand our grammar because they (apparently) can't make use of it, and so are deemed unable to compose. Such was Jackson. His high school stint at Manual Arts in Los Angeles was "an unfolding disaster . . . ill-prepared and unmotivated for academic work . . . socially inept, he was a misfit in a school and a community that prized fitting in above all else" (Naifeh and Smith 122). Even though he was personally supportive of Jackson and his work, Benton not only demeaned his drawing ability, but gave him the lowest marks on ideational skills as well: "He had no verbal facility," Benton claimed. "He had read too little anyhow to be at ease with the subjects discussed" (Naifeh and Smith 238). Benton's (mis)understanding of Jackson was constrained by his own grammar: Benton, the meticulous planner, the artist who re-captured the archly academic Renaissance medium of egg tempra for his murals, a medium notoriously unforgiving and resistant to "thinking on paper" through it; Benton, whose confident, beautifully curving line was in stark contrast to his student Jackson's tortured struggle to master rendering. "Even after two years at the League [studying under Benton], sketching was still not an easy process. Every new piece of paper was another battle with spontaneity, every line laden with risks" (Naifeh and Smith 219). Kozloff's description of Jackson at odds with his compositional surface reads like Shaughnessy as art historian: "It is as if the friction the [paper] itself offered the path of his hand sent him into a rage. The resulting oily turbulences and hectic typographies . . . are of an incomparable strangled brutishness. At every recognition of these failings, Pollock would try to extricate himself by redoubling his furor, which only emphasized them the more" (145). The impression given by his biographers is that Jackson spent the majority of his early years as a painter either sitting in his studio with his head buried in his hands, or angrily yelling, "I'm no damn good!" The image Jimmy Ernst had of him was of "a man looking into the rain, a hard-driving rain" (Potter 71). And Jackson's brother Frank recalls that in the studio the young Jackson shared with his older brother Charles, a much more accomplished, traditional artist, "Jack's work was always turned to the wall" (Potter 42). That correctness of line, how it plagued Jackson, now the Archetypal Basic Writer. To decide to live outside the law of those standards that had been so cruel to him, so unyielding, was very brave; and then, to rise above them, conquering them by avoiding them, living to show there are other ways to produce powerful art.

According to Bois, "it is precisely because Pollock 'did not know how to draw' that he was led to his magisterial invention of the drip, which dealt a radical blow against drawing as it had previously been known" (Review 84). With his formal education under Benton causing a growing sense of betrayal, Jackson had to unlearn what his teacher taught. He had to learn how *not* to render, he had to learn what makes drawing *bad.* Material immersion was his deliverance. One anti-pedagogical strategy he evolved was not to correct errors, but to follow them; he applied neither rules nor models to his mistakes, just materials, working deeper into them rather than through them. As one after another of his official assignments would go bad, he would draw over them. Unable to perfect the undulating line of Benton's hollow-and-bump trademark technique, Jackson would dwell on his crude approximations, doodling unconsciously over them, learning how to veil the representative image he was so inept at rendering. "An outline of a torso would become a skein of swirling lines. . . . Jackson may already have begun to glimpse their significance" (Naifeh and Smith 220). And there was also the extracurricular lessons he was learning through his association with the Mexican muralist Siqueiros, who taught an appreciation of technology and material that was at odds with Benton's traditional academicism. Not just through his advocacy of industrial tools and techniques did he influence Jackson, but in the way he never worked from sketches, "preferring to work directly—in 'partnership' with his materials. He studied the dynamics of paint—its density, its viscosity, its flow rate—in an effort to incorporate those dynamics into the image, letting the paint itself help create the painting" (Naifeh and Smith 287). Jackson was fascinated by

Siqueiros's paint-pouring experimentation, and one night, in 1936, he put a canvas on the floor and tried to replicate the dripped technique of the muralist. What Jackson learned in such personal study was the cynical truth of traditional composition, that it's all about teaching the correct line at the expense of the right line. Jackson became a real compositionist only when he began to follow his heart: discovering he had a vision and voice worth sharing, then realizing he had to abandon his struggle for the correct line and embark on the search for a personally useful and perfectible line to express that inner vision. Traditional composition is oblivious to the value of the right line, it wouldn't even know how to teach it, since it's incommensurate with the standards in place. Traditional composition doesn't consider the text as situationist space for Action Students, a canvas on which they can/must live. With the standards of evaluative criteria firmly in place for most formalist compositionists (who speak *a language they already know*), incorrect writing like Jackson's that seems so obviously to miss the mark seems an easy call. A tangle of dribbles and drools that needs untangling. What Composition would call the Basic Writer's surface became the look that best expressed his statement; as Friedman notes, by 1947, "Pollock had recognized that accidents (spillings, splatterings, puddlings, drippings) incorporated in his work came closest to the look and feel he wanted" (*Energy* 96). A discussion of Jackson and process, then, must spend some time looking at how Composition considers those dribblers and droolers, the ones who "don't know how to write," those for whom instruction seems most adamantly a matter of learning the correct line, the Basic Writer. An obvious text for analysis in this regard becomes Sondra Perl's landmark study of the processes of basic writers, the first to treat such composers, and a study, published in December of 1979, that helps mark the transition from the 'action' spirit of Happenings Composition to the simulationist pedagogy of the post-Happenings. Indeed, Sondra Perl's program for teaching writing amounted to a way to de-Pollock a Pollock: what was needed, she felt, was for a teacher to see "meaning beneath the tangles in [a student's] prose . . . interven[ing] in such a way that untangling his composing process leads him to create better prose" (328).

In explaining her rationale for being the first to undertake a process study of basic writers ("As long as 'average' or skilled writers are the focus, it remains unclear as to how process research will provide teachers with a firmer understanding of the needs of students with serious writing problems" [318]), Perl reveals how the academy portrays the basic compositionist: as in need, deficient, problematical. They are the ones who can't draw. We see this as well in her study's reliance on miscue analysis ("the observer analyzes the mismatch that occurs when readers make responses during oral reading that differ from the text" [323]) as a way of capturing an understanding of the basic writer's process. They are *translated*, then, as mistake-makers, their process existing in some interstitial space of slippage; the locus is *discrepancy*. Basic writers are *les bassesses de* composition. They don't imply contagion, as Rose thought, but rather a denial of the very possibility of healthy communion. The clumsy strangeness of their work when compared to what it should resemble: it's as if done according to the measures Marcel invented, the standard stoppages. Duchamp dropped string onto a table three times and traced the shapes, using them to form his new measures, his new criteria. Basic writers' prose resembles them, in the entropic, degenerative pull of their compositions: the huge, almost magnetically negative heart at the center of their work—it threatens to pull all other writing into it. BW prose is a standard-stoppage in terms of its status as the end of measurable composition. For Bois, any picture, post-Picasso, becomes "a system structured by arbitrary signs" ("Use Value" 28). It was Duchamp who exposed this "semiological repression": "His *Three Standard Stoppages* knocks one of the most arbitrary systems of the sign there is (the metric system) off its pedestal to show that once submitted to gravity, once lowered into the contingent world of things and bodies, the sign does not hold water: it dissolves as an (iterable) sign and regresses toward singularity" (28). Basic writers show not only the flimsiness of our arbitrary systems and signs for writing (which by all means should flow regressively, de-deterministically, into the idea of writing as basic line), but maybe the flimsiness of representation in general, how what is most worth representing (the sublime) can't be represented. A Basic Writer's best come-back line to Traditional Composition now becomes Jackson's line, "I choose to veil the imagery" (Naifeh and Smith 537). Perl's urgency is Modernism's crisis of representation, getting these students able to draw correctly, effecting the proper (arbitrary) resemblance. The "major question" of her study of basic writers is, "What does an increased understanding of their processes suggest about the nature of composing in general and the manner in which writing is taught in the schools?" (317) The key is understanding the process of writing, demystifying it, in order to allow easy replication by even the most unskilled. Perl academicizes the rhetorical scene, then, attempting to restore the fiction of order to the now-ruptured symbolic. Observing a process for her is untroubled, and it leads to direct *increased understanding*, especially given the code she has invented, her representational grammar: "a meaningful and replicable method for rendering the composing process as a sequence of observable and scorable behaviors" (318). That's absurd, of course; or it's true only for very trivial processes. Observing Jackson's process was by no means untroubled. Did he start with the figure, and then use his webs of paint to veil it? Did he really abandon a sense of composition as a process in stages? Was it truly a one-shot deal for him? When and why did he "lose contact" with a work and abandon it? How does he determine its doneness? (He was supposedly "finished" with *One: Number 31, 1950* when Namuth showed up to photograph him painting it. Namuth begged to at least photograph the studio; as Jackson showed him around, he couldn't help returning to the work, dancing and whipping paint around for another half-hour.) Scholars have gone so far as using Namuth's process-research to form computerized composite photographs which might answer some of those questions, but in any event the data didn't really let us figure out composing for Jackson, in terms of understanding it enough to replicate it. What it offered was a vocabulary for talking about the art, insights into the compositionist, and a new, mythic, action-grammar. But Composition has desired of its research, not seeds for myth, but the truth of resemblance (what Werner Herzog, in complaining how "so-called Cinema Verité is devoid of verité," calls "a merely superficial truth, the truth of accountants"). So maybe Namuth wouldn't have been at all the kind of process-researcher Braddock, Lloyd-Jones and Schoer would have loved. But what he lacked in accountancy-truth, he made up for in transformal richness.

> Shooting with available light, Namuth was forced to use long exposures, and the swiftness of Pollock's movements meant that his image was frequently blurred. Some of the photographs from the first session were also blurred by a defect in one of Namuth's cameras. He was initially troubled by these imperfections, but ultimately came to feel that they enhanced the pictures' visual excitement. (Karmel 90)

For Composition, after a veridical composing process is faithfully captured, it's only a matter of how correct imitation can be taught, how the academic can maintain its semblance of order. (Compare this, say, with the sociolinguistic project, which desires only to show how language is used, to capture the shimmering surface's truth of situation.)

Composition's need for a new grammar, a new way of translating the experience, is readily apparent in Perl. Rather than focusing on the idea, the metaphysical statement-value in the writing, she focuses on the text as conventionally articulated, formal structure. Jackson's concern was the inner reality, not the outer form. According to Jackson's friend Reuben Kadish, "Jack didn't go looking for sophistication; he looked for the statement. And he would go for the primitive before the sophisticated" (Potter 106). The focus was on an inner truth that outward material effects couldn't influence; we remember the permission he gave people to walk across his canvases. And Marcel:

> When he learned that the [*Large Glass*] had been shattered, while being transported from a show at the Brooklyn Museum to the Connecticut home of Katherine Dreier, its owner, Duchamp did not appear particularly upset. (Tomkins 129)

If the work exists as statement, idea, its form is ultimately not precious in itself. It doesn't need a perfect surface. Rather than a focus on the inner, lived life, the sense of a text as *dwellable*, Perl focuses on the formal structure, as a particularly defined, reproducible type, with no discussion of that form's potentially enchanting program. The idea of replicating a Pollock occurred often as his fame grew; in fact, fake Pollocks turned up regularly after his death. The British printmaker, Stanley Hayter, lived in the United States during the 1940s, running his famous Atelier 17, where Jackson was a frequent visitor. Hayter realized the folly of trying to replicate a Pollock:

> A lot of our people said [the drip technique] was nonsense, that anybody could do it. That enraged me and I said, "Go to it, and I'll bet you that not one of you can make one square inch of anything that could be mistaken for what Pollock's done . . . " And they couldn't because it's absolutely distinctive, more than handwriting. It's like attempts at faking Pollock: You can't be fooled. (Potter 98)

Dripping seemed somehow not art; any child could do it. It was, unsurprisingly, even equated with the worthlessness of the body, as a common body-process (urination); 'Jack the Dripper' was the pejorative nickname some clever wag of a reviewer gave him. The poetry is missed by an exaggerated formalism made equivalent to replication. Jackson's way of reading was to dwell in the supra-formalist process and content of the work. According to Nick Carone, Jackson

> had a very intimate way of looking at work. . . . He would read things in it, you know, looking as though he's talking to something there, like *he* was painting that picture and on a kind of psychedelic trip of the visual experience. He judged by the unconscious imagery, not by three-dimensional form, reading the pictures in the Jungian sense.
>
> It wasn't verbal so much as an intense communion of the moment, and empathy. (Potter 160–161)

As Goodnough wrote, in his own process-research on Jackson: "He feels that his methods may be automatic at the start, but that they quickly step beyond that, becoming concerned with deeper and more involved emotions which carry the painting on to completion according to their degree of strength and purity" (60). Perl's claims about her coding tool ring false when read against Jackson's process. In hyping her method, she claims "it labels specific, observable behaviors so that types of composing movements are revealed" (320). To define a technology of composition by a 16-item list, made up of 11 basic activity-terms (planning, commenting, interpreting, assessing, questioning, talking, repeating, reading, writing, editing, silence) provides a poor translation scale for process, reducing the context around the production-event to "types" that are vague at best. This counters the more persuasive logic of a site-specific lexicon; with Jackson, for example, there are all those luscious, poetic gerunds like flooding, dripping, dumping.

Indeed, what sort of composing process is it about which a coding instrument can be claimed to depict "the entire sequence of composing movements on one or two pages" (320)? Namuth's coding tool—photographs of the artist in process, along with heartfelt, self-descriptions of the work—was more expansive. Since the process-scene was opened up rather than reduced by his method, it even led Namuth to the use of another instrument—the film camera—to capture that expansiveness. Filming, he said, was "the next logical step. Pollock's method of painting suggested a moving picture—the dance around the canvas, the continuous movement, the drama" ("Photographing Pollock"). The process Namuth was capturing was lived, situationist theatre in a comfortable space Jackson had spent his life searching for; Perl's students, on the other hand, were performing unfamiliar rituals ("composing aloud, to

externalize their thinking processes as much as possible" [318]) in artificial circumstances ("the sessions took place in a soundproof room in
the college library" [318]). When Perl claims her method makes it "possible to determine when students were talking, when they were writing,
when both occurred simultaneously, and when neither occurred"
(320)—and, when we remember traces of Jackson's process that could
never be so easily articulated (Barnett Newman said of Jackson's
process, "Forget hand. It's the mind—not brain, but *mind*—soul, concentration, gut" [Naifeh and Smith 5]; I mean, how do you delineate
that?)—we have to wonder just what sort of measuring tool can do what
she claims; or rather, what sort of writing is so easily observable. Perl, of
course, is not capturing composition; she's generating a simulationist
model, one with an easy unity ("it provides a way of determining how
parts of the process relate to the whole" [320]) that has nothing to do
with the messy, idiosyncratic, existential business of a human engaged in
significant symbolic creation. No doubt, the tool she designed might
have been perfect to capture the trivial, pseudo-academic tasks her students were engaged in: intro social science tasks, for which the student
"reads the directions and the question twice and then begins to plan
exactly what she is going to say, all within the first minute" (321). And
indeed, her subject Tony's process is perfect for the kind of limited genres he's asked to compose. Rather than showing a Pollockian expansiveness, Tony's process is reductive to the point of implosion: as Perl puts
it, "densely packed, tight . . . so full that there was little room left for
invention or change" (324).

The students Perl studies are only too aware that writing has been
defined now as dutiful replication of some existing type. She notes they
all edited far more for form than content. She fails to acknowledge that
her findings in this regard—"most of [Tony's] time was spent proofread-
ing rather than changing, rephrasing, adding, or evaluating the substantive parts of the discourse" (326)—might very well be a logical result of
the academic-formalist curriculum the students have experienced. A
debilitating representational template was obviously strongly instanti-
ated in Tony, as Perl herself discovers: "From the moment Tony began
writing, he indicated a concern for correct form that actually inhibited
the development of ideas" (324). But Perl is blind to her own insight:
she never advocates changing that reality, just assisting basic writers,
with their tangled, miscued processes, to do it better. She plays
Greenberg to Tony's Jackson: seeing only her own formal reality, her

attitude is as patronizing as Clem's upon first looking on Jackson's work: "Being young and full of energy, he takes orders he can't fill" (Greenberg "Marc Chagall" 621). It's up to her to help Tony fill those orders (which are really the academy's). She doesn't seem bothered by the curriculum which produces a Tony, for whom writing is simply re-representing, rather than discovering or being ("there is no point in an act if you already know what it contains" [Rosenberg "American Action Painters" 22]). Steinberg abandoned formalism, after Johns's banal (but thoroughly enchanting) new work forced him to learn other criteria, because he saw greater value in the poetic content of a work—that *statement*, which couldn't be coded by formalist schemes:

> I find myself constantly in opposition to what is called formalism; not because I doubt the necessity of formal analysis, or the positive value of work done by serious formalist critics. But because I mistrust their certainties, their apparatus of quantification, their self-righteous indifference to that part of artistic utterance which their tools do not measure. (64)

This is the part of the work that Perl never mentions, the enchanted part of the work. There's never a question of Tony's writing *sending* Perl. A formalist schema, Steinberg felt, will keep "breaking down because it insists on defining modern art without acknowledgement of its content" (71). Except to note the way her writers quickly took complex topics and turned them into simplistic dichotomies ("classifications . . . made on the basis of economic, racial, and political differences" [325]), Perl finesses away serious attention to the ideational content of her students' work: "No formal principles were used to organize the narratives nor were the implications of ideas present in the essay developed" (325). Had she done so, she might have expressed disappointment that the writing Tony did in no way stretched him spiritually or intellectually. Barnett Newman felt Jackson led "the fight against . . . empty forms instead of real emotions," and implied that good grammar and syntax had little to do with great composition: "Anyone can construct a good-English-sentence kind of picture," he noted; what Jackson engaged in was "painting with a capital P" (Naifeh and Smith 690). Tony's process was hermetic, his standard ploy was "rephrasing the topic until either a word or an idea in the topic linked up with something in his own experience (an attitude, an opinion, an event)" (325), which allowed him simply to re-circulate cynical truisms ("their are men born in rich families that will never have to worry about any financial difficulties . . . " [336]). It reminds one of

Jackson's early, Benton-derived regionalist canvases—conventional images of wagons heading west or landscapes with livestock (Ratcliff calls such work "a slack variant" on Benton's style ["Jackson Pollock's" 105]). Perl finds the "most salient feature of Tony's composing process" not the hermetic canniness of his content but rather its formal "recursiveness" (324). The locus of her commentary on the work is not spirit- or statement-centered, but *techné*-centered. Tony is simply, formally, a builder—whether it's bombs or widgets or exotic pleasure-palaces is immaterial. The builder's routinized, technical actions are what circumscribe his process, the charm or poetry or emotional content is immaterial. (A situationist architect complained, in 1948, one of Jackson's most prolific years: "We have been given the machine for living in, where very often nothing is sacrificed to the only truly human parts of life, to poetry and to dream" [Sadler 7]). Such a definition of process, as formalist replication, limits generic conceptualization. Indeed, Tony's repertoire for editing—non-substantive, formal—ensures he will never reach that moment of textual anagnorisis, that radical re-evaluation of the very work, that Jackson did: Lee recalls, "A little later, in front of a very good painting . . . he asked me, 'Is this a painting?' Not is this a good painting, or a bad one, but *a painting*! The degree of doubt was unbelievable at times" (Friedman "An Interview").

A formalist definition of composition misses the opportunity for the mythic terminology of Jackson's process. There is no real "getting acquainted" period, say, in Tony's process for a given work; each simulationist assignment occasions the same quick routine ("remarkably consistent in all his composing operations" [324]). 'Getting acquainted' would imply coming to know a particular work—an ever-new, site-specific discursivity or productivity—but Tony's process, in the way it simply re-activates the same code or model, is all one long forgetting of the actual text in which he's engaged: "when Tony completed the writing process, he refrained from commenting on or contemplating his total written product. . . . It was as if the semantic model in his head predominated" (327, 328). Writing seems very much a genetic code for Perl; she feels her coding scheme "lends itself to the longitudinal study of the writing process and may help to elucidate what it is that changes in the process as writers become more skilled" (334)—as if the process unfolds (when it doesn't get snarled) according to some inner logic. Perl wants Tony to connect back with the stuff of his writing: not re-work it, enchant it, but rather perfect it, restore it, resolve the "unresolved stylistic and syntactic problems" (328). She wants a basic writing teacher to remove any Pollockian traces from students' prose, straighten out any non-representational dribbles or drools:

> What [Tony] needs are teachers who can interpret that process for him, who can see through the tangles in the process, just as he sees meaning beneath the tangles in his prose, and who can intervene in such a way that untangling his composing process leads him to create better prose. (328)

It is Composition's failure that that canned nothing of a paper Tony wrote, a re-cycling of spiritually empty clichés, wholly devoid of any truly expressive inner reality, can be said to be in any way "meaning"-ful. And that removing the surface errors from it would be in some significant sense "better"-ing it. What rules is not an expressionism, however abstract, but representationalism—the recognizable, the conventional model: for Perl, "consistent composing processes" implies that "the behavioral sequences prewriting, writing, and editing appeared in sequential patterns that were recognizable across writing sessions and across students" (328). No sense of being in a painting, of taking the canvas off the easel to re-configure it as an arena for existential action. That would not be the predictable, measurable, trivial thing, which is what counts now (and needs to be perfected) as process. It is no wonder her five students' processes are so remarkably similar; they have internalized this limited notion of composition as ritual: students get a question, read it over until they figure out a way to connect it to something conventional—usually in the simplistic, dichotomized terms of a sports drama: "Turning the large conceptual issue in the topic (e.g., equality) into two manageable pieces for writing (e.g., rich vs. poor; black vs. white)" (328)—come up with a topic sentence that rephrases the question into a statement, and churn out a few supporting generalizations (activating cultural scripts or phrases). The main concern is getting the representational (not thematic) form right: All of the students observed asked themselves, not 'Is this a painting?', but "Is this sentence [or feature] correct?" (332). To invent and perfect a new process, to discover new materials, to desire a radically new product . . . those were the only things replicable in Jackson's process, and the only things that make composition worth teaching, perhaps.

The waning of process was inevitable, perhaps—even without its trivial reification by process-theorists. Process was seen as inimical to the Modernist program that post-Happenings Composition defined as writing; so Bartholomae complains how

> as a result of the "writing process movement," criticism was removed from the writing course, where it was seen as counter-productive (a "barrier" to writing) and characterized in the figure of the maniacal English teacher with the red pencil. ("What is Composition" 27)

For a theorist like Bartholomae, putting a phrase in quotation marks is the equivalent of consigning it to the psych ward. And, in effect, that was the process movement's fate, its teachers seen as deluded paranoiacs, dangerous enablers, or hopeless dreamers (Rosenberg was right about the inherent ambiguity in the process-encoded product of action-composition). Salon academics triumphed and process was relegated to the pastoral phase of the field's golden years . . . retro, *outré* . . . thankfully matured now into the serious business of historicity, ideology, identity, and discursivity. So, at the 1998 CCCC, for example, there were two sessions that advertised a concern with the composing process. And, really, how would we even teach it? How does one *learn* the avant-garde? Not through traditional schooling, certainly. Jackson was bounced out of every school he attended. But he studied intently what he knew could help him: besides the technologies and materials that interested him, there were things like those copies of *Dial* magazine his older brother Charles sent back home to Jackson and Sande in the early 1920s, both of them pouring over the reproductions of contemporary European painters. On his deathbed forty years later, Sande will reminisce to an amazed Charles about "the spell the Dial articles had cast" over Jackson and him (Naifeh and Smith 99). Jackson's story, then shows the importance of non-mainstream schooling as pre-requisite to learning the avant-garde because, let's face it, Official Composition is a bore. Lee relates how the gallery-mandated practice of the discipline disinterested Jackson, outside of a few contemporaries. ("'I don't believe in art,' said Duchamp. 'I believe in artists'" [Tomkins 129].) What Jackson cared about were local practices, knowing that some nobody was engaged in the act, working out a compositional gospel: according to Tony Smith, "He seldom talked about art, but when he did it was often in relation to his own community—as if it were a form of therapy, or religion. He'd mention some old lady, or a retired broker, who had taken up painting. He would say it in a quiet, solemn way—they had had the call. He cared that they were painting" (du Plessix and Gray 54). Think of the young

Jackson and his friend, Reuben Kadish, re-figuring the LA County Museum in terms of what counts as powerful art,

> searching out works of art that captured the directness, the immediacy, the emotional energy. . . . At the Los Angeles County Museum . . . they bypassed paintings by the old masters and exhibitions of local art and headed for the deserted cellar to wander the "ethnographic" exhibits of South Pacific cultures—glass cases filled with boldly sculptural ceramic bowls . . . carved knife hilts and sword handles . . . tapa clothes in vivid geometric designs. "We had to lie down on our bellies sometimes to see what was in the bottom of the cases," Kadish remembers. "Marvelous things were just stuck back in there. At the time, those things were thought of as mere ethnological data, but we didn't care. We would eyeball them for hours rather than waste our time with the show that the Los Angeles County Art Association was putting on upstairs. We knew where the vigor was, where the real energy was." (Naifeh and Smith 203–204)

Many critics have speculated on how Jackson learned his famous dripped line. Naifeh and Smith trace it to Labor Day, 1924: Jackson's father Roy invites Sande and him for a hike to the Indian ruins in Cherry Creek Canyon. The weather is blistering hot, so they take a brief rest near the creek. Jackson watched "as his father climbed a nearby boulder and urinated onto a flat rock below, creating a distinctive pattern on the sun-baked surface" (101). Greenberg called this explanation "nonsense," but who knows?   The point is such learning is mysterious, unspeakable. Jackson felt art couldn't be taught, only phonies tried. So, there's Jack the Dripper, urinating on a canvas, the Basic Compositionist dribbling out a tangle-trace of prose, incapable of drafting logical sequences. Sometimes, though, the drip-canvas looks more like trails of clotted blood. In 1952, as he danced around the canvas which would become "Blue Poles," late one night, after calling Tony Smith over to talk him out of suicide, Jackson kept throwing the glass basting syringes he used to apply paint against the canvas as they became clogged. They'd shatter on the cotton duck on the floor. In bare feet, both artists worked on, even as the glass shards cut into their skin. Or better still, Jackson at a table in the Cedar Bar, in depressed, drunken solitude, breaking plates and glasses, then playing with the shards, "casually making designs as his fingers dripped blood onto the table-top" (Naifeh and Smith 749), traces of his own literal passage. Kaprow called Jackson's paintings "a kind of diaristic gesture" ("Legacy"

26), capturing the way the work was a record of the life's passage. "Decorate[d] with his own daily annihilation" (49) was how Rosenberg described the action painter's work. Urine, blood, some have even said semen; in Max Kozloff's metaphor, for instance, the drips come from "that aerial sphincter of his consciousness" (146), and Ratcliff agrees: "intimations of all the body's processes appear in Pollock's stained, smeared, encrusted canvases" (64).

Death, blood, despair—that's what's missing from our idea of composition. "Begin with death," says the Dalai Lama, "start from there, and you won't go far wrong" (Heath 41). For the epigram to one of his essay collections, Rosenberg cites Picasso's insight into Cézanne: "What forces our interest is Cézanne's anxiety—that's Cézanne's lesson" (*Anxious Object*). There was anxiety in the White Shoes paper, that refusal "to wear the same type of cleats and the same type of socks" ("Inventing" 150), neglected by the steamrolling power of Bartholomae's critical engine. And Jackson's process was subsumed in anxiety, that endless commitment to new technologies and materials, that breakthrough gospel he left us, which probably helped kill him . . . imagine, for example, being sealed up in that small studio, made as air-tight as possible against a Long Island winter, breathing in the noxious fumes of the Devolac that he used for the black paintings. But even if we discount the materials, it's process itself, with its cumulative force of daily annihilations, that did Jackson in. The incessant need to capture process, the cultification underlying the discourse of action painting, certainly it helped drive him to the breaking point. Namuth's short film took a seemingly endless time to make, outside, in the growing cold of a Springs autumn. On the last day, after shooting for hours, Jackson's hands were freezing; he had grown bitter and surly with this particular tracing of a passage. At 4:30 PM, when they finally wrapped, he tore into the house, poured two tumblers of bourbon, and knocked them back one after another, taking his first drink in two years, and starting the reckless slide leading to his fatal crash. Of course process will wane. How can it do otherwise? By its very nature, it's a sign of the passage of something fleeting. Tension, agony, loss . . . these were always at the heart of Jackson's art. The horrific violence that is birth, the family dinner table he painted over and over that seems like a convocation of cannibals, the naked man with knife suspended, the eyes in the heat, the self-portrait that captured Jackson's on-going anxiety, like Cézanne's, like any Happenings compositionist. All his works are anxious objects, confronting the terror on the other side of the kitchen door, that world that can turn hostile at any moment. And so he responded in kind, with a counter-composition. Lee brings Hans Hofmann, her *maître*, to visit Jackson's studio, which is a chaotic mess. Hofmann uneasily picks up a paint-caked brush, evidence of the state of disgust this room is in, and the coffee can it has dried in comes up with it. Hofmann holds it out to show Jackson, stammering, "With this you could kill a man." "That's the idea," Jackson replies (Naifeh and Smith 398).

To be avant-garde, then, is to be concerned with waste, refuse, impermanence; to see its value, to move through it, to know it is all you can inhabit. To make it your art. The easily accessible, the all-too-available, the unspeakable. Showering down like Roy Pollock's pee, like the enamel housepaint Jackson started using because it was far cheaper than oil paint at Dan Miller's store in Springs (leaving him more money for beer). And earlier, when he used oils, he turned them into Duchamp readymades, squeezing them on directly from the tube. For his canvas, he used unprimed cotton duck, bought in remnant bolts, the kind used for ships and upholstery (he'd treat it before or after with an industrial glue called 'Rivit' to give the canvas a harder surface). None of his materials were bought from an art supplier. When asked "What is Composition?" the voice of CCCC answers with the words of the salon: *a professional commitment to do a certain kind of work with a certain set of materials*; this work must play itself out in *the space on the page, there and not somewhere else.* The space on the page? That's not where Jackson was at; he knew he could gain immeasurable force by connecting more with situational space than compositional surface:

> To eliminate all friction of brush on canvas, Pollock taught himself to pour his colors through the air. . . . To intensify his contact with the painting—the image—Pollock had to break contact with the canvas. Giving up the usual control of his medium, he gained control of a new kind. (Ratcliff *Fate* 59)

Defining composition exclusively, around the parameters of page or canvas, results in that conventional, academic surface. Jackson shows another way to think of the composition—as a record of tracings, of gestures, a result of a body moving through life. This means the abandonment of the salon style, where students learn the established technique and how to work with difficult materials to reproduce rarified genres. It's no wonder Jackson's process was taken by Kaprow and others as a jump-start for the Happenings: they found in Pollock the origin of a different art, one that left the surface entirely, exscribing itself into larger physical space. Jackson and Lee, in a *New Yorker* column from that powerful summer of '50, spoke of how certain critics couldn't understand his gesture, the process-product. Jackson recollected:

> "There was a reviewer a while back who wrote that my pictures didn't have any beginning or any end. He didn't mean it as a compliment, but it was. It was a fine compliment. Only he didn't know it." "That's exactly what Jackson's work is," Mrs. Pollock said. "Sort of unframed space." (Roueché 16)

Such a gesture naturally leads to seeing composition as theatre-notes for the exploding plastic inevitable of our lives. A few years after Pollock's death, Rauschenberg and Johns will come along, the new avant-garde. They'll pick up an idea adapted from Duchamp and Pollock, the idea of the readymade, making art from the easily available, the all-too-quickly-discarded stage properties of our on-going performance piece. And then dumping them into one's compositional surface. I see a urinal, that's art. I see a comb, that's art. I see some Ballantine's Ale cans, from another night of restless drinking, that's art. I see this old quilt, the one on the bed where Jasper and I sleep, that's art. All of these things, so crucial to recording, not recoding, our own passing. "Memories arrested in space" was Jackson's term for his work (Naifeh and Smith 540). "A painting that is an act is inseparable from the biography of the artist" (23). And, where are the intimations of the body's process on CCCC's canvas, the blood on Composition's tracks? Why, covered up with our own wildest fantasies, which aren't really all that wild; to mend the rupture process theory tore in the symbolic order, Rodrigues, for example, desired a re-affirmation of salon-values: "structure . . . models . . . mechanical skills . . . think through ideas . . . revise them . . . write for real audiences and real purposes" (27). But I love it when I get those dashed-off but deeply affecting whirls of rhapsodic prose from students. And it often happens when students get a chance—usually in informal settings like emails or in-class writes, using their own familiar materials—to make a *statement*.

So many avant-garde practices had at their center the use of accessible materials and the rejection of salon techniques, realizing, as Jackson had, that technique was "just a means of arriving at a statement" (Wright). The avant-garde placed a premium on expression, on affording expression to a wider audience than just the select initiates of the academy. Changing the locus of our criticism from the easel to the floor, from the canvas as a space on which to reproduce an object to an arena in which to act, means returning to the idea of a central *revelation* in a work, the *tension*, rather than the formal, aesthetic trappings, the expected pleasures. The surprises of biography, rather than the rituals of mimicry. The statement, rather than the technique. How touching that some young athlete somewhere decides on a new way to wear his uniform, convinces a few other team members how cool it looks, and thereby energizes the team and its fans. Of course that's worth expressing. It changed them. Are our students searching for a way to make the world see the world their way, or, rather, do we insist they be made to show the world the way we think it's supposed to be seen?

Imagine, then, Jackson as a subject for process-research: not like the traditional process-subjects, re-tracing stock academic genres, but one engaged in continual experiment with form and material, trying to realize an inner vision. For that is Jackson's greatest lesson, according to his friend and biographer B. H. Friedman, that one's content, one's statement, "could not be learned or borrowed from outside examples but would have to be found within" (*Energy* 30). "But what are you really *involved with?*" was the question Jackson asked over and over to his friends (Friedman *Energy* xvi), not just 'what are you *working on*,' but 'what are you *involved with*.' If we wanted to learn from Jackson, then, take him as our anti-*maître* (*maître* and *anti-maître*), what would be the verbal rhyme to Jackson's painterly process? What would be a technology of composition that might result in a *prose web* to match Jackson's painted one? To start, we might try to develop in writers an interest in *choosing*, in a context or ethic of *alert waiting* (Rosenberg "American Action Painters" 23). (So many of my students in my writing-about-rap-music class tell me later, "I never actually listened to the words of these songs!"; it's not that they're uninformed, it's just that they need practice in attentiveness, so they can refine their choosing.) And we might keep in mind what other compositionists, also on the bridge to experimentation, learned from Jackson. Look at the influence of MOMA's 1967 Pollock retrospective:

> Minimalist sculptors who had hitherto embraced strict geometric forms soon began creating three-dimensional equivalents to Pollock's painterly chaos. . . . Now sculptors like Robert Morris, Eva Hesse, Barry La Va, Bruce Nauman, and Richard Serra began "doing things" to a range of non-art materials like felt, glass, rubber, and lead. (Karmel 98)

A prose web, then, is writing as *doing things* to a range of materials. Composition as material gesture. It means changing the axis of the image, supplying the (missing, now active) horizontal vector to disable the predictability of composition's strict verticality. But in terms of form, what would it be? Naifeh and Smith remark on the small calligraphic works on Masonite from 1949, in which Jackson has "stripped the web to its fundamental forms—loops, puddles, and spatters—and isolated them like tiny unicelluar organisms fixed on microscope slides" (589). What, then, might be the fundamental forms of action writing? Kozloff provides a way to think further about the prose web, when he taxono-mizes the four areas of accomplishment in Jackson's art. Kozloff makes the point, as so many do, that Jackson embodied the zeitgeist of postwar America, or more exactly, "the time became aware of a vital part of itself through him" (142). Since "there was nothing in the tradition of American art that prepared for any such event" (143) as what Jackson's art accomplished, Kozloff tries to tease out the major components of his innovation. His four areas of emphasis read like the elements of action style: *space* ("limitless . . . planeless . . . a labyrinthine web or screen con-stantly perforated by the eye" [143]); *order* ("the adjectives that describe the relationships of forms in practically all of Western [writing]—con-tained and computed, graded and regulated—do not apply . . . a diffu-sion of attention is equally charged . . . individual or local anarchies are subsumed by a conception of overarching rhythm" [143]); *chance* ("throws into question the very nature of the association of the [writer] and his work . . . what is loosened from conscious manipulation is caught again in a mental network in which every 'accident' is accommo-dated and dovetailed with its mate" [143]); *expressiveness* (the composi-tion's surface "a palimpsest tissue of enormously varied tactile events . . . a graph of [the writer's] movement and his passion" [144]). Trying to capture the all-over quality of Jackson's compositional web, Greenberg characterized the dripped canvases as "filled from edge to edge with evenly spaced motifs that repeated themselves uniformly like the ele-ments in a wallpaper pattern, and therefore seemed capable of repeat-ing the picture beyond its frame into infinity" ("American-Type Painting" 217). And Judd comments on how Jackson's work had "the large scale wholeness and simplicity that have become common to almost all good work" (195). After Jackson, then, we can generally sketch a definition of the prose web: a stretch of textual material designed for intensity; a simple, basic whole, able to capture the author's statement; no dominant/subordinate, hierarchical ordering of the composition's elements; not a clean surface, but one "dumped" with life-residue; expressive, with 'right' lines rather than correct ones; where accident in the service of interest replaces intention; whose overall effect is more *ex*scription into the spacious world than *in*scription on tradition-circumscribed paper, writing now a surface where a contingent order is produced by the dialogue between chance events and ordinary materials, an intense communion of the moment. "It doesn't make much difference how the paint is put on as long as something has been said," Jackson claimed (Wright).

And materially, of course. Our composition must change materially. Jackson's use of new materials, like aluminum fence paint, ensured that the work would represent a profoundly different reality, heretofore unseen: "Pollock uses metallic paint . . . to add a feeling of mystery and adornment to the work and to keep it from being thought of as occupying the accepted world of things" (Goodnough 41). (Clem of course hated the aluminum paint, felt it gave "an oily over-ripeness" to the work [Naifeh and Smith 555].) Lee recalled to B. H. Friedman how one morning on Long Island, before he entered his studio, Jackson told her, "I saw a landscape the likes of which no human being could have seen." Was he talking about a "visionary landscape," Friedman wondered? Lee agreed, adding, "in Jackson's case I feel what the world calls 'visionary' and 'real' were not as separated as they are for most people." If we want students to turn in writing that looks like Roland Barthes' or Richard Rodrigues's or Mary Louise Pratt's, why not just let them use a Xerox machine? Jackson understood this: asked why he turned away from representation, he explained, "the modern artist is living in a mechanical age and we have a mechanical means of representing" (Wright). That necessitated, in Jackson's mind, a different sort of coding for the modern compositionist's program, an abstract expression: "The modern artist, it seems to me, is working and expressing an inner world—in other words—expressing the energy, the motion, the other inner forces" (Wright). The key locus of critique for every composition now is Duchamp's—just the same, does it move? What's dying, what's ruptured a huge hole in the symbolic order, is people's ability to express themselves in artful, intense ways. That we're writing teachers, and we insist on a rarified technique for reproducing stock academic studies, when life is beautiful, the trees are beautiful, the sky is beautiful . . . it kills me.

You know what our problem is? It's a failure of nerve in our myth-making; revealing that about the field might be Jackson's most useful function for CCCC. According to Thomas Hess, "The Jackson Pollock myth is a piece of his art; it reflects an aspect of the content of his paint-ing" (39). Jackson's audacity was bracing; it coalesced the entire culture: as Greenberg notes, "even before [his death] his name had begun to be a byword, soon known to Jack Paar as well as Alfred Barr, for what is most far-fetched in contemporary art" ("Jackson Pollock Market Soars" 42). Greenberg cites British art historian Sir Herbert Read to show the catalyzing power of myth for composition. Read's earlier characteriza-tion of Jackson's work depicted it as the product of a "vacuous nihilism that . . . scribbles a graph of its uncertainty on the surface of a blank consciousness" ("Jackson Pollock Market Soars" 42). But, according to Greenberg, European critics fell prey to the force of Jackson's Brandoesque figure, his "art of raw sensation . . . untutored, barbaric force" (42). And so we have Sir Herbert, in one of his later surveys, treating Jackson, in Greenberg's words, "as he would a consecrated mas-ter" (42). Greenberg wouldn't quibble with that final judgment of Jackson, but he'd take serious issue with the route Read took arriving there. Greenberg's modernism can't learn from myths; the European conception of Jackson (like Rosenberg's) was "a great misunderstand-ing . . . inflated, and exaggerated and distorted" (42). So maybe what is involved in our field is not so much a failure of nerve as a canny distrust in myth, a thoroughly ironic consciousness that refuses to be swayed by poetry. For if Read is right, and scribbled graphs of uncertainty can ulti-mately prove powerful compositions, then the fault lies in our over-mediated consciousnesses. We don't have a blank enough consciousness to comprehend *celui qui fait des gestes blancs parmi les solitudes*; we don't have Stevens' mind of winter to behold the nothing that is not there and the nothing that is. A Modernist analysis like Greenberg's must counter the meta-textual myth of Jackson by revealing his logical place in the procession of Western art's *maîtres*. Rosenberg does the math on what's lost in the move toward establishing Jackson as "a fabricated 'master,'" and the cost is nothing less than the life; critiquing Bryan Robertson's analysis of Jackson, Rosenberg realizes how ridiculous the critical re-styling can be: "In his attempt to inflate Pollock's reputation in terms of current attitudes, Robertson has done everything possible to deprive the artist's life of substance. He has even overlooked his dog, Gyp, and his model A Ford, the companions which served Pollock as equivalents to the frontiersman's gun and horse" ("The Search for Jackson" 58).

And in our field, we continue to let our composition be governed not by mythic figures, or even real lives, but by critical terms, academic forms. But we can't change the fact that it was the *myth* of the "action painter"—that is, the real-time process-record of Namuth's photographs, plus Rosenberg's analysis of the data—which changed a generation of painters, sculptors and critics. What might have given the Action Painter myth its influential charge was the way, as O'Doherty describes it, it's really two classic American myths, the noble savage and the frontiersman, fused to the modern legend of the artist-outcast. Hess agrees with this, referring to the American-ness of the myth: Jackson, riding "out of the Old Frontier . . . the dark, tough, morose Badman" (39). Composition has had no shortage of "noble savage" mythologies, as we've seen with Perl, or as we could see with *Errors and Expectations*, the *Tristes Tropiques* of Composition Studies. But the work of Composition's "noble savage" theorists—at its best—reads like James Johnson Sweeney's backward-looking catalogue introduction to Jackson's first show at Peggy Guggenheim's Art of This Century: "Pollock's talent . . . has fire. It is unpredictable. It is undisciplined. It spills itself out in a mineral prodigality, not yet crystallized. It is lavish, explosive, untidy" (O'Doherty 86). It is composition *manqué*. And though we have a seeming embarrassment of frontier metaphors—horizons, borders, distance, directions, new directions—we realize, in the way Composition never goes on the road, never departs the regional classroom campaign in search of the grand American landscape, that its *frontier* is a virtual simulation. What Composition really lacks is a truly broad definition of artistry, one it could fuse with the outcast-figure, to form the Jacksonian amalgam. With the exception of Macrorie and his ilk, Composition's outcast was set against the social fabric, not out of brooding, tormented genius, but because of plague, disease. Without a sense of an art that commands attention, our outcast myth devolves into a salvation-scenario. Composition's carefully delineated public expectation for writing, rooted as it was to the surface of the page rather than swirling in space, precluded inspired surprise; we would clean the surface of *Full Fathom Five* of all its dumping, de-tangle the crazy beat of *Autumn Rhythm* until it played the nicely-ordered melody of *Broadway Boogie-Woogie*. Our sophisticated irony saw through the truth of romantic myth as something irrelevant, preferring to deal with more manageable half-truths like reified technique. So now, post-process, our symbolic figures are far more modest: the successful writer, the university-inventor—our myth is Horatio Alger fused with a grammar handbook. If I prefer avant-garde practices to academic ones, it's possibly because I teach basic writers, those students so often thought of as the academy's waste, who too often sense their own tragic loss in the midst of an academy that seems always to desire fantasies of excellence (its wildest dream being none of my students on campus any more). Anyway, the academy is craven. Look how quickly they caved in on Jackson's art, how quickly what was once drooly drips of nothing became a Quattrocento masterpiece. Henry McBride, who once thought Jackson's art looked as if "flung," later hopped on the bandwagon when *Life* called him the Greatest Living Painter: the painting still had "a spattered technic," for McBride, "but the spattering is handsome and organized and therefore I like it" (Naifeh and Smith 599); Parker Tyler, who once compared a canvas by Jackson to baked macaroni, now found in it "an impregnable language of image, as well as beautiful and subtle patterns of pure form" (Naifeh and Smith 603). It's not that the work changed, they were just too used to a certain kind of work with a certain set of materials. Myself, I'm always looking for work that sends me, that gives me something I'm not used to, student-writing that enacts the death of academic writing along with its rebirth, and I find that far more frequently with the less-mediated prose of so-called basic writers, writers whose texts are interpretable as meditations on the nature of writing, pursued as if in dialogue with a questioner of ideal innocence and congenital blindness.

If CCCC wants new myths, we could start with this basic choice: either an avant-garde process that continually reactivates itself, exploring new forms and materials in response to the always-rupturing symbolic order, trying to find a line of expressive intensity in order to both chart and inhabit that rupture; or continued salon-simulation, ever-wilder dreams that don't come true so much as crash. If we followed Jackson's choice, when we came upon text-as-diaristic-gestures, seeming at first little more than a tangled snarl, our gaze might dwell a little longer on the rupture, not turn back so quickly to overwrite it with our wildest dreams. We might, initially, fear the death in it, but then begin to suspect it of being a most compelling fantasy. Our evaluative commentary, finally, might sound something like this:

> A boggy, squitchy picture truly, enough to drive a nervous man distracted. Yet there was a sort of indefinite, half-attained, unimaginable sublimity about it that froze you to it, till you involuntarily took an oath with yourself to find out what the marvellous painting meant. (O'Doherty 90, 105)

This describes neither the ideal review of one of Jackson's shows, nor the kind of humane sort of Colesian commentary that would focus on a student's heartfelt statement rather than botched technique, but rather the picture that hung in the Spouter Inn, the symbol of Ahab's quest. O'Doherty (who first connected those lines to Jackson) reminds us of Jackson's interest in Melville, how *Moby-Dick*, that mythic American search, was one of his favorite books.

Surely, though, all this is merely the stuff of one's wildest academic dreams . . . except now that we've moved on to the beautiful world of post-process, why is it that all I can think about is death? 'Post-process,' though? Really? Oh, post-what-became-that-silly-CCCC-process, definitely. But post-*Jackson's*-process? Post-the scrupulous exploration of available technologies? Post-the openness to non-standard materials? Post-the intrepid faith in the personally *right* line over the academically *correct* line? Post-a process (like my own, and most of my students' as well) suffused with equal parts ambition and uncertainty? If you feel we've in some way moved past that . . . that there really is something beyond text as viscous material, hovering for a moment, then leaving behind the sign of one's fleeting passage, the dribble of one's daily annihilation; something more than a bodily intimate writing, in a personally-evolved line, a line that's really nothing more than gesturing with materials but, all the same, capable of expressing a shimmering tension, holding together not just too much with too little but all we know with all we have; the writing course as nothing more (or less) than high school chemistry class, the mad dash for the chemical cabinet . . . . If that's somehow not enough . . . well, may *your* fantasy end better than Ruth Kligman's.

3

SCENES FROM LATE SIXTIES COMPOSITION

> But at times such as
> these late ones, a moaning in copper beeches is heard, of regret,
> not for what happened, or even for what could conceivably have
>   happened, but
> for what never happened and which therefore exists, as dark
> and transparent as a dream. A dream from nowhere. A dream
> with no place to go, all dressed up with no place to go, that an axe
> menaces, off and on, throughout eternity.

> John Ashbery

SCENE ONE:

ROBERT RAUSCHENBERG'S *LINOLEUM* (APRIL 1966, WASHINGTON, D.C.) /

HAPPENINGS

Washington, D.C., April 1966, at a six-day arts festival (designed to be an extravaganza of the most progressive work in theater, dance, and film, and given the suitably pop title of the NOW Festival). Over those six days, festival-goers saw performances by John Cage, the Velvet Underground, Robert Whitman, and Yvonne Rainer. On the opening night of the festival, though, they sat down to the following, a theatre-event entitled *Linoleum*: First, a dancer was seen seated on a Chippendale chair mounted on a rolling platform. She was wearing an old-fashioned wedding dress and in her lap was a pot of cooked spaghetti. Another dancer entered, dressed in a translucent plastic suit, looking like a futuristic lab tech. Adding to that impression was the Fresnellens mask she wore on her face: made of plastic magnifying material, it transformed her face into something out of a surreal dream. She would push the seated bride around on her platform, at times stopping to trace patterns on the floor with pasta. Another performer wheeled himself around the stage with his hands, lying prone in a rolling cage filled with a half-dozen live chickens. He, too, would cease his movements every so often; in his case, to eat fried chicken. Then, shuffling forward in stutter-steps, came another dancer, standing in the middle of a wire-spring bed frame (later in the performance, this dancer would don a strange-looking plaster and wire mesh body covering shaped like a cross between an egg and a haystack).

Finally, there appeared the work's creator, Robert Rauschenberg, also wearing a magnifying mask and plastic suit, described by one writer as "look[ing] like a kind of *commedia del' arte* astronaut" (Sundell 16). He came out and drew chalk outlines around some small, battery-powered, ambulatory sculptures scattered throughout the performance space. As soon as Rauschenberg finished outlining one, it would begin moving. During the performance an American flag on a flagpole was unfurled by Rauschenberg; it kept being unrolled and unrolled, as it was a specially made flag about twenty-some feet in length. The excess was later trimmed off. Throughout the dance, a laundry-filled clothesline was unfurled, and on it was projected Rauschenberg's film, *Canoe*, which he had spliced together from found footage of air force maneuvers and recreational water sports. Rauschenberg's suit had been specially wired, making sounds which varied according to his proximity to a receiver concealed in the flagpole onstage, and which, together with the film's soundtrack, created the score for this piece.

Now, *this* is composition. In its explorations of technology; its collaborative nature; its use of imaginative materials, juxtaposed in interesting, poetic ways (as well as its faith in an audience's ability to make sense of the resulting text); its structure as more performative gesture than hierarchical form (working by intuition and impression rather than by received standards); the homemade aesthetic nature of the piece; and its boldly naive desire to try to make something other than just another dull piece of art, it represents everything I value in composition. And my challenge as a teacher becomes trying to establish a performative space inflected according to such exciting possibilities. What appeals to me most about *Linoleum*, besides the audacious poetic imagery, is the sense that standards and rules have been actively questioned, so that a newly evocative composition can be attempted. *Linoleum* is part of that radical era in visual and performing arts known as the Happenings, which arose out of a feeling in the mid-Fifties familiar to the avant-garde: namely, aesthetic dead end. This was especially true for painters at the time, given the rigid, formalist theory of Clement Greenberg that held such sway, his attempt to rid painting of any effect (such as the literary or sculptural) that wasn't exclusive to it alone, resulting in flatness as the new artistic standard. Artists chafed under such limitations, feeling alienated from what was now accepted work in the Gallery. So, for example, the young American painter Allan Kaprow, creator of one of the first "official" Happenings (*18*

Happenings in 6 Parts), intimately confesses in a 1959 literary review, "I have always dreamed of a new art, a really new art" (Kirby *Happenings* 53). Or French painter and poet Jean-Jacques Lebel, searching for a new "language and long-range technique": "This new language, by the frank way in which it put the question of communication and perception, by its resolution to recognize and explore the forbidden territories which had hitherto halted modern art, had to force a complete re-examination of the cultural and historical situation of art. This language is the Happening" (268–269). Another painter turned Happenings artist, Carolee Schneemann, begs in her notebooks for sheer intensity, for an art that moves: "Notice this insistence on Motion. We cannot capture, hold a moment (impressionism), repeat the moment's verbal content (theater), capture the action itself (futurism): we intensify the perceptions of change, flux, and release them in juxtapositions which grind in on the senses. It is intimate and intense. Happenings: raw, direct, no intermediate crafting, fabricating" (*Meat Joy* 56). Or Oldenburg, another artist, like Kaprow and Schneemann, from a different medium (drawing, sculpture), drawn to the excitement of a new genre: "the 'happening' which was in the beginning a very limited form is bearing fruit as a new physical theater, bringing to the dry puritan forms of the U.S. stage the possibilities of a tremendous enveloping force" (83).

To help them work out a grammar for a new art, the disenchanted looked to the man who remains the most radical formal innovator in American art, and the antithesis of Greenbergian formalism, Jackson Pollock. Kaprow's dreamy desires had led him, two years after Jackson's death, to publish, in the *Art News* of Oct. '58, a poignant reflection on Jackson's legacy, an article that became the Rosetta Stone for those involved in Happenings. Kaprow began by paying homage to the overarching influence of Jackson's mythic status; in almost religious tones he speaks of young vanguard artists as a kind of mystical body of Action Painting: "We were a piece of him; he was, perhaps, the embodiment of our ambition for absolute liberation" (24). But the article is more than hero worship, as Kaprow proceeds to analyze Jackson as avatar of a meta-formalism, one who dispensed with "the idea of the 'complete' painting," in favor of composition as environment, which "gives the impression of going on forever" (26). "What we have then," Kaprow realized, "is a type of art which tends to lose itself out of bounds, tends to fill our world with itself. . . . Pollock's near destruction of . . . tradition may well be a return to the point where art was more actively involved in ritual, magic and life than we have known it in our recent past" (56). When one followed Jackson out of bounds, one was led into the world, into the materiality of Forty-Second Street. Such an aesthetic meant the stuff of art could be found anywhere: Oldenburg, for example, claimed, "A refuse lot in the city is worth all the art stores in the world" (Hapgood 61n). A textuality of the available is fitting for an art inspired by Jackson, who caused a sensation by using relatively cheap enamel house paint and aluminum fence paint in place of academy-preferred oils. Hence, *Linoleum,* and hundreds of other performance works like it, by artists who went out of bounds to pursue new dreams.

Happenings were, as Allan Kaprow defined them, "events which, put simply, happen" ("'Happenings'" 39). They were environments, situations, any kind of non-theatre—created, most often, from piling on poetic images (like Rauschenberg's above), but occasionally out of a kind of Zen minimalism, (e.g., George Brecht's event-scores, mentioned earlier) or simply from a heightened reappreciation of spaces already there (Wolf Vostell's *Cityrama,* for example, in which participants tour the bombed-out ruins of Cologne, according to Vostell's itinerary: e.g., "stand on the corner [of Luebecker Street and Maybach Street] for about five minutes and ponder whether six or thirty-six human beings perished during the night of the thousand-bomber air raid," [Kaprow *Assemblages* 244]). Implicit in Happenings was a faith in the ability to locate meaning everywhere; it was an art more concerned with consumption than actual production. What was more important was the process of appreciation and awareness involved in a textual encounter rather than the commodified product or artwork. As Ann Halprin put it: "There is something going on all the time all around. It's just a matter of being aware—of looking and hearing and putting things together. Something is always happening" (Kostelanetz *Theatre* 67). Or John Cage: "Theatre takes place/ all the time wherever one is and art simply/ facilitates persuading one this is the case" (*Silence* 174). To show art as everyday, Happenings were composed according to the element of chance (Cage, for example, composed according to the hexagrams of the *I Ching;* with Rauschenberg, it was whatever happened to be available), setting in motion events that might enhance our humanity. Even though Happenings might "appear to go nowhere and do not make any particular literary point," the participant in them "feels 'here is something important'" (Kaprow "'Happenings'" 39).

Happenings took cross-disciplinarity to the point of in- or de-determinacy. Take the attitude of Rauschenberg, who worked in both performance and painting: "I don't find theatre that different from painting, and it's not that I think of painting as theatre or vice versa. I tend to think of working as a kind of involvement with materials, as well as a rather focused interest which changes" (Kostelanetz *Theatre* 80). The Happenings, then, were non-theatre artists telling Broadway, telling professional theater—telling the history of performing arts, really— "we can put on an interesting production, too." Soon more and more painters and dancers and other artists were lending their energy to the burgeoning Happenings movement, so that in 1962, cultural vanguardist Susan Sontag could bring the breathless news of "a new, and still esoteric, genre of spectacle" appearing with greater frequency on the New York scene, "a cross between art exhibit and theatrical performance . . . tak[ing] place in lofts, small art galleries, backyards, and small theaters before audiences averaging between thirty and one hundred persons" (263). These artists, desperate to forge some exciting new genre with whatever materials they could scrounge, enjoyed the heady freedom of working without rules. Witness dancer Steve Paxton's comments on Rauschenberg's *Map Room II*, a performance in which he participated:

> *Map Room II* seemed to be a performance-Combine, Rauschenberg's tendency to three-dimensionalize his work finally arriving in four-dimensional expression. . . . [It] was not intended to be a dance as such. It was made for a festival of "Expanded Cinema," which might have meant anything. It was a sign of the times that he, and the other artists involved, were not fazed by the term. Rauschenberg seemed to be trying to follow instructions on the one hand, while on the other delivering works for which no previous instructions existed. (266)

The formative context of the Happenings was richly multiple. Besides Pollock, Happenings artists drew on movements like Bauhaus and Dadaism for inspiration, as well as individuals like Dali, Duchamp, and Schwitters. Ken Dewey identified Kaprow as the single individual who took these influences and themes ("all the casual, instinctive, and scattershot contacts"), realizing "here was something of independent interest," and "ma[d]e it stick as a separate form," to the point where Dewey could say (in 1965), "what we have now are 'forms' coming almost at the rate of synthetic chemicals . . . new methods and new techniques of articulation: ways in which people can express themselves" (208). Kaprow himself traced these "action"-oriented origins for Happenings:

> Futurist manifestoes and noise concerts, Dada's chance experiments and occasional cabaret performances, Surrealism's interest in automatic drawing and poetry, and the extension of these into action painting. All focused in one way or another on the primacy of the irrational and/or the unconscious, on their effect upon undirected body responses, and on the elimination of pictorial and other professional skills as criteria of art. Thus the idea of art as "act" rather than aesthetics was implicit by 1909 and explicit by 1946. ("In Response" 219)

The most commonly agreed-upon point of actual origin for the Happenings is Cage's *Theater Piece #1*, often referred to as the first Happening, a mixed-media performance piece he organized while a member of the faculty at Black Mountain College in the summer of 1952. It took place in the College's dining hall, the chairs of which Cage had re-arranged into four equal triangular groups, formed by X-shaped aisles, with different performance spaces dotting the entire hall. Above the space, Rauschenberg hung some of his white paintings in the form of a cross. With simultaneous events occurring throughout the space, there would be no central focus on the piece, no best seat in the house: "Now, they are all equally good," Cage cracked (Harris *Arts at Black Mountain* 228). Cage planned the piece after lunch one day and presented it that evening, no rehearsals. Each performer was given a specific time bracket, determined by chance, in which to perform. Harris describes the scene, allowing for the way witnesses' memories have become cloudy:

> A general summary of recollections places Cage on a ladder reading either his Meister Eckhart lecture, lines from Meister Eckhart, a lecture on Zen Buddhism, the Bill of Rights, or the Declaration of Independence; [M.C.] Richards and [Charles] Olson reading at different times from another ladder; [Merce] Cunningham dancing in and around the chairs—he was joined in his dance by a dog, who as an interloper, created his own time brackets; Rauschenberg either standing before his paintings or playing scratchy records of Edith Piaf and others at double speed on an ancient wind-up phonograph with a horn loudspeaker; [David] Tudor playing a prepared piano and a small radio; and either Tim LaFarge or Nick Cernovich (possibly both) projecting movies and still pictures upside down on slanting surfaces at

the end of the dining hall. The performance ended with the serving of coffee in cups that had been used as ashtrays during the performance. (228)

Cage's piece was a natural outgrowth of the Black Mountain aesthetic; the school created an atmosphere that would breed a radical redefinition of the theater. For example, in 1936, Black Mountain administrator and painting instructor Josef Albers invited Bauhaus artist Xanti Schawinsky to teach "Stage Studies," and rather than a conventional course in dramaturgy, Schawinsky taught "an investigation into the interaction among essential phenomena such as time, sound, space, movement, and light as manifest in a theatrical setting" (Spector 230). Spector teases out the key performance strategies in Cage's piece, which strongly influenced subsequent artistic practice (and become a good benchmark against which to measure our own compositional criteria): "the use of chance operations and improvisation, the coexistence of independent elements, the employment of projected slides and film, the centrality of the audience, and the lack of any coherent, overarching theme" (230). The response to such an unconventional work (frustrating, as it does, received critical apparatus) was predictable:

> Edgar Taschdijan recalled that, when Cage declared that music "was not listening to Mozart but sounds such as a street car or a screaming baby," he decided that he preferred the music of croaking frogs or the wind whistling through the trees to the commotion of the performance and left. Lou Harrison noted that he found the Happening quite boring, and Viola Farber overheard Johanna Jalowetz remark after the performance, "This is the Dark Ages." (Harris 228)

Such responses are in keeping with the de-determined aesthetic of the work, one oblivious to such traditional criteria such as *boring* or *entertaining*, even using *boredom* strategically to find a really new art (as well as a really new response to it). Rauschenberg: "I'd like it if, even at the risk of being boring, there were an area of uninteresting activity where the spectator might behave uniquely. You see, I'm against the prepared consistent entertainment. Theatre does not have to be entertaining, just as pictures don't have to be beautiful" (Kostelanetz *Theatre* 85).

The desired effect of this kind of aesthetic, one which put everything under erasure, was simply an increase in awareness, a heightened consciousness among the participants, a re-tuning of perception. Perhaps it was postwar commodity malaise, but these artists all felt the world needed re-enchanting, life had lost its sense of innate wonder. These were artists who wanted to change the world, one sensibility at a time. "My art," Rauschenberg said, "is about just paying attention—about the extremely dangerous possibility that *you* might be art" (Spector 227). He summed up the thrill of composition without a net, the excitement of potential trans-formation: "What's exciting is that we don't know. There is no anticipated result; but we will be changed" (Kostelanetz *Theatre* 99). Cage, too, felt he had achieved his compositional goal because, "Many people have told me after a concert that they notice changes in perception of everyday life" (Kirby and Schechner 65). And from the manifesto "Static" written by Swiss avant-garde sculptor Jean Tinguely (with whom Rauschenberg col-laborated): "the only certainty is that movement, change, and metamor-phosis exist . . . our only eternal possession will be change" (Spector 239). For Kaprow, increasing awareness among his Happenings participants meant interrupting, as much as possible, the standard flow of art and life, in order to allow new perceptions to flourish. He felt his "job as an artist [was] to make dreams real" (Kostelanetz *Theatre* 129). It is this smudging of the traditional demarcation between art and ordinary life that most dis-tinguishes the Happenings, whose artists felt a real synergy between the composed and the extant. Kaprow, for example, felt, "*The line between art and life should be kept as fluid, and perhaps indistinct, as possible.* The reciproc-ity between the man-made and the ready-made will be at its maximum potential this way. Something will always happen at this juncture which, if not revelatory, will not be merely bad art—for no one can easily compare it with this or that accepted masterpiece" (*Assemblages* 188–189).

As Greenberg kept insisting, Modernist composition meant limits; but if people didn't want conventional limits in their life, why would they want them in their art? With the two (art and life) indistinct, an expansiveness resulted. Cage gives a sense of this: "From a musical point of view . . . one thing makes everyday life far more fascinating and spe-cial than, say, concert life. That is the variety of sound with respect to all the other things, including space. . . . [I]n our everyday life sounds are popping up, just as visual things and moving things are popping up, everywhere around us" (Kirby and Schechner 65). And so he claimed, "I try to discover what one needs to do in art by observations from my daily life. I think daily life is excellent and that art introduces us to it and its excellence the more it begins to be like it" (Kirby and Schechner 55). Carolee Schneemann wrote in her journal of "our lives themselves as material, stuff for our art or our lives as art containers/ or life the way we shape or discover it being a form of art, the happening an intensifi-cation of our actions in life. The distinctions here swinging between intellection/perception/action" (56). Beyond just an aesthetic choice, there was the sense that by fusing art and life, something ontologically important was happening. If artistic creation could be made like life, and life like artistic creation, it meant that cultural transformation—the dream of the Paris Commune—was possible.

And so, as potential material for composition, in terms of their ability to blur art and life, the Duchampian readymade became useful. Kaprow would claim, "A United States Marine Corps manual on jungle-fighting tactics, a tour of a laboratory where polyethylene kidneys are made, the daily traffic jams on the Long Island Expressway, are more useful than Beethoven, Racine, or Michelangelo" (*Assemblages* 190). The need for new materials is paramount, materials that can produce shock and wonder, that are guaranteed, just by their presence, to result in something differ-ent; materials available almost anywhere—even, as Jackson discovered, from the general store down the road, or even lying around on the ground: a burnt-out match, a dead bee. Anything, as long as it could lift the veil among participants, re-enchant reality to the point where one real-izes the presence of that other world that exists in this one. Some of the most instructive texts on the banal splendor of Happenings materiality are catalogs featuring photographs of Rauschenberg performances. Those images from his theatre work—turtles with flashlights strapped to their backs, crawling among stiffly posed dancers; performers pushing shop-ping carts filled with alarm clocks through the audience; people rolling across the stage in a row of tires; rollerskaters in gray sweatsuits, the para-chutes they wear as backpacks billowing out behind them; dancers wear-ing birds in bird cages around their waists; Rauschenberg himself, in a white dinner jacket, strumming a ukulele, gradually enveloped in the steam from a bucket of dry ice strapped to his waist—are incredible, sub-lime snapshots from the expanded poetic field. Sundell writes,

> Photographs of Rauschenberg's theater pieces reveal the same kind of myste-rious and powerful images that he was able to create with similarly ill-assorted objects in his Combines. The raw material is often identical: objects which embody a sense of the past and the erosion of wear; others, mass produced and banal, which are the stuff of our everyday experience; jerry-built con-trivances of unidentifiable utility; animals; the human body in motion. . . . As in the Combines, subliminal visual and metaphoric associations bind together the most unlikely conjunctions of disparate matter. The works were

performed to a combination of ambient sound, often the electronically
amplified noise made by manipulating one of the props, and scores composed of a collage of taped music and sound-tracks from film or video. (14)

In both the stage properties for his performances, as well as in his
Combines, Rauschenberg practiced an inclusive, quotidian materiality:
"a pair of socks is no less suitable to make a painting than wood, nails,
turpentine, oil and fabric" (Hapgood 18). There is a poignant beauty
open to those who use the domestic or discarded over the rarefied; it
furthers the desired slippage between art and life, generates that
charged dynamic which Kaprow referred to as "a continually active
field, whose outlines are very, very uncertain so that they blend in and
out of daily life" (Kostelanetz *Theatre* 109). But more importantly, legiti-
mating the commonplace as substantive compositional material affords
the status of artist to those who might otherwise find the rarefied nature
of conventional materials a barrier to creation. It means reduction
(really, expansion) of the compositional scene to a simple, available aesthetics of the perceptual (rather than textual) field; with stylistic principles nothing more than a basic combinatory therein for poetic effect. It
puts the emphasis on the ultimate force of the work (Jackson's *statement*)
and not on the formal or conventional qualities. This is Cage as
Venturian architect of the everyday: "We must get ourselves into a situation where we can use our experience no matter what it is" (Kostelanetz
58). It's fast-food aesthetics, hermeneutics-to-go, street-criticism, an
urban style where you don't need any more than you can carry in the
subjectivity-equivalent of a purse or backpack. An open-ended materiality puts the possibility for a Happening, then, potentially anywhere.

Anywhere, to be sure, but some spaces proved more conducive than
others. The less already-determined the better, though, and so the
Happenings artists were anti-architects when it came to the Gallery. The
descriptions of the environments they installed within (and outside of)
institutional spaces shows their work could not be circumscribed by
received standards. Their art had uses beyond the Gallery's strictly curatorial or commercial parameters. For example, a description of Robert
Whitman's attempt to reconfigure the Reuben Gallery's space for his
work entitled *The American Moon* (1960) shows how the institution's aesthetic is deconstructed by the Happenings—in large part at the physical, spatial level: "in order to carry out the first 'gravity-defying event,'
actors would have to wear some sort of harness and be suspended from
a horizontal rope or cable while they 'walked on air' with perhaps only

their legs visible to the spectators. In an attempt to achieve this, large bolts were sunk into the gallery wall to anchor a line" (Kirby *Happenings* 138). Or Kaprow's *A Spring Happening* (1961), for which he also had to radically rework the traditional exhibition-space: "When arriving spectators entered the store[front gallery] with its glass display windows at either side of the door, they found the smaller front section partitioned into a lobby by a seven-foot wall of muslin sheets. One narrow section in the left side of the cloth wall was black. Above the black curtain a man could be seen, apparently walking on some sort of high platform, making arrangements for the performance" (Kirby *Happenings* 94). The space was so charged by shock and surprise, in fact, that "when the black curtain was pulled to one side, and they were asked to enter, many of the people who had made reservations for *A Spring Happening* did not want to go into the narrow, gloomy tunnel; some refused . . . a few made a point of waiting until they could be the last ones—and therefore close to the exit curtain—in the event that the enclosed space became intolerable" (Kirby 94). After being disoriented by the tunnel-like space of narrow blackness, lights would go on and off in short regular intervals. Then a light went on in a red-painted space opposite the tunnel, which participants could view through slits in the muslin. They saw a construction made of chicken wire, newspapers, and cardboard. Through the course of the Happening, booming crashes could be heard, as a man above threw barrels down onto a tile floor; a tape was played of electronic machines making a low rumble; all lights went out, and a bell was heard striking at various points throughout the space; the lights began to flash irregularly again, and the chicken wire construction began to shake violently; the sound of a power saw was heard. The performance went on like that—including performers jousting with tree branches, a floor polisher running back and forth on the roof above the participants' tunnel, shadows moving across the muslin wall, drumbeats sounding. Finally, as Kaprow's impressionistic performance-notes read, "car horn starts constant sound, lawn mower starts, pushed by tar paper figure, moves through all eight rooms cutting swath through leaves blowing them all over" (Kirby 93). It was his desire to evoke scenes and impressions beyond the constraints of the gallery walls that led Kaprow to, more often than not, create Happenings for outdoor spaces.

Beyond merely material considerations, Happenings abandoned formal, generic conventions. Traditional narrative or theatrical constraints were inapplicable. The Happening, as performance art historian and occasional Happenings creator Michael Kirby reminds us, is "nonmatrixed" (*Happenings* 16), i.e., not underscored by classical theatre's time/space/character frame, conventions that control the shape of the drama. Its form was often the result of juxtaposition, a catalogue of sounds, dialogue, objects, and images—database as *de facto* form. Oldenburg's modesty in materials was matched by his basic formal technique; he used parataxis in his Happenings to pile up interesting images until he achieved the disorientation that might lead to a heightened state of awareness: "I throw up images one after another or on top of one another and repeat them until it is evident I am asking, 'What are they, or what do you think you are watching?' My theatre is therefore undetermined as to meaning" (Kostelanetz *Theatre* 154). The goal was life as it unfolds and forms itself in the moments of our existence. Kirby referred to the "compartmented structure" of Happenings as in direct opposition to Modernism's thesis-oriented "information structure" (13). The title of Kaprow's *18 Happenings in 6 Parts*, or Yvonne Rainer's *Parts of Some Sextets* (1965), suggests this no-brand, generic textuality. A paratactic structure can mean numerous tableaux in a composition, some dominated by physical and/or sonic rather than verbal effects, the work becoming a kind of iconic strip mall. The Happenings grammar is an a-logic (which makes it almost anathema to traditional Composition), one in which an author's "private idea structure" does not need to be articulated unambiguously by being "transformed into a public information structure" (Kirby *Happenings* 20). In her work, Rainer treated composition in terms of structural problems that needed solving, which she accomplished by applying a basic temporal pattern to the work, while incorporating unconventional materials: "I resorted to two devices that I have used consistently since my earliest dances: repetition and interruption. . . . So it began to take shape in my head: dance movement of various kinds; activities with mattresses; static activities (sitting, standing, lying); continuous simultaneous actions changing abruptly at perhaps thirty-second intervals, sometimes the whole field changing at the same time, sometimes only a portion of it, but every thirty seconds something changing" (162, 163). Such a method is text as assemblage, which results in a text less loaded, less peculiarly styled. Desire to escape the matrix of conventional grammar and syntax led Dick Higgins to develop his *Graphis* series: "The Graphis series is the result of a feeling that conventional theatre notation in which one action follows another leaves untried an enormous variety of techniques that could enrich our experience. . . . With the Graphises, I was trying to set up a form that was unsemantic, even choreographic, in conception if not in execution" (Higgins and Eisenhauer 123). So he came up with the idea of the *Graphis*, a loosely-delineated, notational performance sketch, a kind of broadly outlined, situational encounter-space-as-the-atre, in which various contexts, characters, or concepts are plotted on a kind of web-like graph corresponding to the performance space. Performers would move through the cycle of notations (according to a complex series of cues). The conceptual score for *Graphis 82* (1962), for example, is no more (or less) than a bunch of curvy, squiggling lines—looking like the first or second layer of a Pollock drip canvas, or a situationist psychogeographic map; an action-text, then, a prose web—overwritten here and there with node-words like "lungs," "lute," "lover," "lizard," "macaroni," which were taken from a Puerto Rican dream-book. For example, a performer would come upon the space for the notation "lungs," and have to develop an interpretive action or idea for that (say, breathing). In Letty Eisenhauer's words, the *Graphis* performance-text grows, when operationalized, into a piece of "complexity, confusion, and visual richness. . . . The more keen the imagination and industry of the performer the richer the piece" (Higgins and Eisenhauer 125, 127). The complexity and confusion were not edited out of Happenings composition because the guiding principle of inflection was the wonderful, the marvelous. As Robert Whitman put it, "[Y]ou could talk about what happens when some person doesn't know what in the hell he's seen, but is excited by it. He doesn't know what it means, but he really doesn't find that important. Something has happened; he's had an experience that's different. He's discovered a world that he didn't know existed before. That's a good thing" (Kostelanetz *Theatre* 238). La Monte Young put the Happenings' bottom-line principle most sublimely: "My own feeling has always been that if people just aren't carried away to heaven, I'm failing. They should be moved to strong spiritual feeling" (Kostelanetz *Theatre* 218).

SCENE TWO:
ERNECE KELLY'S *MURDER OF THE AMERICAN DREAM* (APRIL 1968, MINNEAPOLIS)/
ENGLISH COMPOSITION

To see whether a compositional scene of such textual possibilities and deeply human ends caused any simpatico ripples in our own compositional field, we could unconsign the history of our own field's

avant-garde, starting. perhaps, with CCCC 1968, which was held in
Minneapolis that year, April 4–6, right on the eve of May '68. Sherry
Turkle is an interesting historian for that charmed month of May '68,
and her chronicle of those heady days in France holds true for CCCC.
Turkle speaks of a time when "the struggle and the search was less for
new governmental forms than for oneself. French bureaucratic society
had called forth its antithesis: an antistructural movement which created the context for a radical exploration of the self and a new, more
encompassing mode of human relations" (69). It was a time when even
common graffiti spoke of how "politics had to be made by 'reinventing
language' and that it had to be made in every person" (70); when both
inner and outer experience were fused around language and desire:
"During May, social challenge came to be viewed as analogous to the
analytic experience: as a liberating ritual whose goal is to trace a way
back to a truthful idiom. And this would require the liberation of language. People spoke of May as *la prise de la parole*, 'the seizing of
speech,' and of *l'imagination au pouvoir*, 'power to imagination'" (72).

   Power to the imagination. That could have been the slogan of the
Happenings artists. . . . And so, touring the scene of CCCC '68, a site of
the language arts, we might wish to see the field caught up in that cultural
spirit of the liberation of language, see how well the avant-garde tenden-
cies of a radical populist composition like the Happenings rhymed, if at
all, with thinking in writing instruction. We could start our retrospection
with the "official" fieldnotes to the scene, the CCCC '68 Workshop
Reports. (What a concept, first of all: a textual trace of the everyday at the
CCCC. Populist thinking, as I write this, is trying to recapture that spirit
[e.g., CCCC On-line and those various discussion groups that post anec-
dotal commentary on the conference], but such attempts have yet to
equal the stature of the institutional fixture that the *CCC* Workshop
Reports had.) Those Comp '68 Reporters, recording the passage of a few
people through a rather brief moment in time, reveal themselves as
provocative pedagogues, suggesting welcome new parameters for text-
events—sounding very much, in fact, like Happenings artists. The textual
traces of their workshop-events were open-ended, charged; work(-as-text)
was allowed to be definitively unfinished, as long as it had a buzz: "a spirited, though not easily summarized discussion" (241); "interesting but not
immediately applicable" (240); "we of course reached no conclusions, but
we did have a lively discussion" (245). The avant-garde's suspicion of the
academic can be seen—in Session "4A. The Uses of Stylistics in

Composition Classes," for example, "Some participants seemed to have a traditional hesitancy about rhetoric and stylistics as mere sophistry" (242); or Session "6B. Research in Composition," which suggested "eliminating as much as possible the dangerous aspects of research in composition, i.e., the bias or misunderstandings caused by current measuring devices attempting to measure things considered by some to be immeasurable" (244). At CCCC '68, they were eager to talk intensity at the expense of the formal, concerned as they were about "students who become especially interested in their work" (245) and "the consensus that correctness was only minutely important" (245). They were feeling *la prise de la parole*. For Workshop "5B. Trends in Freshman Composition," "the trend receiving the most attention" was a radical re-thinking of the whole enterprise, "the reassessment of one's own objectives in teaching composition. Indeed, one participant asked, 'How do you know you're doing anything that's right?'" (242). Of course, there was much that was not at all Happening about that year's CCCC: talk of the "non-writer" and how literary analysis or criticism should be "discouraged except in special cases of more perceptive writers" (241), or the felt need among some for "materials . . . devoted to specific types of composition assignments as well as evaluative discussions of texts" (241). But most important, a critical mass of compositionists came together in April of 1968 to consider the possibility of total systemic failure: "Much recent research seems to indicate that students write equally well whether they take a freshman composition course or not—an observation lamented by those present" (246). In fact, that session on "Research in Composition" gave much discussion to a theme prevalent at that time (at all times, it seems), "dropping completely the freshman composition program" (244).

No surprise that CCCC 1968 can be read as a testament to loss, given the historical reality (the far greater loss) of April 4, 1968. Perhaps the most eloquent statement ever made about how and what we lose in Composition Studies was made at that conference when Ernece B. Kelly stood up, the day after Dr. King's assassination, and read "Murder of the American Dream" to the Minneapolis crowd, a short paper on why she was just not having it any more, why she had to leave the conference early. As Kelly saw it, Composition at the time was anything but avant-garde. In her talk, she describes what it's like to sit and watch a tedious performance endlessly unfold during CCCC conventional performances ("I have listened to and have watched the playing out of the kind of drama that continues to be played out each day in this nation . . . a drama which is called variously 'we're making progress' or 'but things *are* improving' or 'we're going as fast as we can'" [106]), all the while knowing that stale drama is really a *trauerspiel* of the loss of hope and opportunity ("the loss of a dream" [106]) when it comes to the status of Black voice and Black style in college writing (and the academy in general). Irmscher was profoundly moved by Kelly's piece, enough so that he published it in the May 1968 *CCC*, noting how well it captured the loss ("Her words suggest how lacking communication is . . .") and hoping her piece might lead us somewhere we weren't, "open channels of communication we do not now have" ("In Memoriam" [105]). The April 1968 conference was purgative, a watershed moment for Kelly, a dislocation/relocation—she came as an English instructor, she says, and she left as a Black woman. Her paper focuses on the cultural counter-trend working against power to the imagination, the academy's pressure against non-traditional style: "I am tired, very tired of being the object of studies, the ornament in professional or academic groups, the object to be changed, reshaped, made-over. I feel sure that thousands of Black students would echo those words" (108). Perhaps Kelly had earlier attended one of the less happening Workshop Sessions, "9A and 9B. Dialect Studies and Social Values," for in her own talk she gritted her teeth about how the conference had met that year, in part, "to discuss the dialects of Black students and how we can upgrade or, if we're really successful, just plain replace them" (106–107). Part of mourning the truth and spirit of Dr. King, for Kelly, was bemoaning the loss to Composition of "the richness and values of the language of the Black ghetto" (107). But those Dialect Studies workshop participants were certainly not mourning the loss of ghetto richness, they were conspiring to supplant it, their report noting the participants' views that "standards of usage were valuable in themselves, that 'taste' ought to be taught and nourished," adding as well that "the popular position was the current one supporting the addition of a standard dialect to the non-standard (still sometimes *sub-standard*) speech of the disadvantaged student" (247). (By "disadvantaged," it was meant "especially Negro students, and the approach that should be taken toward their training in language use" [247].) Their claims were made according to real-world impera-tives, education now conceived, not as being carried away to heaven, but as preparation for future employment: "students had to be made 'employable' by their education and . . . 'standard English,' however that came to be precisely defined, was the kind of speech that made the right impressions in a job interview" (247). However, there were some true Comp '68 types in the crowd at Sessions 9A and 9B to inform the group otherwise: "One participant pointed out that there was a growing feeling that 'black is beautiful' and that any attempt to 'whiten' the dialect of a ghetto Negro was not in the end going to solve any problems. . . . She was supported by another speaker who reported that teachers in Detroit were becoming disenchanted with the bi-dialectal approach" (247). Maybe this disenchantment pervaded the sensibilities of many at CCCC '68; maybe that's why, though she wants to end her cold appraisal with hope, Kelly closes her presentation with "But I think not" (108).

Over in the *English Journal* in May 1968, Macrorie was voicing the same feelings of loss as Kelly, turning away from the same tired impulses: "We ask students never to judge ideas or events out of context, but fail to see our composition classes in any larger world. That is why they are such astonishing failures" (686). Even though the fate of Black students' language put the issue into stark relief, Macrorie knew the waste of young peoples' linguistic richness knows no color. Macrorie could already feel the high walls of Composition's Museum being erected, separating its activity from the larger world, reinforcing rather than blurring the boundaries between art and life. Yet he knew the vernacular value of *la prise de la parole*, of students "communicating with each other and with administrators and teachers in dozens of new ways" (686), so he begged his readers to "look for what is good in [student papers]. . . . Bring [a student] out of his doldrums of fear by honest praise for what he has done well, if only a sentence or paragraph" (692). But such troop-rallying enthusiasm can't hide the fact that Macrorie, like Kelly, was a panic-theorist; they both saw the explosive results of trying to deny discursive alternatives: for Kelly, the sad reality of personal, linguistic richness wasted by CCCC's simulation-drama was that "that very drama is a prelude to continued violence" (106); and Macrorie anticipated student desire and tedium "turning our schools into the shambles remaining after revolutions" (686). The Happenings artists spoke to such disaffection; they existed in large part to reveal the richness in the common, seemingly substandard nothing, as opposed to the overly-determined dullness of official somethings. Cage put best the rationale for this new compositional program of delight in the everyday:

For some things, one needs critics, connoisseurs, judgments, authoritative ones, otherwise one gets gypped; but for nothing, one can dispense with

all that fol-de-rol, no one loses nothing because nothing is securely possessed. When nothing is securely possessed one is free to accept any of the
somethings. How many are there? They roll up at your feet. . . . [I]f one
maintains secure possession of nothing (what has been called poverty of
spirit), then there is no limit to what one may freely enjoy. (*Silence* 132)

And so it is no surprise that the kind of frustration felt by Kelly and
Macrorie over the way formal and institutional constraints limited the
amount of discovery and wonder in a classroom, and an equally similar
desire to intensify perceptions in order to appreciate students' alternative verbal style, led some compositionists of the era, chief among them
Charles Deemer and William Lutz, to turn to the grammar of the
Happenings for Composition pedagogy, in search of a way to transfigure
"the regular sterile classroom" (Lutz "Making Freshman English" 38).

Deemer's article, appearing in the November 1967 issue of *College
English*, was written while he was a graduate teaching assistant at the
University of Oregon. The article reads like a manifesto: interspersed
with bits of text excerpted from radical works by McLuhan, Dewey,
Russell, and others, are Deemer's own stirring rationale and method for
reinventing writing instruction. Formally, as well as conceptually, it
remains one of the best things in Composition's canon. He uses a Paul
Goodman sample to set his context: education defined as "a kind of
inept social engineering to mold, and weed out, for short-range extrin-
sic needs"; it's "in the bureaucratic death-grip . . . of a uniformity of conception and method" (in Deemer 121). Such rhetoric returns us at once
to this bracing era in educational reform, when entire histories of education were tossed out like a bag of stale chips. Compare Deemer's with
a similar manifesto, Jerry Farber's "The Student and Society": "School is
where you let the dying society put its trip on you. . . . Our schools teach
you by pushing you around, by stealing your will and your sense of
power, by making timid square apathetic slaves out of you—authority
addicts" (17). Speaking himself of the conceptual and methodological
rigidity of the school system, Deemer calls English composition "the
rigid child of a rigid parent" (121). Typical of the era, too, a generation-
gap chasm was thought to be inscribed in the classroom's very design:
"the generation behind the podium forever out of touch with the
younger generation in the lecture hall" (123). The standardized dullness of Composition was all the more galling for Deemer because he saw
how it could be "the most influential" of all college courses, a course

central to the very basis of college, "an introduction to what the University is about" (122). Or, as he corrects himself, what the University "should be about" (123). Deemer's desire was to subsume the too distinctly fragmented young/old, active/passive, teacher/student, teaching/learning dynamic of Composition into one undifferentiated impulse (termed now *experience* [122]), in much the same way that Happenings tried to fuse artist and audience into *participant*. He's uncomfortable with the very word *teacher*, always putting it in quotation marks and making asides about the need for a new word for what it represents (122).

So the Happenings became his pedagogy. He shared their same ultimate goal—intensity, the student/audience "actively aware and participant" (123). They shared dramatic strategies as well: Since "shock and surprise are essential features of the happening," Deemer felt they should be "frequent moods" (124) in the composition course as well, helping to jar students out of the tired discursive roles they had fallen into. Deemer knew that students, conditioned by the narrow-bandwidth of university classroom practice, might find his methods odd: "For the student who, *in the classroom*, is not used to participating in any experience at all, the clarity of shock will be quite dramatic when a real experience is presented to him" (124). (*When the black curtain was pulled to one side, and they were asked to enter, many of the people who had made reservations did not want to go into the narrow, gloomy tunnel; some refused.*) Like the situationists, he advocated definite, constructed experiences that the (intensified) student could write out of, knowing students rarely have any wild times in the standard academic real. To change the classroom performance, Deemer not only altered the conception of the performers, but the performance space (speaking from a different part of the room: "the rear . . . or through the side window" [124]) and the script as well ("discuss theology to Ray Charles records" [124]). He consciously offers no specific curriculum for composition-as-a-Happening—simply the rationale, goal, and some broadly sketched strategic moves. He knows for a true Happening to work, it must be a site-specific work shaped by individual teachers and their student collaborators. And the conceptual rewards go beyond the pedagogical alone, as the original Happeners found the greatest gains among their participants to transcend mere theatre: it is, after all, according to Deemer, a matter of "Life over death" (125); namely, "the reengagement of the heart, a new tuning of *all* the senses . . . the first step toward poetry" (125). Wolf

Vostell's aim was the same as Deemer's. Explaining his reliance on the de-contextualing/re-collaging technique of décollage, Vostell could be Deemer: "I'm concerned with enlightening the audience through décollages. By taking everyday occurrences out of their context, it opens up for discussion the absurdities and demands of life, thereby shocking the audience and prompting them to reflect and react" (Berghaus 323–324). Similar to Kaprow, Whitman, et al., Deemer knew space was at the core. He marveled, for example, at the way Timothy Leary could instantly restyle a traditional space "by symbolically stripping out of his establishment gear to preach by candlelight from a stage floor" (124), making the space McLuhanistically *cool.*

Space was the point at which Bill Lutz began his own attempts to make first-year writing a Happening. Lutz, too, doubted anything truly creative could occur in the traditional classroom, given the formal and conceptual limits implied by the space as studio/gallery. "The classroom as presently structured does not provide the environment in which any-thing creative can be taught. Physically, the room insists on order and authoritarianism, the enemies of creativity" (35). Beyond just the Gallery's determinant space, it's the pervasive institutional power of the Museum itself: "Ultimately Freshman English as a Happening calls for the complete restructuring of the university. We would have to break such academic chains as grading systems (including pass-fail) and the absolute authority of the teacher" (35). Lutz, who first delivered his 1971 *CCC* article as a 1969 CCCC paper, catalogues into the published version remarks made in a letter from a friend of his, a University of Wisconsin TA, who heard Lutz present the original paper. That TA artic-ulates the structural auto-erosion needed for first-year comp to become happening: "if enough people let the walls down around themselves and manage in a few isolated places to knock a few institutional walls down, we may really get to have courses like the kind you envision" (35). So small, local gestures are the key. That Wisconsin TA goes on in his letter to theorize a site-specific formalist shift, a new local materiality. "Juxtaposition of the sacred and profane . . . hard core pornography next to pictures and poems about real intense love. If it were legal, we should put joints in the binding. An essay on the birth control pill should include a birth control pill. . . . [Students] seem to flow into each other, and nobody seems to talk coherently anymore. It's juxtaposition, not composition. English Juxtaposition 101" (36).

For his own local detournement of the scene of writing instruction, Lutz replaced standard classroom activities with small-scale Happenings, Deemerian constructed situations, in order to "create an experience about which the student can write . . . in contrast to the usual method of having the student read about an experience someone else has had and then write a theme about it" (36). His first attempt (which he cribbed from the University of North Carolina's 1968–69 FYC Instructor's Manual) was a variety of small event-scores for students to enact, reminiscent of George Brecht. Students received note cards and had three minutes to perform their individual events, then they wrote about what had transpired in the classroom. Activities included:

> Go to the front of the room and face the class. Count to yourself, and each time you reach five say, "If I had the wings of an angel."
>
> Go to the front right corner of the room and hide your head in it. Keep counting to yourself and on every third number say loudly, "Home." . . .
>
> Be an ice cream cone—change flavor. . . .
>
> Walk around to everyone in the room and pat him or her on the back lightly and say, "It's all right." Stop occasionally and say, "Who, me?" (37)

The tasks given the students remind one of the exercises offered art students in Eric Fischl and Jerry Saltz's *Sketchbook with Voices*, where those desiring to find new formal solutions to problems are advised, first (in the words of Larry Rivers and Frank O'Hara) to "Empty yourself of everything" (13), and then invited to undergo a series of tasks suggested by a variety of artists. For example, Jennifer Bartlett suggests the student "Do something that attacks the notion of originality" (132); John Baldessari asks, "What is the smallest drawing that you can make? Make a drawing on a piece of confetti" (49); David Salle offers, "Spend a day talking only in rhyme" (25); Cindy Sherman, "Do your own work but use someone else's clothes" (39); and Dorthea Rockburne, "Try to make something so beautiful it hurts" (43). Like such exercises, Lutz's events had the desired goal of a deeply felt interrogation of compositional form. And, according to Lutz, they succeeded: the resulting classroom megatext—each student's different activity combining into a *de facto* whole during the three-minute period—prompted a discussion of "whether there was a principle of order in operation which they had not seen," culminating in a consideration by the group of "What do we mean by order in writing?" (37).

The success of his initial effort led Lutz to attempt another classroom Happening which resulted in his class being held in a room in the student union, one Lutz had subtly altered to turn into the kind of space in which young people smoked pot in the Sixties (drapes closed; lights off; candle and incense lit; music playing, a combination of rock and head-trip classical such as *Also Sprach Zarathustra* [theme from *2001*] and *Bolero*). For the entire period the class just grooved in the candle-lit, scent-filled dark. Lutz felt he'd put together a successful class that day because his students were carried away to heaven: "when the period was over the students were asked to pick up their books and leave. Some of them did not want to" (38). As Happener, Lutz's goal ("I want to make the student respond directly to his own experience and not someone else's" [36]) sounds like Jean-Jacques Lebel's, who wanted his performances to transform his participants' "old ways of seeing, of feeling, of being" (Berghaus 352), reflecting what Berghaus sees as one of the central tenets of the Happenings: "The Happenings artist is not content with interpreting life, but offers a direct experience of life and allows us to participate in its unfolding in the reality of our existence" (352). In subsequent classes, Lutz tried other methods of altering the classroom to intensify direct experience, including collage, light shows, conducting class discussion in a circle (only with students' backs to the center), asking students "to paint a poem" (which led the class to reflect on whether "the ordering of an experience on canvas [is] the same as ordering that experience on paper with words"), and "rolling around in a room filled with sponge rubber" (38). English Composition as a Happening means turning the writing class into a Lebellian Festival of Free Expression, referring to that series of multi-media events Lebel staged in Europe, which featured everything from a badminton game played with fluorescent racquets, through poetry and films, to a naked woman on a motorcycle roaring through the auditorium (along with more intimate, body-oriented activities). Just as Lutz's students were loathe to leave their newly-charged wonder-space, Berghaus describes the scene after Lebel's *Second Festival of Free Expression* (1965): "Finally, a huge plastic tube in the form of a serpent was inflated, the motorcycle left the hall, and the film screening came to an end. However, the audience carried on with the Happening for another one-and-a-half hours" (357).

Both Deemer and Lutz hoped students might leave the (already-w)rote tedium of conventional expression to experience communication-degree-zero, and for those today also struggling for a way to kill all tedium in their composition classes, the bold naivete of such gestures is endlessly touching. There are several others we could cite here who tried to bring shock and surprise into the Late Sixties' writing class, but it is worth spending some more time on two in particular.

Ken Macrorie is a compositionist not normally associated with the Happenings movement but one whose practices are very much in the spirit of radical performance. His pedagogy advocated leaving the gallery-space ("ask students to place themselves outside of class anywhere they can be alone and quiet" ["To Be Read" 686]); he urged a splashing of all kinds of writing, a fluxus of text—from freewrites, to wordplay, to news articles, to journals, to stories, to sound effects, to parody, to the "record [of] short fabulous realities" (688). It was a curriculum geared to "doing something different for [the student]" (692), in which text would flow like molten metal, the teacher unconcerned as to definable shape or mass, the only evaluative criteria being "the amount of discovery and wonder it contains" (692), i.e., how much light was captured, shimmering there on the surface. His course was run, then, according to the same imperative found in the script directions for Ken Dewey's Happening, *City Scale* (1963): "THE EVENING SHOULD GET MORE AND MORE EXPLORATIVE" (Dewey, Martin, and Sender 179–180). Macrorie summed up his entire quasi-Happenings aesthetic in his 1970 text *Uptaught*, a kind of teaching portfolio as travelogue, detailing his long, strange trip to reach a pedagogy-as-potlatch, where no one needs reshaping, the classroom enterprise being a "time to pursue some truths, when student and professor share their expert knowledge and their experience" (168). His book is a panic-text, apocalyptically reading the scene of instructional theory in writing against the crisis-moment represented by the late 1960s. (It begins, for example, as police in riot gear march off to bust up a student sit-in on Macrorie's campus; he voices his disgust that professors decided not to support the students, or even show interest in the protest, a symptom of how professors "have made the university sick unto death" [2].) Macrorie starts by tracing his own complicity in a system of college writing that results in students producing "mechanical exercises," "all dead" (6). The stock college writing scene (*themewriting*, as Coles will later call it) proved for his students "an insulated act which produced writing no one except a schoolmaster ever read, and he only if forced to" (6). Composition, then, had become as sterile and lifeless as painting for the Happenings artists. Early in the book's chronology, he gets Paul Goodman to judge a campus writing contest, but no prize is awarded because the writing was all so dull. Goodman's comments to that effect help Macrorie form his aesthetic criteria: writing that's "spirited . . . [that] sends me" (17). The same sort of passionate conviction that drove Cage, that daily life was excellent and that composition's purpose was to introduce us to it and its excellence, drove Macrorie: "My students were alive . . . humorous . . . but they wrote dead" (10–11). Macrorie's book is pervaded with the sort of collective, participant spirit of the Happenings, perhaps, because he aggressively loves and admires his students, wants to intensify them and wants to be intensified himself by the encounter the class represents: "Most students are not my equal in experience or knowledge of literature and writing. But in some aspects of each, they may be my superior. I will never know until I let them bring forth themselves full of their own experiences and ideas and feelings, as they are forced to let me bring forth myself" (68). This is a curriculum of *s'exposer, se toucher*. Macrorie spends the book chronicling his attempt to trace a way back to a truthful idiom for his students and himself. He wants to get his students' embodied lives on paper; the grains of their voices, heard in "the bones of the ear" (16); papers with "spirit . . . not written by a drudge" (*Searching* 88). His organizational pattern reads like a Vonnegut novel: short pithy bits of gimlet-eyed common sense.

Models

The professor who wants his student to increase his "sensitivity to art, to people, and to language," calls his textbook *A Program for Effective Writing.*

There is no word the student has heard more and been impressed with less than *effective*, unless it be *important*. (51)

Real Evaluation

A senior student came into my office to tell me how he looks forward to getting out of school so he can once again read with pleasure. He should have put that down in his teacher evaluation. (103)

Encrusted within Macrorie's own prose are not only samples of student papers (a technique he tried as editor of *CCC*), but transcripts of class discussions, and bits and pieces of campus dialogue; the whole work, then, becomes a catalogue of Late Sixties College Composition. One delights in how well his book captures a scene, a lived moment in time. So, for example, four college dropouts stop by his office one afternoon to shoot the shit, vent their frustration, and Macrorie records some of it for us (one, named Brad, says, "I don't give a damn whether the university is burned down or the country goes smash. I couldn't care less. What would be lost?" [152]). Macrorie might have edited *CCC*, but he never really represented the discipline, of course. I think he was misread by even his strongest supporters; his notion of "Engfish," for example, that "feel-nothing, say-nothing language . . . devoid of the rhythms of contemporary speech" (18), was mainly used by the discipline as an editing heuristic to get students to eliminate wordiness, rather than to radically inject life into prose, to transform it into, say, *objects which embody a sense of the past and the erosion of wear, the stuff of our everyday experience; jerry-built contrivances of unidentifiable utility; animals; the human body in motion.* He reaches a point, at the book's end, where he sounds particularly like Joseph Beuys, hoping to change the world through an ethics of heart-and-soul and personal creativity: Every student, he claims, "is capable of seeing the world, human and natural, in a way valuable to others. And capable of learning from others to see it even more sharply" (186).

The compositionist in our field who most poetically embodied the Happenings aesthetic (though by no means affiliating himself with the movement) was Bill Coles. Beginning in 1967 (with "The Teaching of Writing as Writing," which appeared in the same issue of *College English* as Deemer's), he wrote a series of works that expressed his desire to do something different in a writing classroom: to reconfigure the space around "the teaching of writing as art . . . [where] it is not writing that is being taught but something else . . . a way of teaching what cannot be taught, a course to make possible what no course can do" ("The Teaching" 111). Coles's goal was the Happenings' goal—heightened awareness, specifically adapted for a writing class: "intensif[ying] a student's awareness of the relationship between language and experience" ("The Teaching" 111). When he writes about his course's aim, he sounds like Harold Rosenberg: "writing conceived of not as a way of saying something but as something being said, as an action, an extension of being at a moment in time. . . . My object is to keep things open, to pursue an idea in such a way as to allow a student to have ideas of his own, to find himself in the act of expression, to become conscious of himself as becoming" (111–112, 113). Or, as Kaprow put it, "To the extent that a happening is not a commodity but a brief event . . . it may become *a state of mind*" ("'Happenings'" 62). Coles stripped his materials down to a sequence of text-events: conceptual problems or questions to work through, like an Ann Halprin dance workshop, as participants establish an ethic and a vocabulary. Coles generated the sequence of topics for this text-stream according to the principle of "nonsense": "at times they look as though they are creating a sequence, just as at times they look meandering or discontinuous" ("The Sense of Nonsense" 27). Then Coles begins to weave in a range of readings (e.g., Salinger, Darwin, Nicola Sacco, Edward Gorey) which help students further both their ideas and their craft. He created tension between form and formless, pursuing "a peculiar fusion of pattern and anti-pattern, of ordered disorder" (28)—such Zen-like language again recalls Kaprow, who, for example, called his 1964 Happening *Eat* "a reciprocal rhythm between the stable and the unstable" (Kirby "Allan Kaprow's *Eat*" 49). Contexts in a Coles classroom would be set up and abruptly reversed in order to "mockingly invalidate the pat answer, the conventional response," so as to allow something more powerful to percolate: "the wispish suggestion of a meaning which cannot quite be realized, the sense of a sense that is never absent at the same time it is never quite there" ("The Sense of Nonsense" 28). The hope for the participant in his class, "a new awareness of the possibilities of language and of himself as a language user" ("The Sense of Nonsense" 28). His argument—that "nonsense creates its own universe; it is its own point and message" (28)—underscores how much he thought of his assignment sequence as providing students an experience that was different, evoking a world for students they didn't know existed before (at least in the college classroom). The metaphors he uses to delineate his course's dynamic reveal Coles as Mayor of a Secret City, concerned about his citizens' progress through the alleyways of desire: he speaks of "lead[ing] students down dead-end streets," "block[ing] easy escape routes," "butting up blind alleys" (29). The subject of the course was "language" (28), he said, but language as transport from one world to another ("the dead security of an inherited conception of language which will not meet the world they are asked to experience in the course" [29]), a world which phase-shifted in and out around the class-dwellers—now seeming so real, now gone—but real enough that his students would want to fight hard to hold it fast. Coles wanted students to seize speech, to walk out of his semester-long happening not only with a new awareness concerning language, but with a sense of "freedom—from me, from the course, from an earlier self" (34). As such, his aims are perfectly in keeping with the Happenings: if a student wasn't carried away to heaven, didn't leave his class "better equipped to create worlds reflecting what he most wishes to be" (*The Plural I* 181), Coles knew he'd failed.

His major work, *The Plural I*, is a summative description of that late Sixties class he wrote about in various pieces throughout the late Sixties and Seventies. It attempts to recreate that class, through course materials and assignments, student writing and classroom dialogue, on a week-by-week basis. Each chapter, then, is a series of after-the-fact Happenings, writing textbook as event-traces. Coles's intense desire to transform old forms and selves results in the brutal bluntness in his methods with students. From the depiction of one classroom interchange:

> "Couldn't you have gone into some of this on this assignment if you'd really wanted to?"
> "I don't care to go into my personal life that way."
> "Or is that just a cop-out?" (*The Plural I* 39)

But the almost bitter cynicism that wafts in and out of Coles's book obviously stems from the avant-garde's desperate frustration with the emptiness of current culturally sanctioned forms, the "Perfect English Paper (Clear, Logical, Coherent, Empty)" (39). He's not interested in writing that simply makes points; almost Fluxus-like, he advocated a kind of poetic concretism, short touching realities, "writing . . . which created the illusion of something like human beings involved in human experience" (50). So *voice* is a major concept for Coles (as it isn't for post-Happenings Composition); Coles wants writing with a personal style and sensibility, "as though [the writer] were someone you could talk to" (111). What Coles offers his students is a Happening without the wild trappings or costumes. It's a kind of distilled Happening, the coming together, the immersion into craft and meaning and life, the possibility of being changed. It's an action pedagogy: he thinks about "the *activity*" (134) of his class, what they've written/read/discussed/done together enables them to do; it's a matter of the ongoing situational aggregate that develops, "the creation of an atmosphere, a tone" (134). Like Jackson, the site of composition is there, in the air, above the paper. His book makes a writing teacher realize that, in the end, this is college composition: the situations we give our students, the meanings they make and the responses we have to those meanings, then the insights we share with interested others about those situations and meanings (which go to further shape the situations we give . . .). At the conclusion of his book, he knows he's succeeded from the spontaneous end-of-term Christmas party/love-in (complete with parodic, though sincerely meant, carols and gifts) his students stage for him.

Both Macrorie's and Coles's were pedagogies of the everyday, of simple human truths (or short fabulous realities) expressed in a kind of American Plainspeak. This materiality of the commonplace, or found materiality, is central to the Happenings. Take Rauschenberg's *Spring Training* (1965), in which "a watermelon wrapped in a small carpet bearing the image of John F. Kennedy was carried around the stage by a dancer wearing a portable screen onto which slides of canned food, the city skyline, and the Empire State Building, among other things, were projected" (Spector 236). This is an aesthetic of the everyday as juxtaposed, poeticized. Also in that work, Rauschenberg attached small flashlights to thirty turtles and set them loose on stage; the effect, Rauschenberg felt, "was simply more interesting than conventional stage lighting and [he] compared it to 'leaving the TV on in a room with the sound off' in order to create a kind of oscillating illumination" (Spector 237). Such a compositional strategy makes blatant its material logic, but rather than predetermined (often, rarefied) materials deciding the textual outcome, it's in-filling a space with easily available material. Rauschenberg discusses the creation of *Map Room II* (1965): "There was an old sofa on the stage there. I think I make theatre pieces very much the way I make a painting, which is that I simply have to put something into the space. The sofa already occupying part of the space gets to be a member of the cast" (Kostelanetz *Theatre* 83–84). This is information-search, not as a discerning review of the key texts, but as dumpster-diving. It adds a layer of delight to the process. The way Calvin Tomkins describes Rauschenberg's invention-stage heuristics for his Combines and Theater Events, it's the data-search as beach-combing: "Collage for Rauschenberg was a perpetual adventure. It was fun to search the beach or the city for objects he could use. He was always surprised by what he found, and the objects themselves never failed to suggest new possibilities. combinations he might never have thought of otherwise" (88). Besides just sheer availability, the commonplace offered a genuine difference, an ability to reconnect with the enchanted everyday, that never-absent-never-quite-there sense of life. Composition as commonplace meant art as life and life as exciting: the scene of textual activity became just hanging on the beach or street, attentive to stuff, open to being thrilled. Such an attitude was born out of a conviction that rapturous art could no longer be made from the conventional. So Kaprow, for example, drifting among neon lights, smoke, water, old socks, movies, in search of some entirely unheard of happenings. After Lutz, Happening Composition is candlelight-flicker as course material.

Happenings compositionists in our field afforded that basic materiality to students, who were often encouraged to comb through the stuff of
their life to find a genuinely touching moment. "If the truths are no
more than that Dad helped you learn to ride a bike when Mother, sister,
and Sherry didn't," Macrorie told students, "that's what's expected of
you—the deeply felt truth of that experience" (*Searching* 31). The key is
close observation, reflection, searching for some heightened sense.
Robert Whitman's compositional strategy might best be termed *living*:
"It is in the nature of what we do to listen to people and watch them and
see what they are doing, respond to them. If I am making an object and
I want to find the story of that object, one way to do it is to see what people do when they are involved with it, have people involved with it, and
be involved with it myself" (Kirby *Happenings* 136). Macrorie's, too: "In
part, writing is designing or planning," he acknowledges, but the other
part is "watching things happen and discovering meaning" (*Searching*
38). Even when doing research, he advises a logic of the immediate, one
designed, in the spirit of May '68, to set up situations, encounters: "[see]
how the other members of the class and persons in your community can
help you" (89), "get first to living, speaking sources. . . . [S]how everyone how much knowledge resides in any group of people" (90). Of
course, you can do this with a reading-centered course, too. In an infor-
mation-rich culture, texts are perhaps the most easily available material.
And allowing students opportunities to see where the seductive charms
of texts lie seems very happening (there is always the Ray Charles back-
ing track to help the discussion along, too). Most readers, unfortunately,
offer students high-toned instructor-oriented readings that may do
many things, granted, but rarely thrill. They almost never offer students
a spectacular imaginary of writing, one that gets them wide-eyed about
textual possibilities. Topics for composition are as close as our dreams:
"At night when you're beginning to slide off into sleep, and in the
morning when you're coming out of sleep, let your mind receive possible topics" (*Searching* 62).

The available often means the popular. One of Deemer's sound-bites
is a Bertrand Russell quote: "If the object were to make pupils think,
rather than to make them accept conclusions, education would be conducted quite differently: there would be . . . more attempt to make education concern itself with matters in which the pupils feel some interest"
(122–123). We might think, for instance, of Oldenburg's affection for
the materials of the popular, the quotidian: "The goods in the stores:

clothing, objects of every sort, and the boxes and wrappers, signs and billboards—for all these radiant commercial articles in my immediate surroundings I have developed a great affection, which has made me want to imitate them" (26). Popular culture was a defining staple of the pedagogy of Comp '68; articles in the "Staffroom Interchange" of the December 1968 *CCC*, for example, focused on the use of popular media: Dempsey, Maurer and Pisani told how they were "compelled . . . to revise [their courses] and add new material—everything from an experimental film to *Esquire* cartoons" (337); Altschuler explored the use of film: even if she did it out of a desire "to achieve traditional goals," as her title implies, she still felt the need to defer to "student interest" (344). The Happenings, of course, pushed the use of the popular beyond simple content; they sought their grammar and style there as well. Cage, for example, advocates a compositional grammar "following established film techniques" to re-present temporality, using the film-frame as "the basic [compositional] unit" (*Silence* 5). Williamson was on the same wavelength; he advocated, as "an alternative to written composition classes . . . the film-making class. By making films, the student will still get exercise in what is generally agreed upon as the end of composition classes: clear thought and effective expression" (134).

Certainly, I'm aware that many composition teachers today use the popular, but I wonder just what formal and conceptual liberties students have in writing on it, whether, for example, they can use a Cage/Williamson grammar. Students who use a textbook like Allison and Blair's *Cultural Attractions, Cultural Distractions* get to read Public Enemy lyrics and Jill Nelson on Tupac's death, but then, at the end of that unit (after answering the stock "Reading Reflections" questions), they write a very traditional comparison paper. Sometimes, though, a writer's point is nothing more than that they really love Tupac's music, the deeply felt truth of that experience. But that's not enough for Composition: when students get to write on something cool like rock 'n' roll, it must be on rock 'n' roll as something more, something epochal, something befitting inclusion on the Gallery's walls. So they write about how music is "an agent, a shaping force in our lives, that it is more than an expression of thoughts and feelings, that it does more than articulate what is already 'naturally' there" [Bartholomae and Petrosky *Ways of Reading* 725]). To articulate what is naturally there would mean the popular as what helps us pass the time, pop as the soundtrack to our lives. But tracing passages, becomings, contingencies—limning a life as it is lived at some moment to a pop song—is not Modernist Composition's interest at all. Quite the opposite, in fact, as such abstract terms as "agent" and "shaping force" imply something outside the realm of love, sadness, delight, death, or any terms which describe a decisive moment in very real time. As Lefebvre reminds us, the "manifest expulsion of time is arguably one of the hallmarks of modernity" (*Production of Space* 96). The passage, the encounter, the situation, the temporal—that was the great underlying structural dynamic of the Happenings. It's text as becoming: a record, perhaps, of nothing more human than that Dad helped you learn to ride a bike. Ann Halprin was creatively stuck ("I wasn't very stimulated. . . . I wasn't excited about anything"); she was too constrained by the tradition: "I wanted to explore in a particular way, breaking down any preconceived notions I had about what dance was, or what movement was, or what composition was" ("Yvonne Rainer Interviews" 137). This leads her onto Jackson's bridge of experimentation: "Because I didn't know what I wanted to do, or what I wanted to teach, we set up a workshop situation in which I gave myself permission to explore. Even though I was the catalyst of the group and somehow or other the teacher, I still made it very clear that I wasn't teaching in the usual sense. I didn't feel that I had to know an answer and teach it to somebody" (137).

To explore, she turns to the banality of temporal encounters: "I began setting up situations where we could rely on our improvisational skills" (137–138). Working through one piece, *Apartment 6* (1965), a work for three persons that grew out of a very Macrorian desire for deeply felt truth, "a desire to find out more about the human interior" (154), Halprin realizes, "It wasn't until the last, the sixteenth, performance that I felt we had captured what we wanted to do, which was to simply have two hours on that stage of a real-life situation, in which you as a performer and you as a person were completely the same thing" (158). Real-life situations, then, as the ultimate text. This falling back on the basics of situation, of baseline experience, this text-as-passage, allows not only a blurring of art and life, but a blurring of genres as well, every compositional form/genre indistinct, subsumed by the rhythm of temporal movement. As Cage put it, "Time was a common denominator between dance and music, rather than being specific to music as harmony and tonality were. . . . [Dancers] could make a dance in the same structure that a musician was using" (Kirby and Schechner 59).

Genres need blurring, collapsing, because Composition as a Happening demands new syntaxes for essayist prose. It means something like Rauschenberg's Combines as our model of organization, works described by Michael Kirby as "pieces that seem to be personal journals filled with emotionally weighted statements that are not intended to have an explicit meaning or a logical clarity to the observer" (*Happenings* 40). A new organizing principle, then, one inflected according to the inner statement rather than the outer form. Technique, Pollock reminded us, was "just a means of arriving at a statement" (Wright). Jackson's formal logic, the all-over style, became useful to Happenings artists in the way it frustrated a traditional formal reading. Halprin learned to re-formalize her Happenings, focusing on the inner truths of individual gestures: "There was a deliberate avoidance of any beginning, middle, or end, and of fixed time. Instead, we used intervals of action followed by intervals of stillness. Hopefully, everyone in the audience would be able to perceive each element individually and yet discover relationships and events meaningful to his personal experience" (Kostelanetz *Theatre* 67–68). Oldenburg, too, unlearned formal hierarchies in his Happenings: "Well, one action has neither more importance than another, nor a longer duration. I am trying to create a sense of simultaneous activity, as if you could see in one glance all that was going on in a building" (Kostelanetz *Theatre* 154). This is text as *a continually active field*. There is no formal privileging; Rauschenberg felt, "My main problem in constructing a program of a piece is how to get something started and how to get it stopped without drawing particular attention to one event over another. . . . The shape that it takes should simply be one of duration" (Kostelanetz *Theatre* 90). If, as Deemer said, English Composition as a Happening means "taking the first step toward poetry" (125), then contemporary poetry's influence on the Happenings gives us another indicator of syntactic freedoms that must be allowed. "Certainly the general tendency in much modern poetry to base structure on association and implication rather than on traditional formal patterns and sequential logic is a precedent for Happenings" (Kirby *Happenings* 41). As in poetry, significant form can be no more than words or phrases; from Kirby's description of Red Grooms's *The Burning Building* (1959): "A man's voice from behind the set to the left and the girl seated in the chair on the raised platform began to alternate short staccato words and phrases: 'Abraham Lincoln,' one might say; 'Dick Tracy,' the other would answer. Names of states and of comic strip characters were the most common material, randomly mixed. The series had the rhythm and incisiveness of a football quarterback calling signals" (*Happenings* 130). Leave it to a Big Ten teaching assistant to know the score. It's English Juxtaposition 101, in order to capture the everyday. It's the art of juxtaposition, a key strategy to get that multifarious quality, the "x" factor. And not a juxtaposition that inflects one element according to another. Just a simple overlay, the infra-thin frisson of information brushing against information. And "By that brushing," Cage claims, "we will be made aware of the world which itself is doing that" (Kirby and Schechner 71). Cage's process in creating *Theatre Piece* (1960):

> I had been commissioned to write a piece for two prepared pianos, but I introduced an "x" concept of auxiliary noises. Thus I had other groups of noises: one was produced inside the piano, one was produced outside the piano but on it, and then there were noises separated from the piano— whistles. The parts are not in scored relation, they are independent of one another. Then I wrote a lecture to go with them, involving combing the hair and kiss sounds and gestures that made the lecture theatrical. (Kirby and Schechner 61)

SCENE THREE:

LA MONTE YOUNG'S *COMPOSITION 1960 #5* (UNPERFORMED)/

NEW CRITERIA

Post-Happenings Composition, though, returned to the "habits of correct usage" mindset charted by Albert Kitzhaber in his study of college composition (x). In fact, it took error to the next level: it was more than a matter of what makes writing good; in this era of successful writing, writing with power, it became a question of what makes writing better. Error? Given the Happening's "homemade, unsophisticated technical quality" (Kirby *Happenings* 41), it has to be able to absorb the inevitable errors, not futilely try to eradicate them. "The way to test a modern painting is this: If/ it is not destroyed by the action of/ shadows it is a genuine oil painting./ A cough or a baby crying will not/ ruin a good piece of modern music" (Cage *Silence* 161). Static, then, as integral. Happening compositionists, for example, could never author a book like *On Righting Writing*, one of Composition Studies' turn-texts, helping mark the shift from Happenings to post-. The goal was to enjoy, to be intensified—not to judge. "Whitman considered all sounds that occurred, whether intentional or 'accidental,' part of a noise pattern that was an integral element of the Happening. Sound of various sorts was a natural concomitant of the visible occurrences in [the Happening], but equally as prevalent were the sounds made by the performer-stagehands as they made unseen adjustments and preparations" (Kirby *Happenings* 143).

The idea is to work not on righting the writing, but on digging the writing, to perceive it as omen, as change, and see what it gives you, what if offers you, what it teaches you. The rest is fetish for aficionados. Conventions are not only beside the point, they're to be actively avoided. In French, Happenings were called *décollages*, and the artists were *décollageurs*. *Colle* meant glue or paste, so Happenings implied unsticking. The indeterminate nature of Happenings means, for example, La Monte Young's Cagean definition of music as "anything one listens to" (Kostelanetz *Theatre* 203). Composition as a Happening unsticks writing then, (de)defining it as anything one reads.

The Happenings' bet was that new formal criteria could bring about perceptual change. Young planned his *Composition 1960 #5* for a concert of contemporary music at Berkeley. The piece calls for a butterfly (or any number of them) to be set loose in a performance space. The piece is over when the butterfly flies away. The director of the concert program told him it was "absolutely out of the question" ("Lecture 1960" 74). When Young wondered why, what harm there could be in releasing butterflies into an auditorium, one his friends speculated that perhaps the director "thought it wasn't music" (74). Even a colleague of Young's wrote to him saying he didn't understand the piece. Young wrote back: "Isn't it wonderful if someone listens to something he is ordinarily supposed to look at?" (76). Macrorie's aesthetic in the "I-Search" papers, for example, is to have students write something—information sources—they are only supposed to check out from the library. Deemer suggests a classroom text (Ray Charles music) that's only supposed to be listened to back in the dorm. New textual methods imply new criteria, much different than those that would seem fitting for the chief premise of the course as Kitzhaber spells it out historically: "The course exists to provide immediate therapy for students whose academic future is clouded by their inability to manage the written form of English with reasonable ease, precision, and correctness. According to this argument the course must remedy deficiencies of high school training in English and develop each student's writing skill to the level of competence required by college work" (2).

But according to La Monte Young, What Makes Writing Good is also What Makes Writing the Same. Young is more interested in What Makes Writing New: "Often I hear somebody say that the most important thing about a work of art is not that it be new but that it be good. But if we define good as what we like, which is the only definition of good I find useful when discussing art, and then say that we are interested in what is good, it seems to me that we will always be interested in the same things (that is, the same things that we already like). I am not interested in good; I am interested in new—even if this includes the possibility of its being evil" (73–74). Jean-Jacques Lebel knew only too well the force of Kitzhaber's claim, especially in terms of what it meant for the response to Happenings composition: "Art as it evolves, both historically and spiritually, has to face a reaction similar to that which neutralizes the reform of social structures" (268). But the conservative reaction—say, in terms of a professional view taken of things like surface correctness—fights against the deep perceptual change, the focus on inner view, that Happenings were after. Kaprow knew this: "I have not so much given up professionalism as an evil as I have questioned its meaning. No one knows what good craftsmanship is anymore. . . . Each of us is finding that the professional side of our background is not bad but limiting . . . [that] that part no longer has a purpose" (Schechner "Extensions" 226–227). He urges the would-be creator to "give up your training the way saints gave up their worldly lives" (227). The best professional experience needed to do Happenings, according to Kaprow? Be "ripe for a crisis" (227). There comes a point, Kaprow knew, where Composition's obsession becomes a question of What Makes Writing TOO Good: "extremely slick presentations are fascistic because not only do they expect people to be . . . passive . . . but they tune up the information to such density and intensity that everyone's cowed. Some people like to be beaten" (228).

We can get carried away with technologies in terms of their control over inhuman slickness, but we must leave behind the masochistic exercise and get back on the pathway to the deeply felt truth. Beuys, too, was adamantly opposed to the fascism of the surface. As art and theatre historian Günter Berghaus describes it, Beuys's was a desire for a rhetoric grounded in the earthly: "Beuys was extremely skeptical of modern science and felt that technology, in its present application, was reducing human creativity; people mechanized by machines and conditioned by the electronic media had become victims rather than masters of their environment. Beuys drew on the organic warmth of natural materials and used many metaphors of energy and transformation to indicate his desire for a return to a close and immediate contact with the earth" (327–328). In his journal, Oldenburg reflects on the quotidian sculptured objects (e.g., ice cream bar, chocolates in box, blouse, white gym shoes) he'll make to stock the shelves of his gallery/emporium, Ray-Gun Mfg. Co., for his series of Happenings done in *The Store* (1961): "I want these pieces to have an unbridled intense satanic vulgarity unsurpassable, and yet be art. To work in total art is hard as hell" (7). So, abandon working in total art, obviously; don't be afraid of a little vulgarity. It's Macrorie's urgent plea about praising anything at all good in a student's text. If nothing, try again. Bring him out of his doldrums or fear by honest praise for what he has done well, if only a sentence or paragraph" ("To Be Read" 692). Composition is loath to do that, of course, loath to move from What Makes Writing Good to, say, What Makes Writing OK. "Possibly art is doomed to be bourgeois," Oldenburg acknowledges (8), and possibly Composition is, too. Kaprow, though, sounds very Macrorian: "any avant-garde art is primarily a philosophical quest and a finding of truths, rather than purely an aesthetic activity" (Kaprow *Assemblages* 207–208). It's composition more as performative gesture than ultimate text, focusing on the implicit statement. Ken Dewey: "I would say that my training had convinced me that in order to get the play on right, you had almost to forget about the text to get at whatever it is underneath there—the organic thing that unfolds itself and follows a progression. Stanislavsky referred to it as the sub-text . . . . I feel it more as a gesture" (Kostelanetz *Theatre* 167).

Macrorie picked the right guy to judge that writing contest of his. Just why *aren't* Paul Goodman's criteria used more often to evaluate writing, criteria including, among other things, "sends me . . . unique attitude, warm feeling . . . [non-]brainwashed . . . radical . . . indignant . . . compassionate . . . [with traces] of careful, painful perception, personal suffering, or felt loyalty and disgust" (*Uptaught* 17)? The joke of it is, as Greenberg revealed, those are the secret desire-criteria of Modernism anyway. When Cage lists the emotions Rauschenberg evokes in him, it reads like a primer for a Happenings aesthetic: "the feelings Rauschenberg gives us: love, wonder, laughter, heroism . . . , fear, sorrow, anger, disgust, tranquility" (*Silence* 101). Such feelings are in large part a result of the wide-open materiality of Rauschenberg's work, and Cage catches what Leo Steinberg has termed the flatbed effect of

Rauschenberg's work (surface as repository of cultural artifacts) when he says of a combine-drawing's imagery, "it seems like many television sets working simultaneously all tuned differently" (105). We can't say as interesting things about English Composition's (mega)textu(r)al formation as we can with a Happenings architectonics: "every field of art . . . has had some formative influence on Happenings," Kirby acknowledges (*Happenings* 42). La Monte Young took this cross-disciplinary nature perhaps the farthest: "[D]uring my entire Berkeley period, I was constantly talking to people about the form of the wind and the form of fires. Also, I was talking at that time about the sound of telephone poles, and I liked to quote these words from Debussy: 'Listen to the words of no man, listen only to the sound of the winds and the waves of the sea'" (Kostelanetz *Theatre* 192). Happenings become metaphors for thinking differently about the entire compositional scene, from exigency, through materials, to evaluative criteria.

For Kaprow, the implications in Jackson's painting were clear: they led, "not to more painting, but to *more action*" (220). The locus was not the museumified object, but the human, physical act. In Germany at the time, there was the ZERO group, whose name meant to represent "a zone of silence and of pure possibilities" (Berghaus 318). Otto Piene, one of the group's founders, spoke of the "Zero Happenings" they put on: "the event structure permits an exchange of experience between artist and viewer, not possessions. The event as work of art—as process art—is largely anti-materialistic" (Berghaus 318). It's writing as experience-exchange, text as process-action. That compositional notion was popular throughout Europe, seen most obviously in Beuys's concept of Social Sculpture, an "extension of the definition of art beyond the specialist activity carried out by artists to the active mobilization of every individual's latent creativity, and then, following on from that, the moulding of the society of the future based on the total energy of this individual creativity" (Tisdall 207). Speaking of the works of the Paris Action performers, Pierre Restany (the central critic of the *Nouveau Réalisme* school, of which the Action performers were a part) noted, "These action-performances are demonstrations, the purpose of which is to provoke the direct, spontaneous participation of the public in the process of group communication" (Berghaus 314). And, from Piero Manzoni's 1957 manifesto entitled "The Concept of Painting": "[Painting] is no longer valid for what it recalls, explains or expresses (it is more a question of what it founds), and it neither requires nor is able to be explained as an allegory of a physical process: it is valid only insofar as it is: being" (Berghaus 316). About Manzoni, Berghaus remarks: "The actuality of living and being mattered more to him than symbolic communication. In 1960, he wrote: 'There is nothing to be said. There is only to be, there is only to live'" (317). The text, then, as in-process, as still-formative, as the creator. Beuys chose materials (like fat, dead animals, batteries, chemicals) so that his sculpture would be "not fixed and finished. Processes continue in most of them: chemical reactions, fermentations, colour changes, decay, drying up. Everything is in a *state of change*" (Tisdall 7). And in his notebook, Oldenburg wrote, "It is important to me that a work of art be constantly elusive, mean many different things to many different people. My work is always on its way between one point and another. What I care most about is its living possibilities" (51).

This is a central Happenings tenet of Deemer, Lutz, and the rest: that writing is a lived genre, that composition is much more than text processing, it's a way of being. Deemer often cites Dewey (who was also a major influence on Kaprow, as well) on this theme: education as "a process of living and not a preparation for future living" (Deemer 123), or education "conceived as a continuing reconstruction of experience" (123). And so for Deemer, English Composition becomes this mutual experiencing-together, a co-revitalization. Composition "should actually instruct in nothing, in the sense that a 'teacher' reveals and a class digests. What does a 'teacher' know? He is merely human" (123). And I doubt whether Lutz was even half-joking when he claimed that to rethink writing instruction, "We need to look anew at the student, the role of the teacher, the classroom experience, the process of writing, human nature, original sin, and the structure of the universe" (35). In their class immediately following that mellow candle-lit groove held in the darkened Student Union room, Lutz's students reflected on what such an attempt at a Happenings class taught them about composition; it was the fact of writing as heightened existential trip: "We discussed being sensitive to the world around ourselves and being aware of using many of the senses we somehow or other take for granted. The writer, the students decided, must use more than his eye" (38).

In a true action curriculum, every one in the rhetorical scene becomes a do-er, to the point of eliminating, as some Happenings artists did, the audience. Deemer, complaining of "the present fragmentation of the classroom unexperience (as Cummings might say) into 'teaching' and 'learning'" (122), turned to the Happenings to realize his goal of pedagogy as reengagement, "To remove the 'teacher's' authority. To engage the student's active participation" (123). Kaprow was the most famous advocate of a totally participatory theatre: "A Happening with only an empathic response on the part of a seated audience is not a Happening but stage theatre" (*Assemblages* 196). This is Beuys's dream of everyone an artist coming true by default. For Kaprow, the form was ultimately not as important as the doing, the *operation*:

> When we think of "composition," it is important not to think of it as self-suffi-cient "form," as an arrangement as such, as an organizing activity in which the materials are taken for granted as a means toward an end that is greater than they are. This is much too Christian in the sense of the body being infe-rior to the soul. Rather, composition is understood as an operation depen-dent upon the materials (including people and nature) and phenomenally indistinct from them. (*Assemblages* 198)

New technologies, forms, and genres were needed, then, to work against old, accreted forms and allow composition as participatory performance rather than ritual representation. For this was the basic textual difference between the Happenings and more conventional media, this difference between text as the suggestion of an almost-real-ized meaning and text as the reproduction of an extant reality: text as becoming and text as became. So Berghaus notes the difference between *presentation* and *representation* in his discussion of the European Happenings artists. These artists, influenced by the school of European Pop Art called *Nouveau Réalisme*, were among the global group of Late Sixties artists interested in consciously disrupting tradi-tional high/low distinctions in their art. As Berghaus describes them,

> They formed their collages or assemblages from found and processed frag-ments of reality and materials not commonly associated with high art. The appropriation of objective elements of the everyday world and their *presentation* in compressed objects that expressed the material poetics of reality followed a completely different philosophy from the *representation* of reality through the means of conventional realism. They elaborated a new methodology of perceiv-ing and representing the objective quality of contemporary urban life. (313)

To capture Berghaus's *presentation/representation* distinction, a crucial one for the art of the Happenings, we might use familiar examples from American art and consider the difference between Rauschenberg's *Monogram* (1955–59) and a painting by Andrew Wyeth. Or, in terms of the point I'm ultimately trying to make, the difference between a student riffing in an email message on a lyric by Tupac and a conventional academic essay on some traditional disciplinary topic. In his 1964 novel, *The Penultimate Truth,* Dick continues his preoccupation with the theme of simulation, speaking of what he calls "the 'genuine simulated silver' business . . . the universe of authentic fakes" (33). The works and performances I'm subsuming under the name "Happenings" all have this in common: an attempt to move away from simulation; a presentational art, rather than the re-presentational. The parallels between a regimented, rule-driven representationalism and a corresponding social order were obvious to Farber.

> Which rule they make you follow is less important than the fact that there are rules. I hear about English teachers who won't allow their students to begin a sentence with "and." . . . The very point to such rules is their pointlessness.
>
> The true and enduring content of education is its method. The method that currently prevails in schools is standardized, impersonal and coercive. What it teaches best is—itself. If, on the other hand, the method were individual, human and free, it would teach that. It would not, however, mesh smoothly into the machine we seem to have chosen as a model for our society. (20)

English Composition as a Happening implies new presentational acts, new thoughts, and a pleasure in the doing. There is no already-decided life being ritually, dutifully (re-)enacted. Books like *The Plural I* and *Uptaught* are like a series of stained-glass windows depicting the stations of Comp '68's cross, the stages in these pilgrims' progress to redeem writing instruction. In one of his tableaux, Coles depicts his attempt to rip the veil off of collegiate theme-writing for his students. Brecht-like, he reveals the machinery behind the institutionalization of college composition, exposing it as simply "a technique . . . a trick . . . a game you can learn to play" (36).

> "OK, let's play it. Let's see whether you can play it with any subject and whether anyone can play. Let's play Themewriting."
>
> I asked someone to give me a word, any word. "Man," he said to giggles. Then I asked someone else for another: "black." A third student gave me "TNT." I got them on the board and asked who could put them into a sentence that would write a Theme.
>
> "The day that Man invented TNT was the blackest day in the history of humanity." . . .

How does one then proceed? Well, the opener, of course, set everything up. . . . With the sentence on TNT you'd talk first about peaceful uses of the explosive, in mining, railroading, etc., and then you'd turn to killing, particularly the killing of something called wimminenchilren, then to destruction by remote control, and finally to man's inhumanity to you know what with something like this as a windup: "In spite of the many benefits which the invention . . . great achievements . . control of the environment . . . master of the universe . . . . BUT, when weighed against . . . hideous brutality . . . only conclude . . . not master of himself." (36–37)

We still need to interrupt this tedious exchange. Disturbing cultural reification, literally changing the rules of the game through the materials and methods used, was the whole point of Late Sixties Composition. "Screwing things up is a virtue," Rauschenberg maintained (Kimmelan "Irrepressible Ragman" 26). Take Fluxus founder George Maciunas's set of altered ping-pong paddles: he made one with a hole in it, one with a can of water attached, a concave one, and one convex. The idea was, as Stiles put it, to

exhibit the importance of altering objects to redefine behavioral patterns. . . . [T]hey perplex the user and confound the body, requiring its realignment with conceptually implausible behavior as they upset physical and mental connections and conventions . . . insist[ing] that players reconsider the new demands of the game, the skills it once required, and the patterns the players once performed. In short, players must re-perform, must learn to reinvent mind/body orientations, abilities, and actions. (86)

English Composition as a mutual exchange of altered ping-pong paddles: we offer assignments and students offer texts, both honest, heartfelt attempts to interrupt the game of Themewriting, to insist the rules for verbal meaning-making in college and culture be re-thought. Every compositional occasion becomes a "first-time" writing, rather than a conventional routine to learn to represent.

We need, then, a new, plain-speak language for a new, basic-life pedagogy. Rauschenberg reflects on his compositional method in such a street-rhetoric:

The way I begin is by just having an idea and then if that idea isn't enough, I have another idea, and a third, and a fourth, and composition could be described as an attempt to mass all these things in such a way that they don't contrast or interfere with each other, that you never set up a sense of cause and effect or contrast like black or white; but that they either calmly or less calmly

just happen to exist at the same time. So one of my main problems in composing a piece is how to get something started and how to get it stopped without
breaking a sense of the whole unit that more or less should look continuous and
anti-climactic, or—I don't know the word for it when one thing simply follows
another—progressive. Progressive relationship with the elements. (Spector 236)

The Happenings Era was a time of new discourses, new terminologies,
created to describe the text-as-performative-gesture. Action painting,
Combines, Fluxus Events, *Décollages*, and the Happenings themselves.
Carolee Schneemann called her pre-Happenings works (1958–1963)
"painting constructions" because, like some of Rauschenberg's combines, they often had moving or motorized sections (10). Deemer's decision to find "a new word for 'teacher'" (122); also, Ken Macrorie's
neologistic attempts to recast the scene of college writing, his *Engfish*
and *I-Searches*. We need these new methods, this constant de-determining of composition. Take the formal/conceptual method behind a
piece like Cage's essay "On Robert Rauschenberg, Artist, and His Work."
The essay is very much a piece of scholarship on Rauschenberg and so
might have fallen into an academic frame by a conventional default. But
Cage alters the scholarly space immediately through the formal logic of
the piece: the text is a series of commentaries of varying length (some
long paragraphs, some a few lines), operationalized according to the
heuristic Cage provides: "It may be read in whole or in part; any sections
of it may be skipped, what remains may be read in any order" (*Silence*
98). The paragraphs themselves vary among poetically astute reflections
(and even anecdotes) on Rauschenberg,

> This is not a composition. It is a place where things are, as on a table or on a
> town seen from the air: any one of them could be removed and another
> come into its place through circumstances analogous to birth and death,
> travel, housecleaning, or cluttering. He is not saying; he is painting. (What is
> Rauschenberg saying?) The message is conveyed by dirt which, mixed with
> an adhesive, sticks to itself and to the canvas upon which he places it.
> Crumbling and responding to changes in weather, the dirt unceasingly does
> my thinking. He regrets we do not see the paint while it's dripping. (99–100)

> Certainly Rauschenberg has techniques. But the ones he has he disuses,
> using those he hasn't. I must say he never forces a situation. He is like that
> butcher whose knife never became dull simply because he cut with it in such
> a way that it never encountered an obstacle. Modern art has no need for
> technique. (We are in the glory of not knowing what we're doing.) (101)

more general epigrams,

> Beauty is now underfoot wherever we take the trouble to look. (98)

> Gifts, unexpected and unnecessary, are ways of saying Yes to how it is, a holiday. (103)

and self-conscious introspection,

> *I am trying to check my habits of seeing, to counter them for the sake of greater freshness. I am trying to be unfamiliar with what I'm doing.* (106)

> As for me, I'm not so inclined to read poetry as I am one way or another to get myself a television set, sitting up nights looking. (105)

What a hospitable, fascinating template such a strategy might be for students: a loose form in which to record comments about the subject under critical investigation, as well as more personal, reflective prose. Cage's is the performative text, not as representational (*This is not a composition*), but as presentational (*It is a place where things are*). Do we think our students are not like John Cage, don't have the sort of insight that might make such a simple textual arrangement come alive? But that was the pedagogical mission of Macrorie, Deemer and Co., letting them bring forth themselves full of their own experiences and ideas and feelings. Just like the postmodern Museum is now data-site, the Text can be best seen as catalogue, flatbed, a place where things are, a *passagen-werk*. As Oldenburg's *Store*: namely, a compendium of objects, loosely connected around a general function, existing—changing, even; as needs and values change—in space and time. From his notebook for *The Store*:

> My piece is called a store because like a store it is a collection of objects randomly placed in space.

> one's own body the form of change

>> keep form, even after making, in a situation of change
>> not only mechanical but psychological
>> moving sculptures are often all fixed
>> mine are not
>> the law of my work is time
>> change (51)

He referred to his performance work as "a theater of real events (a newsreel)," as "giving hair and muscles and skin to thoughts" (80). So

The Store (and all text) as storehouse of ideas, an experience-exchange, a warehouse in the American Psychogeographic.

Vostell's stated reasons for working in Happenings: they "present a do-it-yourself reality . . . and sharpen the consciousness for the inexplicable and for chance" (Berghaus 320). That consciousness-sharpening potential in a work is what Berghaus calls the *activating* component of a presentational Happening (320), and that's a good way to think about what I respond to in student prose, its power to activate some change in the writer and reader (beyond just mere pleasure or displeasure over whether certain formal conventions have been properly activated). Take the email message I was sent one day by my student Neal C. Ohm. The class had spent several sessions listening to songs by Tupac Shakur and discussing them, as well as reading interviews with the rapper and assorted articles about him. I ask my students to send me traces of their thoughts in email messages periodically through the course, and one day during our unit on Tupac, I received this haunting e-message from Neal:

> What is the difference of our perception of 2Pac opposed to a 45 year old white male's? Not only thinking of you when I ask that (because you are very absorbing/open-minded) but my close-minded father. I asked my dad what he thought of 2Pac and it really disappointed me. He didn't speak from his heart, it was just a repeating (I could tell) from what he read/heard from the News. . . . To show him what I am doing with myself at school, and to mildly influence his one-sided opinion, I let him read the articles you gave us. I actually watched him read them, his facial expressions. What a change.

Neal's note is not exactly academic writing, but when I got it (as is the case with so many of the e-messages I get from students) the small kernel of reality Neal presented thrilled me. It came to me the way, as Kaprow describes, we stumble upon a small, charmed arrangement of simple imagery in the contemporary urbanscape, an arrangement which our perception re-figures into a kind of accidental shrine or fetish, containing all the charmed aura associated with such objects: "slip[ping] out of focus as quickly as it is seized upon . . . burst[ing] blatantly forth out of the nameless sludge and whirl of urban events, precisely where and when it is least expected" (*Assemblages* 164). It made me think of the worlds of both the students and the texts I choose, of the two meeting, and a change being enacted—in Neal's case I can see the change occur, one he tries to further exscribe into his life, his father's life, and mine. Neal becomes a Happener: bored with the cultural recirculation of tired, meaningless forms (his dad's initial repetition of the media line on 'Pac), he plans a little Happening for his audience-participant, leading them through a tour of counter-media materials. Reading Neal's event-score lets me re-enter the action of his compositional scene; it is, as Coles put it, allowing oneself to "be pushed . . . to the edge of irresponsibility, to becoming as a reader what I never figured I'd have to become as a reader of student writing—not better, but more alive" (Coles and Vopat 328). La Monte Young gave the name *event-score* to his pieces, purposefully setting down very sparse scores for his work, so they could be idiosyncratically interpreted in performance. Student writing, then, as concrete, simply-structured event-score: the outline or proto-text for the way the final piece would be realized in one's re-activation of it (through reading, say, or discussion). It was George Brecht who first applied, in 1959, the term *event* to the field of performance. Stiles speaks of "his interest in 'the total, multi-sensory experience' that could emerge from a 'situation,' the 'event' being the smallest unit of a 'situation,'" achieving "maximum meaning with a minimal image" (66). It's English Composition as Fluxus Performance, the scoring methods of which are "predominantly textual in character and are distinguished by clarity of language, economy, and simplicity of words" (Stiles 66). I want to apply Stiles's terminology to student event-scores, seeing them as "practical initiations, invitations to unlimited, or 'open,' interpretation that plunge the reader into a conceptual performance of the text" (67). As Neal's email did for me.

Oldenburg, in describing his own work, also hovers around this notion of form as performative score: "The form here is not so much environmental as fragmental. . . . You are to imagine the missing, that is, what is called negative space or absent matter, counts for something. These are rips out of reality, perceptions like snapshots, embodiments of glances" (49). A possible technique: students move through an interesting collection of materials (rather than, as usual, a collection of essays)—the coursepack then becomes, say, a miscellany of quotations, pictures, poems, advertisements, brief excerpts from novels, cartoons, crossword puzzles, and many other things—then watching the textual progression that happens (even joining in, as I respond to those e-*pensées* I'm sent). Dancer Steve Paxton describes Rauschenberg's technique in performances such as *Linoleum*: "In his choreography, he animated people with tasks in images . . . by couching people within images and then allowing images to coexist, collide, or follow one another" (264). Writing Classroom, then, as Fluxus Festival, animating people with tasks in words, music, and images. Oldenburg's aim with his work on the *Store Days* pieces provides a way of conceptualizing the work students might do in a writing course: "my aim is to develop under these concentrated circumstances a sort of kernel of infinite expansion . . . so that at the end of this season I shall have ten extremely powerful seeds" (83). Happenings composition, then, is students working, under the concentrated circumstances of a college term, on developing kernels, seeds, expandable data-chunks that can flourish later in interesting ways. That's a wholly different way of thinking about form; it means writing not as some verifiable end-form, but writing as growing, changing, maybe even culturally transforming (as Neal Ohm's message worked on me, deepening my appreciation of the true power of rap music in the lives of the current generation). Happenings Composition, then, *literalizes* that basic perceptual shift in the environment of artistic reception. The space of reading a composition becomes a Vygotskyan zone of proximal development. The viewers do, indeed, make the pictures—the "pictures" being the experience, the situation, the theatre in which the work takes place; composition in the now-expanded field. Deemer, too, was focused more on "current media" than "the so-called academic essay" (122). He was an early prophet of the sound-bite, quoting McLuhan on how aphorisms were a much more epistemologically interesting form "just because they are incomplete and require participation in depth" (122).

This transformative intent of Composition as a Happening implies a very different conception of the audience than writing instruction traditionally holds, with its allegiance to the rhetorical triangle. Robert Whitman thought of the audience for his Happenings in terms of trying to evoke the sublimity of artistic expression he felt; anything else was beside the point: "you make available to them the same kind of perception you think you've seen somewhere . . . that thing that exists that you really can't define in any other way except through the piece. [It's] the difference between an artistic experience and something you can talk about; and the last has to do with philosophers and critics and people like that" (Kostelanetz *Theatre* 232). Rauschenberg maintained, "your audience is not a familiar thing. It is made up of individual people who have all led different lives" (Kostelanetz *Theatre* 85). For most of Composition, audience is not made up of individuals, most often it's an undifferentiated, predictable construct, the *reader.* Even concepts like *interesting* or *boring* become more difficult to predict rhetorically when the ultimate goal is perceptual transformation. Rauschenberg: "I'm also interested in that kind of theatre activity that provides a minimum of guarantees. I have often been more interested in works I have found very boring than in other works that seem to be brilliantly done" (85). Happeners saw the audience as environmental rather than judgmental. Kaprow:

> It is not that I object to painting or theatre or music or dance or anything like that. It is that I do not wish to be compared with them, because it sets up all kinds of unnecessary discussions. People say that you're not doing this right, that you're not doing that right. . . . [I]n what I call the normal environment, there are audiences all the time. If we get out and dig up a manhole cover in the street somewhere, as I gather some practical jokers do all the time, and if some people stand around and watch, as they do normally when people are working or something unusual is going on, then that group is a part of the normal environment. They are not audiences coming to watch a performance; they may just pass on very shortly to whatever they have to do. Whereas if we go to the theatre or the rodeo or the circus, we are sitting there not just to watch a show but to judge it with a whole battery of standards. (Kostelanetz *Theatre* 117–118)

In the interview in which Kaprow made that comment, his interviewer, Richard Kostelanetz, realized this implied a nonformal, nonconventional, situationist rhetoric, one interested in extension, in text as seminal: "[W]hat you are creating is a situation opposite that of a book. . . . [W]hat you want to do is create an entity that will in turn stimulate a variety of stories" (119). To achieve composition as a way of being, as action writing, informal writings become a key part of a Happening curriculum, as valid a (non-)genre as the formal essay. Halprin's pedagogy was to explore movement/body possibilities in exercises and phrases that combined into a fixed dance, then it was off onto more experimentation. She called each exploratory phase a "jump." For example, for one dance she was inspired to give every dancer a bamboo pole right before they went out to perform. "We had to do the dance that we'd always done, holding bamboo poles. . . . This was the beginning of our next jump. I became preoccupied with movement in relation to environment" ("Yvonne Rainer Interviews" 141). Composition as a Happening is a series of jumps through forms, problems, materials; exercises that would bring the writing into some new place. Halprin: "I wanted people to have tasks to do. Doing a task created an attitude that would bring the movement quality into another kind of reality. It was devoid of a certain kind of introspection" (142). Yvonne Rainer, who was once a student of Halprin's, recalls,

"I remember that summer I was here with you and you assigned tasks. But as I understood it, the tasks were to make you become aware of your body. It wasn't necessary to retain the task but to do the movement or the kinesthetic thing that the task brought about" (142). So it is with the writing in a Happening classroom: the actual text production is immaterial (*not necessary to retain the task*), it's the awareness (as writing body) the student takes, the awareness of her creative skills. Such a pedagogical dynamic recalls Coles, who wanted "to keep things open, to pursue an idea in such a way as to allow a student to have ideas of his own, to find himself in the act of expression, to become conscious of himself as becoming through the use of language or languages" ("The Teaching" 113).

SCENE FOUR:

ROBERT RAUSCHENBERG'S *FIRST-TIME PAINTING* (1961) /

PROCESS

If writing becomes action, a way of being, Composition as a Happening is Composition as Process: the form equals the making. If modernity tries to banish time, Happenings art counters by being time-encoded. Rauschenberg is again illustrative here, in the way he strove in his art to acknowledge what Spector calls "the durational experience of life itself" (227–228). Cage even called Rauschenberg's *White Paintings* (1951) a "clock of the room," because of the way their plain white surface so vividly registered the minute, gradual effects of a room's changing light (Spector 227). Even more obvious is Rauschenberg's *First Time Painting* (1961), the Combine painting he did onstage during an avant-garde performance concert, with a ticking clock placed in it as a built-in marker of the real-time duration of the actual composition. To further emphasize his process, Rauschenberg placed contact microphones near the surface of the canvas so the audience could hear the work's production evolve. There is a boldness in Rauschenberg simply deciding that here, now, during this performance, I will create; the work becomes much more a record of the doing rather than a planned, traditionally made artifact. Every text, then, as a new work, acknowledging the inherent temporality of its creation. (Rauschenberg wanted that same element of risk in the audience as well: "I'm really quite unfriendly about the artist having to assume the total responsibility for the function of the evening. I would like people to come home from work, wash up, and go to the theatre as an evening of taking their chances. I think it is more interesting for them" [Kostelanetz *Theatre* 85–86].) Such a process-defined composition locates the act of composing very presently, in the now. Neal's email to me about Tupac occurs in a social space far different from Composition's traditional academic timelessness, where students "need to understand the degree to which their writing is not their own," but "part of a tradition" (Bartholomae "What Is Composition" 26). Neal's note, wholly his own, is a journal entry from a life. The under-text is: "This happened to me, and it was interesting. I sat down and read these articles, about a rapper I had known about for a while—I even talked with my father about it—and all at once I could feel time and life intensely for a while." The product is simply a textual trace of its process, a behavior-record of a life, a meditative fragment from an ongoing, lived performance. It is a small canvas of action writing: compared to a well executed salon work, an academic essay, what Neal has done is "American and rougher and more brutal, but he is also completer" (Greenberg, in Friedman *Energy* 96). To talk about it, I find no terms in the discourse traditional Composition makes available; I can only turn to Greenberg on Pollock (sounding very much like Coles on Humphrey) and say Neal "points a way beyond the easel, beyond the mobile, framed picture, to the mural, perhaps—or perhaps not. I cannot tell" (in Friedman *Energy* 96). In any case, I witnessed it, and I changed. As such, it enacts what Kristine Stiles sees as the crux of Fluxus performance: it "compels a reevaluation of the human situation and provides revisionist forms for reevaluating intersubjective connections that enable us to rethink and, thereby, reenact the social world" (65).

The ultimate function of the work, then, is to invite re-entry into the process-site, to reactivate it and capture that sense of becoming. To be hopefully changed. The space of reception becomes the space of production: not a Museum but a transitional space, a passage. The "happening" is a perfect term because that is the very locus of the work: the changing, the occurring, the durational, the situation-ing, the social as a sculpting. In a 1968 interview, Cage speaks of "the world. The real. You say: the real, the world as it is. But it is not, it becomes! It moves, it changes! It doesn't wait for us to change . . . It is more mobile than you can imagine. You are getting closer to this reality when you say as it 'presents itself'; that means that it is not there, existing as an object. The world, the real is not an object. It is a process" (*For the Birds* 80). According to Stiles, it was Cage's combination of Eastern philosophy and Western phenomenology that "allowed the artist to stress behavioral processes as the critical elements that precede the objective state of art as a completed 'thing'" (66). Such "behavioral processes" are rich, holistic. Nancy Spector, for example, speaks of Rauschenberg's work, especially his situational work like the performance pieces and Combines, and notes how the work "exists literally in time or bears the layered traces of its production; it presents the body in motion or reacts to the motion of its audience members; and, above all, it seeks to invoke senses beyond the purely visual" (228). She notes, too, that in Rauschenberg's performance pieces "the performative gesture or corporeal action was emphasized over the discrete aesthetic object" (238). This key focus, the performing body, is one Composition has historically downplayed: rarely has it gone beyond the relatively limited (and usually almost wholly cognitive) bodily metaphor of *seeing* to conceptualize both its production and reception. A more wholly carnated body (moving through banal time) was a central focus in the way process/product issues were theorized in the larger context of performing art history. Spector points out how so much of the performance-based composition of this era—Happenings, Fluxus, Cage, Rauschenberg, the Judson Dance Theater, Zero, and other American and European neodadaist groups—showed a "general shift away from the production of static objects toward the performative gesture experienced in real time" (239). In Composition Studies, the textual performance may have been done at some point in real time, but the aim is to establish that performance as somehow timeless, emblematic of all textual process in any space and time (this, of course, is the very rationale for composing process research). And process and product must be kept distinct (Sommers: "what one has to say about the process is different from what one has to say about the product" [154]). The performance quality of action painting tilts the discursive field around the compositional scene in the Fifties from Greenbergian critical reflection to a performative, process-oriented *this*ness. Structure is beside the point. The process, the doing (within an ethos of intensity) is everything. Cage recalls, "*Theatre Piece* [1960] was composed in terms of what I would call process rather than structure. When we do anything and bring it to a performance, it reaches to a point that becomes realization. At that realization point it can be viewed . . . as structured, though it wasn't" (Kirby and Schechner 63).

Process becomes the indisputable fact of creation—persevering in the work, following a voice, tuning out the influence of interpretation. Composition has spent its time teaching students how to process the feedback given on products, subsuming process in interpretive commentary; rather, we should stress the hard work, the durational reality of composing, the articulate reality of its doing. "The only defense against being trapped in someone's idea of your intention is to keep changing your field and work very hard, so that the *fact* of your creation, which will always be the most important thing, always overshadows its interpretation" (Oldenburg 141).

Time-encoding means space-encoding as well, site-specificity, and it's no accident, I think, that some of the most compelling Happenings-era Composition—like *Uptaught, The Plural I*, Lutz's piece—are accounts rooted in a certain classroom group at a certain time. Many Happenings artists felt strongly about the non-iterable, site-specificity of their Happenings. Rauschenberg, for example, "categorically refused to have [his performance pieces] reconstructed, believing their ephemerality to be a constitutive factor in their existence" (Spector 243n). His most memorable performances all came out of the mix of a certain arbitrary, found set of materials, in a certain space, at a certain time. Rauschenberg's first performance piece, *Pelican* (1963), for example, was a totally arbitrary accident: it was commissioned by mistake, when a pop art festival organizer unwittingly listed Rauschenberg on the program as choreographer rather than his real position on the tech crew (Paxton 263). The ad hoc nature of the piece continued in Rauschenberg's compositional strategies. The festival was to be staged in a D.C. skating rink: "When I heard the piece would take place in a rink I said, why not use roller skates. I favor a physical encounter of materials with ideas on a very literal, almost simple-minded plane" (Spector 234). This is typical of Composition as a Happening. Deemer provides the caveat of site-specificity in his article: "It is with reason I have neglected to present a more explicit blueprint for the happening after which to model a reconstruction of English Composition. In the first place, happenings happen; they are not passed down from one to another. Spontaneity is essential. Each 'teacher' must inspire his own happening" (124).

Kaprow, too, wanted Happenings performed only once, not "passed down," so the process of that one performance, however ragged, became the sole text. "Aside from the fact that repetition is boring to a generation brought up on ideas of spontaneity and originality, to repeat a Happening at this time is to accede to a far more serious matter: compromise of the whole concept of Change" (*Assemblages* 194). Of course, current generations seem raised less on originality, but the concept of Change still holds sway in any transformative pedagogy. Here, process equals an engaged sense of self, an ethical-aesthetic way of being.

Radically different, it cuts far deeper than that notion of process Composition Studies began to fetishize in the post-Happenings era, one which determined "the processes that should occur on the way to the final draft . . . whichever kind of writing you are doing" (Elbow *Writing with Power* 7, 12). This notion of process was not so much a *living on the canvas* as it was a kind of replicable technique, like cross-stitching or preparing a hit of speed (later, of course, it was a kind of mental operational pattern, like the steps one takes in solving a cryptogram). But, as Jackson realized, technique is nothing to fetishize. Rauschenberg, when asked about technique, didn't really know how to respond: "What do you want, a declaration of love? I take responsibility for competence and hope to have made something hazardous with which we may try ourselves" (in Cage *Silence* 101). All Writing, then, as Basic Writing; and Basic Writing as Basic Life.

SCENE FIVE:

RICHARD SERRA'S *SPLASHING* (1968)/

POST-HAPPENINGS

Ah, the Happenings. All dressed up in ice cream and candlelight, they had nowhere to go in Composition. Before we knew it, our goal went from participants in the electric drama reengaging their hearts to having students "appreciate the varieties and excellences of academic discourse" (Lindemann 311). Deemer gave up and went off to write plays. Macrorie and Coles directed their energies more locally, more creatively (Macrorie at writers' workshops, Coles doing young adult fiction). And by 1976, Lutz had been absorbed by the CCCC Executive Committee, writing material that shows how far removed from the Happenings he'd become: reviewing a manual on doublespeak, Lutz '76 is suddenly at a loss ("I am not sure exactly how to classify this book. It's not a collection of essays but a collection of materials—quotations, pictures, poems, advertisements, brief excerpts from novels, cartoons, crossword puzzles, and many other things" ["Review" 97]); confessing the failings of his logical retinality: "Perhaps I like my books too linear, but when I am confronted with a page that consists of nine quotations ranging from people such as Bertrand Russell to Adolf Hitler, along with two cartoons, I am not sure what I would do with the material in class" (98). (Oh, why couldn't he remember the meaning his students took from their Happening, how the writer, they decided, must use more than his eye?) He complains the collection contains "so many bits and pieces that I suspect both students and teachers will have a difficult time making a coherent whole out of the material"; it's simply "a source-book that provides raw material," he says (98). One can't help but think that the William D. Lutz who came upon the collection in 1970 could have built an entire pedagogy of disorientation around such purpose-fully destabilizing raw material, allowing students to comb through detritus and not come up with predetermined coherence. That was 1976, though, and those were different times in Composition. But the disappearance of the Happenings' promise of a new path to poetry and intensity haunts the scene of Composition as no other departed guest has. It's difficult to see Composition of the last thirty years as anything other than a retreat. "Perversions of Form" was the phrase that leaped to Lloyd-Jones's mind in the brief retrospective of the field he gave at the 1997 CCCC in Phoenix.

One of the central moods of this book, then, is disappointment, partic-ularly with what supplanted the all-too-brief era of Happenings Composition, that brand of academic professionalism that dominated the field theoretically in the last quarter of the twentieth century. Clement Greenberg, with his strict formalism, almost willed the Happenings move-ment. It was inevitable artists would chafe as art became more and more determined by theory. It's the same with Composition Studies. No won-der compositionists became starved for formal richness (however kooky and home-grown) when college writing became, as Kitzhaber writes, a place for one "to fix, once and for all, the habits of correct usage and clear and orderly writing so that teachers in other departments need take no special pains about these matters" (x). Italian art historian Franca Mancini offers us a thumbnail sketch of criteria for neo-avant-garde gen-res like the Happenings and performance art when she speaks of "attempt[s] by twentieth century artists, from the historic avant-garde . . . to the present day, to overcome [the limitations of] their specific lan-guage and to interconnect with differing expressive languages—dance, music and the new technologies" (Talalay 5). In that brief phrase, Mancini hits the signature-style criteria of Happenings Composition: anti-conventional, expressive, discursively hybrid, and technologically innova-tive. This is not at all post-Happenings Composition, which is all about conventions; which sees its retreat from expressionism into academicism as some sort of progress; which prefers a purified, taxonomized monophony to hybridity; and consigns discourse on technology to a sub-realm of its discipline. What distinguished Late Sixties Composition is that it reflected the dominant, heady-but-vital art movements of its time. Happenings Compositionists were looking for something startling, active, and non-traditional to wake the classroom up a little: say, the Beatles, "Eve of Destruction," composition-as-film, the Happening itself. Can post-Happenings Composition say the same? In the 1976–79 era, for example, did it have punk or funk or performance art in it? Did it see rap music rising in the late Seventies/early Eighties? No, it elided such rich possibilities totally. And so I read Macrorie today as still delivering the news; I listen to his words the same way I listen to Bob Dylan or Miles Davis, as the still-hippest sounds. It's hard to understand the general indifference that meets his work (or Coles's, Deemer's, et al.) today. I read him the way I do the situationists, (and as the situationists themselves read artists like de Chirico), as having painstakingly laid out bold, poignant blueprints for change, relegated now to libraries and footnotes. Meanwhile, we have class after class of students with their personal inner lives, desires, fears; their variety of interests and abilities; their sometimes strong, sometimes clumsy, sometimes tentative immersion into the material of language.

I wish I could name this as post-Happenings Composition: work from one of my favorite compositional spaces from the Late Sixties (and alas, another loss-site): the Leo Castelli Gallery's storage warehouse, where a new (but maybe not) aesthetic was being ushered in at the end of 1968. Postmodern art historian Douglas Crimp's description of it is suffused with the sadness of roads not taken:

> The site was an old warehouse on the Upper West Side in Manhattan used by the Leo Castelli Gallery for storage; the occasion, an exhibition organized by minimal sculptor Robert Morris; the moment, December 1968. There, strewn upon the cement floor, affixed to or leaning against the brick walls, were objects that defied our every expectation regarding the form of the work of art and the manner of its exhibition. It is difficult to convey the shock registered then, for it has since been absorbed, brought within the purview of normalized aesthetics, and, finally, consigned to a history of an avant-garde now understood to be finished. But, for many of us who began to think seriously about art precisely because of such assaults on our expectations, the return to convention in the art of the 1980s can only seem false, a betrayal of the processes of thought that our confrontations with art had set in motion. And so we try again and again to recover that experience and to make it available to those who now complacently spend their Saturday afternoons in SoHo galleries viewing paintings that smell of fresh linseed oil and sculptures that are once again cast in bronze.

> Of the things in that warehouse, certainly none was more defiant of our
> sense of the aesthetic object than Richard Serra's *Splashing*. Along the junc-
> ture where wall met floor, Serra had tossed molten lead and allowed it to
> harden in place. The result was not really an object at all; it had no definable
> shape or mass; it created no legible image. (150–151)

Serra's *Splashing* literalizes Kaprow's claim that new works, after Jackson,
would extend off the canvas and into the room. In the same way, for
example, Schneemann thought of her 1968 Happening *Illinois Central* as
"an exploded canvas, units of rapidly changing clusters" (167). *Splashing*,
then, is a Jacksonian gesture, a drip composition, an action painting *en
fer*. Such a process-trace, offered as legitimate work to Composition's
Museum, would be treated like the work of a Basic Writer (Crimp, however, turns what would be Composition's response, *The result was not really
an object at all; it had no definable shape or mass; it created no legible image*, into
a point of fascination, not criticism). Happenings artists got used to the
denigration: Schneemann's *Illinois Central* included a scene of bodied
composition, in which the partially undressed performers, blindfolded,
moved towards each other on stage and then began slow physical contact. At least one audience was not having it: Schneemann recalls, "At
Nassau College, male students in the audience went berserk over the
physical contact between the men (performing): they screamed obsceni-
ties, threw basketballs and cups of water at us" (170). Every Gallery, it
seems, tells the same basic story: work is either judged collectible, curat-
able, befitting the Museum's walls, or it's rejected as worthless drippings,
scorned as perversity. Ah, but things are viewed differently in the warehouse: there, simple, bold compositional gestures are made that resonate with some viewers forever after.

It speaks, as well, to the place of art in our curriculum, to how willing
we are (or how strongly we feel the need) to take that next step towards
stirring, deeply affective poetry, or how comfortable we are with a curriculum that seeks only to have students "appreciate the varieties and
excellences of academic discourse" (Lindemann 311), actively banishing
the poetic. Deemer felt "another, and I think more important, advantage
to modeling English Composition after the happening. Western education has long suffered under the delusion that scientific abstraction is
the unique way to knowledge. This, unfortunately, to the neglect of the
poem" (125). The minor status of art in our culture is bad enough, its
almost total absence in our current curriculum, in a field which used to
be known as the language arts, is even worse. Jean-Jacques Lebel:

The extremely limited space assigned to art in society in no way corresponds to its mythical volume. To pass from one to the other—at the risk of breaking the law—is the primordial function of the Happening.

It is avant-garde art that liberates latent myths; it transfigures us and changes our conception of life. If this is a crime, there is no reason why we should deny it—on the contrary, we should claim it for our own. (271)

Our whole aim became to demystify the process of composition, not enchant it. We began to desire not just a clear, replicable process, but a clear way of talking about it. The focus became "develop[ing] control" (Sommers 148). But in Happenings Composition, student writing was seen as much more mystery-dependent; compositionists of 1968 could have been Benjamin's Surrealists: concerned, not with "the logical realm of ideas," but rather "the magical realm of words" (232); "the writings of this circle are not literature but something else—demonstrations, watchwords, documents, bluffs, forgeries if you will, but at any rate not literature" (227). Speaking of Robert Whitman's rehearsals for *The American Moon* (1960), Kirby notes, "Sections were never rehearsed separately. The overall 'flow' was more important to him than specific details" (*Happenings* 140). That sounds like it could be advice to writers. Which flies in the face, for example, of Sommers's insistence on the importance of non-jargony commentary (she chides "the generalities and abstract commands given to students," by "the teacher [who] holds a license for vagueness" [153]); but, of course, words like *flow* really do mean something. Adopting such notions as Sommers's because they seemed so much more rigorous and professional than the hokey romanticism of the Happenings marked the beginning of the end. Then, when those once-arbitrary now-unquestionable notions became the foundational lexicon, scientistic research studies could be run to further extend the simulation, making it seem as if that lexicon actually named a reality (namely, the excellent varieties of academic discourse).

SCENE SIX:
KRISHNAMURTI'S *FREEDOM FROM THE KNOWN* (1969) /
"IT IS RAINING OH MY LOVE"

For some reason, expressionism has become an *outré* term in Composition Studies (though certainly not in any other field of art). The thought of students mining the refuse lot of their own lives to trace moments of becoming, of passages, has become laughable if not downright worrisome in post-Happenings Composition, a solipsistic exercise that takes time away from the crucial interrogation of power and knowledge. But really what more revolutionary content can there be? According to Blanchot, "The everyday is platitude (what lags and falls back, the residual life with which our trash cans and cemeteries are filled: scrap and refuse); but this banality is also what is most important, if it brings us back to existence in its very spontaneity and as it is lived—in the moment when, lived, it escapes every speculative formulation, perhaps all coherence, all regularity" (13). The informal, Blanchot reminds us, is "what escapes forms—becomes the amorphous" (14) It is the site of the insignificant, the unapparent, but also "the very movement of life," and, ultimately, "the site of all possible signification" (14). Happenings Composition prizes the stuff left behind, the otherwise-discarded, because it reveals a particular life. If the class is in any way a Happening, then the ad hoc—the prewriting, quizzes, exercises, notes, journals, email, false starts—is sometimes the most permanently satisfying text of all. Think of Beuys, who used one of his student's discarded works in his piece *Palazzo Regale*; Beuys, who focused on the spirituality of materials, knowing a thing is much more than its exterior might lead one to believe. These too-often forgotten scraps, simply used in Composition as fodder for the final draft, are similar to what Oldenburg calls "residual objects," the costumes and stage properties that might otherwise be tossed when the final performance is over.

> Residual objects are created in the course of making the performance and during the repeated performances. The performance is the main thing but when it is over there are a number of subordinate pieces which may be isolated, souvenirs, residual objects.
>
> To pick up after a performance, to be very careful about what is to be discarded and what still survives by itself. Slow study and respect for small things. Ones own created "found objects" The floor of the stage like the street. Picking up after is creative. Also their parti[c]ular life must be respected, where they had their place, each area of activity combed separately and with respect for where it begins and ends. (110)

Composition has all its prewriting and writing-to-learn activities, but what's prized is the essay; the process-scraps (like Neal Ohm's Tupac riff) are rarely spoken of with the same fascination as the product. Oldenburg knew the spellbinding ethereality inherent in scraps, especially those from the banal world of the everyday: "at the center of my use of pop art is a love for the rejected, inexplicable and simple" (142).

This goes beyond just materials and content to actual language and persons. There is a basic humanity and love always at the core of Composition as Happening. Macrorie knew: "For decades white Americans have livened their language by introducing into it expressions from the streets and nightspots of Harlem, part of the dialect of supposedly ill-educated black Americans. . . . I remember now that when Martin Luther King, Jr., was assassinated, the white, college-educated mayor of Memphis spoke hypocrisies in Engfish and the black garbage workers spoke truths eloquently" (51). *Eloquently* is a term we might sniff at now, as belletristic, politically outmoded. But a true sense of eloquence, in whatever guise, is something to build a curriculum around.

Reader-based prose? Writer-based prose? The distinction is meaningless in Happenings Composition where the viewer makes the pictures. Cage's compositional advice? As much indeterminacy as possible to let interpretation flow: "The structure we should think about is that of each person in the audience. In other words, his consciousness is structuring the experience differently from anybody else's in the audience. So the less we structure the theatrical occasion and the more it's like unstructured daily life the greater will be the stimulus to the structuring faculty of each person in the audience" (Kirby and Schechner 55). Composition, then, the movement of a few people through a brief moment in time and space. For Cage, the temporal, durational dynamic of process (stimulating, reactivating, possibly changing) replaces the information-space product-structure (decoding, processing); he advocated text as a kind of action painting in Jackson's all-over style: "setting a process going which has no necessary beginning, no middle, no end, and no sections. . . . The notion of measurement and the notion of structure are not notions with which I am presently concerned" (Kirby and Schechner 55). Rauschenberg was drawn so heavily to dance and performance due to the "extreme unfixedness in image" it offered (Spector 241). Curator Nina Sundell says of Rauschenberg's *Elgin Tie* (1964)—the piece in which Rauschenberg descends through a skylight on a rope which has a collection of objects and clothing tied to it (things Rauschenberg would employ as he climbed down), into a barrel of water perched on a flatbed truck (a cow is also led on-stage at one point), all to a soundtrack by David Tudor, played on a switch panel, which transformed the performance space's fluorescent lights into bell-sounding audio—"The action, with its allusion to ritual pageantry and its peculiar blend of drama, risk, and absurdity, seems a metaphor for the essence of theater" (12). To pursue Composition as a Happening, must we have students, then, descend from ropes, lead cows into class, be ice cream cones and change flavor? Not really, but in the context of an academic space, they must come as close as possible to that—to text that's a peculiar blend of drama, risk, and absurdity, which seems to me a metaphor for the essence of composition. Dick Higgins saw one reason for the Happenings' demise in the way they grew increasingly grandiose and expensive to make. Higgins counterpointed them to the still-vibrant spirit of Fluxus, whose artists never expected to sell and kept things minimal (Higgins and Higgins). So, then, Composition as Fluxus, letting us repeat the spirit but not the sins of the past. Small subversive gestures, like inviting Neal Ohm to riff on Tupac.

But having students riff on Tupac is certainly not post-Sixties Composition. When I spoke about my writing-with-rap class on an Internet listserv, one of the more famous voices of contemporary composition, posting anonymously, smirked, "you can probably make money betting that the sharks taking courses where the dominant culture trains its young are not studying rap" (S). So, topics controlled tightly now in post-Happenings Composition (according to political and academic goals) as they were prior to the Sixties (for strictly academic reasons). Doing something other, like writing heartfelt *pensées* on Tupac Shakur, for example, is suspected as pandering. But Rauschenberg felt, "There is no poor subject. (Any incentive to paint is as good as any other.)" (in *Silence* 99). Composition cannily embraced politics in the Eighties, but it abandoned aesthetics. What resulted was politically-correct formalism. Abandoning aesthetics in favor of a political simulation ironically meant turning away from the most significant issues of textual politics. In the late Sixties, compositionists were asking the same crucial questions— about what counts as composition, its material base, the relationship between composition and life, and the pressures of institutionalization—that the visual and performing arts asked but never stopped asking. Questions that menace me off and on, every day in my class, in an attempt to see the classroom as a place of human social exchange, resonating with the aesthetic dimensions of common experience. We need Jackson echoing in our ears: "The method of painting is the natural growth out of a need. I want to express my feelings rather than illustrate them." ("Narration"). Jackson leads one right to a rhetoric of human presence. I read the lines from Red Grooms's 1959 Happening *The Burning Building* and I can't see how rhetoric can go any further.

My love my love I am writing my love I am writing you today I am
writing you today as it is raining oh my love my love I must be leaving I must be leaving you today. (Kirby, *Happenings* 122)

Many of our theorists speak knowingly about writing with power, about
the need to "make students proficient users of the varieties of texts they
[will] encounter in undergraduate education," so they don't leave our
class feeling "powerless in the face of serious writing" (Bartholomae and
Petrosky *Resources* 1), but I can only shake my head, knowing the true
power is the power of love, voiced in what Ashbery would call "language
on a very plain level" (*Shadow Train* 3). So, in my quest for a basic passional literacy, I listen in the copper beeches' moaning to a dream from
nowhere. Jackson would understand. Jackson, who heard the sounds in
the grass, who spoke to friends of "the universal energy" and "the reality
. . . in the trees" (Naifeh and Smith 688), who, one morning, on the way
to his studio, tells Lee, "I saw a landscape the likes of which no human
being could have seen" (Friedman "Interview"). And the painting of
that landscape gives rise to the Happenings.

But then who gave rise to Jackson? If Jackson is the Happenings' origin, who's his? Impossible to tell, the influences on him were myriad.
But I want to tease out one, another scene of Late Sixties Composition.
We start in 1929, however, with Jackson in the midst of what would
prove his educational disaster at Los Angeles Manual Arts High School.
Socially inept, unmotivated for academic work, he wouldn't last there
long. But he was fortunate enough to have had one person knock down
a few institutional walls for him, a flamboyant art teacher named
Frederick Schwankovsky. Schwankovsky was a member of the
Theosophy movement, whose members believed the next great
advance in mankind's spirituality was happening in California at that
very time, in the person of the new Messiah, the Divine Spirit,
Krishnamurti. Schwankovsky heard Krishnamurti speak from his camp
in Ojai, California, read his books, and became good friends with him.
He introduced the sixteen-year-old Jackson to him, who was overwhelmed with Krishnamurti's teachings. Preaching the individual path
towards awareness that must be taken, they offered solace to a disaffected youth struggling to create. "For Krishnamurti, the test of all
truth—and later, for Jackson, the test of all great art—was 'Does it flow
spontaneously from an inner impulse?'" (Naifeh and Smith 131).
Jackson spent six days at the camp in Ojai, listening to lectures and
question-answer sessions.

QUESTION: Isn't the theory of individual freedom really anarchy?
KRISHNAMURTI: If the individual is not happy . . . he is creating chaos and anarchy around him, by his selfishness, his cruelty. (Naifeh and Smith 139)

Fast forward.

Well it's 1969, ok
All across the USA
It's another year for me and you,
Another year with nothing to do. (Stooges "1969")

So went the Late Sixties' Ballad of Disaffected Youth, searching for nothing more (or less) than a "real cool time." Or, as the Stooges put it in another song off their eponymous first album, "No fun, my babe, no fun. No fun to hang around, feeling that same old way" (a song covered eight years later, in a more desperate, implosive version, as an encore on the Sex Pistols' American tour, because youthful disaffection, it seems, is always happening).

Krishnamurti understood disaffection. "I don't know whether you have ever seriously faced this issue of why your heart is empty," he wonders at the close of his 1969 classic *Freedom From the Known*. Basically, it's the same work he's always written, a reflection on the search for meaning, energy, intensity, and vitality. He asks the only important compositional question, the question posed repeatedly by Happening artists: "is it possible for a human being living an ordinary everyday life in this brutal, violent, ruthless world—a world which is becoming more and more efficient and therefore more and more ruthless—is it possible for him to bring about a revolution . . . in the whole field of his thinking, feeling, acting and reacting?" (118).

The book could be a blueprint for Happenings Composition as it offers a simple, meditative awareness as the only way to bring about intensity. The answer, apparently, can indeed be heard in the trees' moaning: "Most of us don't know how to look at, or listen to, our own being any more than we know how to look at the beauty of a river or listen to the breeze among the trees" (24). Krishnamurti voices Deemer's desire for reengagement: "There is beauty only when your heart and mind know what love is" (86); and he speaks with the authority of a TA from Madison: "you can tremendously influence the world if in yourself . . . you lead actually every day a peaceful life . . . a life which does not create enmity. Small fires can become a blaze" (118–119). His course requires a mind "always fresh, always young, innocent, full of vigour and passion" (19–20), one which realizes "the intellect is not the whole field of existence," and "that all ideologies are utterly idiotic" (16). In such a curriculum, students would be asked, not to be an ice cream cone and change flavors, for surely the Happenings died of their own kookiness; instead, perhaps, maybe just Macrorie's May '68, Fluxus-like goal of students using available technology "to record short fabulous realities" ("To Be Read" 688). Writing Classroom as NOW Festival.

SCENE SEVEN:

SAM SHEPHARD'S *LA TURISTA* (1967)/

CODA

Let me close with a question. What if we got a text from a student one day that seemed little more than a message, brief and expressionistic? One from a young student, hardly more than a boy, "a dark skinned boy" (Shepard 258), one who came (we think) from a barren part of the Mexican desert? A message from the contact zone, then: the only contact zone I'm interested in; the contact zone where the dark and timeless desert of the primitive meets the brutal, violent, ruthless world of modernity; the one we pass through every day of our lives; the one Sam Shepard explores in every theatre-event he writes. Sam Shepard, who "has said that Jackson Pollock was important to him, but what seems more active in his sensibility," according to Richard Gilman, "are emanations from the 'happenings' phase of painting and sculpture, collage in the manner of Johns and Rauschenberg" (*xiv*). So we read this text, and as we read we realize it's a kind of brief reverie, a short riff about music and the boy's father. He muses lovingly, but in a style of speech unusual in our world, about how they'll be together soon:

> And we'll sit together and smoke by the side of the road, until a truck comes by heading toward my home. And my father will kiss me good-bye and climb on the back and drive off, and I'll wait for another truck going the other way. A pale blue truck with a canvas back, carrying chickens and goats, and a small picture of the Madonna on the dashboard, and green plastic flowers hanging from the rear view mirror, and golden tassels and fringe around the window, and striped tape wrapped around the gear shift and the steering wheel, and a drunk driver with a long black beard, and the radio turned up as loud as it goes and singing Spanish as we drive out into the Gulf of Mexico and float to the other side. (Shepard 276)

If we got such a message, we wouldn't screw up our face because we couldn't "conceive of this writer as at work within a text and simultaneously, then, within a society, a history, and a culture" (Bartholomae "Inventing" 162), right? Cause we'd understand that his message originated "precisely from the breakdown or absence . . . of all such traditions in America" (Gilman *xiii*), wouldn't we? Recognizing this message, in its own small way, as what it is: a chant of paradise, written by a student who just might feel "a counter-cultural need for a new (or perhaps ancient) communal, youthful performative space" (which is how Jeff Kelley accounts for the persistent interest in the Happenings and which sounds to me foolishly like it should describe a writing class [*ix*])? I mean, we wouldn't see this writer as substandard, unproficient, as powerless in the ways of undergraduate writing, would we? Wanting to supplant his dialect with the kind of speech that made the right impression in a job interview? Fearing for him a future where he'll "[eat] nothing but rice and beans all his life . . . [selling] Coca Cola to passing cars" (Shepard 260)? We wouldn't, out of that fear—which is maybe the emptiness of our own heart—cynically fire back a reply like "You'll never make it alive!" (Shepard 276). Would we?

Marcel Duchamp
"Box in a Valise"
1941

Box in a Valise
© 2002 Artists Rights Society (ARS), New York / ADAGP, Paris / Estate of Marcel Duchamp. Philadelphia Museum of Art: the Louise and Walter Arnsberg Collection

Carolee Schneemann
"Chromelodeon"
1963

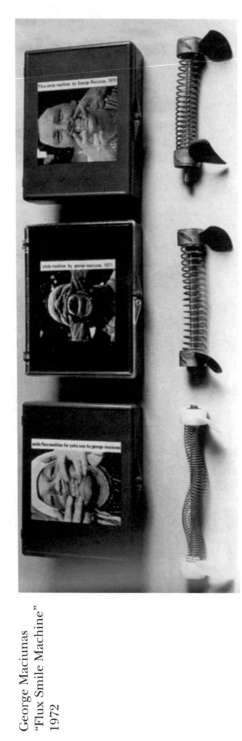

George Maciunas
"Flux Smile Machine"
1972

Smile Machine
Photo by Brad Iverson. The Gilbert and Lila Silverman Fluxus Collection, Detroit.

George Brecht
"Direction" from *Water Yam*
c. 1963

Direction
The Gilbert and Lila Silverman Fluxus Collection, Detroit.

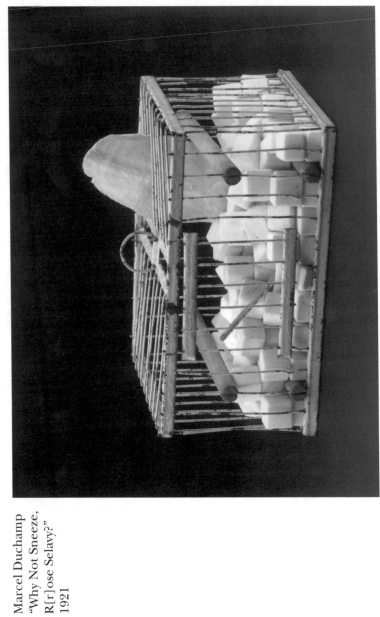

Marcel Duchamp
"Why Not Sneeze,
R[r]ose Selavy?"
1921

Why Not Sneeze?
© 2002 Artists Rights Society (ARS), New York / ADAGP, Paris / Estate of Marcel Duchamp.
Philadelphia Museum of Art: the Louise and Walter Arnsberg Collection

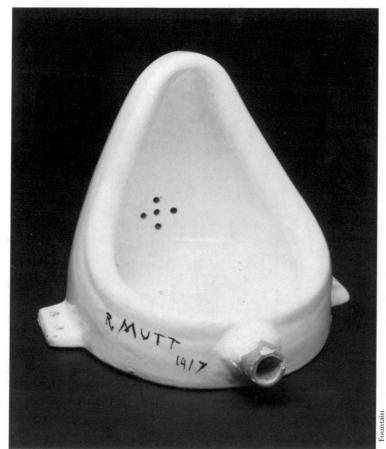

Marcel Duchamp
"Fountain"
1917

Marcel Duchamp
"Rotorelief No. 8 (Hoops)"
1935

Marcel Duchamp
"The Bride Stripped Bare by Her
Bachelors, Even" ("The Large Glass")
1915–1923

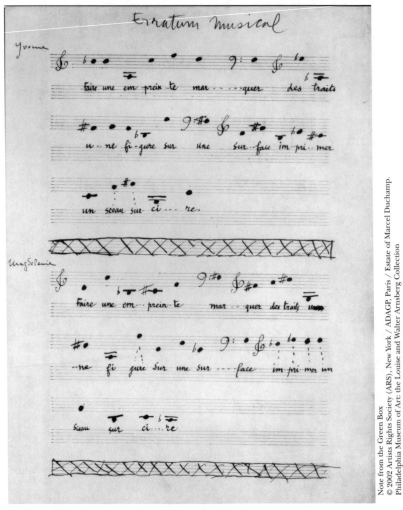

Marcel Duchamp
"A Note from the Green Box"
1934

Marcel Duchamp
"Nine Malic Molds"
("Large Glass, Detail #2")
1941

Nine Malic Molds
© 2002 Artists Rights Society (ARS), New York / ADAGP, Paris / Estate of Marcel Duchamp.
Philadelphia Museum of Art: Bequest of Katherine S. Dreier

Jackson Pollock
Photograph by Hans Namuth

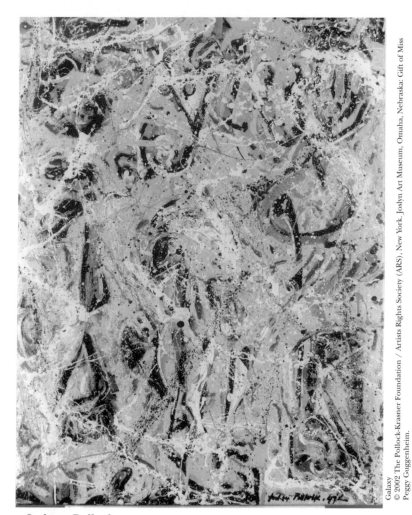

Jackson Pollock
"Galaxy"
1947

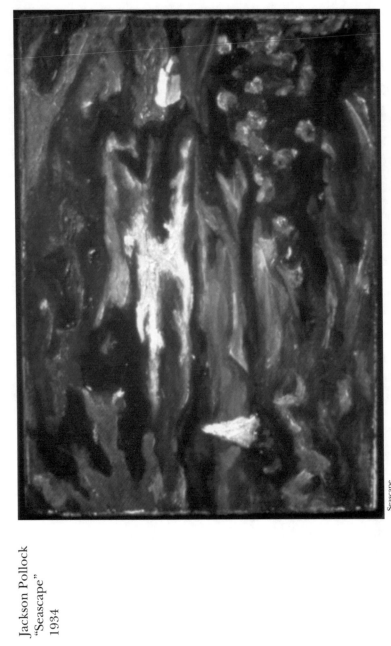

Jackson Pollock
"Seascape"
1934

Jackson Pollock
"Nember 29"
1950

Jackson Pollock in his studio
Photograph by Hans Namuth

Robert Rauschenberg
"Linoleum"
1966

Linoleum
Photo by Peter Moore © Estate of Peter Moore / VAGA, New York

Robert Rauschenberg
"Map Room II"
1965

Map Room II
Photo by Peter Moore © Estate of Peter Moore / VAGA, New York

Robert Whitman
"American Moon"
1960

American Moon
Photo by Robert McElroy. © Regents of the University of California and the University of California Press.

Allan Kaprow
"A Spring Happening"
1961

Spring Happening
Photo by Robert McElroy. © Regents of the University of California and the University of California Press.

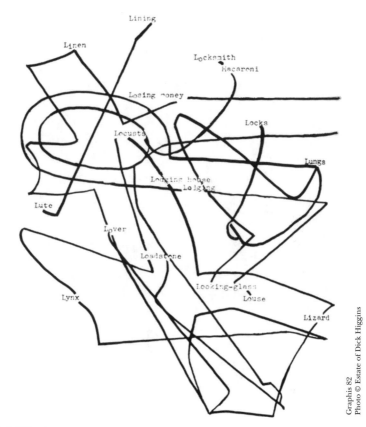

Linen
Lining
Locksmith
Macaroni
Losing money
Locks
Locusts
Lungs
Lodging house
Lodging
Lute
Lover
Loadstone
Looking-glass
Lynx
Louse
Lizard

Dick Higgins
"Graphis 82"
1962

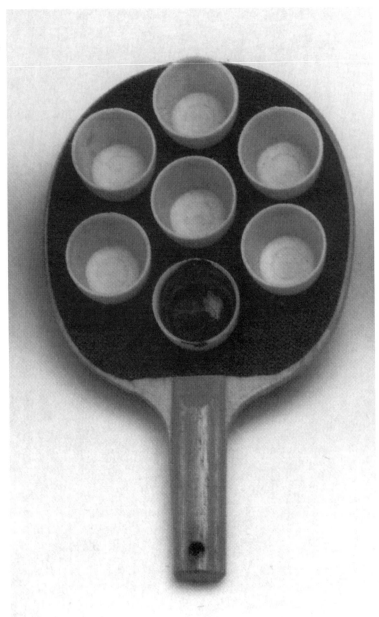

George Maciunas
"Concave Racket"
1972

Nam June Paik
"One for Violin Solo"
1962

Ben Vautier
"Regardez Moi Cela Suffit"
in Nice c. 1962

4

WRITING CLASSROOM AS A & P PARKING LOT

But we are unable to seize the human facts. We fail to see them where they are, namely in humble, familiar, everyday objects: the shape of fields, of ploughs. Our search for the human takes us too far, too 'deep,' we seek it in the clouds or in mysteries, whereas it is waiting for us, besieging us on all sides.

Henri Lefebvre

The shadow of the city injects its own
Urgency . . . Our landscape
Is alive with filiations, shuttlings;
Business is carried on by look, gesture,
Hearsay. It is another life to the city.

John Ashbery

TEXT AS ARCHITECTURE/URBAN PLANNING

Happenings came about, in large part, because Allan Kaprow realized that Jackson Pollock had exposed the central lie of composition. Jackson, Kaprow had understood, realized that traditional notions of form had become entirely beside the point. In Jackson's art, "the confines of the rectangular field were ignored in lieu of an experience of a continuum going in all directions simultaneously, *beyond* the literal dimensions of any work" ("Legacy" 26). Jackson saw the arbitrariness of form: "The four sides of [Jackson's] painting are thus an abrupt leaving-off of the activity which our imaginations continue outward indefinitely, as though refusing to accept the artificiality of an 'ending'" (55). Something—call it the trace of the work—exists on the canvas (on the page), but the real force of the work continues its existence in the mind, the body, in the self as *engagé*. The real composition is in the being. And so, as writers, we must pursue the world beyond disciplinary tradition, "dazzled by the space and objects of our everyday life, either our bodies, clothes, rooms, or, if need be, the vastness of Forty-Second Street" (56). Because of such new concerns, art after Pollock doesn't do well in the more traditional, formalist-inflected architectonics of the gallery space: "it is becoming harder and harder to arrange a show without compromising present needs with older methods. The work never looks quite right; it fits uncomfortably with the glaring geometry of the gallery box"

(*Assemblages* 153). The institutional parameters of traditional exhibition-sites are not conducive to composition as being, as becoming, because, conventionally, their design is inflected away from the relatively undetermined worlds of nature and the street.

> All the marvelous potentials of transformation and interactivity between art, the public, and nature are out of the question. And even when a little of this is made possible, it is so tentative that the old habits of gallery-spectatorship preclude any vital response on the public's part, limit the work's duration to the standard three-week show, and do not prepare anyone for the idea that nature could ever be involved, much less welcomed.
>
> The only fruitful direction to take is toward those areas of the everyday world which are less abstract, less boxlike, such as the out of doors, a street crossing, a machine factory, or the seaside. (*Assemblages* 182)

Kaprow's reading of Pollock's gesture set the tone: performance art historian Richard Schechner, for example, sees as the Happenings' goal "an attempt to bring into a celebratory space the full 'message-complexity' of a downtown street" ("Happenings" 217). Kaprow's own Happenings began to drift out of even detourned gallery spaces, into Bleecker Street courtyards, caves in the Bronx—one even took place throughout three cities (Los Angeles, Boston, and New York) over a four month period. Ken Dewey's *City Scale* (1963), done with Anthony Martin and Ramon Sender, was a five-hour audience tour which Kostelanetz describes as "closer to pure happenings than anything else" (*Theatre* 164). In it, Dewey staged a trip through various scenes of the city, "events . . . purposely ambiguous so that audience members would not have the certainty of knowing whether a given incident had been planned or was happening anyway" (Dewey, et al. 173). These were events (such as a singer in a storefront doing German *lieder;* a couple arguing; a choreographed "car ballet," with gels on the car's headlights; a model seen undressing in an apartment window, and a lone man on top of a billboard) "which impinged upon the life of the city, interacted with it, transformed it, or absorbed it into the structure of the work" (173). The European Happenings artists, especially, favored the cityscape as performance space. One of Wolf Vostell's early Actions, for example, *Der Theatre ist auf der Strasse* (*The Theatre Takes Place on the Street*) (1958), "consisted of a group of people walking down Rue de Tour de Vanves and reading aloud text fragments they found on torn posters" (Berghaus 321). Regarding the connection between the Happenings and the street, Jean-Jacques Lebel was adamant: "Art must literally 'go down into the street,' come out of the cultural zoo, to enrich itself with what Hegel (without humor) called the 'contamination of the casual.' Thus, the first European Happening . . . took place partly in the streets and on the canal of the Giudecca in Venice" (282). The German Happenings artist Bazon Brock knew the power of the street as text: in 1965, in Berlin, he presents an Action entitled *The Street as Theatre*, in which he sets up rows of chairs on the sidewalk of a busy street and sells tickets to the quotidian drama unfolding there (Berghaus 334). Their goal, then, was Macrorie's: the short, fabulous realities of the everyday; the stuff of ordinary social interaction as rich text.

And so, to afford us a better contextual backdrop for the writing class as Happening, I am calling for a new urbanism in Composition Studies. An architecturally-based metaphor, focused around the notion of city planning and city life, seems justified to use in discussing the textual spaces we demand our students inhabit. Bataille, for example, has criticized architecture in the way it imposes an order on people. As Hollier reads Bataille: "Architecture captures society in the trap of the image it offers, fixing it in the specular image it reflects back. . . . Architecture does not express the soul of societies but rather smothers it" (*Against* 47). Such a reading points to my desire for a new urbanism, in the way I find Composition's cultural spaces cramped and uninhabitable. I want to open Composition Studies up to the same urban responsibilities (and possibilities) as architecture. We already draw on the architectural metaphor in our field: we talk about designing curricula, about the classroom as communal space where meaning is constructed socially; we even use the notion of writer as *bricoleur/euse*.; indeed, Halloran has commented on "the very notion of 'structure' [in composition], which suggests a quasi-architectural three-dimensional ordering of parts" (172–73). And anyway, the precedent is already there to read the one theory in terms of the other: Vincent Scully has praised Robert Venturi's *Complexity and Contradiction in Architecture* for "its significant introduction of several important modes of literary criticism into architectural writing" (Venturi *Complexity* 12). Venturi, then, shows it is possible to look at the composition of a building qua composition, to give the building a textu(r)al analysis. I would like to return the favor, in a sense, and use a few ideas in architectural theory (especially as they relate to city-planning) in order to read the scene of the writing classroom. I want to reconfigure the verbalscape of the writing classroom around the very

notion of landscape, cityscape; to reposition the architectonics of college writing more strictly according to architecture. I want to bring the
field back down to earth, to a grounding in everyday life, inflecting our
spatial scene according to the rehumanizing tenets of Jackson's Forty-
Second Street. As part of my discussion, I want to get some Modern and
Postmodern arché-texts speaking to each other: to orchestrate my dialogue, I've chosen Donald Stewart's "modern textbook for freshman
composition" (1), *The Versatile Writer*, along with Bartholomae's
"Inventing the University," as representative of the contemporary practices of university writing instruction (the objection may be raised that
Stewart and Bartholomae should by no means be lumped together, representing as they do the two antinomies of the academic/expressivist
continuum; I hope to show, though, that the Modernist, formalist trend
in our field renders any such distinctions meaningless). Representing
the voice of Postmodernity (overlaid on beats from Venturi, as well as
the French theorists of everyday life) will be some samplings of electronic vox pop—the synchronous online discussion transcripts of some
of my first-year basic writing students, as well as (from the "real world")
the email of an anonymous female worker in a large computer corporation. I want to theorize these arché-texts to show why I feel the need for
a new academic urbanism, one that's more happening, and also to
begin tracing the forms such an urbanism might take. I want to look at
the formal texts of our curriculum as the buildings which comprise our
cityscape, and, as discursive wanderings in and around those buildings,
samplings both from student classroom discussion (in this case, as captured by networked technology) and "real world" professionspeak. The
use of e-discussion transcripts is important because without my experience of teaching writing in a networked classroom—of having a technology that enables more fiercely styled verbal interchange from
students than essayist prose allows—I might never have stopped and
smelled the roses. I offer, then, not so much a theoretical perspective *on*
writing instruction, but a theory *from* instructed writers, one which has
been informed by the ethos of the objects of our practice and has
attempted to read it back into a more general theory of composition.

    First, some notes on the architectural theory of Robert Venturi,
pointing to his desire for new urban concepts. Venturi reacted against
the Modern architectural program, which, according to Vincent Scully,
"came more and more to embody the Greek temple's sculptural, actively
heroic character. Venturi's primary inspiration would seem to have

come from the Greek temple's historical and archetypal opposite, the urban facades of Italy, with their endless adjustments to the counter-requirements of inside and outside and their inflection with all the business of everyday life" (*Complexity* 9). Venturi offered a new architectural program, a "theory of ugly and ordinary" as he called it, reappropriating the very terms that Modernist Philip Johnson used to denigrate his work. Modernism, for Venturi, offered a banal, simplified program of purity, clean lines, and easy unity, which seemed at odds with the Mannerist, Baroque, and Rococo buildings he loved, buildings full of "complexity and contradiction," as he put it in the title of his first book. To Mies van der Rohe's famous Modernist dictum "Less is more," Venturi shrugged, "Less is a bore" (*Complexity* 17).

An architecture that excluded complexity was one at odds with the way we actually live everyday. For example, Philip Johnson's open, clean, almost entirely glass-walled pavilion houses, for Venturi, would be absurd to actually dwell in, in the way they "ignore the real complexity and contradiction inherent in the domestic program—the spatial and technological possibilities as well as the need for variety in visual experience. . . . The building becomes a diagram of an oversimplified program for living—an abstract theory of either/or. . . . Blatant simplification means bland architecture" (*Complexity* 17). History taught Venturi that architecture is rarely simple and pure, that it often reflects life in the way (as Dr. Johnson said of Shakespeare's dramas) "the most heterogeneous ideas are yoked together by violence." And so he developed his "Gentle Manifesto" for "nonstraightforward architecture":

> Architects can no longer afford to be intimidated by the puritanically moral language of orthodox Modern architecture. I like elements which are hybrid rather than "pure," compromising rather than "clean," distorted rather than "straightforward," ambiguous rather than "articulated," perverse as well as impersonal, boring as well as "interesting," conventional rather than "designed," accommodating rather than excluding, redundant rather than simple, vestigial as well as innovating, inconsistent and equivocal rather than direct and clear. I am for messy vitality over obvious unity. I include the non sequitur and proclaim the duality.
>
> I am for richness of meaning rather than clarity of meaning; for the implicit function as well as the explicit function. I prefer "both/and" to "either/or," black and white, and sometimes gray, to black or white. A valid architecture evokes many levels of meaning and combinations of focus: its space and its elements become readable and workable in several ways at once. (*Complexity* 16)

In his first book, a study of architectural form employing the textual methods of literary criticism to read buildings formally, Venturi drew on Pop Art to find meaning in the degraded, commercial aspects of the landscape—what he termed the "honky-tonk elements"—realizing they were not only here to stay, but that they served (and reflected) people's needs and tastes. Where Modern architecture viewed the bastardized architectural hodge-podge of Main Street as an abomination, Venturi asked honestly, "Is not Main Street almost all right?" (*Complexity* 104). As proof, he analyzed the buildings and layout of the commercial centers of town—the seeming contradictions of scale, the use of inflected fragments, and the arrangement of contrapuntal relationships—to find the inherent unity and complexity in the vernacular arché-text.

In his second book (written with Brown and Izenour), Venturi went beyond mere formal analysis, reading architectural design into a theory of the urban symbolic. He went right to the heart of the beast, the center of architectural excess and vulgar commercialism, Las Vegas, in order to see how the modern urban sprawl worked. He sounds the keynote in the document he and Brown used to introduce their project, a studio conducted at the Yale School of Art and Architecture in 1968: "[Our] study will help to define a new type of urban form emerging in America and Europe, radically different from what we have known; one that we have been ill-equipped to deal with. . . . An aim of this studio will be, through open-minded and non-judgmental investigation, to come to understand this new form and to begin to evolve techniques for its handling" (*Learning* xi). The lessons he learned from this project, he urged on his profession, suggesting the need (as Brown puts it) "to learn a new receptivity to the tastes and values of other people and a new modesty in our designs and our perception of our role as architects in society. Architecture for the last quarter of our century should be socially less coercive and aesthetically more vital than the striving and bombastic buildings of our recent past" (*Learning* xvii). Architects' social coerciveness lay in their preference to *change* existing conditions rather than (merely, unheroically) to *enhance* them. It should not be a question of imposing values of classical purity on people's desire for spectacle, but rather learning to make the spectacular speak as well as possible. Modernists refuse the vernacular: "I. M. Pei will never be happy on Route 66" (*Learning* 6).

Venturi found a valid logic, a coherent program, in Las Vegas. It was a logic based on cars and fast movement in open space—meaning, for example, a heightened use of signs (big, bright, eye-catching, able to be seen from the road) and a scaled-down notion of architecture (low buildings to help the air-conditioning, neutral design so they don't detract from the signs). The A&P parking lot became a primal compositional scene for Venturi:

> The A&P parking lot is a current phase in the evolution of vast space since Versailles. The space that divides high-speed highway and low, sparse buildings produces no enclosure and little direction. To move through a piazza is to move between high enclosing forms. To move through this landscape is to move over vast expansive texture: the megatexture of the commercial landscape. The parking lot is the *parterre* of the asphalt landscape. The patterns of parking lines give direction much as the paving patterns, curbs, borders, and *tapis vert* give direction in Versailles; grids of lamp posts substitute for obelisks, rows of urns and statues, as points of identity and continuity in the vast space. (*Learning* 13)

Such a setting, Venturi found, calls for a more complex architectural program, one combining a variety of media beyond simply light, form, and structure in space. It calls for "an architecture of bold communication rather than one of subtle expression" (*Learning* 9). Traditional demarcations get blurred in such an architecture. One watches, for example, in before-and-after photos, the facade of the Golden Nugget become cannibalized by its neon sign until it's unclear whether the building is a sign or the sign is a building. Modernist theory could not read such a facade because it had "abandoned a tradition of iconology in which painting, sculpture, and graphics were combined with architecture. . . . Modern buildings contained only the most necessary messages, like LADIES, minor accents grudgingly applied" (*Learning* 7). Las Vegas called for a reading in which attention was paid to moving, rather than stable, objects; it was inclusive, messy, not exclusive and simple. We only term it sprawl because its inclusive pattern is one we cannot yet read. Possibly because of the messy inclusiveness, the studio-course in which Brown and Venturi's Las Vegas study was done (including 4 days in LA and 10 in Vegas) became a transformative Happenings for the participants, a Deweyesque urban-tour-as-event-scene, one they could even coin with an appropriately mock-theatrical name: "Toward the end of the semester, as the spirit of Las Vegas got to them, the students changed the [course's subtitle] to "The Great Proletarian Cultural Locomotive"" (*xi*).

Now, why do I call for a new academic urbanism? Because I have learned from the existing landscape. Students are *there*, according to

Composition texts, somewhere outside the city limits of writing; we need to get them *here*, to a place where they can do a certain kind of work with a certain set of materials, in a form that will have a payoff in the "real world" (or in our notions of what constitutes their preferred self-development or empowerment). But the spaces we train them to design and inhabit are simplistic, arbitrary, and constrictive. 'Minor accents grudgingly applied'? Not my students; they have words plastered all over themselves, from their clothing brands to their sports team logo's to their concert T's. It's logo as *logos*. Our students represent the grammar and lexicon of Main Street, of the Strip. The sign grammar of Vegas is theirs naturally. As such, they enter the puristic Greek Temples of our classrooms as exiles from Main Street, denied their verbal heritage, their textual homeland. We take away their status as writers immediately. They are "students," a term mutually exclusive from "writer": "You have the choice," Stewart lays down the law, "of thinking like a student or like a writer" (17). We strip from them all the honky-tonk elements they may have brought in with them from Main Street, chastening them for their values in tones patronizing at best:

> How about clothing? Those of us who were children of the Great Depression had no problems. We had one good suit, if we were lucky. Mine was a hand-me-down from my older brother. For school I had one or two pairs of corduroys, two or three shirts to choose from, and one pair of shoes. I didn't even know any rich kids who had wardrobes comparable to those of many college students today. Do you suppose today that somewhere, on some campuses, there are students who have so many clothes that they get up at six-thirty every morning but never get out of their rooms until ten because they are worn out from trying to decide what to wear? (Stewart 6)

It's always troublesome when a self-styled expressivist winds up sounding like Allan Bloom: "What poor substitutes for real diversity are the wild rainbows of dyed hair and other external differences that tell the observer nothing about what is inside. . . . As it now stands, students have powerful images of what a perfect body is and pursue it incessantly. But deprived of literary guidance, they no longer have any image of a perfect soul, and hence do not long to have one. They do not even imagine that there is such a thing" (64, 67). Ironically, it is in the name of authenticity that we rob them of their native Main Street tongue:

> The problem is television trash and commercials. They supply words for you. That is, you do not go through the process of shaping your experience in your own words; you borrow from the stock of television clichés and thus

cheat yourself of the opportunity to put an individual stamp on your experience. You may say, "Well, television clichés are no problem for me because I don't watch much TV. That's for younger kids." So, you were never younger? And you have now obliterated all remnants of TV language from your brain? Perhaps. Then how much time do you spend listening to your stereo? And how do you verbalize your feelings about love and loneliness? In *your* language or in the lyrics of the songs sung by your favorite recording group? Think about it. (Stewart 13)

Donald Stewart will never be happy with "Route 66." Students' self-identification with pop trash is not part of our preferred program for their authentic, empowered voice; neither is working out or buying clothes. Thus we raze the student landscape, until it is as flat as Bloom's "clean slate"; then we give them the blueprints for our temples and demand they (re)produce their new (already colonized) cityscape likewise. It's the (auto)piazzafication of Main Street. How can we expect people to care very passionately about erecting our grand monuments on the still-freshly agent-oranged ruins of their homeland? Heidegger: "Only if we are capable of dwelling, only then can we build" (160). Guiding Composition's practice is what Venturi reacted against in his urbanism and what informal "residual object" texts like e-discussion transcripts often stand in opposition to: a program of the universalization of the existing landscape. Our universal notions of good writing become a totalizing program of design control. Our program is to clone students into Optimal Verbal Technology cyborgs called Versatile or Successful Writers. As architectural critic Kenneth Frampton notes, "Modern building is now so universally conditioned by optimal technology that the possibility of creating significant urban form has become extremely limited," with such conditioning representing "the victory of universal civilization over locally inflected culture" (17). And so he calls for an "architecture of resistance" according to strategies of "critical regionalism," which is exactly the kind of anti-architecture that students use in the unconstrained patois of their online conversations. A program of universalization results from a bland notion of the possibilities of architecture, one that does not admit complexity. To look at architecture in terms of complexity is to see Versailles in the A & P parking lot: it's to see the (other) story that *dwells* in the (purported) story. Letting the other speak (*allos* + *agoreuei*) is the very definition of allegory, and such is the textual strategy Composition Studies refuses in its consideration of student writing. And allegory is precisely the view an architectural reading affords: "an unmistakably allegorical impulse has begun to reassert itself in various aspects of contemporary culture. . . Allegory is also manifest in the historical revivalism that today characterizes architectural practice" (Owens 204). It's the A & P parking lot as *allegory* for Versailles, not metaphor or metonym (which would privilege one referent—allegory neutralizes both/all referents). The relationship is one of displacement or substitution, not reference or representation; it's palimpsestic rather than hermeneutic.

WRITING AS *DÉRIVE* / URBAN LIVING

I chose an architectural frame through which to view my profession because of its central importance (like writing) in determining how people live, specifically how they inhabit their world and how it inhabits them. That latter aspect, the impact of architecture on people, is the aspect most interesting to the situationist theorists. Architecture, for the situationist, is only important in how it contributes to the liberation of everyday life for people, a sentiment expressed, for example, by Ivan Chtcheglov in his "Formulary for a New Urbanism": "Architecture is the simplest means of articulating time and space, of modulating reality, of engendering dreams. It is a matter not only of plastic articulation and modulation expressing an ephemeral beauty, but of a modulation producing influences in accordance with the eternal spectrum of human desires and the progress in realizing them" (Knabb 2). Chtcheglov takes as an example the Surrealist painter Giorgio de Chirico, whose urbanistic vision, because it was not presented in traditional architectural forms and genres, went unused by urban planners, who could not see the imperative for its use in social practice. Chtcheglov, bemoaning the opportunity lost by such neglect, reflects on the way visionary architectural design is the single-most important factor in the project to reshape the world:

> In Chirico's paintings (during his Arcade period) an *empty space* creates a *full-filled time*. It is easy to imagine the fantastic future possibilities of such architecture and its influences on the masses. Today we can have nothing but contempt for a century that relegates such *blueprints* to its so-called museums.
>
> This new vision of time and space, which will be the theoretical basis of future considerations, is still imprecise and will remain so until experimentation with patterns of behavior has taken place in cities specifically established for this purpose, cities assembling—in addition to the facilities necessary for a minimum of comfort and security—buildings charged with evocative power, symbolic edifices representing desires, forces, events past, present and to come. (Knabb 3)

That spectrum of human desires, forces, etc., is referred to by situationists with the term *psychogeography*, defined as "the study of specific effects of the geographical environment, consciously organized or not, on the emotions and behavior of individuals" (Knabb 45). Debord, for example, gives a brief overview of the psychogeographic effects of the general city plan of Paris on human emotions: "The concern to have open spaces allowing for the rapid circulation of troops and the use of artillery against insurrections was at the origin of the urban renewal plan adopted by the Second Empire. But from any standpoint other than that of police control, Haussmann's Paris is a city built by an idiot, full of sound and fury, signifying nothing" (Knabb 5). The situationist program starts from a realization that the grammar of contemporary cities results in impoverished psychogeographic effects. Debord: "First of all, we think the world must be changed. We want the most liberating change of the society and life in which we find ourselves confined" (Knabb 17). If the artist must leave the gallery and go down into the street to create Happenings, the street should not be part of a space that reproduces a sterile geometry. It should be the kind of surroundings Lawrence Alloway (a member of London's quasi-situationist Independent Group) delights in, "the LP environment at airports, restaurants, bars, and hotel lounges, of light and long-lived pop music that extends radio and TV sound outside the house and into a larger environment" (Sadler 15). The urban landscape needs changing, which would affect the life within it, and alienating writing practices represent a key goal in the renewal project: "the only interesting venture is the liberation of everyday life, not only in the perspectives of history but for us and right away. This entails the withering away of alienated forms of communication" (Knabb 33). As Sadler notes, "situationism was founded upon the belief that general revolutions would originate in the appropriation and alternation of the material environment and its space" (13). Hence, the pedagogical revolution hoped for in the material and spatial alterations of Deemer, Lutz, Macrorie, *et al.*

Situationist urban theory can illuminate our understanding of the behavior of the writers we teach. The way students actually inhabit the writing classroom's cityscape is very much in keeping with the situationist notion of the *dérive*, the method used to chart a city's psychogeography:

> The *dérive* (literally, "drift," in the nautical sense) was a matter of opening one's consciousness to the (so to speak) unconsciousness of urban space; the *dérive* meant a solo or collective passage down city streets, a surrender to and

then pursuit of alleys of attraction, boulevards of repulsion, until the city itself became a field of what the L[ettrist] I[nternational] called "psycho-geography," where every building, route, and decoration expanded with meaning or disappeared for the lack of it: for the LI, the *dérive* ("the CON-TINUOUS *DÉRIVE*," LI member Ivan Chtcheglov said in 1953) was to replace work. What the group meant to practice, Debord said in 1959, look-ing back, was "a role of pure consumption"—the total consumption of all images and words of the past, the total consumption of the group's sur-roundings, and ultimately the total consumption "of its time." (Marcus "Guy Debord's *Memoires*" 127)

Apparent in the majority of Composition's arché-texts are efforts to *con-trol* consumption, traffic signals put up to direct the student-*dérive* according to a notion of pedagogical importance or usefulness (i.e., we will never allow our writing classroom's cobblestones to be fully ripped up in order to expose the beach beneath them). Classroom cities are subject to constant surveillance, ready to contain any instance of the stu-dent everyday manifesting itself. So Ken Bruffee, for example, becomes Haussmann when, out of a perceived need to "reapportion freedom" (637), he plasters his cityscape with all sorts of regulatory signs in order to evoke the verbal flow he deems necessary to ensure the success of the collaborative model (his simulation of the social) in student discussion. Students' psychogeographic ramblings within a given textual space (if they can ramble at all) are curtailed sharply. The traffic is strictly one-way, and only on the main(-point) roads:

1. What is the "point" of the paper? What does it say? What position does it take?
2. How does it make its point? What does it do to defend or explain its posi-tion?
3. Is the paper related to any issue raised so far in this course? Is so, which? If not, what context of issues is the paper related to?
4. What are the strong and weak points in the paper? What do you like about it? If what you read was a draft, what suggestions would you make to the writer for revising it? (638n)

But the unwanted trash we vigilantly try to keep off our pedagogical streets turns out to be our most valuable natural resource—exuberance. Those funky, decrepit spaces the situationists loved to explore, like the markets at Les Halles, where Happenings routinely occurred in May '68, were razed, in favor of Modernist buildings. The response of Aldo van

Eyck, radical architect from the Netherlands, to a rationalist city planning that would overwrite the complicated possibilities of a city's old buildings with clean, nicely organized new boxes, could serve as a response to the formalist, essayist prose advocated by most handbooks and textbooks : "Instead of the inconvenience of filth and confusion, we have now got the boredom of hygiene . . . mile upon mile of organized nowhere" (Sadler 32). Desire remains the key component lacking in most Composition theory. Weiner, for example, has eight points to consider in determining the guidelines for setting up an effective moment of collaborative learning; these points all relate to theoretical concepts of task, time, setting, and the like, with no mention of passion or desire ("Collaborative Learning" 60–61). Situationists, on the other hand, offer more useful composition theory; they have only one ground rule for constructing what sound like beneficial models for a writing class, situations in which "the role played by a passive or merely bit-part playing 'public' . . . constantly diminsh[es], while that played by those who cannot be called actors, but rather, in a new sense of the term, 'livers,' must constantly increase," and that guideline is based on deep desires: "The really experimental direction of situationist activity consists in setting up, on the basis of more or less clearly recognized desires, a temporary field of activity favorable to these desires. This alone can lead to the further clarification of these primitive desires, and to the confused emergence of new desires whose material roots will be precisely the *new reality* engendered by the situationist constructions" (Knabb 43). This, by the way, is the most persuasive argument for the use of technology like the synchronous chat program in the composition class: it can channel (and capture) a group of students writing off-the-top-of-their-heads. It provides a textual moment that was never there before and may never be there again, one unmediated by the acculturated crud of received formal ideas regarding writing; maybe it's merely the passage of a few people through a rather brief moment in time, but it's a moment that can be fully inhabited more than most writing assignments. In blurring the distinction between oral and written, creating a kind of creole of conversation and prose, the network allows for writing as *dérive*, allows, in fact, the *dérive* to count as writing, to replace the (uni)formalism of standard exposition. It is a true situationist composing medium. I prefer writing as road map to strange, new places over writing that simply charts again the same, well-worn ground. Classroom collaborative work done according to Bruffee and Weiner, with its conventional task-orientation, is too safe, too already-done—snapshots from a package-tour vacation ("Are we having fun yet?") that's already been taken a hundred times before, now being offered one more time. It's more ritual than lived situation; it can only be acted out, with some students better rehearsed than others. Allowing student-drift into the writing classroom makes possible the allegory of student-as-Jackson-Pollock: even Greenberg could see Jackson's drip canvases as the charged drift-traces of Jackson's journey through modernity, "an attempt to cope with urban life; . . . dwell[ing] entirely in the lonely jungle of immediate sensations, impulses and notions" (Friedman *Energy* 101).

Keep traffic signs in class to a minimum, I've noticed, and the results are charts of the student flâneurian imaginary. One of the first things observed is that the traditional on-task, peer-collaborative response group has maybe a fifty percent chance of staying on-task anyway, and when it does students either give each other pleasantly vague encouragement, manifest their confusion, or engage in harsh instances of conversation-as-confrontation. When they do stay on task, it's with an air of tired duty (Scott: "are we close to done yet?"). The moments when they go off task become more fascinating psychogeographic maps, showing what they feel are the true avenues of attraction: the Strips, naturally—spectacular topics like sex, drinking, drugs, the media, and popular culture (movies, music, TV, ads, and clothes). A conversation between three women students, for example, shows that a lively, gossipy account of the past weekend's romantic encounters is far more interesting than a discussion of their drafts; they're in Strip-mode, re-creating a portable chunk of Main Street—in this case, it's a movie theatre front: the repeated punctuation and orthographic elements dot their prose like lines of flashing marquee bulbs; their sexually suggestive commentary reads like lurid posters used to hype the teen romance now playing; and markered and spray-painted over the theatre front, adding another layer to the urban megatext/ure, are graffiti referring to pop culture:

Kelly: I think that Darrin is a really nice guy, Troy and I are going downhill. He was with her on Friday and Saturday? He told me when I talked to him on the phone that they weren't going out anymore, That little scammer!!!!!!!!!!!!!!!!!!!!! That was Thursday!

Amy: ohhhh noooooooooo its mr bill . . . no, im "GUMBY DAMN IT" kelly stop biting your nails. . . are you nervous???????

Laurie: When did you talk to him on the phone? I'll find out for sure if he is or not from Dan Ramberg

Kelly: Amy I didn't know you were playing now too?

Amy: playing? is this dungeons and dragons PLAYING WITH WHAT?

Kelly: Cool as hell, he told me on the phone Thursday. He gave me his number a while ago, He is always telling me to call him, what should I do???????

Amy: MYYYY Kelly you are really getting to know the computer now you look like a normal secretary.

Kelly: Amy, you better tell me what happened with you and Marty last night, did you fuck or what?

This conversation goes on for four pages' worth of transcript; getting increasingly vulgar and, concurrently, aware of panoptical instructor surveillance policing their desire: "hello," types Amy, at one point, mimicking the teacher, "this is [the instructor] and id appreciate it if everyone would work on their papers instead of screwing around." They will write nothing, of course, this lively in their formal essays. Such conversation, contaminated by the casual, reveals "students . . . speaking in their own voices about things that counted for them" (Macrorie *Upatught* 21). Roger writes a paper on MTV, and in discussion his group blandly, politely circles around it for a few lines until Joel, a neo-hippie who always wears his blonde hair tied in a bandana and sports his NORML button, takes offense at Roger calling people who watch MTV "Deadheads." After Roger clarifies he meant the term as in "dullard," not "Grateful Dead fan," the next two pages leave Roger's paper far behind to rap on the Dead's popularity. In fact, "rapping" is the right word for it; I thought one of the best instances of collaboration, true Composition as a Happening, was when four students dropped peer-discussion and, each taking a turn, did a 20-line rap song on the subject of Mother Teresa.

The networked conversations my students have that seem more traditionally academic are the ones which occur as general discussions around topics that deal with reading they've done. Unmediated by the task-screen of an assigned essay, they're freewheeling *dérives*, showing the precise points of interest and aversion for them in the material. So when we read Allan Bloom, for example, their network discussion becomes an architecture of resistance focused on how wrong Bloom is about the books one needs to have read or the inherent dangers in rock music. In these conversations, the student discourse perfectly mirrors the contemporary urban verbalscape—the operative grammar is the sound bite, the tee-shirt/bumper-sticker slogan, ad copy, graffiti, stadium bannerspeak.

So Pete's take on Bloom: "He says that Rock is a form of masturbation, yet I've never climaxed while listening to ZZ Top," or Dreanna's: "It seems like Bloom was isolated for about 20 years." In another session, Andy gets a little bored with the discussion of how revisionist Vietnam War movies may or may not misrepresent history and drops out to put up a billboard for his current favorite film: "the world's a media circus. get back to nature. see . . . THE BEAR." There's a reality in these discussions that I seldom see in their standard papers. The point doesn't seem so much how we can get them to transfer that natural exuberance to their academic writing, as how we can get academic writing to restyle itself so as to better fit their exuberance. Besides, the larger media culture doesn't bother to expand or elaborate in their glitzy little sound bites, so why should my students?

The problem lies in narrow notions of form and function. Faigley has already shown how, even across a broad range of compositionists, the kind of writing seen as "good" is surprisingly similar ("Judging Writing"). That should come as no surprise, for at the heart of Composition lies an assumption "that certain qualities are common to all effective nonfiction prose[:] . . . significance, clarity, unity, economy, and acceptable usage" (Hairston 1); an affirmation of "a fundamental similarity of values in the forms of discourse throughout the academy" (Marius 28). These qualities and values represent a program of universalization at the level of form and meaning, an aesthetic in service to a very particular beautiful. Macrorie captures the problem with teaching writing under the grammar-of-the-monument when he speaks of the "huge gray result" it produces (*Uptaught* 13). Whether the theorist is an expressivist or a cultural critic, the "real" of writing becomes the form as reproducible, as already written. It is no wonder, then, that Stewart ("accomplished writers develop a sense of which [stylistic options] will work in which situations and then write accordingly" [7]) comes to sound much like Bartholomae (for whom students "mimic the 'distinctive register' of academic discourse [in order] to actually and legitimately do the work of the discourse" ["Inventing" 162]). The very distinction between academic and expressivist writing is bogus because both obey the same logic of structure and function; the texts and students in these courses are always *in service to* empty, boring uses—discoveries of authentic voices or (equally mystic) patterns of discursive power. A true notion of "power" in writing, in the sense of sovereignty, has nothing to do with use and servility: "Life *beyond utility* is the domain of

sovereignty" (Bataille, *Vols. 2 and 3* 198). The so-called expressivist/aca-
demic antinomy represents simply two movements in a single turn in
university writing, in much the same way Bataille saw architecture turn
from being the expression or image of social order to the formal mechanism by which that order was imposed (Hollier *Against* 47). Students
must always "write accordingly" . . . "legitimately": so the official ("real-
world") documentary permanently held over on every screen at the
Composition Multiplex is an anti-parody, a non-allegory—a reverse-
image loony toon in which the Road Runner stars as John Law, vigilantly
patrolling the streets of Vegas in hopes of catching that "common"
(Bartholomae "Inventing" 151) criminal, the Cashinahuan Coyote,
White Shoes (played by Bart Simpson). Situationists declared that modernist architecture "has never been an art" and that "it has on the contrary always been inspired by the directives of the police" (Sadler 50).
Le Corbusier's rationalist program, they felt, was "life definitely partitioned in closed blocks, in surveilled societies; the end of chances for
insurrection, automatic resignation" (Sadler 50). The word Lefebvre
and de Certeau used to speak of the simplistic, clean-lined urban plan
was "'quadrillage,' i.e., a tight military or police control of an area; it
also refers to checkered material or paper, and by extension to the grid
pattern of streets" (Sadler 176).

Both compositionist camps, then, are part of the bread-alone school,
in which writing supplies the necessary, the real—whether an authenti-
cally-voiced solution to a local composing occasion or a Foucauldian
exercise in ferreting out the microphysics of power. But neither man
nor woman lives (or writes) by bread alone, and so these two philosophical camps might as well be one, for all either of them has to say about
the life beyond bread—what Bataille (*Vols. 2 and 3*) variously terms the
miraculous or the divine, and what Lyotard calls the sublime or the
unpresentable. The transformal sublime was the ultimate goal of the
Happenings; we remember the subtext underlying every one of La
Monte Young's performances, people carried away to heaven. The aesthetics of the bread-alone school posit that there is a matching referent
for a given idea; one can only really write if one can reproduce well,
either an authentic passage or an academic tone. A production-as-repro-
duction aesthetic results, for example, in that broad range of Coles and
Vopat teacher-informants Faigley analyzes, all sharing surprisingly similar literary tastes, all using words like "honest" and "true" in their discussions of student texts because their evaluation of writing is based on this

referential correspondence between their experience of the Idea (authenticity, academic register) and the student's written approxima-tion of it as case ("Judging Writing"). Those Hairstonian qualities, then, serve as criteria used to judge a faithful rendering; teaching under such an aesthetic becomes a matter of taste, of evaluating how well the "beau-tiful" (whether romantic or political) is represented. It makes more sense, however, to think of students as writing allegories of composition rather than metonymic representations. Looked at that way, they sud-denly have the coherence Venturi saw in the previously-degraded mega-texture of Main Street: "at one stroke the profound vision of allegory transforms things and works into stirring writing" (Benjamin *Origin* 176). Everyone from Benjamin ("Allegory thereby declares itself to be beyond beauty" [*Origin* 178]) to Bono ("'taste is the enemy of art.' There's a point where you find yourself tiptoeing as an artist, and then you know that you're in the wrong place" [Light 45]) knows beauty and taste are outmoded criteria to bring to an analysis of composition. I bring in Bono because the writing classroom under the bread-alone pro-gram resembles nothing so much as a lame parody of MTV, as seen by the TV show designed, in effect, to be a lame parody of MTV, "Puttin' on the Hits": writing in the bread-alone composition class becomes lip-sync-ing the standards, and teaching becomes a question of judging the authenticity of the imitation. Architectural critic Michael Sorkin's take on that old program sounds very much like the dynamic of the contem-porary writing class, in the way the everyday "autoroboticizes" into hyperreality: "[C]onsecrated to the serial realization of simulation, *Puttin' on the Hits* . . . focuses on the passage of quotidian citizens into the realms of celebritydom by their self-transformation into the figures of rock 'n' roll superstars, . . . judged by a panel of media business oper-atives according to the criteria of 'appearance,' 'lip sync,' and (*sic*) 'orig-inality'" (167–168). But the reality beyond bread has no corresponding figure to reproduce. The sublime, as Lyotard notes, deals with "ideas of which no presentation is possible. . . . [T]hey prevent the formation and the stabilization of taste. They can be said to be unpresentable" (78). The bread-alone theorists, in wanting to supply reality (or, rather, "real-ity"), focus on theories of text *production* (rather than, say, text *consump-tion* or text *seduction*). And so technique—with its etymological origins of bringing forth, producing—becomes the key to their aesthetics. For Heidegger, "the nature of the erecting of buildings cannot be under-stood adequately" (159) in terms of mere technique; the nature of building is caught up in the more sublime notion of "letting dwell" (160). Bread-alone teachers, then, rely on notions of "true" and "honest" because their pleasure lies in the recognition of the representative form. "Ironically, we glorify originality through replication of the forms of Modern masters" (Venturi et al. 148). Even when the unpresentable is acknowledged in their aesthetic, it is as absence, as nostalgia for the (missing) sublime: power, authentic voice, or, say, Bloom's panic-realization that "they no longer have any image of a perfect soul" (67). The sublime is not crucial to their aesthetic, form is (just as power is not really crucial to cultural critique compositionists, merely its discursive patterns). Traditional discussions of literacy, in general, have little of the sublime in them; so one must go outside the formal bounds of Composition—to architecture, for example—in order to better (allegorically) read the field and its students. One of the subtexts of Composition as a Happening is the realization that art criticism in general offers more compelling theory than Composition's canon, particularly (in this case) in relation to the sublime. Take this definition by Joseph Kosuth: "Anything can be art. Art is the relations between relations, not the relations between objects" (Fischl and Saltz 30).

If art today, as Owens suggests, is "unmistakably allegorical" (204), then student-writing-as-art must contain the megatextural element of allegory. Bartholomae's reading of those student placement essays in "Inventing the University" (particularly his reading of the papers by the writers he deems less successful, like White Shoes, for whom there appears no hope, and Clay Model, caught halfway between expressivism and the academic) can serve to trace the implications of Composition's denial of allegory. If allegory is one story doubled by another, then an allegorical reading of White Shoes's paper, written in response to the tedious prompt "Describe a time when you did something you felt to be creative. Then, on the basis of the incident you have described, go on to draw some general conclusions about 'creativity'" (136), might be, "You give me a cheesy writing task, I invest about *this* much time doing it, reaching for the first thing I can think of." But the grammar of the monument crushes such an allegory, treating it solely as representation-manqué, detailing how the naive writer unfortunately imagined himself in the wrong discourse, "the 'great man' theory" (151) of history rather than the (Bartholomae-preferred) power/knowledge theory. And so the paper's entrails are pored over by the high priest to divine further proof of the power of the gods of the monument. White Shoes is a Strip-student, though, far more interested in football than schooling, a student for whom the bread-alone hook of "you must do well on this writing prompt, your scholastic future depends on it" appeals not at all. No one from the Strip could take a topic like that "creative/creativity" one seriously. To flout it makes sense; it's the mandate of Hebdige's street-punks, "throw your self away before They do it for you" (32). Bread-alone theorists can't think beyond the orgy of signification represented by the placement test; but White Shoes is in Baudrillard's post-orgy mode of "What are you doing after the [placement test]?" ("Vanishing Point" 189). Why in the world should he let something like a dull writing prompt interrupt the pleasures of his football fantasies?

Bartholomae tries vainly, like Stewart does with his student Harold, who "thinks and speaks in the language of TV beer commercials" (*vii*), to cram the allegorical excess into the strictly defined representational system of his aesthetics, in which a certain genre can only appear as a certain genre: e.g., "a chair's address is a chair's address" ("Reply" 129), and not, say, a Jimmy Stewart impression (Bartholomae chides North over a CCCC presentation he did one year, on a panel with Pat Bizzell, Cy Knoblauch, and Bruce Herzberg: "Cy, Bruce and Pat gave presentations that were insistently located within a tradition of academic critiques of the academy. . . . You followed with a funny story and an oh-gosh, Jimmy Stewart routine" [North "Personal Writing" 113]). Placement test essays just don't matter for Strip-writers unless they can be allegories of football glory. Excess will always cause implosion in the system which cannot process it. So when the high priests do poke through the entrails of White Shoes's verbal corpse, what they read (and deny) is their own doom: "The allegorical supplement is not only an addition, but also a replacement. . . . Hence the vehemence with which modern aesthetics—formalist aesthetics in particular—rails against the allegorical supplement, for it challenges the security of the foundations upon which aesthetics is erected" (Owens 215). The logic of allegory is not composition's X = X, but X = Y: "any person, any object, any relationship can mean absolutely anything else" (Benjamin *Origin* 175). To those who would refuse the supplement, who would strictly curtail Benjamin's parameters for allegory, an earnest entreaty—less really *is* a bore.

Bartholomae has the right impulses ("I am constantly impressed by the patience and good will of our students" [135]) for the wrong reasons ("He is trying on the discourse even though he doesn't have the knowledge that would make the discourse more than a routine, a set of conventional rituals and gestures" [136]). That is, Bartholomae sees the otherspeak, he sees the second story, but it's as antecedent, as referent, not as excess, not as palimpsest, not as replacement; the other story speaks only as a failed attempt to do the right thing. Smack dab in the middle of the vast expansive texture of allegory's wide-open substitution, Bartholomae stubbornly erects yet another instance of the Modern Composition program, the high enclosing form of symbolism, to be styled, in this case, according to the blueprints for an objective correlative of creativity and some reflexive exegesis. Another modernist franchise soberly towers over the secret life of the city, with writing permissible only on sanctioned streets in the now-occupied territories. Students must place themselves "in the context of what has been said and what might be said . . . [and not] solely in the context of [their] experience" (152). It's writing-as-channeling. Because he refuses the allegorical reading of his placement essays, Bartholomae misses everything outside the bounds of synecdoche; for instance, Bartholomae wants more "'academic' conclusions" from Clay Model's paper (137), but far more tantalizing than any conclusions about the process of creativity in that paper is Clay's brief allusion to the actual model itself, a model of the earth that's "not of the classical or your everyday model of the earth" (135)—academic conclusions are already known, but a new model of the earth sounds wild. The very prompt used to generate the samples in the "Inventing" study, with its description/reflection dynamic, asks students for the dull, bland modernist sort of allegory, striving and bombastic: "conceived of something added or superadded to the work after the fact, allegory will consequently be detachable from it. In this way, modernism can recuperate allegorical works for itself, on the condition that what makes them allegorical be overlooked or ignored" (Owens 215). As a result, Bartholomae's hermeneutics interprets Clay Model's paper only as botched synecdoche, a degraded version of the "'local' instance . . . of working out a general debate in the academy" ("Reply" 130), a franchise-in-ruins. Clay Model, the non-allegory goes, lacks the power/knowledge necessary to turn his paper on creativity into a witty, elegant academic turn, he lacks the arché-tectonics to turn his shack into a monument (to "make the discourse more than a routine" [136]; "to actually and legitimately do the work of the discourse . . . with grace and elegance" [162]). It's the difference between urban and urbane. Bartholomae overlooks (or looks through) the allegory, then, seeing it as mere lacunae, the missing knowledge that would have enabled the academic sublime (just as Stewart claims

Harold "lacks versatility and authenticity" [*vii*]). The palimpsest is ratio-
nalized and erased away, and the only writing left legible is writing that
mimics "our prose" (136). Clay Model becomes the half-way point
between student and writer. He is Frankenstein Monster or cyborg, half
old flesh and half new. It's White Shoes, however, the all-wild, the all-
primitive, the least successful, whose allegory remains inerasable:
"Getting him out of it will be a difficult matter indeed" (151). Like most
compositionists, Bartholomae prefers the cooked to the raw ("I confess
I admire those dense sentences" [159]). In the same way Stewart sees
Harold as thoroughly inhabited by the language of beer commercials,
Bartholomae sees White Shoes as too appropriated by the everyday, that
"conventional rhetoric of the self" (150) that is "so common" (151).
While students like Clay Model appear halfway "to appropriat[ing] (or
be[ing] appropriated by)" (135) *our prose,* they are really halfway to discursive execution; Harold and White Shoes, meanwhile, are fortunately
a whole other story.

All writing courses, regardless of their ideological advocacy, become
Modernist when they close on received notions of form and function.
Venturi speaks for all arché-texture:

> When it cast out eclecticism, Modern architecture submerged symbolism.
> Instead it promoted expressionism, concentrating on the expression of
> architectural elements themselves: on the expression of structure and func-
> tion. It suggested, through the image of the building, reformist-progressive
> social and industrial aims that it could seldom achieve in reality. By limiting
> itself to strident articulations of the pure architectural elements of space,
> structure, and program, Modern architecture's expression has become a dry
> expressionism, empty and boring—and in the end irresponsible. Ironically,
> the Modern architecture of today, while rejecting explicit symbolism and friv-
> olous appliqué ornament, has distorted the whole building into one big
> ornament. (*Learning* 101, 103)

Even when composition classes are styled around an ideology as positive
and humane as feminism, the writing and the peer-discussion around
that writing become "one big ornament" that can be (re)represented
correctly, successfully. Feminist pedagogue Sara Farris bemoans her student James, described as having "brought nothing to the class" because
he and his group refused to write and workshop essays accordingly, legitimately. Farris writes them off, exiles them; as poverty-ridden, they are
ones to be avoided: "James's workshop group demonstrates the problem:

it routinely workshopped four essays in less than fifteen minutes and then looked expectantly at me, waiting for their next task to be assigned. When I talked to them about what I considered to be a dysfunctional group, they insisted that they got out of their workshop exactly what they wanted: nothing. . . . Finally, I just let them be" (306).

If contemporary Composition theory offers a dry, banal, simplistic program, then maybe legitimizing other forms and functions (and teaching to them), even "frivolous" ones like those of an e-chat transcript, might make the landscape less alienating. Because such texts *are* highly functional forms; almost all right, indeed. In a discussion of horror movies, there was one large-group strand going on, and then gradually, after Tracy wondered if anyone had seen *Mommy Dearest* (perhaps because at some level she was applying everything the large group was saying about the genre of horror to that film), a sub-strand opened up in which Tracy and five other students, in about forty lines, did a very nice reading of Joan Crawford as monster. Again, I'm uncomfortable with a response that would say, OK, now get her to write the traditional academic paper on "The Spectacular Horror of Domestic Drama: Mother as Movie Icon as Freddie Krueger." It's almost like they did enough of that paper for now, at least all that's necessary to make the idea a useful one (and the idea *is* a useful one: it helps my movie-viewing now to look at any sort of Spectacular Genre film—like a Hollywood biopic—as horror-allegory). The text of their discussion is readable and workable in several ways at once; multifarious, labyrinthine. Charlie sums up Bloom in a beautiful sound bite: responding to Tom's comment that Bloom's a narrow-minded fool, Charlie explains, "It's because he was raised in the attic of a cheese factory." I almost don't even need to read a ritual analytic paper on Bloom from Charlie now; his comment has stayed with me more strongly than any other single line on Bloom I've read. It's a gospel-comment, an ethic-response; it's about values and truths and inhabited worlds (not mere intellectual forms), and it's sublimely poetic. These discussion transcripts can be read according to a logic named by Lefebvre in the title of one of his early articles: "Fragments of a philosophy of consciousness."

Roger shows that the grammar of the Strip is a comfortable one for him to use in his formal essays. His analysis of MTV, entitled, "WMTV (Whose Music Television???) Or Gnarley TV of the 80s??," reads like it was written in a car, cruising at a real clip, d(é)riving through the subject of the music video network, leaving big signs and little buildings in the wake of his drift. There's no real specific focus; in fact, there's a lot of focuses—about who the MTV audience is, how MTV constructs sexuality, the anti-authoritarian stance of many of its videos, and the representation of African-Americans on the channel. It's a conceptual Main Street, composed according to a logic of bold communication, not subtle expression. None of his points are very well-developed, but the trip down the Strip is well worth the ride, and the (very happening) sign-sentences he uses to dot the street are terrific, wild-style graphic and really flashy, like the airbrushed jean-jackets he does as a sideline:

> [MTV] has appeal, I'm sure, for a certain segment of the population, namely Ferris Buehler and his friends, maybe better described as kids who have nothing better to do.

> In between videos they have commercials like the "*Playboy* Playmate Spectacular Video," a must for young studs, do-nothings, and men of the world whoever they may be.

There's much that's implicit in sentences like that (e.g., the line connecting MTV with Ferris Buehler opens up a critique of class and race and Hollywood films), but do I mind that it's only left implicit? No, because the implicit is often a valid strategy in everyday life, and as Venturi notes, "when form follows function explicitly, the opportunities for implicit functions decrease" (*Complexity* 130). MTV is almost always rhetorically crucial because students often write according to the logic of the televisual, a logic that renders inapplicable Hairston's "qualities [of] effective nonfiction prose." For example, why waste time trying to teach Roger received, rarified truths about transitions between his barely related ideas when they're simply not relevant to his program at all? His effects are best achieved by a different grammar, the rock video's itself, wherein any succession of images yields *de facto* text (Sorkin), instant film-Strip. Oh, where was post-Happenings Composition's Richard Williamson, to write "The Case for Rock Video as Composition"? Juxtaposition is the grammar of the Happenings (e.g., Oldenburg's strategy to simply pile up images "one after another or on top of one another and repeat them"). Roger's compositional question, then, becomes one of simple architectonics (using technology as opposed to mastering technique), mere tinkering with existing material to build a functional dwelling place, rather than grandiose replication and installation. It's students-as-colonized, composing in the bombed-out ruins of their homeland, with nothing to use but fragments, shards. As such, the scene is in keeping with the textual strategy of allegory: "the highly significant fragment, the remnant, is, in fact, the finest material in baroque creation. For it is common practice in the literature of the baroque to pile up fragments ceaselessly, without any strict idea of a goal, and, in the unremitting expectation of a miracle, to take the repetition of stereotypes for a process of intensification" (Benjamin *Origin* 178).

Like video, student-writing-as-allegory employs what Owens calls "structure as sequence" (207). Modernists won't admit the reality of writing done according to paratactic juxtaposition, to allegorical piling-up; they would deny, for example, Virilio's observation that "ours is a crisis of cutting and joining, a crisis of editing; we have passed beyond the crisis of montage" (112). Modernists are precisely in the crisis of montage: how many profess the pastiche? Writing-as-*dérive*, in its randomness, its suggestiveness, styles itself according to nothing except emotional response. The goal is not academic writing's program of retracing the same steps others have traced, but taking wholly new steps, in hopes of finding the unforseeable: one can use the flâneurian stroll of the *dérive*, says Debord, to "draw up hitherto lacking maps of influences, maps whose inevitable imprecision at this early stage is no worse than that of the first navigational charts; the only difference is that it is a matter no longer of precisely delineating stable continents, but of changing architecture and urbanism" (Knabb 53). Student writing as psychogeographic allegory for what they don't like about "our prose."

Despite what you think of the above examples, clearly there is less alienation, less apparent exhaustion, in such verbal texts and interchanges than in, for example, an essay I read by a student at another university, in which a paper was to be written on the topic (not-so-surprisingly similar to Bartholomae's "creative/creativity" prompt), "Define 'boring' and indicate if it is different from 'being bored.'" It's not just me who thinks such a topic can produce nothing but exhaustion, it's the student who wrote on it; in her essay she rambles on for a while, stacking up as many instances vaguely relating to the topic as she can, mind wandering (she even admits), *dérive*-like, through tedious terrain, until she finally arrives at this point in the paper: "When I can't relate to what's going on I go to sleep or my mind starts to wander off into another land. My mind does that when I don't want to do something too. For example, this paper. I really think that this topic is boring because I don't like it and it's making me sleepy. I don't care about boring people." On one hand, a paper like this becomes a perfect economy, with the student using her very exhaustion with the topic as her material text production. But it seems a short-sighted economic base for our curricular cities. Part of the existing landscape we must learn to learn from includes our students' psychogeography. Student e-discussion transcripts, and many of their essays (when desire bleeds into them), let us read what Debord calls "the passional terrain of the *dérive*" (Knabb 50), that vast expansive texture in which all bread-alone topics are reduced to the splitting of hairs as to the difference between boring and being bored. A situationist theory of writing, one responsive to students and the everyday, would say: if the student's *dérive* goes in these various directions (sex, parody, television, clothes, etc.), then the curriculum might best have them theorize those topics rather than count them as unwanted excess. Ivan Chtcheglov, in his "Formulary for a New Urbanism," might be describing our students when he speaks of those "waver[ing] between the emotionally still-alive past and the already dead future" (Knabb 2). Their writing might be necessarily imprecise because, perhaps, they are working out a new life, a future life. Such writing would become, implicitly, a theory of the university, in this case, of the university writing curriculum which would proscribe such topics. Student-*dérive*'s inevitably imprecise navigational chart as urban blueprint (student as de Chirico). Foucault (calling for "a technique of critical demolition"): "The university system, however, can be put into question by the students themselves. At that point, criticism coming from the outside, from the theoreticians, historians or archivists, is no longer enough. And the students become their own archivists" (64). Or their own deconstructionists, dismantling the curriculum at the level of form; for Bataille, "the taking of the Bastille is symbolic . . . it is hard to explain this crowd movement other than by the animosity of the people against the monuments that are their real masters" (Hollier *Against* 47). Student-desire as Godzilla, our curriculum as Tokyo.

CLASSROOM AS PARKING LOT/URBAN FESTIVAL

This discursive excess, this *part maudite*, is really another word for our system's profit, our exchange value, our credit cycle, our slave labor, our money burning a whole in our pockets. The crucial question then becomes our ethos regarding the surplus. Surplus is the basis of allegory. It's allegory's very status as excess—its refusal to be useful, to be in service to—that villifies it: "the allegorical meaning *supplants* an antecedent one; it is a *supplement.* That is why allegory is condemned" (Owens 205, emphasis mine). Bataille builds his theory of general economy—a theory of consumption, not production—around this basic fact of excess-as-profit: "The living organism, in a situation determined by the play of energy on the surface of the globe, ordinarily receives more energy than is necessary for maintaining life; the excess energy (wealth) can be used for the growth of a system (e.g., an organism); if the system can no longer grow, or if the excess cannot be completely absorbed in its growth, it must necessarily be lost without profit; it must be spent, willingly or not, gloriously or catastrophically" (*Vol. 1* 21).

Obviously, based on the number of times I and others have watched classroom discourse go off-task, our curricular system cannot absorb students' energy; they are too much in the everyday—the too-live crew—for our system to process. Does that imply, then, that the system of our curriculum has stopped growing? It seems that way, when we look at the Ozzie-and-Harriet time warp in which we freeze the representation of students and writing. Here's a primal compositional scene from Stewart's screenplay for "[A] [T]ypical Monday": "Later in the day, after eating lunch and attending classes, you find yourself in a meeting of those on the floor of your dorm who are planning the first social event of the fall. You are selected to prepare the first draft of a poster which will tell everyone on the floor what the occasion is, when and where it will be held, and why it will be a lot of fun" (4).

The writing assignments in our curriculum are on a parallel course with the rest of the media, "where the highest function of the sign is to make reality disappear, and at the same time to mask this disappearance" (Baudrillard "Vanishing Point" 188), and so they continue this simulation of student life and identity, disappearing the real desires of our students, constructing body-snatched simulacra who could actually be impassioned to insert themselves into a hoary old *Twilight Zone* plot like Stewart's assignment in Coles and Vopat:

> For this assignment I will ask you to be a twentieth-century Gulliver. You have been shipwrecked and now find yourself forced by circumstances to live in a strange land, one which calls itself Illinois. Specifically, you are living in an urban center named Champaign-Urbana. While you are in this strange city, you take time to observe the customs and rituals of a unique group of persons in the society, a group identified as "college students." Now, in the hope that someday you will return to your native land and report your observations of

these "college students" to your countrymen, you prepare written accounts of the activities of this group. (Coles and Vopat 204)

We can already foresee the blank architecture that will result from such a program of blatant simplification. Assignments currently fashionable under the rubric of "cultural studies," those designed to achieve, as Bartholomae and Petrosky paraphrase it, a Freirean problematization of the student's existential situation (33), are almost grimmer. Constructing a student, as Bartholomae does, who would be impassioned to work on the "general critical project" ("Reply" 130) which he finds intriguing—of how "power and authority . . . are present in language and culture" ("Reply" 129)—makes one's curriculum a pedagogy of oppression and poverty, not of luxury or desire. And as Ross warns,

> a politics that identifie[s] with the victims of poverty, a politics to which intellectuals are prone, [is] doomed to misunderstand the real utopian desires of "class victims" to identify with abundance. If intellectuals today continue to construct a cultural politics exclusively around themes of deprivation, survivalism, oppression, victimage, and alienation, then they will never be able to speak, in a radical accent, the popular language of our times, which is the language of pleasure, adventure, liberation, gratification, and novelty. (115)

The exhaustion in most writing assignments positions our courses at a point on "the edge of ecstasy and decay" (Kroker and Cook 10). Students' conversation (oral or electronic), the point where their exuberant excess encounters the entropic exhaustion of "the difference between 'boring' and 'being bored,'" injects reversibility into our curricular system. The textual results come crackling across like lightning flashes briefly illuminating the dark void of our instructional practices, tracing "a great arc of disintegration and decay against the background radiation of parody, kitsch, and burnout" (Kroker and Cook 8). Students, our blessed inertia, the poison in our inhuman machines, are the only vestiges left of the real in most writing classrooms, which increasingly "leave room only for the orbital recurrence of models and the simulated generation of difference" (Baudrillard *Simulations* 4). Simulation in Composition occurs in the attempt to mask its disappearance of the real under the sign of "real-world" writing. Realism is a key modernist trend; its pervasiveness in Composition makes the field inhospitable to allegory: "by the time Courbet attempted to rescue allegory for modernity, the line which separated them had been clearly drawn, and allegory, conceived as antithetical to the modernist credo

Il faut etre de son temps, was condemned, along with history painting, to a marginal, purely historical existence" (Owens 211). Stewart is *vraiment de son temps*, claiming his book represents "the variety of contexts in which writers work," and promises to share with his student readers "the attitudes, abilities, and work habits of professional writers and the ways in which you might adopt them and thus improve your own writing" (15); and Bartholomae's student has to write in realistic academic drag, "as though he were a member of the academy or an historian or an anthropologist or an economist" ("Inventing" 135). Realism is just not happening; Oldenburg, for example, looked forward to the imaginative as if it were an oncoming evolutionary progression: "Eventually I hope the metamorphic and creative takes over from the realistic as the present takes over from the past" (26). And even so, underlying Composition is not so much Real-World Writing as Real-Wayne's-World Writing: everything is underscored with the parodic *Not!* E.g., the writing you do in Stewart's class will assist you in "acquiring both a more objective and a psychologically deeper sense of the person you are" (Stewart 8). . . . *Not!* Or Bartholomae's students, after learning to be utterly inhabited by academic discourse, will somehow be able to solve "the paradox of imitative originality" (Bartholomae and Petrosky *Facts* 40). . . . *Not!* Our cynical students expect that almost any media voice (except, say, Tupac or Pearl Jam) is also underscored with the parodic opposite (Andy's "the world's a media circus."). For example, one of the texts I used in my first-year writing class is a transcript from a *CNN Crossfire* show which debated the issue of censorship around the question of whether or not 2 Live Crew's record *As Nasty as They Want to Be* should be sold in record stores. In the transcript, Pat Buchanan's blustering tirades, revealing his desire for a simplified, purified, formal program, are patently parodic for students, most of whom either owned the record or were very familiar with it:

> Michael, I don't understand you liberals. You're concerned about a little bit of smog that might get in the air, and you got all kinds of federal rules and regulations, but you're utterly unconcerned about the filth that pollutes the popular culture from which the whole society has to drink. . . . You don't think that this pornography is pollution of the culture and harmful to the individual? Take a look at your society, Michael. It's sick because of what it's drinking from. ("Banned" 12–13)

Students are intuitively hip to Bataille's commonplace: "Everyone is aware that life is parodic and that it lacks an interpretation" (*Visions* 5);

so they can only look with exhausted disbelief at sentiments like Buchanan's in that transcript—or Bloom's: "These are the three great lyrical themes [of rock music]: sex, hate, and a smarmy, hypocritical version of brotherly love. Such polluted sources issue in a muddy stream where only monsters can swim" (74) . . . *Not!* But Bataille is almost right; everyone has learned the truth of parody except bread-alone compositionists, whose architectonics are heavily, simplistically, representational.

In fact, since parody is the only natural response (besides the nothingness of James and his workshop group) to a Modernist writing curriculum, it becomes an exploitable pedagogy. Only if one could do it as parody, for example, would performing Stewart's "Gulliver in Champaign-Urbana" make any sense. For the situationists, parody (in the form of *detournement*, recombining pre-existing textual elements for interesting new programs) was a chief means of text (recycling-as-)production. The situationist slogan "Plagiarism is necessary, progress implies it" speaks to the folly of insisting on a glut of new materials when there's already so much existing stuff that just needs rearranging. For the textually canny situationist,

> it would be possible to produce an instructive psychogeographical detournement of George Sand's *Consuelo*, which thus decked out could be relaunched on the literary market disguised under some innocuous title like "Life in the Suburbs," or even under a title itself detourned, such as "The Lost Patrol." (It would be a good idea to reuse in this way many titles of old deteriorated films of which nothing else remains, or of films which continue to stupefy young people in the film clubs.) (Knabb 11–12)

So, for their parodic scenarios, the situationists put Marxist dialogue into the mouths of truckers at a truckstop and substituted reports of contemporary Klan activities as the new soundtrack of Griffith's *Birth of a Nation* because they were working according to their gospel that "Life can never be too disorienting" (Knabb 13). Comparing the situationist ethos of detourned titles with the standard Compositionist line on the function of titles is illustrative. Operating from an aesthetics of parody, situationists chose titles for the "inevitable counteraction" they could evoke when linked with other texts (visual or verbal): "Thus one can make extensive use of specific titles taken from scientific publications ('Coastal Biology of Temperate Seas') or military ones ('Night Combat of Small Infantry Units'), or even of many phrases found in illustrated children's books ('Marvelous Landscapes Greet the Voyagers')" (Knabb

13). Guiding their impulse was the conviction that "pure, absolute expression is dead; it only survives in parodic form. . . . *Detournement is less effective the more it approaches a rational reply*" (Knabb 10). Bread-alone compositionists are unfailingly rational, about titles as well as everything else: "Just trying to select a title will help you focus, for if you discover that the only title you can think of is vague and extremely broad, you will be forced to realize either that the paper you plan is far too ambitious or that you haven't done enough preliminary work to clarify in your own mind just what it is you want to do" (Hairston 25). A pedagogy geared toward clarification rather than disorientation will never yield the sublime. To build a pedagogy on such a limited notion of titles dooms your curriculum (as well as the writing done within it) right from the start; it's not so much the *banking* as the *bankrupt* concept of education. Rather than even parodies of writing, then—let alone the full-blown possibilities of allegories—students are offered flat fictions: Horatio Alger narratives in which the moral is that if they just follow the neatly ordered, representational program, they'll make it (to the authentic, the academic, the counter-hegemonic, etc.). Our (uni)formalist architecture, then, only offers students the option to (re)reproduce a grand, old (huge gray) monument, one much like Donato's Museum, held together by a similarly noble, airtight fiction about privileged commodities, which, when exploded, creates nothing but a heap of rubble:

> The set of objects the Museum displays is sustained only by the fiction that they somehow constitute a coherent representational universe. The fiction is that a repeated metonymic displacement of fragment for totality, object to label, series of objects to series of labels, can still produce a representation which is somehow adequate to a nonlinguistic universe. Such a fiction is the result of an uncritical belief in the notion that ordering and classifying, that is to say, the spatial juxtaposition of fragments, can produce a representational understanding of the world. Should the fiction disappear, there is nothing left of the *Museum* but "bric-a-brac," a heap of meaningless and valueless fragments of objects which are incapable of substituting themselves either metonymically for the original objects or metaphorically for their representations. (223)

That our curriculum in underscored by the Museum's fiction of representation is seen in Bloom's primal scene for composition: "Imagine such a young person walking through the Louvre or the Uffizi, and you can immediately grasp the condition of his soul. . . . [T]hese artists counted on immediate recognition of their subjects . . . on their having a powerful meaning for their viewers" (63). Judging writing according to the metonymic rather than the allegorical skews our vision of what students are actually doing. In a parodic curriculum, we can see the student as Claes Oldenburg, that classic monument-parodist, who began to distrust the smothering space of the Museum, and so took his work outside, into the public space of urbanity, or rather into urbanity's sublime: Ashton reads Oldenburg as building his "mocker[ies]" of monuments in "spaces grandly imagined to be beyond the realm of possibility" (12). Our students, though, know the penalty for daring to leave the Museum. The Cashinahuan Coyote-writer, White Shoes, is nailed as the least successful writer because he locates himself outside of history and the legitimate work of the discourse, relying on appropriation of commonplace materials for his effect (Bartholomae "Inventing" 150–155). Indeed, he reduces that great onus of history and discourse to a cheap little parody of a Hollywood bio-pic, with himself as the star; Bartholomae sniffs at such naive nerve (or oblivious ignorance) while he puts on the cuffs, shaking his head at White Shoes's attempt to turn a half-assed "act of appropriation [into] a narrative of courage and conquest" (151). But seen allegorically, White Shoes's strategies make sense: "Allegorical imagery is appropriated imagery; the allegorist does not invent images but confiscates them" (Owens 205). Inventing the university seems unnecessarily hard and ultimately tedious (unless inventing a wholly new and different one, not of the classical or your everyday model); confiscating the university is far more intriguing—of course, as the situationist graffiti-slogan suggests, there always remains "ABOLISH[ING] THE UNIVERSITY" (Knabb 344).

So, no, I don't think we spend too much time planning dwellable, exciting spaces to inhabit in our curriculum. (Lutz: "The classroom as presently structured does not provide the environment in which anything creative can be taught" ["Making Freshman English" 35].) Not only do we not offer students textual structures they "cannot help but love" (Chtcheglov), but the notion of students possibly loving our textual worlds "to the point of death" (Bataille) is too depressing to contemplate. Never even considering the possibility of allegory, we only offer composition as a cruel representational fiction of "real-world" writing, affirming a one-to-one correspondence between our writing assignments and students' resultant preparedness to get great jobs and make a lot of money (again, bread alone). But wait. Just what goes on in those beautiful urban high-rises for which we target our students, anyway? Do they have any secrets they want to hide? That is, are there any cracks in the beautifully smooth surface (of authenticity and/or power) our real-world archaeologists of language and authority trace—cracks, maybe, that are big enough to fall into, which might form a labyrinth in which notions of positioning are rendered meaningless? I'd like to offer a few more examples of electronic discourse, these left behind by an anonymous technical writer in a large computer corporation (corporate and personal names changed). Here's her *dérive* through the psychogeography of the crushingly real world, in the form of excerpts from the email messages she steals time away from work to write to an old friend at her former firm:

> David also told me that he was glad I got OUT of Dynastar—that Angela's reputation is very poor (the books are considered to be technically deficient) and that's based on ABC's dealings with her and complaints about the technical inaccuracy of the books. They think she's a fool. (Naturally the books are inaccurate, nobody knows the system and people like Suzanne are working on books!)

> Hi. Don't have a lot of time this a.m., but wanted to caution you on what and to whom you are giving away stuff to (how do you like that syntax?). Do NOT "give" Theresa's group anything—make sure you have yourself covered contractually so that she/they can't appropriate it, and believe me, that's not unknown. (Get a lawyer to draft it). Don't give Tom a preview copy of anything, either. It could have a way of getting duplicated. I know he's a friend of yours, but you have to protect the "product". You simply would not have legal leg 1 to stand on if you don't get a non-disclosure ahead of time.

> Rita Davis looked like hell when I saw her. However, she was drugged out and depressed. I was so sorry to see her that way.

> Speaking of work! I'm up to my ears in it. I'm going to make my deadline— dead or alive, and I'm already down to 114 lbs (via the electronic mail scale in the delivery area). The ONLY good thing about my project is that it's giving me tremendous VISIBILITY throughout the plant.

> I'm looking for another company. I'm tired of Centron. Although this is a lot better than Dynastar, it's become ever-increasingly obvious to me that Centron doesn't give a shit about documentation—no matter what they say. It's still on the bottom of the pile, according to industry listings.

More than 1/3 of the group are talking transfer, but most of the people here have families to support (several women who are heads of the household, etc) and I don't really know what's going to happen. I do know that it's become REAL obvious that there was a mistake made . . . and a BIG one.

That woman is THE most political bitch I ever met. I have taken more courses than ANYONE else in this group on our product and other writers COME TO ME for information now!!! as well as to 'lift' sections from my book!!! Yet she had the balls to tell me that I wasn't a good fit!

One of the few replies her friend makes in the course of the transcript of thirty-some pages of messages is "Take care of yourself, and don't lose any more weight. You'll be looking like a bone with hair, like before." It's almost unbearably touching, this corporate writer's blind business savvy: the more she shrinks, body wasting away to the near-invisibility of bone and hair (like before) from job-induced stress, the more she believes, "it's giving me tremendous VISIBILITY throughout the plant."

But surely we're not surprised at this. We know how many people hate living in the choke hold of our contemporary economy. And the situation seems far from changing, just better-known, thanks to the internet: a recent newspaper article reports, "Thousands of message boards for individual companies have emerged over the last few years, creating a window on what some employees feel but never say publicly. Often the view through this window is rather ugly"; sample ugly messages cited in this article are exactly like those the tech writer above might post, like, "Anyone have any example of the stellar work she has done that earned her the position? She wouldn't know how to fill out a corporate or partnership tax return if her life depended on it" (Abelson 1). Yet curricularly we keep up the mythology that recycling the standard form of academic writing somehow constitutes individual empowerment; that accommodation to its "real world" reality can allow students to position themselves comfortably (or more critically) (or, finally, more firmly?) in that choke hold; that it can, for example, wipe out the racial and gender realities of corporate glass ceilings. Even if it could, what about, you know, the ozone layer, or AIDS? Roger, for example, an African-American convinced AIDS is a government-sponsored plot aimed in large part at his race, mentions AIDS frequently in his e-discussions (e.g., "How is A.I.D.S. going to pop up in *Africa* from monkey shit and there has been monkeys there for millions of years. please

please tell me"), which is more than I can say for academic writing or its sponsors. Despite Bartholomae's conviction that "to teach late adolescents that writing is an expression of individual thoughts and feelings . . . makes them suckers and . . . powerless, at least to the degree that it makes them blind to tradition, power and authority as they are present in language and culture" ("Reply" 128–129), teaching them the rules of academic and professional writing equally suckers, equally disempowers them: it leads students to believe there is a way out of the labyrinth, it suckers them into believing "that *successful* readers and writers [can] actively seek out the margins and aggressively poise themselves in a hesitant and tenuous relationship to the language and methods of the university" (Bartholomae and Petrosky *Facts* 41, emphasis mine). Such a pedagogy becomes Icarian complex: "One of the labyrinth's most subtle (treacherous) detours leads one to believe it is possible to get out, even making one desire to do so. Sublimation is a false exit that is an integral part of its economy" (Hollier *Against* 73).

The situationists make it clear that a curriculum driven by the needs of industry is in no way empowering: "The requirements of modern capitalism determine that most students will become mere *lower cadres* (that is to say, with a function equivalent to that filled by the skilled worker in the nineteenth century)" (Knabb 320–321). The deep, labyrinthine fissures in the surface of power and the political are only too apparent. Bataille has no doubt where ultimate blame lies, in the hands of those who serve to prop up the techniques and politics of utility:

> It has seemed to me that in the end the servility of thought, its submissiveness to useful ends, in a word its abdication, is infinitely dreadful. Indeed present day political and technical thought, which is reaching a kind of hypertrophy, has gotten us ludicrous results in the very sphere of useful ends. Nothing must be concealed: what is involved, finally, is a failure of humanity. True, this failure does not concern humanity as a whole. Only *servile man,* who averts his eyes from that which is not useful, which *serves* no purpose, is implicated. (*Vols. 2 and 3* 14–15)

All a curriculum designed to reproduce uniformity in writing empowers is the system academic writing serves (no matter how counter-hegemonic its ideology, there remain those "reformist-progressive social and industrial aims that it could seldom achieve in reality"). Why conceal it? Why hide the tragedy, covering it up with another dull monument? *Nothing must be concealed:* let's exhume some bodies, then. For example, if some significant part of what our writers in the "real world" are going to be writing is what this corporate writer writes (this shadowy writing which our profession so rarely mentions), why not reveal it, even (especially) teach to it? Why not allow the irrational needs of industry to inform our curriculum? Future businesspeople, for example, might profit by becoming more attentive to email gossip, how to read it, how that writing fits in our culture, whence it arises, and how it represents reality (indeed, the very reality it chooses to represent). It might give students a better sense of control over their futures, show them a side of their future profession that the textbooks don't, show them that the spectacular (say, *Dynasty, Survivor*) just might be a more instructive text for the way business writing actually works than the professional. It might even allow for a discussion of ethics. In fact, we could argue that this discourse is the primal scene of professional writing, the everyday of technical writing, its parking lot or stairwell, writing under the sign of *The Art of the Deal* rather than *The Elements of Style*. Besides, aren't such email messages and gossipy memos the key contemporary documents where policy is really made, rather than the later formalized texts in which policy is ritually presented or even obfuscated? If a curriculum of expressive writing makes our students "suckers" and keeps them unempowered, how crucial a piece of the empowerment puzzle is this kind of discourse to combating suckerdom? Would this tech-writer—who, her messages reveal, graduated from a university with one of the best-known technical writing programs in the country—have perhaps made a better decision about her life and her profession if she had seen samples of this kind of writing as an undergraduate, showing how alienating this labor would be? Does she, I wonder, feel like a sucker for getting into this field?

But even a critique like this keeps the discussion grounded too much in the mythology of the political. The goal of a Happenings composition is the psychogeographical, not the political. From Jean-Jacques Lebel's manifesto: "The political element of its combat, however determining it may be, must never replace the Happening's psychical intent. . . . [Happenings] give back to artistic activity what has been torn away from it: the intensification of feeling, the play of instinct, a sense of festivity, social agitation. The Happening is above all a means of interior communication" (281–282). The need to bring in such texts as that email writing above is most importantly to show the loss, the sacrifice, the waste, that our curriculum, like our culture, denies. Composition's sculptural conceals its sepulchral; those actively heroic Greek temples we teach to are really tombs, masking the dead, disguising the sacrificial victim of the academic order of unified discourse: "Johnny's carefully prepared dead body of a theme, cleaned of all the dirt of the street" (Macrorie *Uptaught* 7). Our concerns for efficiency, versatility, and success align us with the Inca civilization—in Bataille's view, "the most administrative and orderly ever formed by men" (in Hollier *Against* 48). Their urban program of monumental uniformity without ornamentation sounds very Modern, very much the huge gray result of university writing:

> Cuzco, the capital of the Inca empire, was situated on a high plateau at the foot of a sort of fortified acropolis. A massive, ponderous grandeur characterized this city. Tall houses built of huge stone blocks, with no outside windows, no ornament, and thatched roofs, made the streets seem somewhat sordid and sad. The temples overlooking the roofs were of an equally stark architecture. . . . Nothing managed to dispel the impression of mediocre brutality, and above all of stupefying uniformity. (Bataille, in Hollier, *Against* 48)

A small plea then: instead of our current Inca-style academic architecture (the Incas, whose temples disguised their human sacrifices, victims being strangled far inside), perhaps we can at least turn to an Aztec model. The Aztecs, Bataille tells us, were a civilization of total consumption, concerned only with sacrifice: "all their important undertakings were useless" (*Vol. 1* 46). And so, their architecture culminated in their pyramids, at the top of which their victims were sacrificed, out in the open, not denied deep inside. "For Bataille, the world of the Aztecs will remain the model of a society that does not repress the sacrifice that forms it" (Hollier *Against* 47). Our profession may mask the loss and sacrifice on which its verbal monuments are built, but deep within the labyrinth of our "real world" curriculum is the corporate writer above, slowly being strangled by that choke hold our discursive order reproduces (even as it represses it), wasting away, getting thinner and thinner, until, as her friend fears, there will be nothing left but bone and hair.

We could, of course, simply junk the whole notion of power and the political. Contemporary theorists who can precisely chart power's minutest pervasions through discourse and culture begin to sound suspicious; that word rolls too easily off the lips of expressivist and cultural critic alike. They offer not an archaeology of power, but a mythology, which ultimately acts to keep the myth of power alive. As Baudrillard says in his critique of Foucault, "The very perfection of this analytical chronicle of power is disturbing. Something tells us—but implicitly, as if seen in a reverse shot of this writing too beautiful to be true—that if it is possible at last to talk with such definitive understanding about power . . . even down to [its] most delicate metamorphoses, it is because at some point *all this is here and now over with*" (*Forget Foucault* 11). There is no power, there are just the masses (and guns and money and monuments, of course). I ask the political theorists, who seem expert in power's machinations, why they don't effectively operationalize their knowledge beyond the curriculum; I ask them the questions Helen Caldicott asks her lecture audience: Why aren't you storming the White House walls? How many of you are willing to give up your lives to work for your politics? What would Jesus do?—to use the popular cliché most compositionists would find laughable. Christ, now there was a theorist with an ethic of the divine, a gospel of the sublime: a theorist of "by bread alone" . . . *Not!* Perhaps it's time for Composition's archaeologists of power to devise a significant practice for the gospel they speak so beautifully in classrooms and convention halls; they might learn from the cultural studies' scholars of AIDS who have become full-time activists. What would empower students more—teaching them how to accommodate to the rules of academic discourse; or teaching them that if they organized they could demand that they be allowed to write any way they wanted, that they would not have to waste so much time learning to speak like us (their own language being almost all right)? What if they gave a war and nobody came? What if they had an academic discourse and nobody used it? These are the kind of issues the arché-texts of Composition never seem to cover in their chapters on "Getting Organized." From Higgins's "Statement on Intermedia":

> It is difficult for me to imagine a serious person attacking any means of communication per se. Our real enemies are the ones who send us to die in pointless wars or to live lives which are reduced to drudgery, not the people who use other means of communication from those which we find most appropriate to the present situation. When these are attacked, a diversion has been established which only serves the interests of our real enemies. (172)

Besides, ridding our curricula of the mythology of power would leave us more time to think about fun. Theorizing a new urbanism around a notion of Street-Happenings means positioning one of the city's most glorious moments, the carnival, into the new program. And

I think that is ultimately what electronic discourse, by capturing students' passionate *dérives*, does to a classroom: it carnivalizes it. In the classroom-as-carnival, the celebrants dress in the drag of authority not to reproduce it but to mock it, which for Barthes is the very definition of text: "The text is (should be) that uninhibited person who shows his behind to the *Political Father*" (*Pleasure* 53). Carnival is the time when a city comes most wildly, excitedly alive. In their electronic discussions, students costume themselves (either in exaggerated, institutional false faces or just joyous, smiley faces) and, amid lots of laughter, overturn official culture; by doing so, they unmask it, revealing the skeletons in its tomb-like closets. Bakhtin noted what amounts to the carnival's allegorical function as palimpsest of the everyday, in the way it affirms the life of the common people outside of the authority of politics and religion, "a second world and a second life outside officialdom" (6). Since that authoritarian narrative was characterized by "asceticism" and "oppression" (73), this second story becomes the sublime, the beyond-bread. My students continue this tradition; their verbal caricatures of Allan Bloom are as much carnival grotesques as the pompous, overbearing, ultimately laughable demon of *The Closing of the American Mind*. Charlie, for example, kept referring to Bloom in his e-discussions and solo prose as "Plume," which I found very witty, catching the anachronistic nature of his subject. His "It's because he was raised in the attic of a cheese factory" is not academic analysis, it's more like bathroom graffiti; but as pithy, zen analysis, it's also like the clever (and resonant) identity-texts people write on stadium banners at the game-as-festival. (Sara Kiesler, on email in the corporate sector: "It's like all of a sudden there is this park in the middle of my company, and the park is open and there are no hours posted, so anybody can go into the park and cavort" [Bair D1].) The colloquia of carnival opposes itself to the authoritarian word, not accidentally so but purposively so.

But this means that there can be no question of the negotiation or reconciliation between electronic and academic discourse; there will always remain this simple opposition: online chats as glitzy funhouse in the arid Mojave of university writing. As such, then, it resembles nothing so much as Las Vegas. And Venturi reminds us that there's another name for scenes like Las Vegas, oases of fun and enjoyment in the midst of a harsh climate: *pleasure zones*. He taxonomizes their architecture around points that would seem to trace a sweet geometry of the writing class: "For the architect or urban designer, comparisons of Las Vegas with others of the world's 'pleasure zones'—with Marienbad, the Alhambra, Xanadu, and Disneyland, for instance—suggest that essential to the imagery of pleasure-zone architecture are lightness, the quality of being an oasis in a perhaps hostile climate, heightened symbolism, and the ability to engulf the visitor in a new role" (*Learning* 53). We spurn such a design-logic in our curricula (outside of the accidental occurrence of situationist Strip-talk). Our architecture is heavy with the weight of discursive tradition; the climate never turns oasis-like, but stays seriously harsh, either from pedagogies of oppression or psychological self-realization; our symbolic is bland with "real-world" representative mimicry; and the role playing is limited, confined either to shabby suits of socialist-realism or costumes left over from an old TV sitcom. We give students an amusement park, though, to be sure, in the sense of the removal of our curriculum from the real, but it's not very much fun; who could enjoy Stewart's Gulliver-o-Rama in Champaign-Urbana or Bartholomae's Discourse-Pirates of the Freirean? Baudrillard noted that the third phase of simulation, in its gradual envelopment of the real, is how "it masks the *absence* of a basic reality" (*Simulations* 11), and I guess that's what we have, a kind of third-order (third-rate?) Disneyland—Euro(Centric)Disney, then, with Allan Bloom in mouse ears ("Are we perfecting our souls yet?"). Foucault: "Finally, the student is given a gamelike way of life; he is offered a kind of distraction, amusement, freedom which, again, has nothing to do with real life" (65). If we want to be innovative, revolutionary curriculum designers, we might think more about the architectural tenets of pleasure zones when we delineate our "rules" for writers, and we might remember that for the situationists, "Proletarian revolutions will be *festivals* or nothing, for festivity is the very keynote of the life they announce. *Play* is the ultimate principle of this festival, and the only rules it can recognize are to live without dead time and to enjoy without restraints" (Knabb 337). It was not so very long ago we watched another exhausted system overturned by the Velvet Revolution, a name coined from its architects' enjoyment of trashy pop junk like the Velvet Underground. (Vaclav Havel was involved in Happenings in the Sixties. So was Vytautas Landsbergis, who would later become president of Lithuania. And Donald, did they speak of revolution in their own words, do you think, or in Lou Reed's? And, in the end, does it really matter?) In any architecture, systems have lives of their own that do not always follow their intended programs. Baudrillard speculates that cities may be imploding in on themselves because they are no longer responsive to their populace; hence we have power distributed along multiple, unpredictable points, seen by Baudrillard in the actions of Italian students running pirate-radio stations, media-seizers whose actions—as architects of a critical-regionalist resistance to increasing universalization—remind me of some of my students in online discussions:

> That is what continues underground: the implosion of social structure, institutions, power. . . . In Italy something of the same type is in play. In the actions of students, Metropolitan Indians, radio-pirates, something goes on which no longer partakes of the category of universality, having nothing to do either with classical solidarity (politics) or with the information diffusion of the media. . . . In order that mechanisms of such universality cease functioning, something must have changed; something must have taken place for the effect of subversion to move in some sense in the inverse direction, toward the interior, in defiance of the universal. Universality is subverted by an action within a limited, circumscribed sphere, one that is very concentrated, very dense, one that is exhausted by its own revolution. Here we have an absolutely new process.
>
> Such indeed are the radio-pirates, no longer broadcasting centers, but multiple points of implosion, points in an ungraspable swarm. They are a shifting landmass, but a landmass nonetheless, resistant to the homogeneity of political space. That is why the system must reduce them. Not for their political or militant content, but because, nonextensible, nonexplosive, nongeneralizable, they are dangerous locations, drawing their uniqueness and their peculiar violence from their refusal to be a system of expansion. ("Beaubourg-Effect" 13)

The immediacy of new technology in writing classrooms, though, means our students' reversibility becomes increasingly harder to reduce, despite the efforts of Composition's Media Business Operatives to fit it into the political or self-developmental karaoke they offer as the "real."

The choice seems pretty clear as to what we are teaching to, what use will ultimately be made of the compositions we erect on the cityscape. Basically, I see the choice as between the level fields of parking lots and playgrounds, on the one hand, and, on the other, the high, phallic grandeur of institutional monuments (temples, palaces, office towers, universities), hiding their deadly serious business. That is, we can allow students the seduction of texts in a carnival classroom, or we can train them to create writing that can be used in the production and marketing of bombs. But, hey, wait a minute: aren't I wildly oversimplifying? Aren't there really many other safe, neutral, professional capacities, other than the war machine, in which our students could honorably be working—in which they could even be critiquing those systems of hegemony? Perhaps, but they're so few, they're almost not worth mentioning. The use of our excess in the university writing classroom, where the uniformity of the essayist tradition reigns, perfectly mirrors that of our larger culture, in which

> perhaps three-quarters or more of the federal income, over the years, has been spent on "defense" or war-related matters or on servicing the debt on money borrowed for war. . . . [D]uring the forty years of the national security state, corporate America not only collected most of the federal revenue for "defense" but, in the process, reduced its share of federal taxes by twenty percentage points. Was this a conspiracy? No. They all think alike. Yes. They all think alike. (Vidal 90)

They think alike, Vidal claims, because of the universalization of the educational program, particularly for the ruling class (but now, with the increasing use of standardized testing, for all classes, really), in the way it will not admit complexity and contradiction: the education of the ruling class "insures that everyone so educated will tend to think alike. . . . [T]he indoctrination of the prep school alone is usually quite enough to create uniformity of ruling-class opinion when it comes to the rights of property. Since our corporate state is deeply democratic, there are always jobs available to middle-class careerists willing to play the game" (88). Whoever continues to speak of uniformity, say Kamper and Wulf, "today means destruction" (1).

The basic on-the-bus/off-the-bus choice of war or carnival shouldn't surprise; it's as old as the hills. Architecture always boils down to a choice between "the Greek temple [and its] historical and archetypal opposite, the urban facades of Italy, with their endless adjustments to the counter-requirements of inside and outside and their inflection with all the business of everyday life." Bataille reads the historical data for his theory of general economy and finds two extremes in the way excess resources were either "gloriously or catastrophically" consumed: in war and human sacrifice (for which victims were often prisoners of war) on the one hand, and the wasteful squandering of potlach festivals, on the other. The two impulses are at odds: "in general, sacrifice withdraws useful products from profane circulation; in principle the gifts of potlach liberate objects that are useless from the start" (*Vol. 1* 76). I'll take potlach, which represents true luxury, true acquisition. The squandering of resources represented by potlach is similar to what composition teachers from Bruffee to Farris would consider the squandering of productive task-oriented time in the writing classroom, but that's a superficial reading of the situation, one determined by a pedagogy of poverty and the oppressed:

> It is not what is imagined by those who have reduced it to their poverty; it is the return of life's immensity to the truth of exuberance. This truth destroys those who have taken it for what it is not; the least that one can say is that the present forms of wealth make a shambles and a human mockery of those who think they own it. In this respect, present-day society is a huge counterfeit, where this truth of wealth has underhandedly slipped into extreme poverty. The true luxury and the real potlach of our times falls to the poverty-stricken, that is, to the individual who lies down and scoffs. A genuine luxury requires the complete contempt for riches, the somber indifference of the individual who refuses work and makes his life on the one hand an infinitely ruined splendor, and on the other, a silent insult to the laborious lie of the rich. . . [N]o one can rediscover the meaning of wealth, the explosiveness that it heralds, unless it is in the splendor of rags and the somber challenge of indifference. One might say, finally, that the lie destines life's exuberance to revolt. (Bataille *Vol. 1* 76–77)

So no more Versatile or Successful (or Servile) Writers, please; rather Utterly Useless Aztec-Writers, Infinitely-Ruined Splendor-Writers. No more Facts, Artifacts, and Counterfacts; rather Wishes, Lies, and Dreams. Enough of Optimal Technologies already, bring on some Nonstraightforward Technologies for a change. Bataille's reading of splendor is confirmed in my students' e-transcripts: the truly rich, the linguistically exuberant, are often those our profession would deem the textually poor, the grammatically homeless. And just what are the students supposed to be successful professionspeakers or versatile writers for, anyway, if not the festival, the glorious, the miraculous, the too-marvelous for words, the happening? That's what everyone works for: not bread alone, but luxury, enjoyment, *taking it easy.* Bataille: "the worker's wage enables him to drink a glass of wine: he may do so, as he says, to give him strength, but he really drinks in the hope of escaping the necessity that is the principle of labor" (*Vols. 2 and 3* 199).

What is genetically encoded in our curriculum is neither power nor authenticity, but simply the indifference of those affected by it, and its ultimate explosion into exuberance. Or rather, *im*plosion, since that's what condemned buildings do: *the lie destines life's exuberance to revolt.* The lie goes by the name "success," and the scam we work, if students will just enter into our temples as true believers (sacrificial victims?), is *successful* *writing.* 'Successful writing?' Who knows what's successful? Oldenburg: "As far as I'm concerned, when I decide to do something, it's like throwing a switch, and everything that happens from that moment is a contribution to what finally takes place. A happening isn't always successful; and when people ask me whether one was or not, I don't know how to answer" (Kostelanetz *Theatre* 144). Canetti speaks of "the writer's profession" in terms that show both the irrelevance of "success" in our classrooms as well as how blithely we waste our most sublime resources in its name:

> If I now totally ignore what passes for success, if I even distrust it, then I do so because of a danger that everyone knows to exist in himself. The striving for success and success itself have a *narrowing* effect. The goal-oriented man on his way regards most things not serving the goal as ballast. He throws them out in order to be lighter, it cannot concern him that they are perhaps his best things. (243)

Bartholomae himself proves the truth of Canetti's sad prophecy. Boasting of his professional remove from all the give-and-take business of everyday life, he stiffly affirms his role as architect of Greek Temples: "There are parts of my life where I make friends, talk about kids and food and sports (this is my brand of common sense) and take it easy. I try not to write from it, however, or to confuse my professional work with the give and take of common life" ("Reply" 130). As such, he denies the miraculous possibilities of allegory: for him, any person, any object, any relationship *cannot* mean anything else. The everyday cannot substitute for the professional: talk about the kids cannot count as composition theory, just as Stephen North's Jimmy Stewart impression cannot, for Bartholomae, count as a conference presentation *located within the tradition*. The flip side of Bartholomae's aloof reserve is Foucault's claim that what is "academic" is "traditional in nature, obsolete . . . and not directly tied to the needs and problems of today" (65).

And anyway, I think that "talk about kids" can substitute quite well for composition theory. I think, for example, that Mister Rogers offers more sublime composition theory than any "professional" compositionist could ever hope to. What could you possibly build a better composition class on than theory like this:

> As a minister, Rogers has never thought of his television program, or Studio A, or any part of the world as a place to preach. "I never wanted to superimpose anything on anybody," he says. "I would like to think that I can create some sort of atmosphere that allows people to be comfortable enough to be who they are. And consequently, if they are, they can grow from there.
>
> "A lot of this—all of this—is just tending soil." (Laskas 82)

What discursive tradition or authentic voice could ever tell you anything more sublime about how to design a psychogeographical space in which people can reflect on writing? This is bedrock, Lefebvrian shape-of-fields theory, anything else is just too "deep." Compositionists themselves should be read allegorically. When all allegorical readings are permitted, when we can palimpsestically trace the runes of the expressivist ("You have the choice of thinking like a student or like a writer") in the facade of the anti-expressivist ("At an advanced stage, I would place students who establish their authority as *writers*" ["Inventing" 158]), then we can see what little difference there really is between them as compared to a situationist like Fred Rogers. Venturi's list of comparative features charting the differences between the Urban Sprawl ("formally . . . an awful mess; symbolically . . . a rich mix" [*Learning* 117]) and the Megastructure ("a distortion of normal city building process for the sake *inter alia* of image" [*Learning* 119]) provides a handy checklist to distinguish a situationist rhetoric from the dry Modernism of bread-alone's simulation:

Urban Sprawl	*Megastructure*
Ugly and ordinary	Heroic and original
Big signs designed by commercial artists	Little signs (and only if absolutely necessary) designed by "graphic artists"
Auto environment	Post- and pre-auto environment
Takes the parking lot seriously and pastiches the pedestrian	"Straight" architecture with serious but egocentric aims for the pedestrian; it irresponsibly ignores or tries to "piazzify" the parking lot
Promoted by sales staff	Promoted by experts
Feasible and being built	Technologically feasible perhaps, but socially and economically infeasible
Popular lifestyle	"Correct" lifestyle
Process city	Instant city
Looks awful	Makes a nice model
Architects don't like	Architects like
Expedience	Technological indulgence
Vital mess	"Total Design" (and design review boards)
Building for markets	Building for Man
This year's problems	The old architectural revolution
Heterogeneous images	The image of the middle-class intelligentsia
The difficult whole	The easy whole

(adapted from *Learning* 118)

The Total Design theories of Megastructural architects, in reaction to the seeming mess of the urban sprawl, become a misconceived effort to supply the "real" as reality teems around them. They create more impressive models than actual lived spaces: megastructures "are a bore as architectural theory and ultimately, as well as immediately, unresponsive to the real and interesting problems now" (*Learning* 149). Indeed, the sprawl of the Strip is in keeping with the foundation of "process" upon which we've presumably erected our new, humane composition, but "Modern architects . . . do not recognize the image of the process city when they see it on the Strip, because it is both too familiar and too different from what they have been trained to accept" (*Learning* 119).

If only Composition could forget the "real world" that circumscribes it. It is so busy teaching to oppression or the dominant ideology (which students know only too well, from Day One), and avoiding any mention of the sublime, that even if our students do reach a position of power and control and make as much bread as they want, they'll arrive there narrowed, ethic-less, unfestive, all dressed up with nowhere to go. What Composition calls "real" is always in quotation marks, always simulation. The expressivist/academic camps are subsumed by the rhetoric of simulation; their theory makes it sound like language and identity are simply commodity, *prêt-à-porter*, a set of Mouseketeer ears students take on and off at will. Stewart: "Try the new attitude [of writer]. Like a pair of stiff new shoes, it will seem awkward and uncomfortable at first, but you will find it fitting more comfortably with each passing week" (19); Bartholomae: "The student has to learn to speak our language, to speak as we do, to try on the peculiar ways of knowing, selecting, evaluating, reporting, concluding, and arguing that define the discourse of our community" ("Inventing" 134). What they're trying on, really, is irremovable, the straight jackets of formalist grammar and essayist prose, the grammar of the monument that will crush them and bury them. I'm no longer interested in giving students things to try on; I'm more interested now in what they leave behind in the fitting rooms, "the immense human wealth that the humblest facts of everyday life contain" (Lefebvre *Critique* 132). What I see there is a language and identity that is sweet, intelligent, joyous, exciting, available to all, and almost all right, but soon flushed down the abattoir's sewer, as the pure, clean forms of academic writing rush in to cover up the dirty secret of waste at the heart of our discipline. (Irmscher: "In many colleges and universities, Freshman

English still serves its traditional role: to get rid of the ill-prepared, not to help them become better writers" ["Finding" 81].) I'm interested now in the real outside of quotation marks. I don't need Marianna Torgovnick to tell me academic writing is not "exhilirating" (27); I can witness the guillotine-rhythm of Bartholomae's gerunds—knowing, selecting, evaluating, reporting, concluding, and arguing—every day in the academy. All I can do now is refuse to cover up the guillotine's work with another beautiful monument, the way the Palais du Louvre was turned into a lovely Museum after the Terror.

And I can put forward my urban renewal project, built on our basic need for something happening, for non-sense and the nonstraightforward. My project, a polite refusal to be a system of expansion, is offered in the hopes of getting students to be richer writers by seeing a more complex program, by learning more about the textures of their most commonplace materials (there are interesting passages in Venturi's books where he reveals his delight in having a tight budget to work within because it means using the cheapest, most readily available materials; see also Marcel, Jackson, and the Happenings artists), and by using those materials to become the architects of their own aesthetics: building compositions which are more than just picturesque, more than just banal; which may have no enclosure and little direction, but which move in interesting, exciting ways over vast, expansive textures, and which recover an abandoned tradition of rich iconology. And Composition *knew* the value of all this, of course; but we've treated our early architects *worse* than de Chirico, relegating such sublime blueprints as Deemer's and Lutz's to musty stacks in the Library basement. But finally, my urbanism is not a call for a new architecture (no more paradigm shifts, please; Venturi cites Wallace Stevens as to how "incessant new beginnings lead to sterility" [*Learning* 87]); it's rather an anti-architecture, an anti-aesthetic. I want to pressure the cracks in order to bring down the monuments, which "oppos[e] the logic and majesty of authority against all disturbing elements: it is in the form of cathedral or palace that Church or State speaks to the multitudes and imposes silence upon them" (Bataille, in Hollier *Against* 47). Quite often the only technique that makes sense is a technique of critical demolition. Mine is an "architecture-against-itself" to use the term with which Betrand Tschumi labeled his project to turn the old La Villette slaughterhouse into a public park, described by Hollier in terms of the festive and nonsensical that was the park's intent: "As if a donjuanesque architecture would escape finally from the stiff, punitive order of the Commendatore. It would enter into games and begin to dance. 'The program can challenge the very ideology it implied.' Such a project calls upon the loss of meaning, to give it a dionysiac dimension . . . the park, a postmodern 'assault on meaning,' claims as its main purpose to 'dismantle meaning'" (*Against* xi). Hollier, though, remained skeptical of Tschumi's plan to pave over the slaughter-house and erect a park devoted to science and industry, a park that would monumentally attempt to disguise the slaughterhouse that was still there, of course (the persistence of memory), in the form of the slaugh-tered waste of workers' lives represented by the very notion of "industry" the park intended to celebrate. My architectonics of composition, though—representing the scene of the contemporary writing classroom not as temple or fortress (Bloom, Bartholomae), nor as office complex (Hairston's plutography of composition), but simply as baseline firma-ment, as parking lot—insists on the loss and denies the monument. Life, the everyday, is doubled by death and loss, and allegory is the textual strategy that allows us to speak of the one story written over the other (the urban facades of Italy and the ruins of the urban facades of Italy; the skin and the skull beneath); Benjamin: "For an appreciation of the tran-sience of things, and the concern to rescue them for eternity, is one of the strongest impulses in allegory" (*Origin* 223). Benjamin's primal scene of allegory is a perfect one to use for reading our students' coursework: the *trauerspiel*. I want to raze the Inca monuments, then; pave them over and erect *nothing*: parking-lot-as-park, with just an allegorical plaque off to one side, commemorating the waste and sacrifice of those who went before (who are still going—alas, poor James, poor White Shoes, poor Harold, I knew them . . .), a plaque that will tell always of the blood and bone and hair underneath (the sweet, silly ornamentation of those wild rainbows of dyed hair), so we never forget. I don't know, it seems almost all right to me. I mean, our students are *into* cars, even Donald Stewart knew that ("Don't tell me about the various cars I have left out. You know them, probably to the year, and relish that information" 6), so why ask them to leave their rides behind and trek on foot deep within our tem-ples? Let's design our curriculum around the needs of the auto environ-ment. A curriculum-made-happening can become a movable feast, a potlach tail-gate party where all of us nomads can get together to talk about ourselves and our language, sharing what we know, maybe even enhancing the discourse already there in us. It's the confidence of Macrorie, in the unremitting expectation of a miracle: "Out of the corner of my eye these days I sometimes see the glimmer of a world transformed by millions of persons who expect great things from each other" (*Uptaught* 187). And the party is held out in the sun, not in the deep recesses of grandiloquent discursive temples. Think of this as my de Chiricoesque "Arcade" period, in which I feel *empty spaces* like parking lots can create a *full-filled* time. "It is too late to be reasonable and educated—which has led to a life without appeal. Secretly or not, it is necessary to become completely different, or to cease being" (Bataille *Visions* 179). I urge you to stop and smell the stucco roses in the *parterre* of the asphalt landscape.

5

NEVER MIND THE TAGMEMICS, WHERE'S THE SEX PISTOLS?

They said that oblivion was their ruling passion. They wanted to reinvent everything each day; to become the masters and possessors of their own lives. . . . The progress achieved in the domination of nature was not yet matched by a corresponding liberation of everyday life. Youth passed away among the various controls of resignation.

Guy Debord

Our story begins, as always, with lack and desire. It's 1975, the year *On Righting Writing: Classroom Practices in Teaching English 1975–1976* appeared, in answer to the "great concern for the quality of student writing" (Clapp *vii*) expressed in an open meeting on classroom practices at the 1974 convention of NCTE. The preface to this the thirteenth report from the Committee on Classroom Practices informs us that "there was no doubt in the mind of anyone attending the meeting that the improvement of writing instruction should be the theme of this [report]" (*vii*). Whether or not the variety of practices offered in this collection could ever lead to improved writing instruction is anyone's guess. In many respects, any pedagogical notion might provoke good writing, if an intriguing context were also provided. Take Mariana Gibson's piece in this collection, "Students Write Their Own Bicentennial Ballads": she describes a strategy of deconstructing familiar bits of folklore like "Yankee Doodle" with her students, who were then asked to think of contemporary songs that might fit the genre of Americana folk-ballads (she suggests "Ode to Billy Joe" or "The Night They Drove Old Dixie Down"). Afterwards, "the class is ready to write down their own ballads, using topics from our revolutionary era" (94). Depending on the classroom ecology, that might be an interesting class. Gibson's rationale for her lesson was based "upon the fact that much that happened in the fateful years of 1775, 1776, and 1777 was recorded and preserved in song" (93). Indeed, much that happened in the similarly fateful years of 1975–1977 was recorded and preserved in song, too. In fact, compositionists who read Gibson's article a couple years after it appeared might have found even better contemporary songs to explore—

say, "I'm So Bored with the USA" (1977). What's unfortunate about this book—indeed, about post-Happenings Composition in general—is that what's most compelling about the era is what's left out of the scholarship. 1975 was an interesting year in the history of contemporary song; among other things, it was the year in which Malcolm McLaren spotted Johnny Rotten in Sex, his King's Road clothing boutique. I'm not surprised the writers of *On Righting Writing* didn't give that episode much play in their collection because, really, in 1975, who knew? But shouldn't we be surprised that *CCC* of 1977–1980, when it had had ample time to hit, didn't give *any* attention whatsoever to the revolutionary era of the popular that was Punk?

It's an interesting question, the academy's disinterest in Punk, and one that has begun to be taken up. According to Faulk:

> The factors that made the recovery of Punk a belated event [are as] crucial, if necessarily more difficult to articulate, as anything we now have to say about either the music or the subculture. The notoriety of Punk . . . resides not simply in what was said . . . but in what Punk was silenced . . . for saying. (59)

And so I'd like to replay sounds from that silenced era; re-read the almost erased palimpsest of Punk, on which our field's official history has been overwritten; poke around in a cultural parallelism—popular music and Composition theory (which once, in the late Sixties, rhymed in interesting ways)—to see what points can be made about the urges and counter-urges against which we work, and to better understand the powerful pedagogy that was lost when Happenings Composition vanished from our field.

Those who read the old copies of *CCC* 1968–1971 will have no trouble recalling what music flooded the airwaves then and what it meant to its listeners. Happenings Composition found it difficult to form its expressivist pedagogy exclusive of pop. In May 1968, Walker advises, "the bulk of our attention should be given to youth culture . . . if we expect to have an affirmative answer to the question . . . 'Something is happening here, but you don't know what it is, do you Mister Jones?'" (636). The popular was perceived as useful compositional material because it altered the established scene of academic writing. As Deemer urges: "Let the 'teacher' shock the student. . . . Let him discuss theology to Ray Charles records" (124). In December 1968, Kroeger, although grudgingly, realizes "we must know and empathize with our students . . . . Every college English teacher ought to tune in to a local popular radio station once in a while, even if he must shudder throughout the whole experience" (337). And so Kroeger writes about an assignment in which his students do an analytical essay comparing "Eve of Destruction" with "Dawn of Correction." In October 1969, Carter proselytizes that for an instructor concerned with "the problem of getting the freshman to write something he cares about . . . there is in contemporary music a vast and rewarding writing potential for students" (228). And in December 1971, Litz reprints all of Ralph J. Gleason's liner notes for Miles Davis's *Bitches Brew,* tracing the way Gleason was influenced by Miles's phrasing, in order to advocate "a prose form that is a written analog to Davis's new music. This prose form may be called surrealistic writing. . . . [a prose to] break down the barrier which usually exists between writer and reader . . . loose, supple, hip and exactly right for the emotions stirred by the music of the album" (345, 347). (Ah, *Bitches Brew* . . . "'Bitches Brew' by Miles Davis. I loved that album," John Lydon recalls in his autobiography [81].)

For such teachers, popular music seemed an exciting natural landscape through which to chase "the wispish suggestion of a meaning which cannot be realized, the sense of a sense that is never absent at the same time it is never quite there" (Coles "The Sense of Nonsense" 28). Litz took his cue from Gleason ("this music is") to urge an indeterminate response to prose: "let's say it's just writing. This writing is" (354). But gradually such open-ended dreams were abandoned in favor of righting writing; traditional, determinate goals were re-affirmed. Writing could no longer just *be,* it had to be a certain way. That ongoing tension present in all arts, between the academic and the avant-garde, between the high and the low, was shifting in our field. The general debate was nicely dramatized at the 1970 CCCC. There, two convention addresses, one by Robert Heilman and one by Louis Kampf, both meant to articulate the theme of that year's annual meeting, "Foreseeing the 1970s," neatly captured the turn we took from the late Sixties to the late Seventies and today. Heilman, who had been teaching first-year writing since the fall of 1927, used his talk to urge Composition away from its interest in the trendy—its tendency to be "time's slaves, always ready, when slapped, to turn to the other chic" ("Except He Come" 231). (Several months earlier, in November 1969, in a speech at an NCTE meeting, Heilman had made perfectly clear his position on the subject of music in the classroom: "It tends to reduce the amount of reading by creating a thirst for the greater immediate excitement of sound. . . . The classroom is for criticism. . . and it cannot be wise to attenuate it by the substitution of sensory experience which the age already supplies in excess" ["The Full Man" 242–243].) For him, Composition implied mastery of "an objective body of material" (233), one which led, through expertise, to the ordering of texts and selves and worlds. So he inveighed against late Sixties teachers who preached sincerity and relevance at the expense of rules. It was a matter of "indispensable" values: "the trained as against the wild, the tempered as against the raw, the aware as against the ignorant" (236). He closed his speech with a perfect metaphor: "The difference is that between the French Academy and Mardi Gras. . . . The ideal symbolised is civility, and civility is the ultimate victim of the I-want, I-turn-on, my-thing, carnival, id-powered style" (237). (Heilman, then, sounds not-so-uncannily like the British tabloid press in its civility-based outrage at the Sex Pistols: "The Foul Mouthed Yobs," screamed the headlines, "The Filth and the Fury!" "Who Are These Punks?" [Savage 263].) Kampf (who had been led away by the FBI from the 1969 CCCC for his anti-war activity) hated rule-governed composition; he felt rules were "one of our substitutes for the lost authority of church and family" (247) and resulted in "a talent for writing meaningless compositions on order" (246). His address to the opening session boils down to his assertion that "Composition courses should be eliminated, not improved: eliminated, because they help to support an oppressive system" (248). For Kampf, it was not a question of civility but economy: he knew what students were being trained, tempered and made aware for— Composition's implication in a system whereby "higher education . . . has been expanded to allow corporate capital better to exploit the quickening developments in technology" (247). He saw, in other words, how Composition enabled cheap holidays in other people's misery. To replace the academy's oppression he suggests a psychogeographic carnival in which students could simply *become* rather than write: "start by allowing students the free use of the freshman year to discover some things about their lives. Why are they in school? What is their social role? Why do they resent their freshman English teacher?" (249)

Competing presciences, then. But one seems to mirror the reality of the foreseen Seventies, the other a dreamy counter-reality. By the time *CCC* 1976 rolls around, we can see what happened to Kampfian notions of liberating Composition from its institutional thrall: Gebhardt and Smith in February 1976 were cautioning that "'Liberation' Is Not

'License'" in discussing their program called *Self-Awareness Through Writing*. The writing in this program could not be "egoistic, overly personal, [or] chaotic. . . . [It] does not necessitate writing that is too subjective to communicate. . . . No, the key here lies in the discipline" (23). The quest for Heilman's "objective body of material" was in full effect. In the May 1976 *CCC*, Miles begins the ever-popular inventory "What We Already Know About Composition and What We Need to Know," followed by D'Angelo's search, not for wispish suggestions in Composition, but "intelligible structure." In 1978, Lunsford amasses an objective body of material on what we know (and don't) about basic writing, and Bizzell proceeds to shore up academic ramparts ("requir[ing] students to think about what kind of person the intellectual work of college seems to be asking them to be . . . consult[ing] our colleagues in other college departments [to determine whether] the ethos of historians, music theorists, chemists, present any common features" ["Ethos" 353, 355]), at the expense of the popular ("persuad[ing] our students that it is in their best interests to pursue their intellectual work beyond the television image" [355]). The popular was disappeared; it hurt our students: Bizzell, then, shared Heilman's rhetorically oriented distrust of the excess of non-academic sensory experience, blaming "the dearth of extended rational presentation of ideas on television" (351) for students' weak expository skills. Kampf, though, was the Anti-Bizzell; he knew the popular had nothing to do with students' weak writing, it was the fault of the academy's corporate-mindedness: "Our students will attain the confidence to use their language when they are able to face the world with a sense of who they are . . . when we create programs of study which do not require students to turn themselves into marketable products" (249). It's too bad Kampf couldn't have foreseen Punk, because it wound up doing exactly what he wanted Freshman English to do: provide "a resistance culture giving students a sense of a different world" (249). Probably the easiest way to capture the almost hallucinatory non-popular tone of *CCC* at that time is to give examples of the time-warped sampler sayings embroidered on those issue's covers: e.g., the February 1977 issue is decorated with the legend "Snow on a Robin's Tail"; "The Darling Buds of May" adorns May 1977. We read those quaint mottoes now and can only wonder about the world their writers felt was being exscribed.

For Mariana Gibson, then, to remain a pedagogue of popular music in 1975 made her a bold soul. For *CCC* 1976 can now be recorded as the year the music died. Contemporary scholars of Composition Studies might have a difficult time believing that *CCC* 1977–1978 happened at the same time as the Sex Pistols. No surprise, perhaps; lack of enthusiasm for Punk had been institutionalized right from the start: "In the autumn of 1975, the mainstream music industry was not sympathetic to new groups that wanted to make an abrasive sociocultural noise" (Savage 123). For *CCC,* part of the elision lies in our field's general preference for "the tempered as against the raw." And when we do confess a taste for the raw, it's usually rawness *en route* (to authority or voice); it's rarely rawness *en abyme.* Even Elbow threw out all that lovely, foolish prewriting, seeing it merely as steps to the official formal version, "the processes that should occur on the way to that final draft" (*Writing* 7). As Hillocks wrote, the need was to "mov[e] beyond process . . . [to] focus on prewriting activities which help develop skills to be used in ensuing writing . . . something more than discussing general ideas and jotting notes is necessary" (248). Punk didn't discard prewrites, jotted notes, general ideas—it lived off them (in the same way, *CCC* today suffers for having cleared out all the kooky trash—workshop reports, staffroom interchanges, poems, and jeux d'esprit—that makes reading back issues such a lively experience). Composition would reshape rawness out of its insistence on the salvific: we are a *helping* discipline, saving students from their less-than-perfect tongues, affording them access to the privilege and power of SWE. Bizzell spoke for many at the time when she framed our students' problem: they "are socialized in language use much more through watching television than through reading and writing in academic discourse" ("Ethos" 351). Our transmutative language project in the post-Happenings era shifted to academic empowerment, ridding the student-expressive of all traces of the popular so as to ensure postsecondary success and, hence, full access to post-collegiate capital (as Kampf so acutely foresaw it, "train[ing] students for a world in which they will cut each others' throats for their daily bread" [249]). Needless to say, this is not a Punk notion ("Is this writing?" Public Image Ltd. might have asked, "We've been careering" [*Metal Box*]). Why train students for the future when there is no future? Why give them career-oriented writing lessons when career opportunities are the ones that never knock? Punk is not a helping discipline; it doesn't want to reform, but rather to re-form. Like Bizzell, we saw our late-1970s students as pretty vacant and hated it, pitied them. We wanted them to worry about their (our) writing. But Punk students didn't want our pity (or our writing);

they were well beyond being pitied in their feelings. In terms of what counts as Composition, they would care only about the unforeseen possibilities of writing, the process, the play. Any concern for them was returned as accusation:

> You won't find me just staying static
> Don't give me any orders
> To people like me there is no order
> Bet you thought you had it all worked out
> Bet you thought you knew what I was about
> Bet you thought you'd solved all your problems
> But you are the problem . . .
> The problem is you
> What you gonna do with your problem? ("Problems")

We never thought the problem was us; Comp 1977's Lamberg blithely writes of "Major Problems in Doing Academic Writing," and none of the problems are located in the genre or the teacher; they all lie with the students' imperfect mastery, their "lack of self-management skills . . . failure to follow instructions" (26). Even for Britton et al., the problem was that *other* way of teaching, not their own *right* way. Punk, then, acts as a permanent dark-mirror, reflecting back, while at the same time denying, everything we claim. Punk can disgust, sure, but so can we. Even at its most repellent, Punk threw unavoidable questions right back. When Johnny Rotten sang "I'm an abortion," on stage at Winterland, he turned to the audience and dead-panned: "What does that make you?" (Savage 458). No matter how airtight our cynical read of students, Punk's abrasive noise keeps pestering its way in: "You thought that we were faking, that we were all just money-making. You do not believe we're for real, or you would lose your cheap appeal" ("E. M. I."). And Punk, of course, *was* there in Composition 1977. It was present as what leaked out of the system: "It was what your teachers would call you," notes Punk fanzine writer Legs McNeil. "It meant that you were the lowest. . . . We'd been told all our lives that we'd never amount to anything. We're the people who fell through the cracks of the educational system" (Savage 131).

What fell through the cracks became Punk's aesthetic material. Punk knew a refuse lot in the city beat out all the shopping schemes in the world: "'We deal in junk, you know,' said Joe Strummer, 'what we've got is what other people have put in the rubbish bin'" (Savage 235). Punk zines weren't worried about the surface look, just the general ideas. All you needed was knowledge of what your favorite bands, songs, and clothes were—how exciting a life they allowed you to construct out of them. And when Punk composed with official materials, it was always ironically inflected. The art of Jamie Reid, the Pistols' graphic designer, shows that Punk's aesthetic was that of the cut-up, remaking/remodeling the materials of the dominant culture, detourning them from their bland, deadening use into something truly useful. It was a re-fetishization of society's fetishes. Take the official photo of the Queen's Jubilee: only after messing with it—putting the Pistols' logo over the eyes and pasting a safety pin across her mouth (an idea Reid plagiarized from a May 1968 French poster)—could it really signify. (Debord: "We could expect nothing of anything we had not ourselves altered" [31].) This is the Happenings aesthetic, as well: looking upon past works materially, strategically, not with hushed veneration. Cage offers a pedagogical tenet in this regard: "I would not present things from the past, but I would approach them as materials available to something else which we were going to do now" (Kirby and Schechner 54). The grammar of material detournement practiced by Reid was also favored by European Happenings artist Wolf Vostell. According to Berghaus,

> Vostell confronted the spectator with fragments of reality that had been reorganized according to the principles of collage, montage, assemblage, and décollage. The usual continuity of space and time was interrupted, just as modern life is discontinuous and fragmented. He broke through the normal context of the well-known, the habitual, the familiar. Elements of everyday existence were put into a new order so that the ordinary and commonplace assumed a new and strange face. This provoked spectators to take a fresh look at things. It pulled them out of their lethargy and passivity, mobilized their fantasy, and forced them to react creatively with their environment. (319–320)

Vostell's early art, the dé-coll/ages, were amalgams of ripped, weathered posters from the street. Very Punk, that: trying to find beauty from shards of society's (particularly the media's) rotting excess. And just as Kaprow had claimed for Jackson, the space of art went from the wall into the street: Vostell's dé-coll/ages gave way to dé-coll/age Actions. His early Action, *The Theatre Takes Place on the Street* (1958)—in which a group of people were directed to walk down a street and read the text fragments they found on torn posters, using body language to interpret them; tearing the already torn posters even further to expose covered layers or suppressed media text, creating a catalogue-text of handbill detritus—was designed to stop a traffic line in the participants' lives; as Berghaus writes, "The participants were able to go beyond the level of contemplating a work of art to reflect critically on themselves and their relationship to reality by being involved in a change of their environment" (321).

The Queen's Jubilee poster, then, was only *materially* interesting for Punk. Post-Happenings Composition revered the past as art, and so became concerned with reproducing it, with writing as an iterative gesture, free of irony; an unconscious dynamic of repetition, blithely unconcerned with whether the forms it advocated were the right ones to re-cycle in terms of human need and desire. Hillocks, for example, writing in 1986, determines "the most effective mode of instruction" to be

> activities which result in high levels of student interaction concerning particular problems parallel to those they encounter in certain kinds of writing, e.g., generating criteria and examples to develop extended definitions of concepts or generating arguable assertions from appropriate data and predicting and countering opposing arguments. . . . [It] places priority on structured problem-solving activities, with clear objectives, planned to enable students to deal with similar problems in composing. (247)

It became writing as a way to activate the codified scripts of academia, those similar problems in composing (and so Bizzell's call for a "taxonomy of academic discourse" ["Ethos" 355]). The search for intelligible structures is over; the goods have been found and now they need only be routinely delivered. Punk wanted the only-too-conscious repetition, the last repetition, using it all up so it could never be used again. The goods were unpacked, found revolting, and then fucked with. Rather than a taxonomy of discourse, it preferred a pastiche (e.g., Punk fashions were a melange of looks from an assortment of trends, the jumble sale aesthetic). In 1946, in his pre-bicentennial ballad "The Great Trouble with Art in This Country," Duchamp—the "original" Punk, the one who painted a mustache on the Mona Lisa and entered a urinal in an art show—articulated his boredom with composition as he knew it, and it was precisely with art as perfected repetition. He wanted not the ongoing, unified academic narrative of a tradition steadily unfolding, but rupture, an historical-material detournement such as punks practiced in their re-fetishization. His comments explain not only his own artistic strategies, but the Punk boredom with, say, the Rolling Stones:

there is no spirit of revolt—no new ideas appearing among the younger artists. They are following along the paths beaten out by their predecessors, trying to do better what their predecessors have already done. In art there is no such thing as perfection. And a creative lull occurs always when artists of a period are satisfied to pick up a predecessor's work where he dropped it and attempt to continue what he was doing. When on the other hand you pick up something from an earlier period and adapt it to your own work an approach can be creative. The result is not new; but it is new insomuch as it is a different approach. (123)

About twenty years later, Macrorie would feel a similar dissatisfaction with Academic Composition as he knew it, also desiring irruption: "I should have realized that a cataclysmic event was needed to break a student away from the dead language of the schools—some severe displacement or removal from the unreal world of the university, like drunkenness" (*Uptaught* 11). And ten years after Macrorie, came Rotten: "I'm watching all the rubbish, you're wasting my time. I look around your house, you've got nothing to steal" ("No Feelings"). This is precisely the spirit of the Happenings, whose artists spoke of boredom matter-of-factly. Asked why he preferred Happenings to traditional theatre, Robert Whitman was frank about how little the mainstream theatrical culture offered in terms of interest or usefulness: "I've seen it all before. I haven't read a modern play that has anything to do with what I think is interesting, exciting, or meaningful in my life. They just haven't been pertinent to the problems I face" (Kostelanetz *Theatre* 234).

Unlike Composition's, Punk's performance was not judged according to standard criteria: "'Whether they were *good* or not was irrelevant,' says [a fan who watched the first Sex Pistols gig in late 1975]: 'I *wanted* to be excited and they filled a spot.' [Punk p]erformers are only as interesting as the emotions that they generate, or the situations that they catalyse" (Savage 142). A focus on 'error,' for example, was anathema. Lydon could be talking about mainstream Composition instead of boring rock bands when he speaks of the folly of focusing on surface perfection instead of the bold energy of the statement:

> We had to learn our skills from a live perspective. It wouldn't have worked any other way. That's what was wrong with most of those bands then—and still is. They were too much into the perfection of it all. . . . We had something none of [those] people had—energy and sheer, brazen honesty. We

couldn't give a fuck what people thought because we felt what we were saying was much more relevant. (94)

The key genres of Punk are those which made sense only when written in large letters on the media of collective space—fashion, graffiti, music, crime (these, of course, are the same discursive-sites as the negation-soundtrack of today, gangsta rap). *CCC* 1977 chose more exclusive, insular media. The social became simply a representational trope. Instead of stimulating situations, it simulated them; rather than scene, there's scenario, case. Hairston shows how to begin the fictification, explaining the way to achieve a rhetorical effect as if it were assumed the reader knew what s/he wanted, just not how to reproduce it: "Begin by asking these questions . . . Who is my audience and what assumptions can I make about them?" (2nd ed. 2). The Sex Pistols were just the opposite: "Don't know what I want but I know how to get it" ("Anarchy in the U.K."). Teachers at that open meeting in 1974 wanted improved writing instruction, perhaps, because they found, as Macrorie, Kampf, and Co. had, that the academy has an incredible propensity for turning something—a good idea, compelling material, an interesting medium, a student's life—into nothing. Punk, however, has the uncanny ability to turn absolute nothing into something amazing:

> In the United States, primitive enclaves had formed across the country (nightclubs, fanzines, record stores, a half-dozen high school students here, a trio of artists there, a girl locked in her room staring at her new haircut in the mirror)—though perhaps less in response to the thrill of hearing $10 import copies of the banned "Anarchy" single than to newspaper and TV features about London teenagers mutilating their faces with common household objects. Real discoveries were taking place, out of nothing ("The original scene," said a founder of the Los Angeles punk milieu, "was made of people who were taking chances and operating on obscure fragments of information"); for some, those discoveries, a new way of walking and a new way of talking, would dramatize the contradictions of everyday existence for years to come, would keep life more interesting than it would have otherwise been. (Marcus *Lipstick Traces* 36–37)

Punk just couldn't be represented in the narrative of *CCC* 1979, not like the Beatles or "Eve of Destruction" were in *CCC* 1969. Despite the title of Barry McGuire's hit, he wasn't rooting for the end of the world, he was dreading it ("Can't ya feel the fears I'm feelin' today? . . . Take a look around you boy, it's bound to scare ya' boy" [Kroeger 338]). And

Beatles music was appealing because it was a way to keep alive the myth ". . . that the system worked, that the class system wasn't as repressive as some critics contended. It also proved that 'art' and the attitudes fostered in English art schools could produce 'higher' values, enabling a working-class lad to rise above his common station and the grim reality of his childhood background" (Graham 103). So Steven Carter sells *CCC* 1969 readers on the Beatles by citing accolades from Aaron Copland, Leonard Bernstein, Ned Rorem, and Wilfred Sheed, and reinforces the high/low dichotomy by assuring that "young people grow into the Beatles as they are growing out of the wasteland of popular music—the top forty—which the Beatles have transcended" (229). Punk, as toxic-wasteland, didn't care about the high/low, tempered/raw dichotomy: Rhetoric of the Open Hand vs. the Closed Fist? How about the Rhetoric of the Middle Finger? The Sex Pistols sang about "no future" as if they'd discovered the most wonderful thing in the world— its ending. *CCC* 1979 couldn't allow Punk in because it would negate *CCC* 1979 and all the Composition it was attempting to prefigure, where discipline-based discursive patterns are rehearsed and reinforced. How could late Seventies *CCC* permit "Don't be told what you want, Don't be told what you need" ("Anarchy in the U.K."), when that's what we were all about doing? We were hyping our objective body of material as what students needed to succeed in college as well as the professions, but Punk, meanwhile, was taunting, "You won't find me working nine to five. It's too much fun being alive" ("Problems"). Punk wanted the world of the Paris Commune, a world that desired to "forever erase the divisions of faith, work, family, and leisure" (Marcus *Lipstick Traces* 141). The Commune's is a palimpsest as indelible as Punk's:

> The Commune was the biggest festival of the nineteenth century. Underlying the events of that spring of 1871, one can see the insurgents' feeling that they had become masters of their own history, not so much on the level of "governmental" politics as on the level of their everyday life. . . . [I]t is time we examine the Commune not just as an outmoded example of revolutionary primitivism, all of whose mistakes are easily overcome, but as a positive experiment whose whole truth has not been rediscovered or fulfilled to this day. (Debord et al. 314–315)

Think of all those Eighties *CCC* pieces about how writing on the job worked. Will knowing how a biologist writes help bring about the Paris Commune? Ah, but what about how a biologist drinks, dreams, envies?

The sweet, cracked desire to explore lives and possibilities marked the re-emergence of *CCC* 1968; as Deemer put it, that "reengagement of the heart, a new tuning of *all* the senses. Taking the first step toward poetry" (125). This meant hearing the unheard of, permitting any material that might afford that poetry. Marcus:

> Punk to me was a form of free speech. It was a moment when suddenly all kinds of strange voices that no reasonable person could have ever expected to hear in public were being heard all over the place. . . . [I]t was the Sex Pistols who gave people permission to say anything—I mean, if this ugly, hunched-over kid could stand up and say, "I am the Anti-Christ" and make it believable, then anything was possible. ("Punk and History" 231)

Punk, then, echoes May 1968 in Paris, when "the country stopped, and suddenly everybody began to talk. . . . For a month everybody spoke to everybody else. You could talk about anything. People who had never stood up in front of more than two people, were standing up in front of thousands; fifteen-year-old girls, seventy-year-old men were trying to talk, haltingly, but in sometimes very eloquent ways, about how they wanted to live" (Marcus in "Punk and History" 232).

I don't mean to romanticize Punk, but rather to heuristicize it, to trace what I feel is its most useful, essential thread. Of course, Punk could genuinely repulse. Sid Vicious was in many respects pathetic; but pathetic people can be interesting, especially when they wield negation, which can turn their bullshit into an ethos. The hope, of course, is that negation under the politics of boredom will find no real reason to corrode what's interesting (is, say, John Coltrane, in any way the enemy?). The destructive urge goes beyond morality, ideology, aestheticism or experimentation, but when welded to the politics of boredom, one expects constructive destruction. "When we hit San Francisco . . . Sid was just into chaos for the sheer hell of it. Destroy everything. That's well and fine, but you don't destroy things offhand and flippantly. You've got to offer something in its place" (Lydon 261). Punk's famous battle cry, then—"I can't stand listening to this junk any longer!"—is presumed to result in more interesting junk. Was Punk politically suspect? *Fronts* attract obsessives, especially apocalyptic *fronts* designed to change the world. The local politics at punk clubs, for example, could be violent, awful. But the larger national politics in England at the time, the system Punk tried to undo, were worse. Punk racist? A case could probably be made. (Is a naive rhetoric of anti-racism ultimately guilty of racism? "[As was] pointed out at the time, '[Punk's] use of terms like rats, scum, plague, vermin, disease make racists appear inhuman, outside society and history.' This rhetoric of impurity exactly paralleled that of the fascists themselves" [Savage 518]), but the charge can certainly be brought immediately to bear against Margaret Thatcher, who mused in a TV interview, "People are really rather afraid that this country might be rather swamped by people with a different culture" (Savage 480). Insight into Punk's politics can be found, as usual, in the sign system that crucially signified for Punk, its clothing, especially the tee-shirts. Punks wore their politics on their chests as well as their sleeves (those swastika armbands). Charges of Punk's homophobia must deal with the conscious gay aesthetic of Punk: e.g., the tee-shirt McLaren sold on which two cowboys, one adjusting the other's bandanna, both naked from the waist down, penises just barely not touching, have the following exchange:

> Ello Joe, Been anywhere lately?
> Nah, its all played aht Bill,
> Gettin to straight. (Savage 101)

"There's too many closets," sang the Pistols ("Holidays in the Sun"), whose very name traced a homoerotic fantasy: "It came about from the idea of a pistol, a pin-up, a young thing, a better-looking assassin, a Sex Pistol" (McLaren "Punk and History" 225). Misogyny? Then you need to factor in things like the Sex tee-shirt of a woman's breasts, which afforded males an instant trans-gender opportunity; as well as the countless women drawn to Punk, on stage, in the music press, and in the audience (according to music journalist Caroline Coon: "The punk movement was the first time that women played an equal role as partners in a subcultural group" [Lydon 72]. And musician Chrissie Hynde recalls: "The beauty of the punk thing was that from January to June of 1977, nondiscrimination was what it was all about. There was little or no sexism or racism" [Lydon 153]). Finally, to determine Punk's politics, we might consider McLaren's 1974 manifesto tee-shirt, emblazoned with the legend "You're gonna wake up one morning and *know* what side of the bed you've been lying on!", listing below all the hates and loves of the movement coalescing around 430 King's Road. The entries show that Punk ideology described fairly traditional far-left politics— hates included dull rockers (of course), as well as liberals, media monopolies, the racist National Front, lousy politicians, and all who "profit by bad housing"; loves included not only proto-Punks like Iggy and black musicians like Trane, Shepp, and Marley, but Alexander Cockburn, Lenny Bruce, Joe Orton, anti-capitalist articles in *The New Statesman*, and even Walt Whitman (Savage 84–85).

McLaren was an ethnographer of the situationists and May 1968. So the slogans, the spectacle, detournement—all became the stock strategies of Punk. As did the ideology (which might as well have been Louis Kampf's):

> The radical critique and free reconstruction of all values and patterns of behavior imposed by alienated reality are its maximum program, and free creativity in the construction of all moments and events of life is the only *poetry* it can acknowledge, the poetry made by all, the beginning of the revolutionary festival. . . . *Play* is the ultimate principle of this festival, and the only rules it can recognize are to live without dead time and to enjoy without restraints. ("On the Poverty" 337)

To ensure no dead time, Punks would use *informe*, in the form of their corrosive spit—a precious Punk fluid (Bataille: "The formless . . . serves to bring things down in the world . . . [it] amounts to saying that the universe is something like a spider or spit" [*Visions of Excess* 31])—to break down the institutions which prevented the carnival. The Pistols rallied their generation when they announced "you'll always find us out to lunch" ("Pretty Vacant"): they were vacant only in society's (hollow) eyes, in reality they were plotting their Permanent Mental Health Day. For Happenings Composition, the academy was a key institution needing as much spit as one could gob to bring it completely down: "Ultimately," Lutz realized, "Freshman English as a Happening calls for the complete restructuring of the university" (35). May 1968's short and sweet academic critique could be read in situationist graffiti: ABOLISH THE UNIVERSITY. Despite its purported nimbus of helping students, situationists saw the academy acting only to perfect itself: "they fall back into professorial morality . . . *through a real rationalization of the teaching system.* . . . The university has become an institutional organization of ignorance; 'high culture' itself is being degraded in the assembly-line production of professors, *all* of whom are cretins and most of whom would get the bird from any audience of high schoolers" ("On the Poverty" 320). Macrorie confirmed that assembly-line's potency: "I was beginning my teaching, and, naturally enough, developing a protective blindness" (*Uptaught* 11). The academic system left the student a bored, ignorant spectator: "The whole of his life is out of his control, the whole of *life* is beyond him. . . . [H]e parades his very ordinary ignorance as if it were an original 'lifestyle'; he makes a virtue of his shabbiness and affects to be a bohemian" ("On the Poverty" 322). Foucault, in 1971, saw the sham: "The student is put outside of society, on a campus. . . while being transmitted a knowledge traditional in nature, obsolete, 'academic' and not directly tied to the needs and problems of today. . . [there's] this kind of artificial, theatrical society, a society of cardboard, that is being built around him" (65). Or as the Sex Pistols sneered, "cheap dialog, cheap essential scenery" ("Holidays in the Sun"). No wonder, then, the Pistols' worst audiences were university students, parading their ignorance by sitting on their hands at some of the most interesting performance events in history: "It was excellent fun to confront an audience and watch them just stare. The best gigs we'd ever done was when the audience didn't even bother to clap. Those gigs were usually at the universities. Outside of the universities, you'd find that people were a bit more understanding. Isn't that odd? Our worst enemies were university students" (Lydon 87).

CCC 1977 cast out rock 'n' roll, preferring the high road of discipline, mastery, intelligible structure. *CCC* 1977, then, means *no fun*. According to Patti Smith: "Rock's creed is fun. Fun forms the basis of its apocalyptic protest. . . . The work ethic produced the A-bomb. It must be abandoned" (Graham 87). The new class that developed in the 1950s, the teenager, was meant to consume, not produce. Its fun was in large part erotic, "not connected to reproduction . . . mocking parents' belief in sexual repression, marriage, and work as necessary for salvation" (Graham 86). The turn from *CCC* Late Sixties to *CCC* Late Seventies can be traced in the choices made: the work ethic over leisure, production over consumption, the reproductive over the erotic, the salvific over the diabolic, the positive over the negative, the individualistic over the collective, the representational over the expressive, the professional over the amateur, the past over the contemporary, resolution over conflict, appreciation over disgust, and integration into cultural systems over their disruption. Stephen North worried in *CCC* 1978 about the whole enterprise—"the broad absurdity of the whole thing . . . it's rather like lying on your back in the backyard on a clear summer night and calling that astronomy" ("Composition Now" 178). Exactly! Punk pedagogy was DIY. One of the Pistols' crowd, Debbie Wilson, affirms the virtues of the anti-academic, "I was still finding my way. I don't think anybody really knows their way with clothes at fifteen. We created the style by not being educated about dress" (Savage 207). Lydon agrees: "You don't need to be technically proficient at your so-called art to write songs. If you are musically proficient, usually you won't be any good at writing songs because you won't be able to express your feelings. You'll be bogged down in the technology of note perfections, set patterns, and set ideas" (230). Punk found the best educational theory scrawled on a Paris wall: "*Prenez vos desirs pour realité,*" or embroidered on the shirt of some mega-lomaniac entrepreneur from King's Road: "BE REASONABLE. DEMAND THE IMPOSSIBLE." In this topsy-turvy pedagogy, "to succeed in conventional terms meant you had failed on your own terms" (Savage 140). *CCC* 1977 went on to discover successful writing, the way, the process, the cognitive key to righting writing. Its dream was a time when "Lord God have mercy/ All crimes are paid" ("God Save the Queen"). Punk's key to righting things? Take your pick: "How many ways to get what you want/ I use the best/ I use the rest/ I use the enemy/ I use anarchy" ("Anarchy in the U.K."). To re-festishize the swastika armband was a way to force an interruption, one which might provide a space to wonder whether Punk was only articulating a more general inchoate social reality; to wear a bondage suit in public was simply to bring sexual repression to the surface; to "give a wrong time, stop a traffic line" might allow one a delay to reflect whether one's future dream really did amount to no more than a shopping scheme. When McLaren was asked on a TV interview why the Pistols were so sick, he answered they had to seem sick, "people are sick everywhere; people are sick and fed up with this country telling them what to do" (Sex Pistols *We've Cum*).

Listening to Punk was only "a *preliminary* stage" (Graham 103), it was music you listened to in order to take further action, records to play *en route* to the ultimate rejection of records, in favor of making one's own music. We never taught that, we never taught writing as a way of hating writing (except people like Kampf). Ours was a passive curriculum of music appreciation. It was a way of purifying writing, loving writing; the simple, unconscious art of the fetish. Punk Composition doesn't care about perfection—where there's no sense, how can there be error?—it's interested in *passages*, "teenagers chang[ing] their lives in pop acts of transformation" (Savage 192). So Allan Kaprow, for example, is ultimately not Punk. He didn't want his Happenings to bring about an end to theatre (the way, say, Duchamp wanted to make paintings that would put an end to painting); he was more 'big tent' than replacement: "I think of theatre in broader terms than most theatre people. This doesn't mean that the traditional theatre of the last few hundred years has to be moved out. Let's just add to it. . . . I don't want to put anyone out of business" (Schechner "Extensions" 229). European Happenings, born out of a strong social malaise, were far more Punk, and doubtless obvious precursors to it. Jean-Jacques Lebel describes those post-Pollock days of European anomie:

> All that was left of "action painting" was action. We were determined to become one with our hallucinations. We had a feeling of apocalypse, an insuperable disgust with the "civilization of happiness" and its Hiroshimas. Everything which had not become irremediably meaningless revolved—and still revolves—round two poles: Eros and Thanatos. It is a question of giving form to the myths which are ours, while falling prey as little as possible to the alienating mechanisms of the image-making industry. (272)

So part of both the European tradition of the Happenings as well as its later manifestation in Punk is the tradition of the spectacular-poetic political protest. To get to Johnny Rotten spitting, as Marcus's *Lipstick Traces* shows, we need to start, at least, at the Paris Commune, move through the barricades, and down to (as Lebel notes) Hans Arp blowing his nose in the French flag and Jean Duprey pissing on (and, hence, extinguishing) the eternal flame at the Arc de Triomphe. "In spite of everything, an art which does not face up to the principle of reality is one which has agreed to cheat, to compromise, to go down on its knees" (Lebel 272). And in Japan at the time, there was the guerilla theatre group Zenkaguren, who specialized in fashioning loosely-sealed cellophane bags of shit—called "truth grenades"—which they would lob at the police. Lebel definitely caught their spirit:

> It's time for mass shit-ins. Hit the impeccably toilet-trained "adult" civilization where it hurts—in its heavenly cleanliness. The sooner everyone realizes that
>   ART IS $HIT
> the better. From then on, it's pure spontaneity. (283–284)

Rather than analyzing or improving some horrid aspect of the culture, punks knew it was often just simpler to gob spit (or lob shit) at it: "A lot of people feel the Sex Pistols were just negative. I agree, and what the fuck is wrong with that? Sometimes the absolute most positive thing you can be in a boring society is completely negative. It helps" (Lydon 77). Take Wolf Vostell's very Punk Happening *No-Nine dé-coll/ages*

(1963), which performs, let us say, the ultimate analysis of televisual media. Where a post-Happenings cultural-studies curriculum might use a nice, tidy, theory-based, ad analysis to "deconstruct" media representation, Vostell took a different, more direct route: "After being driven to a quarry where Vostell had set up a TV set, the audience settled down to watch a popular quiz show which Vostell, from the upper part of the quarry, constantly jammed or 'décollaged.' Finally, he blew up the television" (Berghaus 323). At a later festival in 1963, in New Jersey, he buried a TV. This is the difference between Composition's official attitude of cannily deciphering and critiquing systems of cultural representation and Punk's ultimate response, which figures "why bother?" The system deserves no more than to be fucked with, blown up, and then—if you're feeling generous—buried. Anything more would legitimize it, encourage it. Vostell, in fact, purposefully noted his distinct difference from Kaprow. In an "action lecture" the two of them gave in New York, in 1964, Vostell saw his goal as *informe*, the opposite of Kaprow's sunnier expansiveness: his interest, he stated was "decomposition of the life principles that surround us, whilst you [Kaprow] . . . build up and construct" (Berghaus 324).

We can see the Punk/Happenings connection in Fluxus founder George Maciunas's 1962 manifesto "Neo-Dada in Music, Theater, Poetry, Art." In this essay, Maciunas champions what he terms a concretist notion of art, implying "unity of form and content, rather than their separation . . . the world of concrete reality rather than the artificial abstraction of illusionism" (156). He wants to return to an art of material reality, and so even the sound of a piano becomes illusionistic, as opposed to the more materially concrete sound "produced by striking the same piano itself with a hammer or kicking its underside," a sound "more material and concrete since it indicates in a much clearer manner the hardness of hammer, hollowness of piano sound box and resonance of string" (157). Take proto-Punk Pete Townsend's guitar-destroying finales to his concerts with the Who, acknowledged by Townsend to be influenced by Fluxus artist Gustav Metzger's 1962 lecture at Townsend's art school. Or Nam June Paik's *One for Violin Solo* (1962), which consisted of him destroying a violin, a performance termed "action music" (Smith "Fluxus" 26). Paik's piece went utterly counter to traditional concert-hall aesthetics, which, by festishizing the violin, abstract it from basic humanity. Stiles writes, "Paik's performance visualizes how oppressive elite cultural 'art' objects may be when their affective presence is over-determined against the value of human presence. Fluxus performances in general resoundingly support human presence and enactment over the *in-itselfness* of objects or the 'affective presence' of fine art" (85). Punk was desperate to return to a human presence, suffocating rubber bondage shirts worn on stage and safety pins stuck into bodies became a constant reminder of the body as baseline. To achieve concretism, Maciunas put forth the very Punk concept of art-nihilism or anti-art. The anti-art-forms he advocated read very much like Bataille's *informe*, and would seem to burn off the simulation of affective presence and bring about a desired re-connection with the human-scaled real:

> The "anti-art" forms are directed primarily against art as a profession, against the artificial separation of a performer from audience, or creator and spectator, or life and art; it is against the artificial forms or patterns or methods of art itself; it is against the purposefulness, formfulness and meaningfulness of art; anti-art is life, is nature, is true reality—it is one and all. Rainfall is anti-art, a babble of a crowd is anti-art, a flight of a butterfly, or movements of microbes are anti-art. They are as beautiful and worth to be aware of as art itself. (157)

Both Punk and the Happenings realized the interdependence of creation and destruction. Vostell first used *décoll/age* to name his Happenings when he read the term used in 1954 by *Le Figaro*, to describe the take-off and immediate crash of an airliner. And Jackson, of course. The drip paintings are nothing if not Punk:

> Perhaps initially Pollock was expressing, acting out, the tension between his frustrations and his rebelliousness by spilling paint. Perhaps he wanted to destroy the entire history of painting and to start fresh, screaming now, as during much of his life, "Fuck you," screaming this at the world, at history, with the most intensely positive and negative meaning, simultaneously loving and angry. . . . Like a naughty boy, Pollock may have wanted to make a mess, to disturb everything neat and orderly and faceless about the canvas, its clean surface, its regular texture, its rectangular shape, all reminiscent of dining tables he'd cleared and cleaned as a child and at the League, of dishes he'd washed and wiped until sparkling, of laundry on the line, of shirts he'd been told to tuck in, of rules of cleanliness, rules of composition. (Friedman *Energy* 98)

English Composition as Punk would have meant English Composition as Neo-Avant-Garde, resulting in a movement away from the Modernist representational program in which it languishes, a movement seen by Foster as distinctive of vanguard contemporary arts in their "shift in conception—from reality as an effect of representation to the real as a thing of trauma" (146). It was a natural for writing classes: when *Rolling Stone* writer Charles Young first met John Lydon in England, in the Summer of 1977, his reaction to "the idea of this sickly dwarf bringing the wrath of an entire nation down on his shoulders . . . [was that] if someone this powerless could cause that much uproar, maybe words still mean something" (73). A British Mariana Gibson might have had her students writing Queen's Jubilee ballads in 1977. And if John Lydon had been one of her students, he'd have done brilliant. No surprise: as Gibson knew, "The more familiar the theme is, the easier it will be for students to catch the creative mood" (94). And the theme of Lydon's Jubilee ballad, "God Save the Queen," was very familiar to him: "As for 'God Save the Queen,' there's always going to be this aristocratic segment of English society who are untouchable and unflappable. They wouldn't know what you were talking about should you attempt to even comment on their atrocious behavior. They just don't see it" (186). So, of course, that familiarity let him easily catch the creative mood: "I wrote 'God Save the Queen' at the kitchen table. . . . I wrote it one morning waiting for my baked beans to cook. I wrote the lyrics in one sitting" (81). Lydon had facility with the composing process perhaps because of a conception of his writing as exscription into life rather than solipsistically recycling a simulation: "This is how I write most of my songs. There is no set format, I tend to think a long time before I put pen to paper. When I'm ready, I'll sit down and write it out in one long piece, more like an open letter than a song. It becomes valid confrontation. There's an element of glory to it" (82). Lydon, then, would have provided Composition with a wonderful student-exemplar of the composing process as energy made visible. Music journalist Caroline Cook might have been speaking for a compositionist when she marveled at the freshman-aged writer's expressive power: "I loved his talent for writing, which was a combination of nerves and ambition. Here was somebody, nineteen, writing poems. That's what makes someone an artist. It's what moves you" (Lydon 114).

Alas, though, no Rotten Writing in *CCC* 1977. But Punk does just barely exist in the bowels of late Seventies Composition, fleetingly, as a wispish suggestion of unfortunately underused writing material: Lunsford mentions in passing that in one of her research studies, "About half of the twenty-two basic writers' essays . . . focused on punk rock and disco" ("Content" 283). There was a potential, then, in Punk, like Happenings Composition, that can't be forgotten, which makes its erasure that much harder to swallow. "It was a good time. It could have gone anywhere at one point. It kept people on edge. . . . At the end there was a pointless rerunning of a B movie, packed with the obvious. It shouldn't have been. It could have been something very courageous, and an absolute change. And yes, we could have won" (Lydon in "Punk and History" 231).

Exploiting Punk in CCCC 1977–1980—allowing students to write against the inhibitory—would have meant teaching the Deemerian allegory "English Composition as Cabaret Voltaire"; it would have meant Composition according to "the notion that in the constructed setting of a temporally enclosed space—in this case, a [classroom]—anything could be negated. It was the notion that, there, anything might happen, which meant finally that in the world at large, transposed artistically, anything might happen there, too" (Marcus *Lipstick Traces* 241). The program of the Cabaret Voltaire sounds like something those who want literacy as social action might like to explore: "Night after night, unknown people climbed out of the crowd to speak, to recite poems they had treasured all their lives or made up a few minutes before, to sing old songs, to make fools of themselves, to take part, to change" (Marcus 212). To a curriculum like this, one that tells unknown people they can "be free, elegant, smart, independent, the owners of all that they say," post-Happenings Composition knowingly sniffs, "sentimental realism" (Bartholomae "Writing" 70, 69). (It's reminiscent of how Greenberg dismissed the Action Painter, as if he had "come out of nowhere and owes practically nothing to anything before him. It's as though art began all over again every other day" ["How Art Writing" 143]). But from 1977 on, Composition was not busy converting the writing classroom into a Dadaist cabaret; rather its project was ridding the verbalscape of all traces of the carnival, erecting the classical facade of the New French Academy. There would be no abandoning of the work ethic in CCCC's foreseen Seventies. After all, it is only to pinheads like "Mr. Little-Know and Mr. Strong-Feel [that the Academy] is likely to seem only the original school marm, and Carnival the ultimately free secular Beulah Land," according to the trained, tempered, aware Robert B. Heilman, who wasn't against Carnival *per se*, only when it threatened to completely restructure the university, "only when it pops up all year round in classroom, study, and library" ("Except He Come" 237).

CCC volume 29, number 1, appeared in February 1978, one month after the Sex Pistols' gig at the Winterland, their last as a group. Just as the Pistols were going through their own long-overdue death-throes (one observer at the concert recalled: "It was a zombie performance, people who were already dead, reanimated for a while, going through their motions. They were media-saturated, they'd run out of message to deliver" [Savage 457–458]), a similar death-rattle finally sounded in our field. In that number of *CCC*, the still-barely-animated zombie of Happenings Composition is finally brought down: Robert Connors reviews Ken Macrorie's *Vulnerable Teacher*, using the review as an opportunity to nail the coffin on the spirit of Comp 1968. He brings in enough cynical power to ensure Macrorie's death by exposure: e.g., "We are given, for the umpteenth time, the tale of his pedagogical death-rebirth experience of May 5, 1964, with its famous battle-cry, 'I can't stand reading this junk any longer!'" (108). Connors consciously casts this ideological clash as a Sixties vs. Seventies thing, just as Punk itself did—"getting rid of the albatross . . . still the spirit of '68" (Public Image Ltd. *Metal Box*); or, as the seventeen year-old Punk spat at the twenty-nine year-old hippie, "We like noise, it's our choice, it's what we wanna do. We don't care about long hair, I don't wear flares" ("Seventeen")—except Connors comes off as a kind of Anti-Punk, shaking off Sixties nonsense to get back to Heilmanian business: "The bright lamp of Sixties radicalism, which Macrorie hefted so confidently in *Uptaught . . .* has dimmed and begun to gutter in the harsher realities of the Seventies" (108). Connors ends the review with a patricidal dream-image, that of "the pragmatic Seventies hav[ing] wounded Macrorie's Panglossian humanism unto death" (109). So, Punk a part of the burgeoning of post-Happenings Composition? "Give 'Em Enough Rope" on the cover of *CCC* 1978, instead of "Travelers' Warming: A Blizzard of May Blossoms"? No way. Post-Happenings Composition was built to last, to have a permanent aesthetic and callistic form; it's part of the evolving tradition. Punk, as music, as medium, was built to self-destruct faster than snow on a robin's tail, to have the *informe* of decay and disgust. It's a gamble, of course, to refuse to reproduce old writing, to be so seized by the desire to create a new thought that one is desperate enough to try to wring meaning out of even such nothing junk as safety pins, to hope to disgorge ethereal spirit from common household objects agonizingly available to all. Formally, it's a gamble one is sure to lose.

There's an inexorability, a doom-equation at the heart of negation's drama, which results in Punk's pathetic end. Few artists—only Duchamp comes readily to mind (who called some of his texts "wrotten writtens" [*morceaux moisis*] *vii*)—have been able to marshal enough inner resistance to continuously exploit negation for more than a matter of years. Hebdige notes that Sid and Nancy's story "obeyed the laws of narrative[,] and inevitably, given the status of the protagonists, they remained, first and foremost, events within representation" (39). Indeed, they *are* characters—in "The Ballad of Sid and Nancy" (a cautionary tale, of course):

> For naughty boys who swear and break
> All boundaries and try to make
> Pain out of pleasure, pleasure from pain
> Look on Sidney; think again. (Hebdige 38)

The Pistols couldn't maintain nihilism's pitch; by the time they toured America, their negation-value was only exploitable as ad-copy hook: "They said no one could be more bizarre than Alice Cooper, or more destructive than Kiss! They've not seen the Sex Pistols!" was how the cornball radio commercial hyped their Dallas show (Sex Pistols *We've Cum*). Sid and Nancy, Hebdige continues, were "victims of their own drive to coherence, in bondage to a fantasy of absolutes in a world where they simply don't exist" (40). Negation, in taking on everything, proves a demanding strategy, "curdl[ing] into the nullities of dogma, cynicism or self-destruction" (Savage 478). So there, on stage at San Francisco's Winterland Ballroom, on January 14, 1978, Punk caught up with itself:

> On stage, all one saw was an ugly, unlikely youth declaring his time as a pop star had come to an end: you could see it happen, hear him deciding to quit. "Ah, it's awful," he said in the middle of "No Fun," his last song as a member of the Sex Pistols, even his loathing leaving him. . . . The disgust that the band had been built to talk about had finally . . . overtaken the one whose job it was to talk about it. . . . All one saw was a failure; all one saw was a medium. . . . The show had gone as far as a show can go. (Marcus *Lipstick Traces* 123)

"Ever get the feeling you've been cheated?" Lydon asked from the Winterland stage at the end of the Sex Pistols' last concert. (Should that be the last question on our students' course evaluation forms?) If Lydon's disgust became self-realization, what about *CCC*'s tradition of pedagogical critique: victims of our own drive to coherence, in bondage to our own fantasy of absolutes—what do we do when we realize it's our own pedagogy we've been critiquing, it's our own body we've been mutilating?

Worse, and infinitely more worrisome, what if we never realize it? The Sex Pistols imploded partly because they stopped loathing the rock star system and began coveting it, re-novelizing themselves into its institutional narrative. Such is one of many contradictions at the heart of Punk: after killing rock 'n' roll, they attempt to find their identity in it. They transgressed the democratic impulse of Punk for industry elitism; as the Carnival became *played aht*, they decided to check out the Academy. The legend scrawled on Steve Jones' amp, "Guitar Hero," at some point lost all irony. That dangerous impulse—to become our worst nightmare, to forget to remember the politics of boredom—is always present in CCCC. "We're all prostitutes," sang some Punk band nobody hardly remembers.

Punk in *CCC* 1977? Of course it was there. In fact, it was there even earlier, in the early Seventies. *CCC* 1968 failed, like pop at the time, to transform the world because it neglected to definitively unfinish the institution. Trimbur, for example, sees process theory's failure in its inability to escape belletrism. As the hippie era became post-, a hollow sense of ritual set in: "Style replaced content; clothing became costume" (Savage 6). The ritualistic pervaded Composition; writing-as-iteration existed only to perfect. So I close with another tale of lack and desire, the one about the scholar bored by the increasing staleness of the same old song in Composition pedagogy, reflecting back on his first semester teaching Freshman English, in 1973, and his grim realization of NO FUTURE regarding his students and his curriculum: "I knew from the first week that I was going to fail them; in fact, I knew that I was going to preside over a curriculum that spent 14 weeks slowly and inevitably demonstrating their failures" (Bartholomae "Tidy House" 5). But some abrasive sociocultural noise breaks through the otherwise bland sounds of the early Seventies for that teacher, in the form of a student paper composed of little more than boredom and spit, a sound that twenty years later this teacher still cannot get out of his head. In fact, he claims, "it was the only memorable paper that I received from that class [in 1973] and I have kept it in my file drawer for eighteen years, long after I've thrown away all my other papers from graduate school" (6). The teacher was a young graduate assistant named David Bartholomae, the student was a young . . . what? Basic Writer? Loser? Nihilist? Punk? named Quentin Pierce. The paper is a self-canceling text, a self-failing gesture. It's the auto-mutilation of the student's last frontier: the body of his own writing. "The body becomes the baseline, the place where the buck stops," Hebdige said, describing the British punks. "To wear a mohican or to have your face tattooed, is to burn most of your bridges. In the current economic climate, when employers can afford to pick and choose, such gestures are a public disavowal of the will to queue for work, throwing yourself away before They do it for you" (32). Bartholomae dwells on the Punkish surface of Quentin's body: "the handwriting is labored and there is much scratching out . . . crossed out sentences" (5–6). But it is, of course, the slogans contained within Quentin's manifesto that Bartholomae cannot shake. Quentin leaves the ritual of post-hippie positivity behind to say "fuck you" to his writing teacher, his paper, his future, himself ("my entrance, my own creation, my grand finale, my goodbye" [Public Image Ltd. *Public Image*]). He injects the whole enterprise of post-Happenings Composition with instant entropy, or rather he exposes the entropic decay inherent in it through his refusal to enable the ritual further. After a few halting attempts at an answer to the ultra-academic prompt "If existence precedes essence, what is man?" his paper makes the turn for oblivion (*his ruling passion*):

> Man will not survive, he is a asshole.
> STOP
> The stories in the books or meanless stories and I will not elaborate on them
> This paper is meanless, just like the book. (6)

Quentin's negation fails himself before They have a chance to:

> But, I know the paper will not make it.
> STOP. (6)

Bartholomae continues his still-shook reverie:

> At the end, in what now begins to look like a page from *Leaves of Grass* or *Howl*, there is this:
>> I don't care.
>> I don't care.
>> about man and good and evil I don't care about this shit fuck this shit,
>> trash and should be put in the trash can with this shit
>> Thank you very much
>> I lose again. (6)

Whitman or Ginsberg—maybe. But they sound even more like the lyrics of a Sex Pistols song. As Punk, Quentin's self-negation works as *informe* to undo Bartholomae's curricular theory: "I was not prepared for this paper. In a sense, I did not know how to read it. I could only ignore it. I didn't know what to write on it, how to bring it into the class I was teaching" (6). Quentin, then, is the excess that our pedagogy cannot process, the poison in our human machine. But Quentin is also the flower in our dustbin, one whose seed lay not-so-dormant (*the only memorable paper*) for eighteen years until it blossomed in "The Tidy House." No need to worry, therefore, about Punk in CCCC. It's inescapable, forming a permanent theater of tension—the dominant culture vs. the underground, the academic as against the avant-garde. The pragmatic Seventies may well have wounded all Panglosses unto death, but what about the Anti-Pangloss? Punk might have imploded as a medium, as a show, but as *a state of mind?* As that, it's going nowhere. Punk's historical implosion is beside the point—I mean, big deal, the Paris Commune imploded, too: one could "easily prove that the Commune was objectively doomed to failure and could not have been fulfilled. They forget that for those who really lived it, the fulfillment *was already there*" (Debord et al. 316). The Pistols knew: "Too many people had the suss/ Too many people support us/ An unlimited amount/ Too many outlets in and out" ("E. M. I."). Punk—under whatever name—is here for the long haul, as long as modernity lasts; Lefebvre tells us, "to the degree that modernity has a meaning, it is this: it carries within itself, from the beginning, a radical negation" (Marcus *Lipstick Traces* 184). So Punk, finally, as part of the burgeoning of post-Happenings Composition? Why, it's the part we remember best.

6

ENGLISH COMPOSITION AS A HAPPENING II

PASSAGES

This book has shown my interest in work that explores practice: work that can be used to think about pedagogy, texts, materials, issues of production and reception, and particularly issues of form and content (what's used in Composition, what's not, and what other fields with the idea of composition at the center are using). I've especially been interested in recuperating ideas from the past—most obviously those figures like Duchamp, Pollock, the Happenings artists, the situationists, and the Sex Pistols, all of whom I consider compositionists-at-large; but also, in terms of the field of Composition Studies, from compositionists I've loosely grouped under the rubric Happenings Composition, referring to a time when our field seemed more open to broader material concerns. And I can't help but compare Composition of that vibrant era to that which supplanted it, as a kind of chronicle of loss. Take, for example, two very different textbooks, Ken Macrorie's *Searching Writing* and Bartholomae and Petrosky's *Ways of Reading*, which seem like such key transition texts to me: one the last gasp of the spirit of Late Sixties Composition, the other central in establishing the curriculum of the academic, analytical essay that currently holds sway. As scholar-teacher, I like to wander through such pedagogical scenes, hoping to inspire my practice (or reconfirm it), searching for ways I can best present forms and occasions for writing that might allow my students' spirit of inquiry and poetry to flourish in interesting ways.

In *Searching Writing*, the problem with college composition for Macrorie is almost wholly material: "In classes, the experiences in textbooks and lectures belong to others. Students are expected to see the relevance of this material to their new lives, but their old lives are seldom allowed into the discussion, and half-people learn poorly" ("Preface"). *Searching Writing* was designed to reinvent the research paper (that academic arch-genre) as "I-Search" paper, an expressive, experiential inquiry-quest a student undertakes out of some nagging personal need, "searches in which persons scratch an itch they feel" (14). In fact, the topics for such inquiry needed to be so idiosyncratic, so deeply felt, that Macrorie urged a kind of receptivity that would allow them to bubble up out of semi-conscious, quasi-dream states: "Walk around for a couple of days letting yourself think of what you feel you need to know. At night when you're beginning to slide off into sleep, and in the morning when you're coming out of sleep, let your mind receive possible topics" (62). (Macrorie's student, then, as surrealist-in-training; Benjamin speaks of "Saint-Pol Roux, retiring to bed about daybreak, fix[ing] a notice on his door: 'Poet at work'" [*One-Way Street* 226–227].) The textbook's basic methodology: after a series of freewrites to hone a personal, expressive style, the student identifies a topic, figures out the key information sources to check (usually people and current pamphlets, not books), and then writes up the story of the search. The overriding ambiance hovers around those *outré* terms "honesty" and "authenticity," with Macrorie psyching the student: "Say to yourself, 'What goes down here is going to be truth of some kind, nothing phony'" (6). It's a stubborn search for truth, for the conditions that might lead to it. The book's subtitle could have been "Only Connect," offering us the writing course as this basic human encounter between teacher and student: "The two must meet, bringing with them their own experiences and searches, their own effort and commitment" ("Preface"). The writing class, for me too, is, yes, all about that meeting, two experienced souls on their individual quests, their searches, stopping for a brief encounter, passing the time, then moving on, reinvigorated for the journey by their time spent chatting together.

An absurd idea, I know; that's the writing class as coffee bar, acquaintances meeting for an hour or so, looping through the verbal traces of their respective passages. Mere chit-chat is utterly forbidden, no casual conversation when there's all that required work to do. Shooting the breeze is not a currently sanctioned curricular practice: "There is nothing worse than a class where discussion is an end in itself—where a lively fifty minutes is its own justification" (Bartholomae and Petrosky *Resources for Teaching* 4). Such self-justified rap sessions, though, formed the highly unprofessional pedagogy of Happenings Composition:

> Halfway through the semester now in all my classes, I begin the two-hour session by saying, "What's on your mind today?" . . . One day when I [asked it] . . . Miss Edick, who had frequently launched the class into a good discussion,

started to speak, looked sad and confused, and then said in a low voice, "*I don't know—this may sound awfully strange. Maybe I shouldn't ask, but I've had to think about death lately, and I just wonder what you think of it.*" (*Uptaught* 177)

Mine, then, is nostalgia for the pre-professional, the pre-disciplinary. My sense now of Composition is of a field that all reads the same books, shares the same notion of what counts as professional knowledge; this auto-replicating homogeneity of the professional becomes the material discriminator for *Ways of Reading*: reading selections based on "the sorts of readings we talk about when we talk with our colleagues" (iv). Trimbur dutifully acknowledges this *de facto* canonicity—"all the work in cultural studies, feminist studies, postcolonial studies, literacy studies, African American studies, gay and lesbian studies, and so on that it seems irresponsible not to follow"—as the price we pay "for better and for worse, [to feel] part of a profession that has arrived" ("Close Reading" 137). We may have arrived, but what we've left was the joyous potential of our idiosyncratic status as anti-discipline, concerned only with students' inner lives, helping them craft some meaning on their own anxieties. When the overall imperative, then, was just to love them; the goal simply that "deeply felt truth" (Macrorie *Searching* 31).

Ways of Reading is designed to be a program "where students are given the opportunity to work on what they read," a "place to work on reading" (iii). Itchy topics are not scratched in the course, neither do ideas for investigation percolate through from half-sleeping states. They are controlled according to the set list of readings a student works through in the course: it is, then, a classic composition-reader-based course. The particular spin *Ways of Reading* applies is that students work through texts that will supposedly help them read the university, see how the discourse and inquiry of scholarly writing works. Texts chosen are bedrock critical theory classics—Barthes, Berger, Fish, Kuhn—as well as other similar literary monuments. Think about that scene for a minute: some of the most prized works by true icons in contemporary literary and critical thought, and these things somehow need to be *worked on* ("and [the students] work on it by writing" [iii])? Now, these works are pretty famous, have a pretty firmly established critical rep; do they really need *more* work done on them? And just what sort of work would that be, that our students could do it? What they're doing, of course, is materially extending those masterpieces further into the discourse. It's a kind of conservancy work, extending the scope of the works' power, preserving their reputation in the scholarly tradition by weaving them tighter and more firmly into the fabric of critical thought: making it more and more unmistakable, more obvious, that when one writes about the tradition of Western thought, the names that will repeatedly recur are Barthes, Berger, Fish, Freire, Kuhn, Anzaldúa, etc. This is burnishing the works, glossing them, tending to their critical apparatus, making sure the investment in them remains sound. The standard space for such a scene? It's the museum curator's office.

Bartholomae, then, is the Sherman Lee of Composition. In the history of American museums, Lee, as curator of the heavily endowed Cleveland Museum of Art, was someone who could afford to withstand the pressure Thomas Hoving, the Metropolitan's director, put on the museum world to stage huge blockbuster shows in order to increase attendance. Lee wanted the museum to "remain immune to community pressure, [so] he defended the critical and preservationist role of the museum against what he regarded as a misguided interpretation of the institution's civic responsibility" (Conforti 22). Lee fought to strengthen the museum's cultural ramparts against the popular, the spectacular. All those blockbusters were taking the curator's time and resources away: "Traditional activities surrounding the care and interpretation of the museum's permanent collection had been disrupted. The priority once granted to conservation and scholarly publications had been undermined; galleries were no longer places for the quiet contemplation of works of art" (Conforti 22).

For most of my career as a composition instructor, I was uncomfortable with my status as academic gatekeeper. I bristled at that role of mine in an institution whose goals I saw as somberly conservative. But I've since learned to approach my role strategically. Take Hans Haacke, who creates highly prized installations, exhibited in museums and galleries, which are deeply critical of the museum and its corporate-sponsored ability to fix form and content, not to mention helping to shape the larger cultural ambiance. When asked why he showed his work in museums, since he hated them so much, he answered: "You have to be part of the system in order to participate in a public discourse. . . . As soon as you exhibit your work in galleries and museums, you are part of the system. I have always been part of the system. I am of the opinion that you cannot act outside the system, or be on your own, and participate in a discourse" ("School" 23).

As composition teachers, we mount exhibits, prize certain works, neglect others, and in so doing, lead our local patrons through a tour of form, content, and larger questions of cultural ambiance. We are, indeed, curators, but as such, we need to do our job well. SFMOMA's Bruce Weil feels his job as curator is to work against the museum's role as repository of the culture's finest, positioning the institution instead as a more neutral information provider for people: art as ideas, data, rather than (overly determined) objects. As curators of academia, then, we can exploit the possibilities of our status, exposing students to a range of culturally valid forms as well as non-mainstream content; in so doing, we provide our audience with a host of possibilities for worlds and forms to inhabit. What I see in many *Ways of Reading*-derived curricula, though, are a lot of weak, safe shows; shows with less-than-risky themes, all showing the same kind of middle-brow art. Most all of the composition readers I see carry on some version of the Sherman Lee project, trying to continually gloss the canon of our permanent collection, inviting students in to study the great works and contemplate "the way the text positions them in relationship to a history of writing" (Bartholomae "What Is . . . ?" 21). The titles of the shows we mount all sound like the titles of those bland, corporate-sponsored traveling exhibits: *How We Live Now, Re-Reading America, Gender Images, Our Times.* I eagerly await textbooks with titles like *Environments, Situations, Spaces; In the Spirit of Fluxus; Formless: A User's Guide,* or *Sounds in the Grass.* What *Ways of Reading* teaches is traditional Art Appreciation, recharging the masterpieces for a student, re-enchanting them. It's pedagogy as docency. The questions the text asks about a work are designed to make it come alive for students, to make them learn to savor it the way we in academia (supposedly) do, to make the work's discursive field viral, recombinant: "We have learned that we can talk about [these works] with our students as well" (Bartholomae and Petrosky iv). *Ways of Reading,* then, places students in the huge white cube of the contemporary museum gallery, walls dotted with some of the greatest works ever thought and felt. This is a vastly different space from *Searching Writing*— Macrorie locates his student on the street (in a camera shop, a fire station, a zoo): "Go to people. They're alive this year, up to date" (89).

Macrorie's idea of the *deeply felt truth* has resonated so strongly in my practice because it is the aspect of my students' writing I like best, the aspect I think represents their strongest work. Take Greg White, a student for whom writing an essay is a tenuous process; he shows his true voice, his heart and insight, in short works, in in-class writings and in the email messages he sends me. Here, for example, in an email with the subject heading "been there, done that!" he reflects on the discussion we had earlier that day of some Tupac Shakur songs:

> dear mr. sirc
>
> i'm in class today were talking about 2pac and not so much disappointed, however the people in class don't understand 2pac the way i do. see my life is very different from what people think. it pissed me off to hear people in our class talk but not from experience. but from what they learne by the media. 2pac song "keep ya head up" is so true. how do i know? because everything he said i've been through remember when you said you can't listen to this song wihtout having a tear come to your eye. well it did because it hurt for 2pac to be so much on point. the things this man said was so true for instance he said he blame his mother for turning brother into a crack baby. my mother had a child who is my brother who has down syndrome from my mother drinking. and then he goes on telling how he tries to find his friend but their blowing in the wind. when i went home i trie to find my friends the one's who i was hanging with when i was young they were around just always out of reach i understand when pac said he people use the ghetto as a scapegoat i love my ghetto i'm not just talking about the people i'm talking about the place. the people most of the people are good to me. the rest want to see my fell i have so many mixed feelings right now i can't stay focused on what i'm saying i guess that's another down fall us people from the "ghetto" have sometimes the feelings as pac fuck the world attitude and other times i say i'm going to show all these mother fuckers what i can do so many obstacles so little time makes me frustrated. so i can't focused i what i supposed to do.

I have many students like Greg, and my challenge, I feel, is to have these young writers burnish not Jane Tompkins's essays, but their own form of powerful *pensée*, while, certainly, at the same time learning some kind of basic prose styling to help them avoid verbal pitfalls at the university. It is a tough struggle, doubtless because it is the key tension in all fields throughout modernity with the idea of composition at their center: the tension between the academic and the avant-garde. This is the focus of Composition as a Happening, on the institutional space that enframes the human scene of written expression. As such, it fits with what art theorist Hal Foster sees as the crucial difference between the historical and neo-avant-gardes: "the historical avant-garde focuses on the conventional, the neo-avant-garde concentrates on the institutional" (17). So Deemer, Lutz and the rest of Composition's historical avant-garde took as their focus the conventions of the texts students produced, opening them up to the passional possibilities of new forms like those generated by the Happenings; as Lutz declared, "We must as teachers of writing concentrate first on the creative aspect of writing" ("Making Freshman English" 35). Our concern in the second wave of Composition's avant-garde is on the over-determined classroom scene, the university's imperative and how it is allowed to invent itself, replicate itself, in the work done in that space. We are not so fortunate, perhaps, to live in the heady times of the historical avant-garde. As Foster shows, those were times when the rhetoric was anarchistic. He cites the language of Daniel Buren's 1971 essay on "The Function of the Studio," calling for "total revolution" and "the extinction" of the studio (25); and in our field, again from Lutz, we have a call for "the complete restructuring of the university" (35). "Our present is bereft of this sense of imminent revolution," as Foster acknowledges; hence, contemporary artists engaged in the institutional critique of the neo-avant-garde "have moved from grand *oppositions* to subtle *displacements*" (25). So the goal becomes ways to pressure the academic context in firm but subtle ways. We might start, as I do, with figuring out new strategies for allowing the voice and concerns of Greg White to become a part of the academic verbalscape. This means I reflect on the central question of to what extent essayist academic prose must remain the focus of my practice? Despite my affinities, I can't look to Macrorie's I-Search genre for a resolution to this tension. There's often a thin-ness about the quest in Macrorie's students' papers, a chipperness; his student Elizabeth King's paper, for example, "A Camera Right For Me," begins "'What do you want for a graduation present?' my mom asked. I hadn't even thought about graduation, let alone a present, but that's my mom—always ten months ahead of time. 'How about a good camera?'" (67). He prizes a melodramatic belle-lettrism far more than I do, and so occasionally his own prose cloys: "That's why so many lectures and textbooks are dry—they lack the blood, muscle, rain, and dust of stories" (99). He can't shake that Hirschian obsession for cutting excess verbiage—even though he does sell editing with a gimlet eye: "Wasted motion irritates or infuriates us because at bottom we know we're going to die at seventy or ninety and we want to make good use of the time we have left" (39). And his formalism leads him, not just to offer a four-part template for the I-Search paper, but even, of all things, to a gratuitous put-down of Peter Handke's "The Left-Handed Woman," calling it "sloppy and confusing to a reader" (130). I love Ken's spirit, then, but not always his letter.

So, where do I go? Where I wanted to go, what made the most sense to me personally, was here:

[1. MARGINAL NOTES]

The bride stripped bare by her bachelors even.
to separate the *mass-produced readymade* from the *readyfound*—the separation is an operation.

Kind of Subtitle
Delay in Glass

Use "delay" instead of picture or painting; picture on glass becomes delay in glass—but delay in glass does not mean picture on glass—
    It's merely a way of succeeding in no longer thinking that the thing in question is a picture—to make a delay of it in the most general way possible. (Duchamp 26)

To Marcel Duchamp's *Green Box* (1934), and the idea of the prose catalogue. Text as a collection of interesting, powerful statements. A kind of daybook or artist's notebook. The way I myself work—jotting notes on the fly, sound-bite *aperçus* that sound good by themselves but can become workable bits in a larger structure. A basic compositional tool; a medium I feel students like Greg White could work well within. Jean Suquet has some relevant, deeply engaging commentary on this amazing work:

In Paris, in 1934, an edition of a hundred or a hundred and fifty copies of the *Green Box* was published—so named because of its green flocked cardboard cover and the assonance between "vert" [green], "verre" [glass], and "ouvert" [open]. Ninety-four scraps of paper bearing plans, drawings, hastily jotted notes, and freely drawn rough drafts were delivered in bulk. It was up to the reader to shuffle these cards as he or she pleased. There was no author's name on the cover; the work appeared anonymous and as if offered to the blowing winds. In light of this, I had not the least scruple, when opening it for the first time in 1949 at the request of André Breton, in making it speak (with Marcel Duchamp's consent) in my own voice; and out of its sparkling randomness, I began fishing words that resonated with something I felt deep inside me, something obscure yet promising illumination. One should refrain from saying "I." One should say "we." It is indecent and pretentious to appropriate body and soul, blood and sweat, the work of another. If an interior journey goes deep enough, at some point it arrives where all roads meet.

I was twenty. I dreamt—with due reverence—of taking up the journey where the previous traveler had left off. ("Possible" 86)

Suquet, then, had an encounter with Duchamp, a meeting, to which each of them brought their own experiences and searches, their own effort and commitment. He saw Marcel as a fellow-traveler, and their encounter changed Suquet's life, evoked in him a grand dream, a life-long itch. His whole scholarly career became an endless We-Search paper on the *Large Glass*. Duchamp was able to effect this vocation in Suquet, perhaps, because the technology of composition he used was different, interesting, human-scaled. Formal requirements were left open, *ouvert*; the focus was on the idea behind the composition, the statement it made: "I considered painting as a means of expression," Marcel said in an interview, "not an end in itself. . . . [P]ainting should not be exclusively retinal or visual; it should have to do with the gray matter, with our urge for understanding" (135–136). Duchamp, then, as Action Painter, concerned with the revelation contained in the act, that tension. It's the same tension, between the formal and the transformal, that Macrorie felt: "In part, writing is designing or planning; in part, it's watching things happen and discovering meaning" (38).

But not every student is caught up in working on a *Large Glass* that they need to make a mess of notes and drawings about. That is probably not an itch of theirs. But rap music most definitely is. That email from Greg White was written in the basic writing class that I center around hip hop. It's a course students have begged to get into for the past 6 years I've been running it. Some students have waited an entire year to get into it. No surprise, hip hop is a rubric for some of the most exciting cultural media available to young people today, transcending perceived distinctions of age, gender, race, and ethnicity. My goal as academic curator is to mount a hip hop exhibit that will satisfy the masses' itch, as well as leave them with an intense formal, verbal, and conceptual experience, one that will give them cultural and discursive capital to do with as they see fit. Like Bartholomae, I am a preservationist; one of the curator's duties, according to Weil, is to preserve the fragile works that threaten to disappear (said regarding both Daniel Spoerri's resin-covered foods from the 60s, which are rotting today; as well as much of the recent net-art tied to links—the perils of archiving, offline, art that was conceived to evolve online). I'm tired of seeing so many Greg Whites come and go in my courses and not have their heartfelt work archived in some culturally meaningful way. A course on writing about rap is one obvious way the classroom can be remade as a Happenings space—witness the email another student, Angela Bates, sent me at the end of our course one semester, an evaluative comment that seems to hearken back to Lutz's class in that incense-filled room in the student union:

> The best of your class is that we can listen to rap and talk about how we feel about particular aspects of the song and all and we can use the lyrics in the papers. The most enjoyable project was the paper on Tupac I love tupac and I was able to show my love on a different level where people can respect him as a person and as an artist the same way that I do so I tried to incorporate some [of] my emotions and convictions into the paper.

But as Happenings performance space, then, we need to, as Oldenburg reminds us, attend to those "residual objects" left behind. So the performance-document, the trace, is important; leaving behind the score or theatre-notes for your project, so others can appreciate and learn from your group's efforts. (Coles and Macrorie, with their book-length collections of the scores, notes, and residual objects from their own performance spaces, seem to have intuitively understood this.)

To attempt such a trace-capturing in my class, as a way to allow student desire to subtly pressure academic writing, I've been drawn to another catalogue of passionate inquiry, Benjamin's record of his thirteen years of research into the cultural preoccupations of nineteenth-century Paris, *Das Passagen-Werk (The Arcades Project)*. It is a work similar to Duchamp's, a definitively unfinished project that one is intended to extend, "at best a 'torso,' a monumental fragment or ruin, and at worst a mere notebook, which the author supposedly intended to mine for more extended discursive applications" (Eiland and McLaughlin x). The English translators of the work offer a nice capsule overview of Benjamin's project, sort of a Bartholomaen text-driven I-Search of not simply scholarly classics but an entire culture, centered around the Macrorian street. The subject of the *Arcades* quest was the *slow study and respect* of the residual objects left behind from the ongoing performance piece called "Paris of the Nineteenth Century":

> diverse material [from the literary and philosophical to the political, economic, and technological] under the general category of *Urgeschichte*, signifying the "primal history" of the nineteenth century. This was something that could be realized only indirectly, through "cunning": it was not the great men and celebrated events of traditional historiography but rather the

"refuse" and "detritus" of history, the half-concealed, variegated traces of the daily life of "the collective," that was to be the object of study, and with the aid of methods more akin—above all, in their dependence on chance—to the methods of the nineteenth-century collector of antiquities and curiosities, or indeed to the methods of the nineteenth-century ragpicker, than to those of the modern historian. Not conceptual analysis but something like dream interpretation was the model. The nineteenth century was the collective dream which we, its heirs, were obliged to reenter, as patiently and minutely as possible, in order to follow out its ramifications and finally, awaken from it. (Eiland and McLaughlin ix)

So we find entries such as the following from the convolute (or grouped sheaf of notes) on "[Boredom, Eternal Return]":

Child with its mother in the panorama. The panorama is presenting the Battle of Sedan. The child finds it all very lovely: "Only it's too bad the sky is so dreary."—"That's what the weather is like in war," answers the mother. Dioramas.

Thus, the panoramas too are in fundamental complicity with this world of mist, this cloud-world: the light of their images breaks as through curtains of rain. [D1,1]

"This Paris [of Baudelaire's] is very different from the Paris of Verlaine, which itself has already faded. The one is somber and rainy, like a Paris on which the image of Lyons has been superimposed; the other is whitish and dusty, like a pastel by Raphael. One is suffocating, whereas the other is airy, with new buildings scattered in a wasteland, and, not far away, a gate leading to withered arbors." François Porché, *La vie douloureuse de Charles Baudelaire* (Paris, 1926), p. 119 [D1,2]

The mere narcotizing effect which cosmic forces have on a shallow and brittle personality is attested in the relation of such a person to one of the highest and most genial manifestations of these forces: the weather. Nothing is more characteristic than that precisely this most intimate and mysterious affair, the working of the weather on humans, should have become the theme of their emptiest chatter. Nothing bores the ordinary man more than the cosmos. Hence, for him, the deepest connection between the weather and boredom. How fine the ironic overcoming of this attitude in the story of the splenetic Englishman who wakes up one morning and shoots himself because it is raining. Or Goethe: how he managed to illuminate the weather in his meteorological studies, so that one is tempted to say he undertook this work solely in order to be able to integrate even the weather into his waking, creative life. [D1.3] (101)

A vector analysis of almost any page from the *Passagen* gives an idea of the various genres he's working in: quotation (of passages of varying lengths), summary, short critical reflection, more extended quotation and/or analysis, sound-bites, notes to himself. In terms of the material content, it's far more open, more lived—among the myriad topics covered are history, urbanism, desire, horror, shopping, pleasure, conspiracy, art, architecture, prostitution, gambling, engineering, even transcriptions of names and signs (I like how the translators use the word *torso* because truly there is a body moving in this space, a desiring body). He achieves, then, the true daybook, one whose method implies "how everything one is thinking at a specific moment in time must at all costs be incorporated into the project at hand" (*Arcades* 456). Finally we can note the preconception of writing as hypertext: that entry above, with the " Dioramas " tag, for example, in the "[Boredom, Eternal Return]" convolute, anticipates readers who can click the selection, taking them to the "[Panorama]" convolute.

Why am I drawn to this method, and how do I use it? First, it's the idea of sustained inquiry, of the search as project. It's basic Macrorie: "Anyone can learn to search and write in a way that furthers thought and reflection, that builds and sees" (*Searching* "Preface" np). The *Passagen*, though, is *form ouvert*, far more open than Macrorie's; it's a minimalist building structure, that "slender but sturdy scaffolding" the historian erects "in order to draw the most vital aspects of the past into his net" (Benjamin 459). Currently, as one attempt at Composition-as-a-Happening, my students are involved in an arcades project trying to permeate the phantasmagoria of rap's drama because, as a curator, I want my gallery-space to be thought of as an important information-source for the student-audience. Each class member selects a convolute, based on desire (old school, cultural roots, the socio-political, gender, race, gangsta, 2Pac, the industry); some general theory and background is read and annotated; then more specialized reading; then contemplative field work. Audio and video as necessary. Brief works constellated together into the larger interactive project. Writing that works minutely, from the inside out, to develop a statement. So Scot Rewerts, for example, begins his own Arcades Project on rap and politics by recording and reflecting on a text snippet on Malcolm X he found on a hip hop website and some Rage Against the Machine lyrics:

    -El Hajj Malik El Shabazz aka Malcolm X was assassinated on
    February 21 1965 but his connection to Hip Hop has been a long
    and strangely eerie one. The man who once ran the streets of

Harlem, lived the fast life and spent time in prison was a bona fide Hip Hopper of sorts back in the days of his youth. Malcolm went to all the latest shows, hung out with all the coolest music cats. He was up on the latest happenings as they were emerging from the streets. Back when he was a youth, Hip Hop of his day was known as Be-bop and Malcolm who was always known for keeping it real was down with the whole scene. (Davey D's Newsletter)

A direct correlation with one of the most powerful black men that ever lived to hip hop, shows how truly political hip hop is. In a Rage Against the Machine song Zach rap/rocks "Ya know they murdered X and tried to blame it on Islam!" (http://www.musicfanclubs.org/rage/lyrics/wakeup.html)

-Background: 'Black nationalism'
               'He may be a real contender for this position should he abandon his supposed obedience to white liberal doctrine of non-violence . . . and embrace black nationalism' 'Through counter-intelligence it should be possible to pinpoint potential troublemakers . . . and neutralize them' (http://www.musicfanclubs.org/rage/lyrics/wakeup.html

This is in the background to Rage's song "Wake up." This, even though not really thought to be a hip hop genre of music, is extremely political in reference to the Civil Rights movement.

Here are some selections from Peter Prudden's Rap Arcades Project on the topic of whiteness in rap music:

-"What had been proven in the 1960s, particularly by Motown, was that R&B-based music by black singers could easily be sold in massive quantities to white teens, creating a lucrative commercial-cultural crossover" (3).

[Nelson] George brings up a very good point in this quote. I believe this is a foreshadow for the success of the rap industry. White teens indulge in gangsta rap simply because it takes them from their middle-class suburban homes and into the heart of the inner city. More importantly, it opens their imaginations to drugs, sex, guns and violence, the very things they are sheltered from in their daily lives.

-"The heroin invasion . . . empowered a new vicious kind of black gangster. Heroin emboldened the black criminal class. Hip hop would chronicle, celebrate, and be blamed for the next level of drug culture development" (George 35)

From the words of Notorious B.I.G., "either your slingin crack rock or you gotta wicked jump shot." Over time, the African-American male has been notoriously rocked with this assumption.

I can't leave the topic of rap and white folks without offering up this memory. It is summer 1995 and I am spending the long Labor Day weekend at a house out on the tip of Long Island. To my surprise, in a local publication I spot an ad for a Run-D.M.C. gig at the Bay Club in the Hamptons' town of East Quogue. Along with two other old-school hip hop colleagues, Ann Carli and Bill Stephney, I drive to the club, where we encounter a large drunken crowd of college-age and young adult whites. The club is jam-packed and the narrow stage swollen with equipment.

When Run, D.M.C., and Jam Master Jay arrive onstage, the building rocks. The 99.9 percent white audience knows the words to every song. "My Adidas," "Rock Box," and "King of Rock" are not exotic to this crowd. It is the music they grew up on. I flash back on Temptations-Four Tops concerts that are '60s nostalgia lovefests. Well, for these twenty-somethings, Run-D.M.C. is '80s nostalgia. They don't feel the music like a black kid from Harlem might. No, they feel it like white people have always felt black pop—it speaks to them in some deep, joyous sense as a sweet memory of childhood fun. In a frenzy of rhymed words, familiar beats, and chanted hooks the suburban crowd drinks, laughs, and tongue kisses with their heads pressed against booming speakers. It may not be what many folks want hip hop to mean, but it is a true aspect of what hip hop has become. (74–75)

This quote [from Nelson George] depicts the classic stereotype of the white suburban teen seeking a revolutionary moment derived of independence, attitude, style, and tough guy mentality. I realize this image simply because I have fallen under these circumstances countless times. As a teenager living in a middle class society with rules and regulations operating in every arena the feeling of rebellion against the norm is consistently present. Others and I view rap as an escape to a world unimaginable to our Abercrombie & Fitch lives, where the biggest thing we must decipher is whose house we will watch Dawson's Creek at. The fact is driving down the street with the windows down in the parent's expensive car with the latest track blaring and the bass bumpin presents a bad boy thuggish image. The truth is we as adolescent white kids have absolutely no indication of what it means to live the life of the lyrics we feel associate with our lives. On how many occasions have you heard of a 14-year-old white child shot to death for his Air Jordans? The reality is never, we dream and paint pictures in our minds of what life is like in the inner-city through these albums. I enjoy listening to rap music, but to say I can relate or I feel for those who lives are filled with drugs, guns, violence, poverty, and sex is completely asinine.

The Macrorian quality to my use of the *Passagen* is how the student finds an already-enchanted space and wanders through that (the museum now conceived of as populist, audience-responsive data-site). In

Ways of Reading, students inhabit those expansive, relatively empty spaces, far removed from their own world; they don't awaken from the dream of academic discourse, they learn to speak it and keep dreaming it. But an even keener difference between the *Passagen* and *Ways of Reading* is that sometimes the search *is*, indeed, about a text, and sometimes it's even about a "long, powerful mysterious piece like John Berger's 'Ways of Seeing'" (Bartholomae and Petrosky *Ways of Reading* iii), but oftentimes it's not. Oftentimes the search is about a personal project that's being worked on that has far more to do with beats and rhymes than with a John Berger article. And sometimes the search is even more basic, Greg White as Miss Edick: "*I don't know—this may sound awfully strange. Maybe I shouldn't ask, but I've had to think about death lately, and I just wonder what you think of it.*" *Given that . . . ; if I suppose I'm suffering a lot . . .* was how Duchamp phrased Miss Edick's low murmur (23). The *Passagen* is not the student's clever response to a docent-guided tour through the great works of literary culture, but simply a re-representation of the students' own self-guided tours through cultural detritus that fascinates, which maybe holds clues; as Macrorie termed these material searches, "stories of quests that counted for questers" (*Searching* "Preface" np). Texts in such a curriculum become paratactic assemblage, with an intuitive structure based on association and implication, allowing the reader to fish out of them words that resonate with something felt deep inside (*an escape to a world unimaginable to our Abercrombie & Fitch lives*). Writing *apassionato e con molto sentimento*. I really don't think it's up to me to teach students how to process that "serious writing, . . . the long and complicated texts" (*Ways of Reading* iii) of the academy; if certain disciplines feel the need to use those texts, they're free to teach students their intricacies. Composition as a Happening means the displacement of such texts from the writing class, substituting a basic awareness of how to use language and information, a cool project, and a sense of poetry. This, after all, is a highly respectable curatorial mission: "to reinvest art with a new humanism, using basic forms of symbolism, allegory, figuration, and language . . . ask[ing] us to think about how we feel about the world we live in" (Auping 11).

THE TEA CEREMONY

Compared with the way post-Happenings Composition defines the classroom enterprise of college writing instruction, as *a professional commitment to do a certain kind of work with a certain set of materials,*

Composition as a Happening is far less mediated, looser. It silences that tedious, already-wrote drone of *knowing, selecting, evaluating, reporting, concluding,* and *arguing.* It is a pedagogy designed to un-build our field's spaces, a standard-stoppage, a composition theory (like Schoenberg's) that values the eraser end of the pencil (or the delete key). If post-Happenings Composition demands a commodity to hang on its gallery walls, Happenings Composition offers, as anti-commodity, Rauschenberg's most sublime work, his erasure of a de Kooning pencil sketch. Disappearing becomes our new production strategy: "But I want to slim things down, get rid of things, reduce stocks. To escape fullness you have to create voids between spaces so that there can be collisions and short-circuits. For the traditional imagination, that is not acceptable. It's a sacrilege" (Baudrillard, qtd. in Gane 38). Erasing dull, overdetermined words would open up the gaps between them, until the words form a new syntax, representing their new relations, inexpressible by the concrete, alphabetic forms of language. Baudrillard knows that in contemporary communication systems

> there is no time for silence. Silence is banished from our screens; it has no place in communication. Media images . . . never fall silent: images and messages must follow one upon the other without interruption. But silence is exactly that—a blip in the circuitry, that minor catastrophe, that slip which confirms the fact that all this communication is basically nothing but a rigid script, an uninterrupted fiction designed to free us not only from the void of the television screen but equally from the void of our own mental screen, whose images we wait on with the same fascination. (*Transparency of Evil* 12–13)

Silence, then, can be an ethical weapon, a last-ditch attempt to savor shards of the unmediated real. In a rhetoric of silence, the necessary preparation isn't planning but rather forgetting; instead of brainstorming, it's brain-emptying. Oldenburg's desire becomes heuristic:

> I would love to do a happening based on another dream, where I say to myself, "On the 24th of January I'm going to do a happening," and my entire preparation consists of forgetting that I had promised to do this piece on the 24th of January. When the time comes, I get into a cab and I go to the theatre and there I am with the audience before me. Whatever I did would be the piece. I haven't had the nerve to do it but in a way all pieces are like this. (Kostelanetz *Theatre* 147–148)

Post-Happenings Composition takes silence as its origin, not its terminus: "A course . . . must begin with silence, a silence students must fill"

(Bartholomae and Petrosky *Facts* 7). Silence there is simply the *nihilo* that needs to be *ex*-ed. A clean-slate prerequisite for something—say, a conventional, "authorize[d]" (*Facts* 7) Margaret Mead allegory. The post-Happenings Composition student needs something to say, has to more or less approximate a preconception; it can't be that the student-as-John-Cage has nothing to say and he is saying it and that is poetry as he needs it, or that the student-as-Johnny-Rotten doesn't know what she wants (to say) but knows how to say it. What we leave behind when we depart from silence, from nothing, is a sense of the sublime. As Cage reminds us, "When going from nothing towards something, we have all the European history of music and art we remember and there we can see that this is well done but the other is not. So-and-so contributed this and that and criteria. But now we are going from something towards nothing, and there is no way of saying success or failure since all things have equally their Buddha nature" (*Silence* 143). Composition today can never be common, can never use the commonplace; "the use of platitudinous 'common wisdom' and received opinions" stigmatizes the Basic Writer (Miller Review 93). Always rarified, reshaped, made over, Composition stubbornly rejects the readymade. Its goal is the special sight, the special vision; there is our sight and there is our students' sight, and the goal is to have students approximate our preconception (Coles calls such presumption "consciousness-razing" ["Response" 207]). Since we do not want "a classroom situation where any reading is seen to be as good as any other reading," we must "get the students to move beyond" (Miller "Fault Lines" 402) their own interpretations and to approximate ours. Thus, a post-Happenings Compositionist like Richard Miller is happy when his student writes a paper in which the student's old vision is renounced and a new sense of moral rectitude is pledged (dutifully using Pratt's institutionally-sanctioned metaphor): "I can now see [Anzaldúa's] strategy of language and culture choice and placement to reveal the contact zone in her own life. . . . I feel I need to set aside my personal values, outlook and social position. . . . I must be able to comprehend and understand the argument of the other" (406). It reads like English Composition as Loyalty Oath. Post-Happenings Composition never wakes from the dream of *Successful Writing*, of *What Makes Writing Good*. Composition as a Happening refuses that fantasy: "Rafael Mostel tells a story of returning to the Bang on a Can festival with John Cage after a dinner break. As they made their way to their seats, some friends urged them to come sit in the back, claiming, 'The sound is better back here.' Cage laughed and went to his previous seat, saying, 'Imagine, a sound being better.'" (Gann 84). Post-Happenings Composition's insistence on distinctions, on distinctive writing, means the museumification of the classroom space rather than institutional displacement. Bizzell, despite her sympathy to " 'texts' of all kinds" ("Contact Zones" 168), is simply a traditional Sherman Lee style curator with a slightly trendier art of exhibition: "I am suggesting that we organize English studies not in terms of literary or chronological periods, nor essentialized racial or gender categories, but rather in terms of histor-ically defined contact zones. . . . Time periods can be short or long, litera-tures of different groups, languages, or continents can be considered together, all genres are admitted, and so on" (167). The galleries have been given new names, but the museum is still there. All genres admitted, Patricia? Even La Monte Young's "form of the wind or the form of fires. Also . . . the sound of telephone poles"? Maciunas's anti-art forms like rainfall and crowd-babble? Bizzell's brand of composition gets us further entrenched in *culture* and less involved with the *real*. The Happenings sought an escape from culture by seeking refuge in the real. Lebel:

> The man/world equation is an open one, to which each Happening brings a new and evolutive solution. The Happening tries to loosen the labyrinthine knot of the Real; it is, above all, a deliverance from the tangled thicket of the knots of culture. Each participant has a different interior mandala, and thus communication takes place transconsciously. It would appear that there is a transition from inorganic to organic matter, and that, in the same way, the inorganic matter of thought—the pulsion—is transformed into an ideo-graph, a language, an action. Caught by and in the Happening in its rough pregrammatical state, the thought-process is freed and undistilled . . . the manifestation of the "cosmic link." (274, 276)

Post-Happenings Composition names no other site but culture, that is where its compositionists labor, getting further and further entangled in its thickets. There is never talk of a cosmic link to another "realer" reality. Think of Yves Klein's *Aerostatic Sculptures* (1958), in which "one thousand and one blue balloons were released into the Parisian sky to let the immaterial sensibility permeate and impregnate the world" (Berghaus 314). English Composition as a Happening is Student Text as Blue Balloon. Where is the place for spiritual intensification in main-stream Composition's curriculum? Just as Jackson's paintings were for their maker and viewers (Patsy Southgate, for example: "Jackson let us see his guts, and in so doing the giving up his life. The encounter with

Jackson changed my view of art and my way of seeing all things. It changed my way of relating. Jackson changed my life" [Potter 193]), so were the Happenings spiritually therapeutic for their creators and participants. For Vostell, "a happening is *direct* art in a cathartic sense: realization of raw experiences and psychic recovery through conscious use of the inner freedom in man" (Berghaus 323). Post-Happenings Composition insists that only determinate, closed-form text really means—the kind of work Kozloff claimed Jackson destroyed, "contained and computed, graded and regulated," work in which each "passage or episode is compared with another" (143)—but Jackson's art, as well as the Happenings themselves (as well as a punk riff or gangsta sample), show that open-ended, indeterminate texts mean quite well and might actually be more effective to bring about the ends Vostell was after, the striving for a sense of the infinite. The emphasis on a simple spirituality of the human heart as key Happenings criteria is not too surprising. From Tristan Tzara's "Lecture on Dada" (1922): "Dada is not at all modern. It is more in the nature of a return to an almost Buddhist religion of indifference" (Motherwell 247). Jackson Mac Low perceived how Vostell's *décoll/ages*, in similarity "with disciplines such as those of Buddhism, Vedanta and Smkhya Yoga . . . strip away the relatively illusory world of 'form' and 'name'—of phenomena—in order to see the 'really real' . . . to show us an 'in-between' reality, hidden by the ordinary surfaces of things" (Stiles 70).

Post-Happenings Composition, when it talks about writing, never seems to talk about the amount of discovery and wonder it contains. Usually content comes to mean text by Rodriguez or Douglass or Anzaldúa, never, say, blue balloons, rainfall, or getting a new camera. The irony is that in its rarification, Composition becomes bland, dull. The further irony—it is the commonplace that proves most useful in attuning perception: the rich poverty of the everyday helps cultivate a useful principle of forced selectivity. In 1961, for instance, on the Merce Cunningham tour bus, Rauschenberg announces a fact about himself: "I tend to see everything." What cultivated such panoptical power? Steve Paxton, a Cunningham dancer with whom Rauschenberg often collaborated in his own performances, felt it was poverty: "In the early days, in unrenovated downtown Manhattan, he scoured local stores and streets for materials. He had to appraise everything in his search and decide what to take home. This period of poverty lasted long enough to provide a thorough schooling in looking, seeing, and visual sorting" (262).

Instead of Rodriguez's way of reading Hoggart ("Hoggart provided a frame, a way for Rodriguez to think and talk" [*Ways of Reading* 3]), why not Tzara's way of reading a newspaper (or was it a poem)? In Dada, "[e]veryday life was brought onto the stage. Announcing the title of a poem, Tzara read an article from the newspaper. . . . Under the pressure of absolute theories that applied to life rather than to a specific art, the distinction between performing and not performing began to break down for the Dadaists" (Kirby *Happenings* 29). Late Sixties Composition's materialist egalitarianism in drawing on the common, charging it with undreamed-of evocativeness, made its Happenings pedagogy possible. It found the most sacred not in the culturally expensive and intellectually high-toned, but in the most available, the already-dumped—Ray Charles records, or the Iron Butterfly. It's the de-determinate response to the over-determined nature of things, stripping composition of all the acculturated crud of tradition to see it as uninflected, as *organization of words* or *gesturing with materials*, the basic problem of expression. John Lydon: "I'd never had any inclination to become a musician. I still don't. I'm glad I'm not. I'm a noise structuralist. If I can remember how to make the same noise twice, then that is my music. I don't think you need the rest of the fiddly nonsense unless you're in a classical orchestra. Instant pop with access to cheap emotions" (50). Masterpieces can be dull; actions, processes can keep things lively: "it is so difficult to listen to music we are familiar with; memory has acted to keep us a-ware of what will happen next, and so it is almost im-possible to remain a-live in the presence of a well-known masterpiece. . . . [This] is not the case with Feldman's music. We are in the presence not of a work of art which is a thing but of an action which is implicitly nothing" (*Silence* 136).

A return to process, to action writing, means a restorative reflection on all those process pre-writes, those simple dumpings (which, if ever re-used, had to be reshaped and made-over into acceptable college writing). Informal writings are central to a Happenings curriculum because students learn more about their personal style and statement in those open forms. Writing on glass, then, or any material . . . writing on ceramic, even. Jackson painted bowls during the Depression because they were one of the few art-works people could afford then. But also appealing to him was the genre's remove from the academic. Easel painting's technique was marked for Jackson: "Canvas and easel were circumscribed by formalities; they bore the burden of training, of classes, of composition. . . . A bowl or plate, on the other hand, was an invitation to play—a cheap and disposable license to spontaneity in which he could safely explore his own artistic future" (Naifeh and Smith 322). Currently, electronic texts threaten to go the same way—email messages, list-posts, MOO logs, and e-conference transcripts seen as relatively worthless little drips and drools of discourse when compared to formal assignments. But those liquid words, mere spit or bile forming itself, they certainly can shimmer, can't they? In their seeming *bassesse*, light is caught, it glistens, and for a moment, perhaps, an epiphany. And please let us agree on this: what more can a composition do? Composition as *Shimmering Substance*, then. Such was the lesson learned by Robert Childan, to finally discover the *wu* in what he previously thought were miserable, small, worthless-looking blobs, lacking any trace of discursive historicity: "To have no historicity, and also no artistic, esthetic worth, and yet to partake of some ethereal value—that is a marvel . . . that, Robert, contributes to its possessing wu. For it is a fact that wu is customarily found in least imposing places, as in the Christian aphorism, 'stones rejected by the builder.' One experiences awareness of wu in such trash as an old stick, or a rusty beer can by the side of the road." (172)

Post-Happenings Composition, as we remember from Donald Stewart, sees nothing of value in the Budspeak of beer cans, only a commonplace register of discourse that must be eradicated from his student. So let's resolve to dwell in the nothingness of the process-trace. Let's remake Jean-Jacques Lebel's *Funeral Ceremony of the Anti-Procès* (1960) for our first Happening, the one in which the "Anti-Procès manifestation [is] dead and buried" (Kaprow *Assemblages* 228). Let's make the form of formlessness a design for sequential writing assignments. Maybe a term's coursework is all just one long assignment, a bunch of scraps, ideas, plans—some finished pieces, maybe; but mostly definitively unfinished: a diaristic gesture, like Duchamp's *1914 Box*, like Kaprow's reading of Jackson's canvases, like Peter Prudden's Rap Arcades Project; all done, to use the terms Hebdige uses to refer to his own writing, as "the discontinuous jottings in a traveler's diary . . . [having] the uneven consistency of writing on the run" (8). Cool journals full of seemingly worthless blobs were the stuff of Happenings Composition: From Buell comes a pedagogy of pop and the everyday: "Frequently the best results come from recording observations, feelings, random notions, family and personal things. One sixth-grade student, urged by his father to keep a summer journal, spent a number of days copying down Beatles' lyrics. But then,

to the delight of his father and to his own surprise, he wrote the following and other entries like it . . ." (45–46). And please, let's not try to start
our institutional displacement by worrying about what our colleagues
across the campus want a first-year writing course to do: if we have to
answer to them for teaching students an intensified awareness of language, then they have to answer to us for the ecocide, economic immis-
eration, racial and gender insensitivity, and corporate ethics-lessness of
their professions.

We can begin, grammatically, to make a few alterations in the physical
arrangements. Rauschenberg's paintings offer a reconceptualization of a
work's method and reception: "pieces that seem to be personal journals
filled with emotionally weighted statements that are not intended to have
an explicit meaning or a logical clarity to the observer" (Kirby *Happenings*
40). Cage, we remember, loved the utterly fresh, life-like heterogeneity of
Rauschenberg's combine-drawings: "The message changes . . . the work is
done on a table, not on a wall . . . there is no oil paint . . . I imagine being
upside down . . . it seems like many television sets working simultaneously
all tuned differently" (*Silence* 105). Writing as assemblage, with a structure
based on association and implication; piling stuff on to create a spellbinding, mesmerizing surface, like staring into the *Rotary Demisphere* and seeing
what's evoked. Such would make a text less loaded, less determined, less
peculiarly styled, more open to possibilities, rather than closing on conventional notions. Crimp, like Steinberg, Cage, and so many others,
appreciates Rauschenberg's radical gesture in turning the surface of the
painting into a dumping-ground, a "flatbed," offering not a natural representation, but an idiosyncratic collection: "This flatbed picture plane is an
altogether new kind of picture surface . . . a surface that can receive a vast
and heterogeneous array of cultural images and artifacts that had not
been compatible with the pictorial field of either premodernist or modernist painting" (47). Such a surface could accommodate the multivalent
text-flow desired by Macrorie in '68, that "record [of] short fabulous realities" ("To Be Read" 688). Again, we might look to something purposively
other, like Eric Fischl's exercise book for artists, to find a useful classroom
text for assignments that take notions of the sublime as their goal:
"[Write] something that undermines expectations" (26), "Start with a
premise and then somehow invert it" (27), or, to paraphrase Vito
Acconci's assignment, "You've written an A paper, but you're going to die
as it's read. What do you do? What's the paper? How do you want to both
begin and end?" (53) Or we could simply appreciate student performance

as writing-in-itself, as readymade, rather than raw material needing re-shaping to mimic the masterly style, to (be)fit its frame (say, the massive Baroque gilt of Hoggart). The student's engagement with textual materials as *encounter*—with all the give-and-take dialogue and discovery that visits (especially those tinged with interest) can hold. *Shortly the stranger leaves, leaving the door open* (Cage *Silence* 103). It's a way to achieve that rhetoric of unfamiliarity desired by Irmscher, who calls the sublime of writing one of "the irreducibles" (*Ways* 10), and warns that too much analysis of writing destroys its scene; his metaphor is taking a kaleidoscope apart and trying to understand it (11). The common *flâneur* becomes the new celebrant; the Grand Ethical Poetic is Any Interesting Situation. Rather than being politically correct or professionally responsible, topics for essays are chosen simply because they thrill (e.g., given the choice, punk will *always* be chosen as topic by half our students). The populist *informe* undoes the walls and disseminates art *as it pleases*. Poor Composition. All those endless new beginnings, new paradigms, new metaphors, new directions, new inquiries. *The town may be changed, but the well cannot be changed.* Or, as Oldenburg put it, explaining his use of the Store as production/reception-site, "The studio for making art goes thru different guises, now a store, next year perhaps a factory" (141). Or perhaps a punk club, or a rap concert. Maybe even a college writing classroom. From an artistic statement by Happenings artist Robert Whitman, arises a rhetoric of writing as *s'exposer:* "The intention of these works has to do with either re-creating certain experiences that tell a story, or presenting experiences that tell a story, or showing them. You can re-create it or present it or show it. You can expose things. All these things have to do with making them available: you make them available to the observer, so called" (Kirby *Happenings* 134). His goal is very much Cage's, who felt that the whole idea was "to demonstrate what I know about, what I think people need to know about" (*Silence* 136). Form becomes the simple record of personal experience. In an interview with Richard Kostelanetz, concerning the composition of her influential Happening, *Birds of America* (1959), Ann Halprin shows how such a record can generate potentially transformative text:

> I had been inspired to work on this piece as a result of a personal experience. One day as I was sitting for a long time outdoors in our wooded dance-deck, I became aware of light on a tree, a red berry that fell at my side, a fog horn in the distance, and children shouting; and I wondered if they were really in trouble or just playing. These chance relationships, each independent of the other, seemed beautiful to me. I composed *Birds of America or Gardens Without*

Walls according to that experience. Each thing was meant to take a long time, so stillness was an essential ingredient. It was intended for the audience to become so relaxed, if you will, that they could just see and hear and not have to interpret and intellectualize. They could let each thing be what it is as pure physical, sensory experience. Also, inherent in this personal experience was the possibility of discovering in chance relationships some new ways of releasing the mind from preconceived ideas and the body from conditioned or habitual responses. (Kostelanetz *Theatre* 67–68)

This is very much what I call bottom-line, parking-lot rhetoric. Very personal, very expressive, just being, becoming; very much the opposite of what passes for text in contemporary Composition: Whitman and Halprin are not doing the discourse's work, whatever that is; nor are they doing a discipline's, they're not the happy laborers off to work in a subject-field. They're just humans, out in the world, perceptive, observing things. English Composition as a Happening, then, might start simply with affording students the opportunity to render their world as Whitman and Halprin do, possibly even seeing new connections.

So the tour is over; no more galleries, then, unless they are galleries-without-walls. Writing leaves the Museum now, or rather, the wall-panels slide away and the outside is let inside. Instead of walls . . . floors, refuse lots, the stage at Winterland, the vastness of Forty-Second Street. Post-Happenings Composition extends the notion of matrixed performance to its preferred classroom metaphors—community or contact zone (that hyper-form of community, the panic-community). But to call the classroom even a *culture* already mystifies. How about just classroom as society? Of Independent Artists, perhaps: Writing Classroom as General Exhibition. In search of that tradition-loaded historicity and authenticity, the Japanese consumers in Philip K. Dick's *Man in the High Castle* abandoned their heritage, their old ways—notions like *shibusa*, for example, "the highest expression of aesthetic attainment in Japan" (Sawada 1). A recuperative effort to recapture such concepts does not stem from a mere conservative nostalgia for old ways, however; rather the strategy is that of the neo-avant-garde, attempting "to *re*connect with a lost practice in order to *dis*connect from a present way of working felt to be outmoded, misguided, or otherwise oppressive. The first move (*re*) is a temporal one, made in order, in a second, spatial move (*dis*), to open a new site for work" (Foster 7). So Daiyo Sawada, for example, feels that a reconnection with Japanese aesthetics, with concepts like *shibusa*, "could have a profound and perhaps unexpected influence on the way we live, the way we learn" (2). *Shibusa* finds poignancy in the rough, the quiet, the modest, the natural, the implicit, the simple. It concerns itself with anti-architecture, the un-building of walls, the blurring of inside and outside—seen, for example, in the sliding wall-panels of the Japanese house, bringing the outside in, bringing the inside to the outside. A *shibusa*-inflected theory of education would question how schools "are often constituted of exterior walls which in their massiveness act as boundaries for separating the living (learning) space from outside (everyday) space in rather emphatic ways. There is no intent that the walls be an invitation for that which is outside to come inside nor for the inside to venture outside" (3). A *shibusa* space, one where silence is heard meaningfully, is seen in "the quiet of the Japanese tearoom which attains a serenity of spirit through the stillness of gently boiling water and the hush of the swishing tea brush . . . in saying nothing, everything is invited. It is an invitation to become" (5).

So forget even the Happenings. Dick Higgins acknowledges the Happenings died from the weight of their own commodified fetishism. He much preferred the subtle displacement of Fluxus performance, in which small, banal actions became heightened through the participants' selective focus (Higgins and Higgins). So Composition as Tea Ceremony (as Fluxus Performance). Owen Smith traces the gradual transformation in the Fluxus theory of performance, speaking of such late Fluxus events as Brian Buczak's "'Falling down on the icy sidewalk' Parts one and two," which, according to Buczak, "consisted of slipping and falling down on the sidewalk when least expecting to do so." For Smith,

> The lack of framing in this piece . . . demonstrates the recognition in some later Fluxus actions and events of the performative aspects of *all* activity—even when such activity is not separated and presented as "performance." While at first glance some of the later Fluxus events seem to resemble semiprivate activities or parties, it was precisely in these events and gatherings that the performance activities of Fluxus came closest to one of the central aims of its agenda: the merging of art and life, or the abandonment of art. With a minimum of self-conscious performance, these later Fluxus events became a celebration of the unpretentious pleasures to be found in life. (36)

Let our tea ceremony become a funeral tea-ceremony of the anti-process, then, for a work of *shibusa* is more process, more the nothingness of an art-and-life-blurred residual object than Official Something Product: "it emerges as a *by-product* of ongoing life. . . The concept of the by-product is a most significant yet most difficult concept to appreciate when we are continually shown that the way to produce something is to know the specifications . . . *operational specifications* of criteria which define the production of the desired products. Production of this kind . . . is best done by machines" (Sawada 6–7). (As Jackson intimated, there are modern, mechanized means of representation, if all you want is *a certain kind of work with a certain set of materials.*) Instead, *shibusa* prizes the irregularities seen in nature, textures beautifully imperfect. It implies success measured only in terms of the possible: *shibusa*, "in having no mechanical regularity of quantitative precision, invites participation by the observer because it suggests rather than commands; it opens up new possibilities because it is inherently unfinished" (9). The goal is nothing more than a feeling of intensity, the new view in your heart. Let each thing be what it is as pure physical, sensory experience. Let's say it's just writing. This writing is. The desperate poignancy of simple pleasures. "Taking momentary pleasures to their limit is a way of transcending history and death, and, in a doomed world, is even inevitable" (Graham 89).

That's what's needed, what Krishnamurti offered Jackson, the grounding for the basic stylistic he tried so hard to craft, a rhetoric of the heart. Instead of tracing the shape of cultural tradition, Composition needs to penetrate to the core of human emotion. This is what Macrorie and Coles pursued so stridently, so fervently. Fluxus artist Dick Higgins, writing in his 1966 "Statement on Intermedia," saw how it should have all come down in Composition circa 1976: "Could it be that the central problem of the next ten years or so, for all artists in all possible forms, is going to be less the still further discovery of new media and intermedia, but of the new discovery of ways to use what we care about both appropriately and explicitly? . . . We must find the way to say what has to be said in the light of our new means of communicating" (172). But post-Happenings Composition wasn't interested in new ways to express basic cares. It fell to extra-curricular scenes like Punk to find a way, however crudely (but how awfully excitingly), to say what had to be said. Or someone like Coles, whose incredible 1981 piece "Literacy for the Eighties" is pedagogy in the form of a rant from an old codger at the end of the bar, desperately hectoring the young breed about how it was all going wrong:

> One of the first things you want to get straight about teaching writing is the vital importance of the question of what you're going to make the whole thing mean, for your students as writers, for yourself as a teacher of writing—what you're going to make it mean and how you're going to keep that central. Against what sea of troubles do you see yourself taking arms as a teacher? In

the name of what do you fight? And if there is no sea of troubles for you, no fight to fight, why bother? Why not just sell shoes? (249)

That last line sounds like it came off a tee-shirt sold in a Kings Row boutique. What Coles was after was a return to the ultimate foundation of the enterprise, the central energy. How else would we define that except in terms of a basic human expressionism? Which is how the Happenings artists tried to undergird their program of the re-enchantment of the real. Theirs was a theory of textuality that tried to get in touch with energies in things, to renew people's engagement with the world; that took perception and life's intensity for its aim, not *art* or *discourse* or *discipline.* That preserved the mystery.

> I know that down to the last simple detail experience is totally mysterious. The only person I know that tried to prove the simplest thing in the world, like a piece of candy, was utterly mysterious was Chirico (in his early days). But I guess its what every still-life ptr worth anything tried to show, too. With me of c. well I am living in the city, a particular city, in a different time, and my subjects are as apt to be depictions of the real thing as the real things (even real pie these days does not taste like pie). Still, what I want to do more than anything is to create things just as mysterious as nature. (Oldenburg 49)

It's retuning all compositional spaces according to a sacred economy. It's the exchange-value of the Official Museum Culture vs. the use-value of Human Life. What this means for the Happenings compositionist is the de-reification of the "craft and design" of a formalist curriculum in favor of a sense of enchantment. More from Oldenburg's notebook:

> This elevation of sensibility above bourgeois values, which is also a simplicity of return to truth and first principles, will (hopefully) destroy the notion of art and give the object back its power. Then the magic inherent in the universe will be restored and people will live in sympathetic religious exchange with the materials and objects surrounding them. They will not feel so different from these objects, and the animate/inanimate schism mended. What is now called an art object is a debased understanding of a magic object. When our vision is clouded by bourgeois values and by removal from an actual functional situation (through museum-civilization) the power of the object wch was a functioning object becomes suspended and only its artificiality, that is its craft and design (which are the lowest and easiest of creations), are noted. This is "art." Think how many children a day are being perverted into art and their natural recognition of the magic in objects stamped out! (60)

A student's heart-felt email, coming out of the energy of daily life, so often has a magic, transformal power that a dutifully-written academic essay rarely achieves. This is what overwhelmed Bill Coles about his student George Humphrey's writing. It was the way in which Humphrey captured the profound sense that one particular moment—spouse asleep on a couch as you write at your desk, while outside the window you hear the rapid transit rumbling by; the train's sound directs your gaze out that window, where you see 2 pear trees in a garden below, as well as a power plant; for some reason, the memory of conversations about D. H. Lawrence struck up with someone in your building's elevator drifts into your mind—holds clues to the mysterious workings of the world. That essay offered Coles proof that writing could be transformative. Oldenburg goes on for over three pages in his notebook for *The Store*, articulating his ethos as a series of *pro*'s that try boldly to de-determine art around a baseline humanity, delineating the *What Makes Writing* of English Composition as a Happening. For example,

> I am for an art that is political-erotical-mystical, that does something other than sit on its ass in a museum.
> I am for an art that grows up not knowing it is art at all, an art given the chance of having a starting point of zero.
> I am for an art that embroils itself with the everyday crap and still comes out on top.
> I am for an art that imitates the human, that is comic, if necessary, or violent, or whatever is necessary.
> I am for an art that takes its form from the lines of life itself, that twists and extends and accumulates and spits and drips, and is heavy and coarse and blunt and sweet and stupid as life itself. (39)

or

> I am for the art of neck hair and caked teacups, for the art between the tines of restaurant forks, for the odor of boiling dishwater.
> I am for the art of sailing on Sunday, and the art of red and white gasoline pumps.
> I am for the art of bright blue factory columns and blinking biscuit signs.
> I am for the art of cheap plaster and enamel. I am for the art of worn marble and smashed slate. I am for the art of rolling cobblestones and sliding sand. I am for the art of slag and black coal. I am for the art of dead birds.

I am for the art of scratchings in the asphalt, daubing at the walls. I am for the art of bending and kicking metal and breaking glass, and pulling at things to make them fall down. (40)

Composition, as I write this, seems subsumed in the politics of its practitioners. But its politics are more rote ideology than the breathtaking principles of the human heart. What could be a more basic, principled ethos than the de-determining of perception, which is the *de facto* politics of the Happenings artists? Theirs was a politics that skirted ideology to focus on the basic needs for a life lived in mental and spiritual splendor. When Kaprow piles up a courtyard full of old tires, when Rauschenberg combs the trash for his stage properties, when Cage feels that the best music is whatever you hear going on in the world around you, there's a very radical politics embedded there, an implicit critique of an over-mediated, over-commodified culture, whether explicitly stated or not; a culture the newly intensified perceptual shift of Happenings art will, hopefully, transform. Lebel: "We can no longer be satisfied with loopholes and cracks in the System; we can no longer accommodate ourselves with the pseudo-liberation of a profit-oriented economy which winds up controlling not only the distribution but the actual conception and materialization of the theatrical vision" ("On the Necessity" 283). It is not just the idea of supplement or alternative, but replacement of the current social scheme. Take Fluxus founder George Maciunas, who saw as Fluxus's "pedagogic function" the "step by step elimination of the Fine Arts . . . to redirect the use of materials and human ability into socially constructive purposes" (Stiles 69). As Owen Smith said of the Fluxus artists, "Ultimately, Fluxus does not refer to a style or even a procedure as such, but to the presence of a totality of social activities and a desire to participate in life without fixed goals or definitive characteristics" (36). Late Sixties Composition staked this social transformation on an aesthetics, based in an embodied spirituality; currently, Composition's more ideological theorists and practitioners stake it on a (often mean-spirited) thought-and-language-based textual politics. When Berghaus describes the intentions behind the Happenings and Events of Milan Knížák, founder of Eastern Europe's AKTUAL group, it sounds like the best possible political curriculum:

[His] impulses for artistic creation were simple, practical, and direct in meaning. Hedonism and the enjoyment of positive life forces were combined with a sense for the poetic and sentimental. Knížák was a man of great optimism, sensuality, and *joie de vivre*. Spontaneity and immediacy meant more to him than aesthetic finesse. The demonstrations were designed to bring to the fore the inner forces that have been repressed or suffocated by social conditioning and material preoccupations. (359–360)

A politics without wonder and poetry, without a deep sense of sublime joy, will never be enlightening, will never be anything more than a scolding complaint. What we are (or what we should be) are poets. Lloyd-Jones describes a new, discursively hybrid writing program they created at Iowa, "a program for a broader range of writers" (5), one which sounds very Happenings, based on simply working with materials in the spirit of baseline human intensity; a curriculum based on craft, but one fully engaged in the world:

> Journalists came to our courses as well as poets, graduates as well as freshmen, biologists as well as literary critics. They all came to perfect their crafts; we claimed that the craft we offered allowed them better to define themselves as crafters, to govern their own materials, and to relate to the rest of the world. Our craft, we said, is as complicated as life itself, and it engages any question a human can care to ask. (5–6)

This is very much Coles's aim of *new awareness/new possibilities*. Lloyd-Jones realizes his identity as a compositionist: "I prefer to classify us as poets, primeval makers, enabling the culture to know itself and connect its people into a productive wholeness" (6). Deemer's classroom was not an ideological space. It wasn't a question for him of students learning the truth of new opinions or the folly of old ones, but simply a delay: "Rather the student should experience the difficulty of holding *any* opinion" (124). Rather than coming across as politically charged, "Should the 'teacher' chose to reveal (unmask) his own inadequacy (humanness), the revelation might prove efficacious and distinctly human" (124). "An art of ideas is a bore and a sentimentality," Oldenburg wrote, "whether witty or serious or what. I may have things to say about US and many other matters, but in my art I am concerned with perception of reality and composition. Which is the only way that art can really be useful—by setting an example of how to use the senses" (48). Composition in the Empire of the Senses. Students working in whatever medium, trying to do something that sends one to heaven. Ah, the heavens . . . way up there, those swirling stars, dark and transparent as a dream. The Milky Way as fitting topic for a *Ways of Reading* course, then? Not likely, of course. We know only too well the Modernist reaction to starry-eyed sublimity in composition: too suspect,

of course, too commonplace. Greenberg loathed the non-academic freedoms Duchamp represented: if Duchamp were right, and anything could
be art, why

> In this context the Milky Way might be offered as a work of art too.
>
> The trouble with the Milky Way, however, is that, as *art*, it is banal. Viewed
> strictly as art, the "sublime" usually does reverse itself and turn into the
> banal. (Greenberg "Avant-Garde Attitudes" 303)

My point: obviously, if we can't tell the banal from something as sublime
as the Milky Way, we must stop viewing composition strictly as art.

The moment, I know, seems to have passed. Late Sixties Composition
gets mustier and mustier on that shelf deep within the dark interior
stacks of my institution's library. But, of course, the moment hasn't really
passed at all for some, those for whom the return to convention in the
Composition of the 1980s can only seem false, a betrayal of the processes
of thought that our confrontations with Composition-as-a-Happening
had set in motion. I'm speaking of those who wonder about the single-
minded professionalization surrounding the teaching of writing, its need
to reproduce and represent in a work, to charge it with the aura of institutional tradition, of potential master status. Who wonder if our institution exists to enable writing or if the writing works in service to the
institution, if "perhaps a writer's meaning ought to be a guide to the
appropriateness of a convention rather than the other way around"
(Coles, "Response" 208). Who wonder about "the freedom to abandon
reason and aesthetics and to just be" (Stiles 77). Who wonder if students
could do pieces of writing that weren't "writing." Who wonder why
Composition has to be *a certain kind of work*; why it can't, instead, be more
like a celebration of the unpretentious pleasure found in life. Who wonder where we might end up if we took that first step toward poetry. Who
wonder about the wonder, the discovery, the wispish suggestion, that
imagined sense of being upside down, of being more alive. Such wonder-
ing will never cease. The Museum is most certainly in ruins. Despite fervent attempts by post-Happenings Compositionists to keep building the
permanent walls, writing-as-*informe* uncongeals walls and moves art outside into the museum-without-walls. Malraux's museum-without-walls is
"curated" in terms of its availability, its reproducibility, its status as infor-
mation-site. Its system of patronage is simply the popular. Malraux's "permanent" collection was slides, photos, no objects outside of their
representations. So now, not only are the walls gone, but all the prize

works of monumental classical sculpture are gone, too, cleared from the entryway's space; only the rotunda's fountain-as-*Fountain* remains, that radical negation there at the beginning. But even the *Fountain* doesn't really remain. The "original," "signed" by R. Mutt himself, doesn't "exist" anymore, it was either broken, stolen, or lost. It exists only as a state of mind, an idea, a wispish suggestion. *Fountain* was the original unoriginal artwork; since it "originally" exists only in its reproducible form as Stieglitz photo, it's the perfect piece to commence our post-post-Happenings Museum-Without-Walls' impermanent download data-site collection. That original auratic presence—that "historicity" that we, like Dick's Japanese, are mad for—is a phantasm. "In our time," Crimp realizes, "the aura has become only a presence, which is to say, a ghost" (124). There are other ghosts, too, in our field, very agitated poltergeists, making weird sounds, knocking things over, causing cold chills to pass over the inhabitants. They will never be exorcised, never stay buried, never stop haunting us. They come with the house. We can only offer them what they want: an invitation to become. We'll keep remaking Composition-as-a-Happening, then, until we get it right. Oldenburg, realizing in 1968 that what Happenings artists had been doing for the previous ten years still hadn't been understood, could just as well have been speaking for Duchamp, Pollock, the situationists, or the Sex Pistols when he remarked, "The understanding of what we all have done is still not cleared up yet" (Kostelanetz *Theatre* 141). Charles Deemer's (un)original allegory has been a pleasure to cover. I salute the next remake of *English Composition as a Happening*, on and on through *n*-dimensions. A great era of the legend continues.

REFERENCES

Abelson, Reed. "By the Water Cooler in Cyberspace, the Talk Turns Ugly." *The New York Times* 29 Apr. 2001: sec. 1, p. 1+.

Allison, Libby and Kristine Blair. *Cultural Attractions, Cultural Distractions: Critical Literacy in Contemporary Contexts.* Upper Saddle River, NJ: Prentice Hall, 2000.

Altschuler, Thelma. "Using Popular Media to Achieve Traditional Goals." *College Composition and Communication* 19 (Dec. 1968): 340–344.

Amerika, Mark. "Avant-Pop Manifesto: Thread Baring Itself in Ten Quick Posts." <http://marketplace.com:70/0/alternative.x/manifestos/avant.po.manifesto.txt.> (20 Sept. 1996).

Armstrong, Elizabeth and Joan Rothfuss. *In the Spirit of Fluxus.* Minneapolis: Walker Art Center, 1993.

Ashbery, John. *Shadow Train.* New York: Penguin, 1981.

———. *Flow Chart.* New York: Knopf, 1992.

Ashton, Dore. "Monuments for Nowhere or Anywhere." *Idea Art.* Ed. Gregory Battock. New York: E. P. Dutton, 1973. 11–17.

Auping, Michael. *Jenny Holzer.* New York: Universe, 1992.

Bair, Jeffrey. "Electronic Messaging." *Minneapolis Star Tribune* 28 Feb. 1992: D1–D2.

Bakhtin, Mikhail. *Rabelais and His World.* Bloomington: Indiana University Press, 1984.

"Banned in the USA." Transcript of CNN *Crossfire.* New York: Journal Graphics, Inc., 11 October 1990.

Barthes, Roland. *S/Z.* Trans. Richard Miller. New York: Hill and Wang, 1974.

———. *The Pleasure of the Text.* Trans. Richard Miller. New York: Hill and Wang, 1975.

Bartholomae, David. "Inventing the University." *When a Writer Can't Write.* Ed. Mike Rose. New York: The Guilford Press, 1985. 134–165.

———. "A Reply to Steven North." *PRE/TEXT* 11.1–2 (1990): 121–130.

———. "I'm Talking About Allen Bloom: Writing on the Network." *Network-Based Classrooms: Promises and Realities.* Ed. Betram C. Bruce, Joy Kreeft Peyton, and Trent Batson. Cambridge: Cambridge University Press, 1993. 237–262.

———. "The Tidy House: Basic Writing in the American Curriculum." *Journal of Basic Writing* 12.1 (1993): 4–21.

———. "What is Composition and (if you know what that is) Why Do We Teach It?" *Composition in the Twenty-First Century: Crisis and Change*. Ed. Lynn Z. Bloom, Donald A. Daiker, and Edward M. White. Carbondale: Southern Illinois University Press, 1996. 11–28.

———. "Writing With Teachers: A Conversation with Peter Elbow." *College Composition and Communication* 46 (Feb. 1995): 62–71.

———, and Anthony R. Petrosky. *Facts, Artifacts and Counterfacts*. Upper Montclair, NJ: Boynton/Cook, 1986.

———, and Anthony Petrosky. *Resources for Teaching Ways of Reading An Anthology for Writers*. 2nd ed. Boston: Bedford Books of St. Martin's, 1990.

———, and Anthony Petrosky. *Ways of Reading: An Anthology for Writers*. 2nd ed. Boston: Bedford Books of St. Martin's, 1990.

Bates, Angela. "Number 5." Personal email. 4 June 1997.

Bataille, Georges. *Visions of Excess: Selected Writings, 1927–1939*. Ed. Allan Stoekl. Minneapolis: University of Minnesota Press, 1985.

———. *The Accursed Share*. Vol. 1. New York: Zone Books, 1988.

———. *The Tears of Eros*. Trans. Peter Connor. San Francisco: City Lights, 1989.

———. *The Accursed Share*. Vols. 2 and 3. New York: Zone Books, 1991.

Baudrillard, Jean. "The Beaubourg-Effect: Implosion and Deterrence." *October* 20 (1982): 3–13.

———. *Simulations*. New York: Semiotext(e), 1983.

———. *Forget Foucault*. New York: Semiotext(e), 1987.

———. "Beyond the Vanishing Point of Art." *Post-Pop Art*. Ed. Paul Taylor. Cambridge, MA: MIT Press, 1989. 171–189.

———. *The Transparency of Evil: Essays on Extreme Phenomena*. Trans. James Benedict. London: Verso, 1993.

Benjamin, Walter. "The Work of Art in the Age of Mechanical Reproduction." *Illuminations*. Ed. Hannah Arendt. New York: Schoken Books, 1969. 217–251.

———. *Charles Baudelaire: A Lyric Poet in the Era of High Capitalism*. Trans. Harry Zohn. London: NLB, 1973.

———. *One-Way Street and Other Writings*. Trans. Edmund Jephcott and Kingsley Shorter. London: NLB, 1979.

———. *The Arcades Project*. Trans. Howard Eiland and Kevin McLaughlin. Cambridge: Belknap Press of Harvard UP, 1999.

———. *The Origin of German Tragic Drama*. Trans. John Osborne. London: Verso, 1977.

Bergahus, Günter. "Happenings in Europe: Trends, Events, and Leading Figures." In Sandford. 310–388.

Bizzell, Patricia L. "The Ethos of Academic Discourse." *College Composition and Communication* 29 (Dec. 1978): 351–355.

———. "Cognition, Convention, and Certainty: What We Need to Know about Writing." *PRE/TEXT* 3 (Fall 1982): 213–243.

———. "'Contact Zones' and English Studies." *College English* 56 (Feb. 1994): 163–169.

Blanchot, Maurice. "Everyday Speech." *Yale French Studies* 73 (1987): 12–20.

Bloom, Allan. *The Closing of the American Mind.* New York: Simon and Schuster, 1987.

Bois, Yve-Alain. "The Use Value of 'Formless.'" In Bois amd Krauss 13–40

———. Review of "Jackson Pollock: Early Sketchbooks and Drawings." *Artforum* Feb. 1998: 82–84.

———, and Rosalind E. Kruass. *Formless: A User's Manual.* New York: Zone Books, 1997.

Braddock, Richard, Richard Lloyd-Jones and Lowell Schoer. *Research in Written Composition.* Champaign: National Council of Teachers of English, 1963.

Britton, James, Tony Burgess, Nancy Martin, Alex McLeod and Harold Rosen. *The Development of Writing Abilities (11–18).* London: Macmillan Education Ltd., 1975.

Bruffee, Kenneth A. "Collaborative Learning: Some Practical Models." *College English* 34 (Sept. 1973): 634–643.

Buell, Thomas C. "Notes on Keeping a Journal." *College Composition and Communication* 20 (Feb. 1969): 43–46.

Burroughs, William. *Naked Lunch.* New York: Grove Press, 1959.

Cabanne, Pierre. *Dialogues with Marcel Duchamp.* Trans. Ron Padgett. New York: Viking Press, 1971.

Cage, John. *For the Birds.* Boston: Marion Boyars, 1981.

———. *Silence.* Hanover: Wesleyan University Press, 1973.

———. *X: Writings '79–'82.* Middletown: Wesleyan University Press, 1983.

Camfield, William. "Marcel Duchamp's *Fountain*: Aesthetic Object, Icon, or Anti-Art?" *The Definitively Unfinished Marcel Duchamp.* Ed. Thierry de Duve. Cambridge: MIT Press, 1991. 133–178.

Canetti, Elias. *The Conscience of Words.* New York: The Seabury Press, 1979.

Carter, Steven. "The Beatles and Freshman English." *College Composition and Communication* 20 (Oct. 1969): 228–232.

Clapp, Ouida H., ed. *On Righting Writing: Classroom Practices in Teaching English 1975– 1976.* Urbana: NCTE, 1975.

Coles, William E., Jr. *The Plural I:* The Teaching of Writing. New York: Holt, Rinehart and Winston, 1978.

———. "The Teaching of Writing as Writing." *College English* 29 (Nov. 1967): 111–116.

———. "The Sense of Nonsense as a Design for Sequential Writing Assignments." *College Composition and Communication* 21 (Feb. 1970): 27–34.

———. "Response to William E. Coles, Jr., 'Teaching the Teaching of Composition: Evolving a Style.'" *College Composition and Communication* 29 (May 1978): 206–209.

———. "Literacy for the Eighties: An Alternative to Losing." *Literacy for Life: The Demand for Reading and Writing.* Ed. Richard W. Bailey and Robin Melanie Fosheim. New York: MLA, 1983.

———, and James Vopat. *What Makes Writing Good.* Lexington, MA: DC Heath and Co., 1985.

Conforti, Michael. "Hoving's Legacy Reconsidered." *Art in America* June 1986: 19–23.

Connors, Robert J. Review of *A Vulnerable Teacher. College Composition and Communication* 29 (Feb. 1978): 108–109.

———. "Basic Writing Textbooks: History and Current Avatars." Theresa Enos (ed). *A Sourcebook for Basic Writing Teachers.* New York: Random House, 1987. 259–274.

Crimp, Douglas. *On the Museum's Ruins.* Cambridge: MIT Press, 1993.

Crosby, David. *If I Could Only Remember My Name.* Atlantic SD 7203 1971.

D'Angelo, Frank J. "The Search for Intelligible Structure in the Teaching of Composition." *College Composition and Communication* 27 (May 1976): 142–147.

Danto, Arthur C. "Whatever Happened to Beauty?" *The Nation* 30 Mar. 1992: 418–421.

Debord, Guy. Soundtrack of "On the Passage of a Few Persons Through a Rather Brief Period of Time." *Situationist International Anthology.* In Knabb 29–33.

———, Attila Kotànyi and Raoul Vaneigem. "Theses on the Paris Commune." *Situationist International Anthology.* In Knabb 314–317.

de Duve, Thierry. "Given the Richard Mutt Case." *The Definitively Unfinished Marcel Duchamp.* Ed. Thierry de Duve. Cambridge, MA: MIT Press, 1993. 187–230.

———. "Echoes of the Readymade: Critique of Pure Modernism." *October* 70 (Fall 1994): 61–97.

———. *Kant After Duchamp.* Cambridge, MA: MIT Press, 1996.

Deemer, Charles. "English Composition as a Happening." *College English* 29 (Nov. 1967): 121–126.

Dempsey, Ann, Mary Lou Maurer, and Rosemary Pisani. "English—Everything from an Experimental Film to *Esquire* Cartoons." *College Composition and Communication* 19 (Dec. 1968): 336–337.

Dewey, Ken. "X-ings." In Sandford 206–210.

———, Anthony Martin, and Ramon Sender. "City Scale." In Sandford 173–181.

Dick, Philip K. *The Man in the High Castle.* 1962. New York: Berkley Medallion, 1974.

———. *The Penultimate Truth.* New York: Belmont, 1964.

Donato, Eugenio. "The Museum's Furnace: Notes Toward a Contextual Reading of Bouvard and Pecuchet." *Textual Strategies: Perspectives in Post-Structuralist Criticism.* Ed. Josué V.Harari. Ithaca: Cornell University Press, 1979. 213–238.

Duchamp, Marcel. *Salt Seller: The Writings of Marcel Duchamp.* Ed. Michel Sanouillet and Elmer Peterson. New York: Oxford UP, 1973.

Ede, Lisa. *Work in Progress: A Guide to Writing and Revising.* 2ⁿᵈ ed. New York: St. Martin's Press, 1992.

Eiland, Howard and Kevin McLaughlin. "Translators' Foreword." In Benjamin *The Arcades Project* ix–xiv.

Elbow, Peter. *Writing With Power: Techniques for Mastering the Writing Process.* New York: Oxford, 1981.

———. "Reflections on Academic Discourse." *College English* 53 (Feb. 1991): 135–155.

Eliot, Alexander. "Handful of Fire." *Time* 26 Dec. 1949: 26.

Eliot, T. S. *Selected Essays.* London: Faber and Faber, 1932.

Faigley, Lester. "Judging Writing, Judging Selves." *College Composition and Communication* 40 (Dec. 1989): 395–412.

———. *Fragments of Rationality: Postmodernity and the Subject of Composition.* Pittsburgh: University of Pittsburgh Press, 1992.

Farber, Jerry. *The Student as Nigger: Essays and Stories.* New York: Pocket Books, 1970.

Farris, Sara. "'What's in it for Me?' Two Students' Responses to a Feminist Pedagogy." *College Composition and Communication* 43 (Oct. 1992): 304–307.

Faulk, Barry. "Tracing *Lipstick Traces*: Cultural Studies and the Reception of Greil Marcus." *Works and Days* 11.1 (1993): 47–63.

Fischl, Eric and Jerry Saltz. *Sketchbook with Voices.* New York: Alfred van der Marck Editions, 1986.

Foster, Hal. *The Return of the Real.* Cambridge: MIT Press, 1996.

Foucault, Michel. "Rituals of Exclusion." *Foucault Live (Interviews, 1966–84)*. Ed. Sylvere Lotringer. New York: Semiotext(e), 1989. 63–72.

Friedman, B. H. "Interview with Lee Krasner Pollock." In Namuth and Rose n.p.

———. *Energy Made Visible*. New York: McGraw-Hill, 1972.

Frampton, Kenneth. "Towards a Critical Regionalism: Six Points for an Architecture of Resistance." *The Anti-Aesthetic: Essays on Postmodern Culture*. Ed Hal Foster. Port Townsend, WA: Bay Press, 1983. 16–30.

Gane, Mike, ed. *Baudrillard Live: Selected Interviews*. London: Routledge, 1993.

Gann, Kyle. "The Last Barbarian." *The Village Voice* 9 Nov. 1993: 84.

Gebhardt, Richard C., and Barbara Genelle Smith. "'Liberation' Is Not 'License': The Case for Self-Awareness through Writing." *College Composition and Communication* 27 (Feb. 1976): 21–24.

Gervais, André. "Connections: Of Art and Arrhe." *The Definitively Unfinished Marcel Duchamp*. Ed. Thierry de Duve. Cambridge, MA: MIT Press, 1993. 397–426.

Gibson, Mariana. "Students Write Their Own Bicentennial Ballads." In Clapp 93–94.

Gilman, Richard. "Introduction." In Shepard xi–xxvii.

Goodnough, Robert. "Pollock Paints a Picture." *Art News* May 1951: 38+.

Graham, Dan. *Rock My Religion*. Ed. Brian Wallis. Cambridge: MIT Press, 1993.

Greenberg, Clement. "Marc Chagall, Lyonel Feininger, Jackson Pollock." *The Nation* 27 Nov. 1943: 621.

———. "'American-Type' Painting." *Art and Culture: Critical Essays*. Boston: Beacon Press, 1961. 208–229.

———. "The Jackson Pollock Market Soars." *New York Times Magazine* 30 Apr. 1961: 42+.

———. "Modernist Painting." *The New Art*. Ed. Gregory Battcock. New York: Dutton, 1973. 66–77.

———. "The Case for Abstract Art." In O'Brian, 75–84.

———. "After Abstract Expressionism." In O'Brian 121–133.

———. "How Art Writing Earns Its Bad Name." In O'Brian, 135–144.

———. "Jackson Pollock: 'Inspiration, Vision, Intuitive Decision.'" In O'Brian, 245–250.

———. "Interview Conducted by Lily Leino." In O'Brian, 303–314.

Hairston, Maxine. *Successful Writing*. New York: Norton, 1981.

———. *Successful Writing*. 2nd Ed. New York: Norton, 1986.

Halloran, S. Michael. "From Rhetoric to Composition: The Teaching of Writing in America to 1900." *A Short History of Writing Instruction from*

Ancient Greece to Twentieth Century America. Ed. James J. Murphy. Davis: Hermagoras, 1990. 151–182.

Hapgood, Susan. *Neo-Dada: Redefining Art, 1958–62*. New York: American Federation of Arts, 1994.

Harris, Joseph. "After Dartmouth: Growth and Conflict in English." *College English* 53 (Oct. 1991): 631–646.

———. *A Teaching Subject: Composition Since 1966*. Upper Saddle River, NJ: Prentice Hall, 1977.

Harris, Mary Emma. *The Arts at Black Mountain*. Cambridge: MIT Press, 1987.

Heath, Chris. "U2: Band of the Year." *Rolling Stone* 18 Jan. 2001: 36+.

Hebdige, Dick. *Hiding in the Light: On Images and Things*. London: Routledge, 1988.

Heidegger, Martin. "Building Dwelling Thinking." *Poetry, Language, Thought*. New York: Harper and Row, 1971. 145–161.

Heilman, Robert B. "Except He Come to Composition." *College Composition and Communication* 21 (Oct. 1970): 230–238.

———. "The Full Man and the Fullness Thereof." *College Composition and Communication* 21 (Oct. 1970): 239–244.

Herzog, Werner. "Lessons of Darkness." Manifesto delivered during Regis Dialogue. Walker Art Center, Minneapolis. 30 Apr. 1999.

Hess, Thomas B. "Pollock: The Art of a Myth." *Art News* Jan. 1964: 39+.

Higgins, Dick. "Statement on Intermedia." In Armstrong and Rothfuss 172–173.

———, and Letty Eisenhauer. "Graphis." In Sandford 123–129.

———, and Hannah Higgins. Lecture. Walker Art Center, Minneapolis, 30 June 1998.

Hillocks, George, Jr. *Research on Written Composition: New Directions for Teaching*. Urbana, IL: NCTE/ERIC, 1986.

Hollier, Denis. *Against Architecture: The Writings of Georges Bataille*. Cambridge, MA: MIT Press, 1989.

———. "The Use-Value of the Impossible." *Bataille: Writing the Sacred*. Ed. Carolyn Bailey Gill. London: Routledge, 1995. 133–153.

Hopps, Walter and Susan Davidson, eds. *Robert Rauschenberg: A Retrospective*. New York: Abrams, 1997.

Irmscher, William F. "In Memoriam, Rev. Dr. Martin Luther King, Jr., 1929–1968." *College Composition and Communication* 19 (May 1968): 105.

———. *Ways of Writing*. New York: McGraw-Hill, 1969.

———. "Analogy as an Approach to Rhetorical Theory." *College Composition and Communication* 27 (Dec. 1976): 350–354.

————. "Finding a Comfortable Identity." *College Composition and Communication* 38 (Feb. 1987): 81–87.

"Jackson Pollock: Is He the Greatest Living Painter in the United States?" *Life* 8 Aug. 1949: 42–45.

Judd, Donald. *Complete Writings 1959 – 1975.* Halifax: Nova Scotia College of Art and Design, 1995.

Kamper, Dietmar, and Christoph Wulf, eds. *Looking Back on the End of the World.* New York: Semiotext(e), 1989.

Kampf, Louis. "Must We Have a Cultural Revolution?" *College Composition and Communication* 21 (Oct. 1970): 245–249.

Kaprow, Allan. *Essays on the Blurring of Art and Life.* Ed. Jeff Kelley. Berkeley: University of California Press, 1993.

————. "The Legacy of Jackson Pollock." *ARTnews* October 1958: 24+.

————. "'Happenings' in the New York Scene." *ARTnews* May 1961: 36+.

————. *Assemblages, Environments and Happenings.* New York: Abrams, 1966.

————. "In Response." In Sandford 219–220.

Karmel, Pepe. "Pollock at Work: The Films and Photographs of Hans Namuth." *Jackson Pollcok.* Ed. Kirk Vardenoe and Pepe Karmel. New York: Museum of Modern Art, 1998. 87–137.

Kelley, Jeff. "Introduction." In Kaprow *Essays* xi–xxvi.

Kelly, Ernece B. "Murder of the American Dream." *College Composition and Communication* 19 (May 68): 106–108.

Kimmelman, Michael. "Life is Short, Art is Long." *The New York Times Magazine* 4 Jan. 1998: 19–23.

————. "The Irrepressible Ragman of Art." *The New York Times* 27 Aug. 2000: sec. 2, p. 1+.

Kirby, Michael. "Alan Kaprow's *Eat.*" In Sandford 48–50.

————, ed. *Happenings: An Illustrated Anthology.* New York: E.P. Dutton, 1965.

————, and Richard Schechner. "An Interview with John Cage." In Sandford 51–71.

Kitzhaber, Albert R. *Themes, Theories, and Therapy: The Teaching of Writing in College.* New York: McGraw-Hill, 1963.

Knabb, Ken, ed. *Situationist International Anthology.* Berkeley: Bureau of Public Secrets, 1981.

Kostelanetz, Richard. *The Theatre of Mixed Means: An Introduction to Happenings, Kinetic Environments, and Other Mixed-Means Performances.* New York: The Dial Press, 1968.

————, ed. *John Cage.* New York: Praeger, 1970.

Kosuth, Joseph. "Art After Philosophy, I and II." *Idea Art.* Ed. Gregory Battcock. New York: Dutton, 1973. 70–101.

Kozloff, Max. *Renderings: Critical Essays on a Century of Modern Art.* New York: Clarion/Simon and Schuster, 1969.

Krauss, Rosalind E. *The Optical Unconscious.* Cambridge: MIT Press, 1993.

———. "Horizontality." In Bois and Krauss, 93–103.

Krishnamurti, J. *Freedom From the Known.* Ed. Mary Luytens. San Francisco: HarperCollins, 1969.

Kroker, Arthur and David Cook. *The Postmodern Scene: Excremental Culture and Hyper-Aesthetics.* New York: St. Martin's, 1986.

Kroeger, Fred. "A Freshman Paper Based on the Words of Popular Songs." *College Composition and Communication* 19 (Dec. 1968): 337–340.

Kytle, Ray. "Prewriting by Analysis." *College Composition and Communication* 21 (Dec. 1970): 380–385.

Lamberg, Walter J. "Major Problems in Doing Academic Writing." *College Composition and Communication* 28 (Feb. 1977): 26–29.

Laskas, Jeanne Marie. "The Good Life—and Works—of Mister Rogers." *Life* Novemeber 1992: 72–76, 78, 80–82.

Leavis, F. R. *The Great Tradition.* Garden City, NY: Doubleday, 1954.

Lebel, Jean-Jacques. "On the Necessity of Violation." In Sandford 268–284.

Lebel, Robert. *Marcel Duchamp.* Trans. George Heard Hamilton. London: Trianon Press, 1959.

Lefebvre, Henri. *Critique of Everyday Life.* Vol. 1. London: Verso, 1991.

Lefebvre, Henri. *The Production of Space.* Trans. Donald Nicholson-Smith. Oxford: Blackwell, 1991.

Light, Alan. "Behind the Fly: Bono—The Rolling Stone Interview." *Rolling Stone* 4 March 1993: 43+.

Lindemann, Erika. "Freshman Composition: No Place for Literature." *College English* 55 (Mar. 1993): 311–316.

Litz, Robert P. "this writing is: Ralph J. Gleason's Notes on Miles Davis' *Bitches Brew.*" *College Composition and Communication* 22 (Dec. 1971): 343+.

Lloyd-Jones, Richard. "Poesis: Making Papers." Paper presented at the Conference on College Composition and Communication. Phoenix, 16 Mar. 1997.

Lunsford, Andrea A. "What We Know—and Don't Know—About Remedial Writing." *College Composition and Communication* 29 (Feb. 1978): 47–52.

———. "The Content of Basic Writers' Essays." *College Composition and Communication* 31 (Oct. 1980): 278–290.

Lutz, William D. "Making Freshman English a Happening." *College Composition and Communication* 22 (Feb. 1971): 35–38.

———. Review of *Doublespeak: Language for Sale.* *College Composition and Communication* 27 (Feb. 1976): 97–98.

Lydon, John. *Rotten: No Irish, No Blacks, No Dogs.* With Keith and Kent Zimmerman. New York: Picador, 1994.

Lyotard, Jean-Francois. "Answering the Question: What is Postmodernism?" *The Postmodern Condition: A Report on Knowledge.* Minneapolis: University of Minnesota Press, 1984. 71–82.

Maciunas, George. "FLUXUS." In Sandford 94.

———. "Neo-Dada in Music, Theater, Poetry, Art." In Armstrong and Rothfuss 156–157.

Macrorie, Ken. "To Be Read." *English Journal* 57 (May 1968): 686–692.

———. *Uptaught.* Rochelle Park: Hayden, 1970.

———. *Searching Writing.* Rochelle Park, NJ: Hayden, 1980.

Marcus, Greil. "Guy Debord's *Memoires*: A Situationist Primer." *On the Passage of a Few People Through a Rather Brief Moment in Time: The Situationist International 1957–1972.* Ed. Elisabeth Sussman. Cambridge, MA: MIT Press, 1989. 124–131.

———. *Lipstick Traces: A Secret History of the Twentieth Century.* Cambridge: Harvard UP, 1989.

Marius, Richard. "On Academic Discourse." *Profession 90:* 28–31.

McLuhan, Marshall and Quentin Fiore. *The Medium is the Massage.* New York: Random House, 1967.

Miles, Josephine. "What We Already Know About Composition and What We Need to Know." *College Composition and Communication* 27 (May 1976): 136–141.

Miller, Richard E. "Fault Lines in the Contact Zone." *College English* 56 (Apr. 1994): 389–408.

Miller, Susan. Review of *Errors and Expectations. College Composition and Communication* 28 (Feb. 1977): 92–94.

Molderings, Herbert. "Objects of Modern Skepticism." *The Definitively Unfinished Marcel Duchamp.* Ed. Thierry de Duve. Cambridge: MIT Press, 1991. 243–265.

Morris, Robert. *Continuous Project Altered Daily: The Writings of Robert Morris.* Cambridge: MIT Press, 1993.

Motherwell, Robert, ed. *The Dada Painters and Poets: An Anthology.* New York: Wittenborn, Schultz, Inc., 1951.

Murray, Donald. *Write to Learn.* New York: Holt, Rinehart and Winston, 1984.

Naifeh, Steven and Gregory White Smith. *Jackson Pollock: An American Saga.* New York: Clarkson N. Potter, 1989.

Namuth, Hans. "Photographing Pollock." In Namuth and Rose, n.p.

———, and Barbara Rose. *Pollock Painting.* New York: Agrinde, 1980.

Nesbit, Molly. "The Language of Industry." *The Definitively Unfinished Marcel Duchamp.* Ed. Thierry de Duve. Cambridge, MA: MIT Press, 1993. 351–384.

———. "Her Words." Walker Art Center. Minneapolis, 8 Nov. 1994.

North, Stephen. "Composition Now: Standing on One's Head." *College Composition and Communication* 29 (May 1978): 177–180.

———. "Personal Writing, Professional Ethos, and the Voice of 'Common Sense.'" *Pre/Text* 11.1–2 (1990): 105–119.

O' Brian, John, ed. *Clement Greenberg: The Collected Essays and Criticism. Vol. 4: Modernism With a Vengeance, 1957–1969.* Chicago: University of Chicago Press, 1993.

O'Doherty, Brian. *American Masters: The Voice and the Myth.* New York: Universe Books, 1988.

Ohm, Neal C. "#2." Personal email to author. 27 Jan. 1997.

Oldenburg, Claes. *Store Days.* New York: Something Else Press, 1967.

Olsen, Lance and Mark Amerika. "Smells Like Avant-Pop: An Introduction, of Sorts." http://marketplace.com:70/0/alternative.x/memoriam/1.txt. 20 Sept. 1996.

"On Poetry, Language, and Teaching: A Conversation with Charles Bernstein." *Boundary 2* 23.3 (Fall 1996): 45–66.

"On the Poverty of Student Life." In Knabb 319–337.

Owens, Craig. "The Allegorical Impulse: Toward a Theory of Postmodernism." *Art After Modernism: Reconsidering Representation.* Ed. Brian Wallis. New York: Museum of Contemporary Art, 1984. 203–235.

Paxton, Steve. "Rauschenberg for Cunningham and Three of His Own." In Hopps and Devidson, 260–267.

Perl, Sondra. "The Composing Processes of Unskilled College Writers." *Research in the Teaching of English* 13 (Dec. 1979): 317–336.

Phillips, Donna Burns, Ruth Greenberg, and Sharon Gibson. "*College Composition and Communication*: Chronicling a Discipline's Genesis." *College Composition and Communication* 44 (Dec. 1993): 443–465.

Pollock, Jackson. "Narration Spoken by Jackson Pollock in Film by Hans Namuth and Paul Falkenberg 1951." *Pollock Painting.* Ed. Barbara Rose.

Potter, Jeffrey. *To a Violent Grave: An Oral Biography of Jackson Pollock.* New York: G. P. Putnam's Sons, 1985.

Prudden, Peter. Class Reading Notes. 25 Jan. and 15 Feb. 2001.

Public Image Ltd. *Metal Box.* Virgin, 1979.

———. *Public Image.* Virgin, 1978.

"Punk and History." *Discourses: Conversations in Postmodern Art and Culture.* Ed. Russell Ferguson, et al. Cambridge: MIT Press, 1990. 224–245.

Rainer, Yvonne. "Some Retrospective Notes on a Dance for 10 People and 12 Mattresses Called *Parts of Some Sextets*, Performed at the Wadsworth Atheneum, Hartford, Connecticut, and Judson Memorial Church, New York, in March 1965." In Sandford 160–167.

Ratcliff, Carter. *The Fate of a Gesture; Jackson Pollock and Postwar American Art.* New York: Farrar, Strauss, Giroux, 1996.

———. "Jackson Pollock's American Sublime." *Art in America* May 1999: 104–113.

Repp, John, ed. *How We Live Now: Contemporary Multicultural Literature.* Boston: Bedford Books of St. Martin's, 1992.

Rewerts, Scot. Class Reading Notes. 23 Feb. 2001.

R. E. M. "So Fast, So Numb." *New Adventures in Hi-Fi.* Warner Bros, 1996.

Roberts, Francis. "'I Propose to Strain the Laws of Physics.'" *Art News* Dec. 1968: 47.

Roché, Henri. "Souvenirs of Marcel Duchamp." *Marcel Duchamp.* Robert Lebel. Trans. William N. Copley. London: Trianon Press, 1959. 79–87.

Rodrigues, Raymond J. "Moving Away from Writing-Process Worship." *English Journal* Sept. 1985: 24–27.

Rodriguez, Richard. "Ganstas." http://www.mojones.com/MOTHER_JONES/JF94/rodriguez.html. 9 Sept. 1996.

Roen, Duane H., Stuart C. Brown and Theresa Enos, eds. *Living Rhetoric and Composition: Stories of the Discipline.* Mahweh: Lawrence Erlbaum Associates, 1999.

Rose, Barbara. "Introduction: The Artist as Culture Hero." In Namuth and Rose, n.p.

———. "Namuth's Photographs and the Pollock Myth." In Namuth and Rose, n.p.

———. "Pollock's Studio: Interview with Lee Krasner." In Namuth and Rose, n.p.

Rosenberg, Harold. "The American Action Painters." *Art News* Dec. 1952: 22+.

———. "The Search for Jackson Pollock." *Art News* Feb. 1961: 35+.

———. "Action Painting: Crisis and Distortion." In *The Anxious Object.* 38–47.

———. *The Anxious Object: Art Today and Its Audience.* New York: Horizon Press, 1964.

———. "After Next, What?" *Art in America* Apr. 1964: 64–73.

Ross, Andrew. "The Rock 'n' Roll Ghost." *October* 50 (1989): 108–117.

Rubenfeld, Florence. *Clement Greenberg: A Life.* New York: Scribner, 1997.

S. "S –> gs/t." PRE/TEXT List. http://www.pre-text.com/ptlist/sirc3.html 4 Dec. 1994.

Sadler, Simon. *The Situationist City.* Cambridge: MIT Press, 1998.

Salter, James. *Light Years.* San Francisco: North Point Press, 1982.

Sandford, Mariellen R., ed. *Happenings and Other Acts.* London: Routledge, 1995.

Savage, Jon. *England's Dreaming: Anarchy, Sex Pistols, Punk Rock, and Beyond.* New York: St. Martin's, 1992.

Sawada, Daiyo. "Aesthetics in a Post-Modern Education: The Japanese Concept of Shibusa." Paper presented at the annual meeting of the American Educational Research Association. San Francisco, 1989.

Schechner, Richard. "Happenings." In Sandford 216–218.

———. "Extensions in Time and Space: An Interview with Allan Kaprow." In Sandford 221–229.

Schneemann, Carolee. *More Than Meat Joy: Performance Works and Selected Writings.* Ed. Bruce R. McPherson. New York: Documentext, 1997.

"School for Scandal." Interview with Hans Haacke by Deborah Solomon. *The New York Times Magazine* 26 Mar. 2000: 23.

Schwartz, Jospeh. Review of Francis Christensen's *Notes Toward a New Rhetoric. CCC* 2/68, 41–42.

Sex Pistols. *Never Mind the Bollocks Here's the Sex Pistols.* Warner Bros., BSK 3147, 1977.

———. *We've Cum for Your Children (Wanted: The Goodman Tapes).* Skyclad, (sick) SEX 6 CD, 1988.

Shepard, Sam. *Seven Plays.* New York: Bantam Books, 1981.

Smith, Danyel. "Holler If You Hear Me." *Village Voice* 1 March 1994, Pazz and Jop Supplement: 20.

Smith, Owen. "Fluxus: A Brief History and Other Fictions." In Armstrong and Rothfuss 22–37.

Sommers, Nancy. "Responding to Student Writing." *College Composition and Communication* 33 (May 1982): 148–156.

Sontag, Susan. *Against Interpretation.* New York: Farrar, Strauss, and Giroux, 1966.

Sorkin, Michael. "Faking It." *Watching Television.* Ed. Todd Gitlin. New York: Pantheon, 1986. 162–182.

Spector, Nancy. "Rauschenberg and Performance, 1963–67: A 'Poetry of Infiniste Possibilities.'" In Hopps and Davidson 226–245.

"Statements by Jackson Pollock 1944/1947." In Namuth and Rose n.p.

Steinberg, Leo. *Other Criteria: Confrontations With Twentieth-Century Art.* London: Oxford UP, 1972.

Steiner, Robert. *Towards a Grammar of Abstraction*. University Park: The Pennsylvania State University Press, 1992.

Stewart, Donald. *The Versatile Writer*. Lexington: DC Heath, 1986.

Stiles, Kristine. "Between Water and Stone: Fluxus Performance: A Metaphysics of Acts." In Armstrong and Rothfuss 62–99.

The Stooges. *The Stooges*. LP. Elektra, 1969.

Sundell, Nina. "Rauschenberg/Performance." *Rauschenberg/Performance, 1954–1984: An Exhibition Organized and Curated by Nina Sundell*. Cleveland: Cleveland Center for Contemporary Art, 1984. 6–22.

Talalay, Marjorie. "Introduction." In Sundell 5.

Tisdall, Caroline. *Joseph Beuys*. NY: Solomon R. Guggenheim Museum, 1979.

Tomkins, Calvin. *Off the Wall: Robert Rauschenberg and the Art World of Our Time*. Garden City, NY: Doubleday, 1980.

Torgovnick, Marianna. "Experimental Critical Writing." *Profession 90*. 25–27.

Trimbur, John. "Close Reading: Accounting for My Life Teaching Writing." In Roen et al. 129–141.

———. "Taking the Social Turn: Teaching Writing Post-Process." *College Composition and Communication* 45 (Feb. 1994): 108–118.

Turkle, Sherry. *Psychoanalytic Politics: Freud's French Revolution*. Cambridge: MIT Press, 1981.

Vardenoe, Kirk. "Comet: Jackson Pollock's Life and Work." *Jackson Pollcok*. Ed. Kirk Vardenoe and Pepe Karmel. New York: Museum of Modern Art, 1998. 15–85.

Venturi, Robert. *Complexity and Contradiction in Architecture*. 2nd Ed. New York: Museum of Modern Art, 1977.

———, Denise Scott Brown, and Steven Izenour. *Learning From Las Vegas*. Rev. Ed. Cambridge, MA: MIT Press, 1977.

Vidal, Gore. "Time for a People's Convention." *The Nation* 27 January 1992: 73, 88, 90–91, 94.

Virilio, Paul. *The Lost Dimension*. New York: Semiotext(e), 1991.

Wallace, David Foster. "E Unibus Pluram: Television and U.S. Fiction." *Review of Contemporary Fiction* 13.2 (Summer 1993): 168.

Walker, Jerry. "Bach, Rembrandt, Milton, and Those Other Cats." *English Journal* 57 (1968): 631–636.

Weil, Bruce. Lecture. Walker Art Center, Minneapolis, 7 Apr. 2000.

Weiner, Harvey S. "Collaborative Learning in the Classroom: A Guide to Evaluation." *College English* 48 (Jan. 1986): 52–61.

———. *Reading for the Disciplines: An Anthology for College Writers*. New York: McGraw-Hill, 1990.

"What I Learned in School." *Life* Sept. 1998: 50+.

White, Greg. "been there, done that!" Personal email. 26 Jan. 1999.

Williamson, Richard. "The Case for Filmmaking as English Composition." *College Composition and Communication* 22 (May 1971): 131–136.

"Words." *Time* 7 Feb. 1949: 51.

Workshop Reports. *College Composition and Communication* 19 (Oct. 1968): 240–260.

Wright, William. "An Interview with Jackson Pollock." In Namuth and Rose, n.p.

Young, Charles M. "Rock is Sick and Living in London: A Report on the Sex Pistols." *Rolling Stone* 20 Oct. 1977: 68–75.

Young, La Monte. "Lecture 1960." In Sandford 72–81.

"Yvonne Rainer Interviews Ann Halrpin." In Sandford 137–159.

Bonus Track

FUNERAL CEREMONY OF THE ANTI-PROCÈS II
A happening for CCCC

(WARNING: *Contains sampled material*)

Heterogeneity names the writing instruction we want. Exasperation names our reading of Composition Studies. This is what we wish we could say: "More recently, a large body of diverse compositions . . . employs a variety of materials and objects in an equally varied range of formats, completely departing from the accepted norms required by 'writing' as we have known it." But, as regards the need for a happening to be performed at CCCC, "this new work has brought sharply into focus the fact that *the convention hall's concurrent session room has always been a frame or format too,* and that this shape is inconsistent with the forms and expression emerging from the work in question." For those who feel the frame of the format:

Forget about packing a suitcase full of clothes for CCCC. Simply wear the same costume—body wrapped, mummy-like, in a roll of toilet paper—over the span of the convention's four days. In place of clothes, then, fill your suitcases with the following, which you can spend all day Wednesday arranging throughout the convention center as your own personal Pre-Convention Workshop (entitled "Anti-Intellectual Property"): *auto parts, dolls, bedsteads, television antennas, washing machines, fragments of building ornament, lawn sculptures, grass mowers, tangles of muffler tailpipes, hubcaps grouped liked stars, venetian blinds splayed out in circular rays, and silver-foiled twigs resembling icicles against the blackened profusion. . . artificial flowers . . . and shrines—one of them to John F. Kennedy.*

And mirrors, of course; bring as many mirrors with you to CCCC as you can, to place throughout the convention center at key locations, because *mirrors, ingeniously placed, abruptly confuse the space and add to the complexity that already issues from the masses of objects.*

For the entire duration of the conference, sit for fifteen minutes in the same spot in the convention hall (just outside the book exhibit) every four hours (one hour per C) and eat fifteen pages of a different complimentary composition textbook during each interlude, with a different environmental tape providing loud background accompaniment (some of the environments recorded might include the sound of wind or the sound of fire). Then turn to your fellow conventioneers when you've finished eating and cry, "But meanwhile, the rest of the world has become endlessly available[!]"

For your presentation, do not talk about whatever you've originally proposed for your session topic, but instead spin a number of Duchamp's *Rotoreliefs* for your audience, asking them what they see in the whirling images (*a breast with a slightly trembling nipple? an eye staring outward?*), writing their responses on your by-now tattered toilet paper shreds (in ink made of one part each blood, urine, and tears). Then, through a vocoder (the only piece of AV equipment you should request, besides Duchamp's *Rotary Demisphere*, which you'll need to spin the *Rotoreliefs*), advise your audience members of the range of methods and materials their students can use in their writing assignments. Tell them: *Materials [for academic essays] may be obtained by cutting up all the items listed in a random selection of pages from the telephone company's "Yellow Pages." These are stirred into a pot and are picked out [by students] one after the other, blindfolded, up to that number fixed by a previous chance operation.* Clothes, gas, spiderwebs, sky, river, *and* boxes *are examples. . . If the selection includes twenty tons of gold dust or three hermaphrodites with red hair, it may be quite difficult to come by them, and so in such instances, one must pick some more slips of paper from the pot.*

Next, give a brief demonstration of how to use the *I Ching* to respond to student writing.

Finally, pass out a series of small cards to the audience members, cards which will have a variety of sample student paper topics on them (e.g., *THREE LAMP EVENTS: on. off./lamp/ off. on.*). Instruct the audience members to assign their given topic to a writing class (the only composition principle/instruction given to students being "Extension"), asking them to send you the results (which you will read/exhibit/perform/screen/remix the following year at CCCC). Spend the remainder of your allotted time using the vocoder to read a prepared text: *A wall of trees tied with colored rags advances on the crowd, scattering everybody, forcing them to leave. Eating is going on incessantly, eating and vomiting and eating and vomiting, all in relentless yellow. There are muslin telephone booths for all, with a record player or microphone that tunes everybody in on everybody else. Coughing, you breathe noxious fumes, or the smell of hospitals and lemon juice. A nude girl runs after the racing pool of a searchlight and throws water into it. Slides and movies, projected in motion over walls and hurrying people, depict hamburgers: big ones, huge ones, red ones, skinny ones, flat ones, etc. You push things around like packing crates. Words rumble past, whispering dee-daaa, ba-ROOM, lovely, love me; shadows jiggle on screens, power saws and lawnmowers screech just like the subway at Union Square. Tin cans rattle, soaking rags slush, and you stand up to shout questions at shoeshine boys and old ladies. Long silences when nothing at all happens, when bang! there you are facing your- self in a mirror jammed at you . . .*

If there are any questions from the audience after your session, you will have prepared the following six answers for the first six questions asked, regardless of what they are:

1. That is a very good question. I should not want to spoil it with an answer.
2. My head wants to ache.
3. Had you heard Marya Freund last April in Palermo singing Arnold Schoenberg's *Pierrot Lunaire*, I doubt whether you would ask that question.
4. According to the Farmers' Almanac this is False Spring.
5. Please repeat the question . . .
   And again . . .
   And again . . .
6. I have no more answers.

INDEX

ABOUT THE AUTHOR

Geoffery Sirc works in composition at the University of Minnesota, General College.